# THE 21 ESCAPES

# ESCAPES

OF LT ALASTAIR CRAM

# THE 21 ESCAPES

# OF LT ALASTAIR CRAM

A compelling story of courage and
endurance in the Second World War

## DAVID M. GUSS

MACMILLAN

First published 2018 by Macmillan
an imprint of Pan Macmillan
20 New Wharf Road, London N1 9RR
Associated companies throughout the world
www.panmacmillan.com

ISBN 978-1-5098-2956-9

1 3 5 7 9 8 6 4 2

A CIP catalogue record for this book is available from the British Library.

Map artwork by ML Design

Typeset in Janson Text LT by
Palimpsest Book Production Ltd, Falkirk, Stirlingshire
Printed and bound by CPI Group (UK) Ltd, Croydon, CR0 4YY

Visit **www.panmacmillan.com** to read more about all our books
and to buy them. You will also find features, author interviews and
news of any author events, and you can sign up for e-newsletters
so that you're always first to hear about our new releases.

*For Kate,*
*Through the wire*
*& home*
*together*

# Contents

# List of Illustrations

I never hear the word 'escape'
Without a quicker blood,
A sudden expectation
A flying attitude!

EMILY DICKINSON

escape as a need, as a spiritual necessity

ALASTAIR CRAM

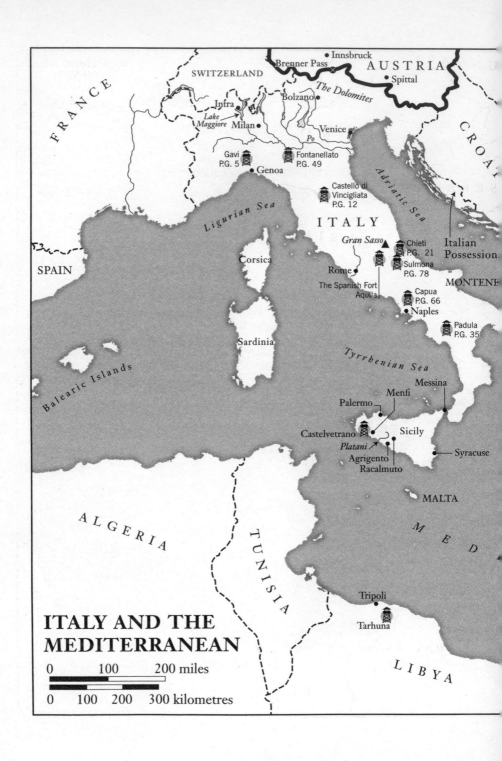

INNSBRUCK
SWITZERLAND
Brenner Pass
AUSTRIA
Spittal
The Dolomites
Intra
Lake Maggiore
Milan
Bolzano
Venice
Po
FRANCE
Gavi
P.G. 5
Fontanellato
P.G. 49
Genoa
CROA
Ligurian Sea
Castello di Vincigliata
P.G. 12
Adriatic Sea
ITALY
Gran Sasso
Chieti
P.G. 21
Italian Possession
SPAIN
Corsica
Rome
Sulmona
P.G. 78
The Spanish Fort
Aquila
Capua
P.G. 66
MONTENE
Naples
Sardinia
Padula
P.G. 35
Tyrrhenian Sea
Balearic Islands
Messina
Menfi
Palermo
Castelvetrano
Sicily
Platani
Agrigento
Racalmuto
Syracuse
MALTA
ALGERIA
M
E
D
TUNISIA
LIBYA
Tripoli
Tarhuna

# ITALY AND THE MEDITERRANEAN

0     100     200 miles

0   100   200   300 kilometres

UNGARY

SERBIA

ALBANIA

R O M A N I A

B U L G A R I A

German
Occupation

REICHSKOMMISSARIAT
UKRAINE

Black Sea

T U R K E Y

GREECE

Aegean Sea

...ian Sea

DODECANESE
(Italian Possession)

Crete

CYPRUS

M E D I T E R R A N E A N    S E A

Derna

Benghazi

Tobruk

CYRENAICA

Sidi Rezegh

EGYPT

───── Greater Germany

- - - - Other borders

⛫ Prisoner of War camps

# GERMANY AND CENTRAL EUROPE, 1943

SWEDEN
Copenhagen

DENMARK

North Sea

Bal

Barth
Stalag Luft I

Hamburg

Ravensbrück

Marlag und
Milag Nord

Elbe

Wesser

Bergen-Belsen

Amsterdam

Brunswick
Oflag 79

Berlin

HOLLAND

Hannover

Köthenwald
Klinikum Wahrendorff

Luckenwalde
Stalag IIIA

Bad Oeynhausen

GERMANY

P

Warburg
Oflag VIB

HARZ MTNS

Brussels

Fulda

Rossla

Sagan
Stalag Luft III

BELGIUM

Nordhausen

Leipzig

Spangenberg
Oflag IX A/H

Dresden

Colditz
Oflag IVC

Rhine

Rotenburg an
der Fulda,
Oflag IX A/Z

Frankfurt-am-Main

Petschek
Palace and
Pankrác

Prague

Mährisch Trüb
Oflag VI

SUDETENLAND

Sulíkov

PROTECTORATE OF
BOHEMIA & MORAVIA

Brn

Eichstätt
Oflag VIIB

Strasbourg

Danube

Moosburg
Stalag VIIA

Passau

ALSACE

Munich

Linz

Vienna

FRANCE

Salzburg

Bruck

Zurich

AUSTRIA

Spittal
Stalag XVIII A/Z

SWITZERLAND

Maribor

ITALY

Milan

Zagr

CROAT

Königsberg

EAST
PRUSSIA

Danzig

REICHSKOMMISSARIAT OSTLAND

Thorn
XXA

Vistula

Bialystok

Warsaw

Lodz

GENERAL
GOVERNMENT
OF POLAND

Katowice

Cracow

Nisko

Lwow

REICHSKOMMISSARIAT UKRAINE

Ostrava

SLOVAKIA

TRANSNISTRIA

Cernauti

lava

Budapest

HUNGARY

ROMANIA

| 0 | 100 | 200 miles |
|---|---|---|
| 0 | 100 | 200 | 300 kilometres |

Preface

# Finding Alastair Cram

I never met Alastair Cram, and if I had, I'm not sure he would have enjoyed being the subject of a book. He was such a private person, so reserved and modest, so relentlessly uninterested in talking about his many adventures. And yet he did leave a paper trail beginning with a set of journals written immediately after the war. Even these were nearly impenetrable. Written in pencil with little punctuation and words often running into one another, they were the work of a man possessed with the need to get it all down. He toyed with the idea of publishing it, wondering if it might not serve as a manual for escape. 'This book,' he wrote in one entry, 'is a record of one individual's ventures outside the wire, its excuse being to represent as faithfully as possible the background of escape in Europe in this war for the adventures related here were typical of those experienced by many hundreds of officers and men of the United Nations.' Of course, Alastair's experiences were anything but typical, nor did he ever try to publish it. He simply took the foolscap and cheap school notebooks he'd written on and stuffed them into an envelope, never to be looked at by him again.

When I discovered them sixty years later, there were pages missing, some torn and others misfiled. Almost all of them were nearly illegible, and even with the help of an amateur crypto-grapher from Texas, took several years to decipher. I knew long before then, if not immediately, that his was a story I had to tell. I had known of Alastair since childhood, a legendary figure haunting the escape literature I began devouring in large quantities from the age of twelve. It's what turned me into a reader and lover of books, and eventually into a researcher as well. Such works were readily available to British children of a similar age, but I lived in America, where only a handful of the most famous titles like *The Great Escape* and *The Wooden Horse* were to be found.

A mathematics teacher with the improbable nickname of 'Butts' came to my rescue. He had been ordering rare Lewis Carroll books from England for years and offered to add my list to his own. Today, when almost anything can be purchased over the internet with the promise of next-day delivery, it's hard to remember that incomparable joy in receiving a long-anticipated package which had travelled by ship across the Atlantic. It wasn't long before I began writing to the authors, peppering them with questions and advice about other titles. None was more generous than Pat Reid, who had described his own hair-raising escape in *The Colditz Story*. Having grown up reading escape literature from the previous war, Reid understood my fascination and responded with long, sensitive letters, often accompanied by a book or photograph.

Then I went to college, and the Vietnam War took over, cooling my interest in anything related to the military. I wrote poetry, studied art, lived with an indigenous group in the headwaters of the Orinoco, published books on South American mythology and eventually became an anthropologist. Busy with teaching and research, it was years before I thought seriously about escape again. But on a visit to the local public library one day, I wandered over to 940.54, the Dewey Decimal System's classification for the Second World War and escape. To my surprise there were a number of new titles I'd never seen before. Unlike the first generation of books written immediately after the war, these were by men who had recently retired or simply wanted their stories recorded before they died. I pulled Tommy Calnan's *Free as a Running Fox* off the shelf and started reading. In no time at all I was back with my old friends in the tunnels and trains with their disguises and subterfuges.

I decided to contact Pat Reid. It had been twenty-five years since we were last in touch and I wanted to let him know what had become of me and to thank him for all he had done. Unfortunately, I was too late. He had died several years earlier at the age of seventy-nine. All of this reignited my interest in escape narratives. I read a handful of the newer books and, while some were excellent, the one story I couldn't find was that of the Baron, Alastair Cram. Once referred to as the Harry Houdini of the Second World War, Alastair escaped, or at least attempted to by his own account, twenty-one times, more than any other prisoner of war. Up till then, much of what I knew about him came from a detailed MI9 report as well as George Millar's *Horned Pigeon* and Jack Pringle's *Colditz Last Stop*. Yet I was certain that anyone who had accomplished what Alastair had would have left some sort of record, either written or taped.

Although he had died in 1994, I believed that his widow, Isobel, might still be alive twelve years later. To my amazement, a single letter to the Scottish Mountaineering Club – which Alastair first joined in 1930 – was all it took. Isobel, I learned, was living in Edinburgh, and other than severe arthritis, was in relatively good health. And yes, Alastair had left a collection of journals detailing his various wartime exploits, all of which had just been transferred to the Mountaineering Club's archives for safe keeping. I was welcome to consult them, though warned that they were impossible to read. I was also told that there was a great deal of other material that might be of interest to me. That August, my wife, Kate, and I visited Edinburgh, timing our trip to coincide with the 2007 Fringe Festival.

We adored the city and had a blast at the festival, yet what we loved most of all was Isobel. Smart and witty, with an outrageous opinion about almost everything, she welcomed us into her Stockbridge home with a warmth usually reserved for the most intimate of family members. Over the next nine years we certainly felt as though we had become that, regularly exchanging letters and calls and visiting as frequently as possible. And all the time talking about Alastair as only Isobel could. Whether it was growing up in Perth, the war years, his time as a prosecutor in Germany, the Mau Mau in Africa, or their many climbs across the globe, there was no greater guide than Isobel. Nor was there anyone more excited about finally having his story told. 'Alastair was a modest man,' she wrote when we first met. 'But he does deserve credit for his deeds and it is reassuring to know he will receive it.'

She told us many things about Alastair, some of which I doubted he would have shared himself. But she had always been the talkative one in their relationship, and he the solitary figure, reluctant to speak about his various adventures. 'He was a well-known loner,' Isobel said, 'and I respected his silences. If he opened up and let you in, you could follow him there. But he was deeply private.' Ironically, these were the same qualities Pat Reid identified as essential to the DNA of the successful escaper:

> For, when you escape, you court loneliness – the loneliness of a hunted animal! And even for the escaper there comes an urge, aided by fatigue and hunger, to give himself up in order to regain lost companionship – if only of other prisoners. Here, then, is the big question: Are you gregarious, or can you take being a loner?

While the need for solitude may not have been the motivating force behind Alastair's numerous escapes, it was certainly a welcome by-product. It also helps explain why they all seemed to turn into hikes. Other escapers took trains and buses, but Alastair always preferred to walk and, wherever possible, climb. He went back to peaks he had explored in the 1930s, often as a guide. He would eventually see mountaineering and escape as part of the same process, each leading to a similar emancipatory 'catharsis', in which all bonds of attachment were severed and fear vanquished. Only then could individuals discover their full potential. It was transformation by danger, which Alastair claimed could be realized in any number of ways. 'We are all prisoners inside the barbed wire of attachment,' he wrote, 'with sentries of desire and fear guarding us from our freedom. Luxury, comfort, lust for life, vanities are the Detaining Powers of the spirit of every man.'

Alastair never gave up the spiritual search that preoccupied him throughout his twenties. As Isobel noted more than once, 'He was a contradiction in terms. He had the lawyer side, very rational and all. And then he had the ethereal side.' Both of these were carefully braided together in the journals, which Alastair prefaced with a subtle directive: 'This is a plain tale of personal adventure, although perhaps the more discerning may perceive a secondary experience interwoven of spiritual progression.'

As Kate and I retraced Alastair's extraordinary odyssey through Europe over the course of several years, it too became a pilgrimage. Starting as he did in Sicily, we visited Castelvetrano and Racalmuto, where the old men of the Società di Mutuo Soccorso still remembered Carlo and the Maresciallo. From there we went on to Padula and, like George Millar, were awed by the power of the Certosa di San Lorenzo. Gavi required multiple visits, aided considerably by Andrea Scotto and the Friends of Gavi. Travelling through the Brenner Pass with stops in Bolzano and the Dolomites, we circled around Munich, ending up in Prague instead. There, Colonel Kulfánek gave us a moving tour of the Gestapo Museum in the former Petschek Palace. Getting into Pankrác, which is still an active prison, proved more difficult. In Mährisch Trübau, however, the staff at the military academy in what was once Oflag VIIIF couldn't have been more welcoming. It was a short ride from there to Sulíkov, the village where Alastair and Jim Gaze stopped for help in May 1944. Nothing had changed, and other than two white horses and a man smoking meat, there were no signs of life. One of our last trips was to Bad Oeynhausen, the ageing spa town where Alastair spent several years as a prosecutor with the War Crimes Group. We were surprised by the level of resentment still simmering just beneath the surface more than sixty years after the Occupation.

I am grateful to Alastair for taking me on this journey and for providing me with what I needed to tell his remarkable tale.

After more than fifty years of immersion in the literature of escape, I could hardly imagine a better gift. At the same time, it saddens me that Isobel, who contributed so much to this book, is no longer alive to see its publication. She died in January 2016 at the age of ninety-six. Shortly after our first exchange, Isobel sent a letter to Robin Campbell, archivist for the Scottish Mountaineering Club, in which she wrote, 'Let us hope that we have done the right thing in entrusting Alastair's history to a US Professor.' That trust and friendship have sustained me throughout this long project and remain one of its greatest rewards.

# 1

# The Mountain

He arrived by plane on Christmas Eve, looking like any British tourist happy to be spending a few winter days by the sea. And while it's true that Alastair Cram had always wanted to visit Sicily, he never imagined it would be quite like this. Just four weeks earlier he had been threading his way through burning tanks at the Battle of Sidi Rezegh when an explosion knocked him cold. The Germans had overtaken the artillery observation post he and three others were using to track enemy movements. It was the fourth day of Operation Crusader, the Eighth Army's plan for relieving the garrison at Tobruk, under siege for seven months. It started with an attack on the Axis airfield at Sidi Rezegh; then quickly turned into a back-and-forth that lasted for days. When it was finally over in early December 1941, it had become the largest tank battle to date and Operation Crusader the first Allied victory. The losses on both sides were devastating, especially after Rommel launched a final, desperate attack. That's when Alastair's position was overrun and he was left for dead.

He awoke to find a teenage boy in an oversized Afrika Korps uniform standing over him. One hand was shaking his shoulder while the other was nervously clutching a Luger. '*Verwundete?*'

he kept yelling. 'Wounded? Are you wounded?' Alastair wasn't sure. His helmet had a huge dent, which helped explain the ringing in his ears as well as the terrible headache and double vision. Then a slightly older German appeared and, like an actor who's been waiting in the wings to deliver a single line, proudly said in his best Gymnasium English, 'For you, the war is over.' But, as Alastair soon discovered, 'a new personal war was just beginning'.

Three days later he was handed over to the Italians, as it was agreed that they would be responsible for all prisoners captured by the Axis forces in North Africa. They were, after all, still nominally in charge of the campaign. The newly formed Afrika Korps was sent by Hitler solely to support his southern ally as the British pushed further into Libya. Ferrying prisoners the short distance across the Mediterranean was also much easier and less costly than transporting them all the way to Germany. Unfortunately, many drowned when British submarines unwittingly torpedoed their boats.

Before Alastair even embarked at the Libyan port of Benghazi, he had already made two escape attempts. One was at Derna, where he was discovered crawling through the wire and barely avoided being shot. Now, with more than 300 other prisoners, he was marched onto an Italian destroyer and locked in the forecastle. The space, airless and dark, with the noxious odor of fuel wafting through, was too small to hold even half their number. When the steel cover slammed shut, Alastair knew there would be little chance of surviving an attack. But Allied submarines weren't the only thing they had to worry about. No sooner had they manoeuvred past the sunken ships that sat like small islands throughout the harbour when a violent storm broke out. Huge waves picked the boat up, rocking it from side to side until it nearly turned over; or so it seemed to those stuck below. Almost everyone became sick, moaning and vomiting till the entire floor was covered with a putrid, yellow liquid. Mixed with the faeces of those suffering from dysentery, it washed over them each time the boat listed. Some compared it to the Napoleonic Wars with their deadly prison ships, or worse still, the Middle Passage.

One of the few who didn't become ill was the Senior British Officer (SBO), an old Australian buccaneer named 'Skipper' Palmer, also known as 'Pedlar' or 'Pirate'. A large, colourful man with a big heart and an oversized personality, Skipper became famous for running the blockade at Tobruk. In fact, he was so successful in resupplying the besieged troops that the Germans put a price on his head. What made his feat even more remarkable was that he did it in a three-masted schooner captured from the Italians. In 1916, he had set out for England on a similar ship, which the Germans sank, leaving him in a lifeboat for three days. Following service in the Royal Navy, Palmer eventually found his way to China, where he worked on schooners up and down the coast. Now back in uniform once again, he was asked to employ similar skills in North Africa – landing commandos, picking up spies, eluding blockades, smuggling weapons and moonshine. There was a reason they called him 'Pirate', an epithet he happily embraced with his skull-and-crossbones flag. If there was anyone who refused to go into captivity without a fight, it was Skipper Palmer.

Now, with conditions quickly deteriorating below deck, the Italians began opening the steel cover to let ten prisoners up at a time. That's when Palmer introduced a plan to take over the ship and sail to Malta. While there were two machine guns on deck, only one – a double-barrelled weapon – was permanently manned. The other, located under the half deck, was hidden beneath a large canvas spray cover. Palmer promised to take the most dangerous role, leading a charge on the bridge where the double machine gun was set up. A second team, which Alastair was to be part of, would seize control of the other gun and with it, the ship. Finding enough healthy volunteers proved difficult. Alastair estimates that by this point there were no more than twenty able-bodied men left. Among the many sufferers was a young artillery officer named Leslie Hill, who glibly summed up the prevailing misery: 'Most of us army types were too sick to help. I would have been delighted if the destroyer had sunk with all hands, particularly myself.'

Illness wasn't the only problem. As Palmer circulated, trying to drum up support for his plan, he was shadowed by his second in command, a South African Army captain named MacQuarie. No sooner had he explained his idea than MacQuarie began disparaging it, insisting it was too dangerous, if not suicidal. Palmer was furious, calling him a fifth columnist and worse. If he'd had a gun, he probably would have shot him. 'That SOB ruined a perfect escape,' he later said. But the moment had passed. Sensing that something was afoot, the Italians handed out extra weapons and increased their vigilance. Finally, with the storm worsening, they decided to turn round and head back to Libya, this time docking in Tripoli. Palmer, who was still fuming, would never get a chance like that again. In September 1944, a year after losing his arm jumping from a train in Germany, he was repatriated.

Trucks were waiting at the pier to drive them south to Tarhuna, where they spent the next three weeks in a makeshift camp removing lice and listening to their stomachs growl. Many were too hungry even to get out of bed while others were simply too depressed as the impact of becoming prisoners finally started to sink in. Michael Ross, captured after a 150-mile trek through the desert, expressed the general sense of despair and hopelessness when he wrote: 'I felt guilty and ashamed at the terrible and utter waste of it all. I was suddenly a useless, almost helpless being, a parasite destined to be fed and housed until some day, mercifully, I should be set free.' Alastair was also aware of the damaging physical and psychological effects of being imprisoned. At thirty-two, he was somewhat older than most of his comrades, and with a law practice back in Edinburgh might have been mistaken for a sedentary professional. Nothing could have been further from the truth. An avid mountaineer and distance runner with a demanding exercise routine performed daily since childhood, Lieutenant Alastair Cram of the Royal Artillery was in perfect physical condition. While becoming a prisoner left some immobilized in a temporary state of shock, it increased Alastair's resolve all the more, as he later confirmed in his journal:

The first months of captivity press heavily on morale. A life of ceaseless activity at a blow is modified to one of monotony and complete inactivity. Worst of all to bear was the vision of the seemingly unending barren months; all one thought of was years of captivity, for it was patent to everyone that this war would not soon end. I felt a kind of horror at the effect on the will, mind and spirit that imprisonment must inevitably have unless the ennui was most desperately fought . . . Beyond these sterile years loomed the spectre of returning, cowed and broken to the bright, busy, uncaring world probably incredibly altered to meet persons who would have advanced, experienced, succeeded. Hopes, dreams, ambitions crumbling to bitter dust turned inward, remorseless. Humiliations and physical hard-ships were but small inconsequential things before the true spectre of physical decay, mental ruin and moral collapse. Those who did not succumb even temporarily were fired by a wild urge to regain all, by the one means left – escape.

On 24 December a fleet of ambulances arrived to take them back to Tripoli, where they were loaded onto Savoia bombers. Now the threat was the RAF in Malta, which they avoided by flying as close to the water as possible. Their destination was the small town of Castelvetrano, famous for its olives and for the ruins of Selinunte, one of Europe's greatest archaeological sites. Sacked by the Carthaginians and then levelled by an earthquake, Selinunte was the perfect Greek city, albeit in Sicily. They were housed in a seventeenth-century convent located in the centre of town. Originally constructed for San Francesco di Paola's Order of Minims, it was stripped bare during the unification of Italy, and after that used as a barracks, school, refugee centre and now a prison. It still retained a powerful aura of sanctity, at least when its latest inmates arrived on Christmas Eve. Follow-ing their first good meal in weeks, they started singing carols while a priest offered communion to a hushed line of men. Almost everyone was moved as the faded murals shimmered and came alive under the soft glow of candlelight. Combined with the thick straw bedding that covered the floor, many, including Alastair, were given a new appreciation of the meaning of the Nativity.

In the morning the air was sweet and cool and filled with the

scent of plants and flowers, a relief after Tarhuna and the dull-
ness of the desert. Best of all was the sight of mountains rising
in the distance. 'If I could reach them,' wrote Alastair later, 'I
would be safe.' From the age of four, when he made his first climb
up Craigellachie in the Cairngorms, the mountains had been his
refuge, a place of healing and rebirth, or as he once wrote:
'Mountaineering is a means to an end and that end is merely a
beginning.' By fourteen he was climbing alone in the Highlands
and not long after in the Alps as well. The local papers treated
him as a celebrity, describing each of his feats in detail – the
attempted rescue of two stranded climbers in the winter of 1928,
summiting the Matterhorn in a storm, guiding the Cambridge
University Club in the Alps in white-out conditions, completing
the cycle of Munros, co-founding Perth's Junior Mountaineering Club. What still eluded him was the chance to climb
Everest. He had hoped to be part of a 1939 expedition, but that
dream vanished, like so many others, with the advent of war.

For Alastair, mountaineering and escape would be inextric-
ably linked. It wasn't just that so many of his schemes involved
mountains and the same climbing skills; it was that both drew
upon a similar emotional and mental transformation, what he
referred to as 'the unspeakable heightening of perception. An
entry into an awareness consciously sought.' Castelvetrano,
where an escape route revealed itself almost immediately, was
a perfect example. The bathroom, reached by walking through
an ancient kitchen, was in the rear corner of the convent. Its
roof – which offered a fine view of the stars – was almost
non-existent. And although the back wall was fourteen feet high,
it had plenty of good holds for a rock climber like Alastair, who
would have no problem scaling it. On the outer side, a mound

of dirt had built up over the years, reducing it to a simple nine-foot jump. For the first few days a guard was assigned to patrol the area. Then, out of boredom or loneliness, or simply because he was too cold, he moved inside, monitoring access to the bathroom from the warmth of the kitchen.

Alastair told no one, not even Skipper Palmer, of his plans. He knew that his fellow prisoners would have thought him crazy. In fact, he thought so himself. He had no civilian clothes, nor any papers, maps, or compass. As for food, he had a little chocolate and a pound of dates. His idea was to head for the mountains and, after walking south for several days, make for the coast, where he would steal a fishing boat and sail over 125 miles to Malta. On the 28th, four days after arriving, he was ready to go. Slipping into the bathroom took some time. The guard would open the door for each person, then wait attentively until they came out. Alastair patiently stood in the shadows for well over an hour. At last the guard was changed. The new one was a short, overweight private more interested in warming his hands by the stove than controlling traffic to the loo. Men passed back and forth as he looked the other way. Alastair quickly slid behind a tall officer, his 5'8" frame concealed as they entered the bathroom together. The door closed. In seconds, he was up the wall and over. No one heard him as he leapt to the ground. Even the barking dogs weren't enough to give him away. He crouched down as he crossed the road and disappeared into the well of night.

Within ten minutes he reached a ravine and immediately felt his body come alive as he scrambled over the sharp limestone ledge. This brought him into an endless series of olive groves, where each gnarled tree – some more than 1,000 years old – vied for attention. Enchantment soon turned into something much more sinister, pushing Alastair to get through them as quickly as possible. He finally came to a grove filled with ripe oranges, and for the first time since climbing over the wall, stopped and rested. Listening for possible pursuers, he remained standing as he ate two dozen oranges one after another. It wasn't long before he arrived at the Belice River, heavily protected with barbed wire, spiky reeds and thick nettles. He tried to ford it, but had to give up and swim across. With dawn approaching, and the mountains still ten miles away, he broke into an abandoned barn to spend the day. He was wet, cold and exhausted, and could barely stop shivering. But he was free.

He was awakened by the sound of search planes flying close to the ground. He found them oddly comforting, an affirmation of his success. Just before dusk he set out again, following the shoreline to avoid the small town of Menfi. Workers were leaving the plantations and vineyards with blankets draped over their heads. Alastair quickly joined them, covering himself in the same way. He felt secure beneath this new disguise until a young man mistook him for his sweetheart, and gently started calling: 'Maria, Little Maria. Wait, wait.' Alastair began walking faster with the love-struck youth hot in pursuit. When the road looped around a gorge, he left it and started to climb: 'I did a quick traverse, across and up the rocky walls, which seemingly were steep enough to cool the ardour of love. I wondered what the youth thought of his athletic mistress. Maybe I spoiled a promising affair but it was a lesser shock for him than if he had caught up with me.'

He eventually came to an old cobblestone path which he followed up to the snow line. By now it was pitch black and difficult to see. He was hungry and cold, and desperate to find shelter. That's when Alastair experienced what many escapers have felt: the sensation of not being alone, of being guided by a greater force or presence. Perhaps it's what led him to a stone hut tucked inside a hollow. Hanging by the door was a large pail of fresh milk covered with a heavy crust of cream. He put his face in and drank. A small boy opened the door and invited him in. They huddled together for warmth until morning, when an old man appeared. Alastair, still in his British uniform, claimed to be a German soldier, lost after being separated from his comrades. To his surprise, the old man spoke good German, having been a prisoner in Austria during the last war. When the subject of Mussolini came up, he spat on the ground and rubbed it in with his foot. Later, two other men arrived, carrying a large loaf of bread and some olives. The old man made cheese, which he moulded into a lump the size of a fist. He placed it in Alastair's hands, along with a glass of dark wine. They talked cautiously, barely raising their voices loud enough to be heard. His hosts were generous by custom rather than conviction. They refused any money and hardly turned their heads when Alastair said goodbye with a Nazi salute. Halfway up the trail he turned to look back, but none had watched him leave.

Alastair remained high in the mountains, alone except for the occasional shepherd or two – elusive beings who lived in caves and dressed head to toe in sheepskins, which they also used for bedding and even as makeshift doorways. They drank sheep's milk and ate sheep's cheese. More comfortable with their flocks than with humans, they could be heard serenading them with pan pipes, or calling in a strange ovine tongue as the animals came to lick the salt from their hands and faces. When Alastair tried to approach, they quickly disappeared. Yet Alastair too was a 'child of the mist', a Highlander whose father was a Buchanan from Callander with ties stretching back to Rob Roy and the Mac-Gregors. They were the ones who emerged from the mountain mists to steal cattle and wreak revenge upon the thieves who had taken their homes.

As dusk approached, he scrambled down to greet a young man working in the fields. Once more he claimed to be a German soldier who had lost his way. The man, covered in sweat and dirt, and dressed in a patchwork of different materials, invited him to spend the night. His stone hut, similar to the one Alastair had stayed in before, was much darker and smelled a lot worse. Only when his eyes adjusted to the dim light did he realize why. In addition to the old man and small boy seated by the fire were the many animals who also shared the space – the dogs and chickens, the two oxen, a donkey and even a goat.

They ate olives, fresh figs and bread, washed down with strong red wine. Then, to Alastair's surprise, the old man turned to him and asked: 'Can you speak English? You look a lot like an Englishman.' Alastair replied slowly in his best German-inflected accent, telling him he had learned a *leetle beet* in school. The old man went on talking about New York, where he had lived for many years, saving money to buy the land they were now on. He loved America but had promised to return to his native land, a move he now regretted and would never have made had he known how oppressed Italy had become:

All our gold was taken away. My wife's jewellery. Now they take our grain and oil and wine. Up here in the hills it is calm but down in my village there are Carabinieri and Blackshirts. We work very hard, the land is rich, but we receive little, and boots and clothes are dear. Sometimes I think we would be better off independent. We are happy people, loving music and leisure and wine. We love the land. We are not soldiers. To us an empire is only a loss. We are not like the people in the North, boastful and arrogant, cruel and treacherous. We have our feuds and hurt one another, for we are hot blooded. Every Sicilian woman keeps a knife in her stocking. But war is too large for us to grasp. All we wish is to be left alone . . . What do you think, signore? You are not like the others we have met.

Alastair left at daybreak before most of the menagerie was even awake. By mid-morning he had arrived at a series of canyon-like passes with steep walls rising on both sides. As he entered the second one, a dramatic rock spire suddenly came into view. The temptation to climb it was simply too great, and while he had some feelings of guilt, the emotional benefits easily outweighed them: 'I climbed it by the East face. It was of course madness. It was my plain duty to press on. But in those days escape was a joyous venture, not the grave and serious business it became later.'

It was New Year's Eve, the last day of 1941, a year the Allies would rather forget. The trails leading down to the valley floor were filled with families on their way to town to celebrate. After a long nap in an orange grove, Alastair joined the procession. He was soon stopped by two young men demanding to see his papers. German soldiers, Alastair informed them, did not show their papers to Italian civilians. And where were their papers, he

asked in a threatening tone. They didn't have any? Then perhaps they'd like to join him on a visit to German headquarters.
That was enough to put an end to their officious meddling,
though Alastair doubted whether they believed his story.

By now he had settled into a routine of selecting a house to
approach at dusk just before dinner. He was invariably invited
in and given a bed for the night. This often meant no more than
a pile of straw shared with several family members and their
animals. It didn't matter how poor they were or how little they
had, the Italian peasants, or *contadini*, were generous to a fault,
and without exception welcomed him into their homes.

The next day, after trudging up a long, narrow valley, he found
himself at a house so derelict it was hard to believe anyone could
live in it. Surrounded by aged fruit trees and prickly pear, it
leaned dangerously to one side as though waiting for a good
breeze to blow it over. Seated on a rickety chair in front was an
equally ancient dwarf. The man's wife had gone to Bivona to visit
family and he was grateful for some company. He brought out
large bowls of pasta, along with bread and wine. For dessert they
drank Marsala, which the old man had also made. By then it was
dark and an evening chill was settling in. As they drew closer to
the fire, Alastair marvelled at the beauty of the old man's face, a
landscape of ridges and glens like a topographic map. He was
curious about Alastair's family. What were his parents and siblings like back in Germany, and didn't he miss them? Alastair,
who was an only child, was happy for the chance to invent an
ideal sister as well as several other imaginary relatives. The old
man seemed satisfied and, after staring in silence at the fire,
offered his own theory about Nordic women, sexual repression,
and the origin of war:

The young men are crazy about blonde women. But they pursue them for what they imagine is there but is not. The dark force of passion. They are intrigued because they are 'frigid', but when they break down that reserve – and few can do that better than our hot-blooded young men – they find tepidness. When I was young we sought a girl with hair so intensely black it contained blue flames in the sunlight. She is like our Sicilian wine, fire and power. But if you cannot satisfy her beware, for her receiving energies will turn to jealousy. For love of you, she will try to kill you. For our women folk carry knives from childhood, and if you try to escape from her, her family will make a vendetta against you. So try. You will escape and then – 'slick!' the razor edged knife in the dark. And your women folk, how is it with them? They are mainly blonde, I am told. Ah you Germans, your women are so lukewarm you are compelled to find excitement in war. It is the same with the English. For if their women were like ours you would want to stay at home.

They shared a bed, slick with oil and dirt, and only one threadbare blanket between them, which they fought over most of the night. As he prepared to leave, the old man warned him that he might have trouble crossing the Platani River as the bridge had recently washed away. Alastair thanked him and set off for Agrigento. Like Selinunte, it was one of the great cities of Magna Graecia, the Greek expansion that helped transform ancient Italy for ever. Alastair was confident he could find a boat in one of the small fishing villages along the coast, and from there sail to Malta. It wasn't long before he heard the sound of the river as it pushed its way through a gorge hundreds of feet below. By then, he was travelling along a thin goat path when suddenly, out of nowhere, a man slid down from above, nearly knocking him over. Unlike the two who had stopped him on New Year's Eve, this one was a legitimate member of Mussolini's fascist militia, the Blackshirts. He demanded to see Alastair's papers and laughed when he said he was a German soldier trying to get back to his unit.

'You're no German,' he answered. 'I fought in Spain. You're an Englishman.'

To which Alastair replied, quite honestly, 'No, I'm not.'

'You're coming with me now,' the Blackshirt barked in a feeble attempt to sound intimidating. It soon became clear that his intrepid captor was afraid of heights. When the path shrank to little more than a foot, the terrified Italian began to panic. With a clear drop on one side and a sheer wall on the other, he grabbed on to Alastair for dear life. That was foolish, as all Alastair had to do was give him a good shove, which he did, sending him over the edge into the riverbank below.

Alastair hurried on, passing the spot where the stone bridge once stood. A group of men were busily at work constructing a new one beside it. To his relief, a temporary wooden crossing had already been installed. Rushing across unseen, he immediately returned to the safety of the hills. By now he had been walking for over a week, with each day bringing him closer to that magical zone he would inhabit so often while on the run – the exhilaration of freedom, the threat of danger, the electrified senses of the fugitive, the unfiltered smells and sounds experienced when alone in nature, even the delirium caused by lack of food and sleep combined with physical exertion. Together, they created a pathway to the 'higher realms of perception', a parallel route to the joy of mountaineering.

He walked across fields that had just been ploughed for a new planting of oats and wheat. There were poppies and fennel and Queen Anne's lace, and in the distance carpets of yellow broom that reminded him of home. The almond trees too were starting to blossom with a delicate scent that filled the valley. Higher up, he came to an area bursting with orange trees but fled when a girl called out to him from a ladder. Her black hair shimmered with blue flames in the sun and, while he didn't see it, he was sure she had a knife in her stocking. He remembered the old man's warning. 'I had enough trouble on my hands,' he said, 'without figuring as enemy number one in a first-class vendetta.' Finally, he reached the top of the ridge where he entered the garden of a ruined cloister. The air was crisp and clear with a perfect view far out to sea. In the distance was Malta. He hadn't realized it would be visible, and was as surprised as anyone when he saw it quietly sitting on the horizon. For the first time he actually believed he was going to succeed.

It took him two days to reach the sea. The first night he slept on the floor of an abandoned house. By morning a storm had moved in and didn't let up until he finally arrived, cold and hungry, around 1 a.m. The beach was deserted as the winds from the storm continued to blow. He found two boats up on rollers, both of them locked and dismantled. Their masts, sails, rudders and oars were in a separate hut 500 yards away. Alastair checked the door but that was locked too. He'd need another person to help him get a boat in the water. But that wasn't the only problem. The Italians had placed restrictions on all non-military craft, limiting the hours they could be at sea as well as their distance from shore. Any boat discovered over twelve miles out would be sunk without warning. Alastair, who learned to sail as a child in Perth, did a quick calculation: at six knots, and with sunrise at five, he'd be twenty miles out when the day's first search planes flew over, an easy target. There was also the issue of food. He'd barely eaten for two days and would need provisions for the trip to Malta. He decided to go back to the hills to forage for food. After that, he'd return to the beach and launch one of the boats.

The sky was still overcast and the path pitch black as the rain turned into a cold, piercing sleet. He was light-headed and half starved, aware that this was when judgement was compromised and mistakes were made. An hour later he heard the bells from a mule train. When he finally overtook it, the driver – a small, toothless man whom he could barely understand – nearly died of fright. But he agreed, after some haggling, to take Alastair 'home', or so he thought. They travelled all night and the next day too, using goat paths and trails that only a mule driver would know. It was already dark as they struggled up a cobblestone walk and entered a small town. By then Alastair was almost delirious and paid little attention when they turned into the doorway of a large brick building. Once inside, the lights flipped on and he realized he was standing in the middle of a police station.

He feigned outrage at being detained, insisting that they let him go at once. Couldn't they see he was a German soldier?

'Doesn't Cosentino speak German?' somebody asked. 'He was a waiter in Budapest. Go and call him.' Minutes later, a tall, spindly man in his forties rushed in, looking as though he should be carrying an order of goulash. His German was limited to what was on the menu, and after struggling to converse with Alastair, he assured everyone that he was indeed a member of the Wehrmacht.

To be certain, they woke the local schoolmaster and dragged him in for a second opinion. His German was even worse than that of the waiter, leaving everyone to wonder what exactly he was teaching their children.

Then the sergeant major in charge got through to Palermo, nodding as he repeated, 'Five foot eight, blond, curly hair, blue eyes, ruddy complexion, athletic build.' Covering the phone with one hand, he looked up, and with a huge smile announced: 'He fits the description of the escaped British officer exactly.' To which everyone, except Alastair, cheered. Wine and cake were brought out and they celebrated as if their football team had just won the championship. Nothing like this had ever happened in Racalmuto.

## 2

# Enter the Baron

Word of the miraculous appearance of the British officer spread quickly through the small mining town. By mid-morning, a line of women carrying baskets filled with fruit and cakes had formed outside Racalmuto's police station. Everyone wanted to get a glimpse of Alastair, who by now was affectionately referred to as 'our Englishman'. Among the first to arrive was the mule driver responsible for his capture. Dressed in his Sunday best, he came to ask for Alastair's forgiveness. Had he known that he was British, he would never have turned him in. But Alastair himself claimed to be a German, and one could only assume that he was a deserter as well.

Most visitors were content simply to watch in amazement as he consumed one enormous plateful of food after another. There were some, however, who insisted on placing their children on his lap, as if he were a visiting Santa with the magical power to grant wishes. At around 10 a.m. a district commander from the Italian army pulled up in a black Fiat. Like most Italians, he was amazed that anyone would want to leave the safety of a prison camp to return to combat. 'Why escape?' Alastair was frequently asked. 'It's very dangerous. Stay here, eat, drink, sleep. After the war you'll return to your home. You'll see your mother, you'll have a beautiful girl. If you die, it will all be over.'

The district commander grilled Alastair about his plans. How was he going to get out of Sicily? Where was he heading?

Finally, as if confessing a deep secret, Alastair said in a near whisper, 'Siracusa.'

'And then what?'

'Swim to Greece.'

To which the Italian exploded in disbelief, 'You must be crazy! It's impossible. It's miles and miles away.'

'Oh,' Alastair said sheepishly, 'I thought there was just a narrow channel.'

That night he was taken to the basement and locked in a small, windowless cell without heat or light. He had been on the run for two solid weeks and, while the showcasing of his extraordinary eating abilities had blunted the initial trauma of recapture, it now hit him with full force:

Nothing so completely underlines loss of freedom than the closing of a heavy door, the grinding of the locks and bolts, the echoing retreat of footsteps and of silence and solitude . . . Recapture is bitter but the disappointment does not become apparent immediately, rather there is a sense of relief from strain. Not until that moment does one realize that for days, hour by hour, one has been living at a high pitch with every muscle and nerve strained and tensed for the uttermost effort. The body and brain, driven, channelled by some of the most powerful urges one can experience, have known surge after surge of energy and power against the physical difficulty of hills, rivers, rocks, scrub and weather . . . Day and night one has lived in the character of a part, thinking and speaking another so that one may seem to speak and act like another. Sweet it is to recover one's identity. Rest and mindlessness. Then the bitterness of realization. Then the restless seeking spirit begins to search again and one prowls the cell, exploring. Vain quest.

He remained in Racalmuto for several days, awaiting the arrival of the carabinieri who would escort him to Palermo. By then he had gained back the weight he had lost and also befriended many of the locals, in particular the sergeant major's family. His wife was a lovely Genovese who, along with her four children, was a constant presence at the station. Alastair was especially fond of Carlo, their precocious eight-year-old son. The sergeant major even asked if the boy could visit him in England after the war. His departure was filled with tears and hugs. Extra food was secretly slipped into his pockets while Carlo held his hand all the way to the station. As the train pulled out, the sergeant major screamed: 'Don't try and escape. If anything happens to you, what shall I tell Carlo?'

Palermo was much less inviting, and after several lengthy interrogations he was glad to be on his way again. His escort was increased considerably. Instead of two carabinieri, there were now five, each of them elaborately costumed with cocked hats, capes and swords. Alastair's reputation as a dangerous prisoner was taking shape. It was a sullen and sleepy trip, at least, until they reached the Bay of Naples. Sandwiched between a breathtaking sunset on one side and an equally spectacular view of Mount Vesuvius erupting on the other, Alastair could forget for just a second that he was a prisoner and imagine himself a young aristocrat on a Grand Tour of Europe.

Their destination was Capua, twenty-five miles north of Naples, where a transit camp had been set up on a barren, water-soaked field. There were several thousand prisoners, almost all of whom had been captured in North Africa. Finding permanent homes for the glut of new arrivals was taking time, leaving many stuck in a camp that was never meant for prolonged stays. They were cold, damp, crowded, hungry and bored, with no amenities such as a library, theatre, or playing field. There were Red Cross parcels but they were treated like precious jewels, brought out only for special occasions. Many were too weak to even get out of bed, and yet sleep was equally difficult as bedbugs and lice were endemic. Everyone was depressed. Michael Ross said that 'Capua was about as miserable a place as could be.' Alastair called it 'a muddy, dreary camp', and was shocked when he finally saw his friends from Castelvetrano, moved the morning after his escape:

I found my late comrades pinched and wan. They were packed in wooden bungalows, bed to bed. The cold was intense. The lavatories outside and the food meagre in the extreme. In spite of minor hardship I was well fed, tanned and hard as nails and more than ever determined to escape. Capua looked an easy nut to crack. The double apron wire, the bad lighting and stupidity of the sentries promised well. Three factors made me delay. Lack of food, the appalling weather of raging winds, sleet and blinding rainstorms, and lack of local knowledge.

Alastair was more concerned than ever about the soul-destroying nature of imprisonment. And yet, there were some, like Eric Newby, who appreciated the irony that it also provided unprecedented freedom. Every need was taken care of. There were no obligations, no decisions, no financial responsibilities, no job. According to Newby, 'We were certainly much more free than many of us would ever be again, either during the war or after it. And as prisoners we did not even suffer the disapprobation of society as we would have done if we had been locked up in our own country. To our own people we appeared as objects worthy of sympathy.'

For Alastair, it was this lack of responsibility and engagement that threatened to drain one's vitality and 'insidiously sap the will'. George Millar, a lieutenant with the Rifle Brigade, worried about this as well, claiming that in the most extreme cases one 'lost interest in everything inside the prison and everything outside it. You stifled, you stagnated, you sulked.' And eventually you couldn't even get out of bed. Alastair knew right away that escape was the surest and most powerful form of resistance, especially when combined with his demanding mental and physical regimen. He spent hours studying and copying maps, taught a course in German for escapers and pumped guards for as much local information as possible. He also amassed a good supply of food, saving part of every meal, no matter how small. Self-discipline, he said, was its own reward, paid out in psychological benefits.

His physical conditioning began every morning at 7.30, when, regardless of the weather, he took off all his clothes and performed a series of movements known as the Müller System. While all but forgotten today, J. P. Müller was once considered the most famous Dane after Hans Christian Andersen. A former soldier and sanatorium inspector, Müller developed a simple

31

fifteen-minute programme that combined a mixture of stretches, bends, squats, push-ups, leg lifts and sit-ups. To achieve the maximum benefit, he insisted they be performed naked or in what he called an 'air bathing costume'. Concluding with a vigorous and thorough rubbing of the body from head to toe, there was little that the Müller System couldn't cure; or so a 1916 ad in *The Times* claimed:

> There are reports from thousands of men and women on the Müller System as a remedy for Digestive and Intestinal Disorders, Nerve Maladies, Obesity, Thinness, Throat and Lung Complaints, Uric Acid Troubles, etc., and as a delightful process of real rejuvenation.

Published in 1904, *My System, 15 Minutes' Work a Day for Health's Sake* became an international best seller and was soon translated into more than twenty-five languages. One of his most devoted followers was Franz Kafka, who did his Müllers stark naked in front of his window at least twice a day. The System was also adopted by the British army during the First World War, when soldiers were ordered to do them in the trenches. Müller eventually moved to London where he published a slew of other books with titles like *My System for Ladies*, *My Breathing System*, *The Daily Five Minutes* and *Morals, Sex, and Happiness*. Following the deaths of his wife and two sons, he retreated to a medicinal spring near Moesgaard, where he devoted his remaining years to spiritualism and the occult. Despite predictions of longevity, he died of bronchitis in 1938 at the age of seventy-two.

It's unclear when Alastair was first introduced to the Müller

System, though it probably coincided with his growing interest in climbing and the desire of a teenage boy to develop his strength. By the time he enrolled at Edinburgh University, he was already a dedicated practitioner. While there, he not only received several Blues in cross-country and track, but also briefly held the Scottish record for the half mile. When he was named vice captain of the team in 1933, the student paper ran a profile under the heading 'Cross-Country Personalities'. It made special mention of Müller's influence:

> The undoubted excellence of our Vice-Captain as a runner across country can be attributed both to the fact that he combines the stamina and endurance of the expert climber with an unusual turn of speed, and to the fact that he is invariably in magnificent training. Surely there never was a man more fit than Cram – he positively radiates vitality. Muller is his private deity, and his exercises sacred rites, performed at 7:30 a.m. with a sacred fervour which sleepy Cowan men well know. He has, too, a missionary zeal which has produced surprising effects in the section.

Alastair expanded his routine at Capua to include a mile run in between the Müller exercises and the cold sponge bath and rub. It was the spectacle of his naked contortions as he vigorously rubbed his body that everyone who was a prisoner with him recalls. George Millar described the unusual sight in his memoir, *Horned Pigeon*, written immediately after the war: 'At first Cram used to have an excited, sometimes a caustic, audience when he did the rubbing, which consisted of starting low down on each leg and rubbing in strangely voluptuous movements right up to

33

the base of his neck.' Although impervious to any comments, they changed considerably as his reputation as an escaper grew. By now the story of his fourteen days spent wandering around Sicily was legendary. What everyone wondered was what his next move would be, as it was certain to come. Some said he was 'fanatical', while others proclaimed him 'an escapologist'. Then suddenly, everyone started calling him the Baron.

The title was borrowed from one of Germany's most popular pre-war athletes, Baron Gottfried von Cramm. Born just a month before Alastair, in July 1909, von Cramm was a leading figure on the international tennis circuit of the 1930s. He was also a major heart-throb, tall and elegant with the kind of manners that could seduce anyone. He had already won the French Open twice and been a finalist at Wimbledon three years running when the event he's best remembered for took place: the Davis Cup of 1937. Although he lost to Don Budge after blowing a 4–1 lead in the final set, many consider it one of the greatest tennis matches ever played. It was also the high point of von Cramm's career. Up till then, the Nazis had tolerated his refusal to join the party, believing that his international success was compensation enough for his quiet resistance to the regime. He was also a national hero, much too popular and well connected to arrest. His immunity came to an abrupt end in March 1938, when he was accused not only of having a homosexual affair with a Jewish actor named Manasse Herbst but also of illegally sending him money in Palestine. Von Cramm served five months in prison, after which he moved to Sweden. He returned to the Fatherland, however, when war broke out and eventually won an Iron Cross for service in Russia. Despite some closed doors, he resumed his tennis career after the war, playing competitively well into his forties.

It didn't matter, of course, whether or not one knew the origin of Alastair's new title. He wasn't simply the Baron because of his German namesake – though that was the inspiration; he was the Baron because of his accomplishments. If, as Adrian Gilbert claims, 'escapers were the military elite of the POW world', then it makes sense that Alastair would be awarded noble status. His next stop certainly turned out to be worthy of a baron.

Alastair had been at Capua for only a few weeks when he was told to get ready to leave at 6 a.m. the following day. He was being sent to Aquila in the Abruzzi to be punished for his prior escape. The two soldiers who came for him weren't very bright, nor did they seem concerned that he might try to get away. He forced them to lower their guard even further by pretending to be lame and barely able to walk. It was a shameless performance, and yet it seemed to work. No one who yelped and groaned as loudly as he did could possibly be considering an escape. Within half an hour, both guards were sound asleep. As for Alastair, he was too excited to even think of taking a nap.

It was an old train and very cold inside. The heating, if it ever existed, had broken down long ago. The other passengers had come prepared with warm coats and blankets wrapped around their shoulders. As they chugged along into the Apennines, a heavy snow began to fall. The conductor, who was a cousin of one of the guards, came by and gently tapped him on the back. They weren't going to make it to Aquila, he said. There was too much snow with giant drifts blocking the track. It wasn't the first time this had happened either. Another train had been dispatched although they'd have to walk quite a way to board it. Could the Englishman manage, he asked. He had been told that his legs were bad.

An hour later, they screeched to a halt. There was mass confusion as everyone stood up at once to gather their belongings. The conductor's cousin rushed out to walk ahead, while the second guard changed seats to get a better view. Alastair quietly stood up and, using the other passengers for a shield, worked his way to the opposite end of the car. Then, as everyone was being helped from one side of the train, he jumped out from the other. As he sank down, he knew right away that he was in trouble. Snow that fresh and deep would be impossible to cross without proper shoes or skis. But since he'd come this far, he might as well continue. Snow was still falling and visibility poor; both would work in his favour as he headed straight uphill towards a stand of trees just a hundred yards away. He'd gone only a short distance when he heard the alarm being raised behind him. Already well above his waist, the snow seemed to be getting thicker the higher he went. Then the two guards started screaming that they'd shoot if he didn't stop at once. It hardly mattered. His legs were completely stuck and he couldn't move at all. Just as well, since the guards had also forgotten to load their weapons.

They eventually reached the new train, and as they thawed out, the guards expressed their amazement at Alastair's sudden recovery. His legs didn't seem to bother him at all any more. They still hadn't figured it out. However, they did make him a proposition. If he didn't mention their failure to load their rifles, they wouldn't report his escape. Fair enough, said Alastair, as he was handed a large piece of bread and cheese.

The castle, when they finally arrived late that night, emerged from the mist like a ghost ship, its giant prow jutting out over the city. Built by Aquila's sixteenth-century Spanish rulers, it sat inside four great bastions, a symbol of power and fear. Though its original occupants had left long ago, it was still known as the Spanish Fort and remained just as imposing. It certainly was to Alastair as he stared up at its massive stone walls, dripping with water. His reverie was quickly brought to an end by the two guards, who nudged him forward with a simple 'Andiamo'. Crossing over a deep moat amid swirling gusts of wind and snow, they passed through a heavy door to enter into another universe.

A captain in an impeccably tailored uniform welcomed him into a wood-panelled room filled with high-backed chairs and silver chandeliers. 'Come, stand by the fire,' he commanded in perfect English. 'You must be tired after such a long journey.' As he offered him a cigarette and a glass of wine, Alastair noticed that he was wearing a British Victory Medal from the Great War. Would he prefer chocolate or biscuits, the captain asked. Unfortunately, the cafe from which he was to order his meals had already closed.

From there he was brought to see the commandant. Tall and handsome with salt-and-pepper hair, he was a full colonel, though he might well have been the dean of a major university. Alastair, he graciously announced in Italian, had been sentenced to thirty days' imprisonment, 'tutto di Convenzione di Geneva', all in exact accordance with the Geneva Convention, neither more nor less.

'It was fantastic,' said Alastair when he was finally shown to his room. While his companions at Capua were enduring the worst possible conditions, he had been sent to a punishment camp that resembled nothing so much as an exclusive men's club. With its tiled floor and fireplace, the room would have been luxurious under any circumstances, especially given its furnishings. Included among the tasteful arrangement was a small desk, chest of drawers, antique armoire and, best of all, a huge four poster bed with a spring mattress and night table and lamp beside it. For any additional needs, a servant had kindly been provided.

For the first few days he remained locked in his room, save for two hours of daily exercise as stipulated by Convention rules. That soon changed as many of the Italian officers were curious to meet him. In fact, it wasn't very long before they started showing up with bottles of wine and other treats. They usually appeared around eight and would often sit in front of the fire talking well into the night. They all desperately missed their families – their mothers, children, wives, a best friend, even a horse. None could understand how Alastair, thirty-two and with a steady income, wasn't married. In the end, they blamed it on the coldness of English women, an argument he'd heard before.

They tended to steer clear of politics, though as time wore on, the anti-fascists among them made their sentiments known. The Abruzzesi hated Mussolini according to one of the officers. So much so that he began giving Alastair money and, even better, the addresses of people who might help him should he manage to escape. One contact in Rome was the sister of a philosophy professor from Edinburgh whom Alastair knew quite well. The officer apologized for not doing more but it was simply too dangerous. He and others like him were waiting for the tide of war to change. In February 1942 it began to look as though it never would. Rommel had already retaken Benghazi and was on his way to Egypt. The Germans were also rolling across the Crimea and almost at the Volga. Burma had been invaded by the Japanese. And, in one of the worst defeats of all, Singapore had just surrendered.

Although a guard was assigned to follow him everywhere, Alastair was soon permitted to come and go as he wished during the day. He especially liked walking along the battlements with their spectacular views of the Gran Sasso, the highest peak in the Apennines. After the first week, another prisoner joined him, a lieutenant with the Italian Air Force who was serving thirty days for a very different kind of transgression. While flying over Spoleto he had buzzed two girls on bicycles, setting off an air raid alarm. 'A crime of passion,' he said dismissively, 'not worthy of punishment'. A Sicilian with an English aunt and Polish background, Marcello was practically a parody of the Latin lover. Tall with big white teeth and black hair combed straight back under a double layer of pomade, 'his one interest in life was the other sex'. Not only did he regale Alastair with endless stories of his many conquests, he even found a way while serving his sentence at Aquila to add to them.

Every day small groups of young women, between seventeen and eighteen, passed by the castle, giggling and chattering on their way to a nearby school. Not one to miss an opportunity, Marcello borrowed a pair of binoculars from one of the guards and was soon tossing love notes across the moat. Among the group of admiring girls was an extremely attractive brunette who always wore a red scarf around her shoulders with a matching hat. Her name was Gisella, though Alastair called her La Bambola Rossa, 'The Red Doll'. Before long he was sending letters of endearment himself, to which Gisella happily replied. Marcello, meanwhile, had become obsessed with a skinny blonde named Nanella. His proclamations of love were soon so unrestrained that the commandant, whose room was directly below, called up for him to be more quiet. The colonel didn't disapprove of the relationship. He simply objected to the noise.

Marcello eventually convinced a guard to let him meet Nanella inside the moat. He kindly asked Alastair if he and La Bambola Rossa would like to join them as well. This led to several intimate visits until one day Gisella invited Alastair home to spend the night. He told her that to do so, he'd need civilian clothes, especially if he planned to leave the castle after dark.

'Don't worry,' she replied. 'My brother's in North Africa. You can use a suit of his.' But there was another problem; Alastair was about to escape.

Marcello had showed him a small hinged window on the floor below. Once through it, Alastair was able to climb up to the battlements and by walking through the guards' sleeping quarters reach the drawbridge over the moat. While exploring the route, he discovered a wardrobe full of new uniforms, one of which he took. Since they had arrived there, the castle had become an assembly point for fresh recruits. With so many new faces passing in and out, he felt confident he wouldn't be challenged if he crossed first thing in the morning. He planned to remove the hinges from his door and start in the middle of the night – first through the window, then up to the battlements, silently past the sleeping guards, dressing in his uniform, and over the bridge by 6 a.m. He had money, contacts, warm clothes, and a rucksack full of food. His goal was Switzerland and with any luck, he should make it. He would wait, however, as long as he could for the weather to improve.

Gisella, who had already wrapped up her brother's clothes, was becoming anxious. Why was Alastair taking so long? She knew that he was reluctant to put her in danger but had repeatedly assured him that it didn't matter. She finally sat down and wrote a long letter describing her feelings and the life she imagined they would have together. She was desperate and acting erratically by the time she arrived at the castle. When she didn't see Alastair or Marcello, she walked up to the gate and asked the guard to deliver her letter. The captain with the British Victory Medal happened to be there and offered to take it.

That afternoon, Alastair's room was searched and the stolen uniform discovered. He was eventually tried for theft and sentenced to a year in civil prison. He never served it, though, as Mussolini soon declared a general amnesty to celebrate twenty years in power. Extra guards were now posted in front of his door and he was let out only to see the commandant. Avuncular and professorial as ever, he calmly expressed his disappointment in Alastair's childish behaviour. Then, in what may or may not have been an attempt at humour, he announced that Alastair had been punished enough and would depart for another camp the following day.

The train was already in Naples by the time Alastair learned where he was going: Padula, an ancient farming community so old that it was said to have been visited by Hercules. That was when it was still called Cosilinum, before the malarial swamps – which gave it its new name – were drained by Carthusian monks. Arriving at the beginning of the fourteenth century, they also built a giant monastery with the largest cloister in Europe. Named for a martyr slowly roasted to death over a barbecue pit, the Certosa di San Lorenzo had been a national monument since 1882 and would eventually be declared a UNESCO World Heritage Site. Its exquisite architecture wasn't wasted on the prisoners, many of whom had come directly from Capua. Tom Straker, a major with the New Zealand Infantry Brigade, noted with some irony that entering the newly baptized Prigione di Guerra 35, was an uplifting experience: 'We felt our spirits rise as we passed inside.' George Millar, who had studied architecture at Cambridge, was even more effusive: 'Worn out though I was by a long journey and by the tediously strict search we were obliged to undergo on arrival, I still count my entry into the vast court-yard of the monastery at Padula as the second greatest moment in my twenty-month career as a prisoner of war. The greatest moment came at the end.'

There were many ways in which it was the ideal space to be converted into a prison. It was already conveniently divided into two parts with each serving a function similar to its original one. The maze of offices, chapels, kitchens and store rooms in the front half had been the realm of the lay brothers who acted as an interface for the monks living in complete isolation in the cloister behind. Most monks arrived by the age of fourteen, the second sons of noble families who were given no choice in what amounted to a life of solitary confinement. They lived in one of twenty-four apartments lining an enormous grass-covered courtyard with a fountain in the middle. Meals, slid through a small opening, were eaten alone, and other than chanting at prayer, all speaking was forbidden. They wore hoods and lowered their heads when venturing outside their rooms. The second floor was composed of one great corridor with twenty-foot-high ceilings and interior-facing, glassless windows. Damp and either too hot or too cold, it served as an ambulatory where the Carthusians could occasionally exercise. This too was done alone.

The apartments, each of which had housed a single monk, were converted into suites for as many as eight senior officers at the rank of captain and above. The others, who numbered at least 400, were placed in the unpartitioned ambulatory. With beds and a small cupboard placed no more than two feet apart, there was little privacy and lots of noise. What most remember best, in fact, was the snoring, a nightly cacophony of ear-splitting wheezing that often made sleep impossible. Connecting the two floors was a double marble stairway that swept back and forth like a sail before reaching its destination beneath an equally oversized dome. Lining the steps were enormous, open windows that framed a different view with each twist and turn – the Valley of Diano, fields full of wheat and corn with animals grazing at the edge, orchards and olive trees, the foothills of the Apennines covered with flowers, and hanging above it all, the village of Padula with its red roofs and balconies strung with laundry. For the prisoners, like the monks before them, this was the only portal into the other world. Apart from the playing field that sat just beyond the stairs, they were entirely confined to the cloister.

News spread quickly of the Baron's arrival and it wasn't long before he had his first suitor. Jack Pringle, a captain with the 8th Hussars, wanted to escape and was looking for a partner. Alastair had never considered teaming up with anyone. He was too much of a loner. In fact, it was one of the first things that people usually recalled about him. When Tommy Macpherson was asked about Alastair, whom he knew at Gavi, his response was typical: 'Alastair was of course another matter. Actually he was so reserved, so much his own man, that I don't believe anyone knew him really well.' And yet, he was perfectly amiable and could always be counted on for a good story when needed. But he had few close friends, and they were all climbing partners, like Edward Machonochie, the bank teller's son who was with him in the Cairngorms in 1928 when they discovered Thomas Baird, stranded and dying in the snow. His dearest friend was Kenneth McDougall, from whom he was inseparable throughout the 1930s. English-born, though educated in the US and Scotland, Dougal, as he was commonly known, was both a zoologist and veterinarian. A strong climber and visionary, it was Dougal who introduced him to the Darlings and their Island Farm experiment. When he was killed with the Devil's Brigade in southern France in 1944, Alastair felt as though he had lost a brother.

Jack knew that Alastair had little interest in having anyone join him on an escape. 'I had to convince him that I was serious,' he said. After all, Alastair already spoke German, French and Italian, was familiar with the landscape, and could perform physical feats that few others could match. He also knew how quickly one needed to make decisions while on the run, and worried about getting involved in drawn-out deliberations. Winning his confidence took time, although it helped that Jack had made one escape and even had a plan for getting out of the monastery. Alastair was also impressed with Jack's Italian, which he spoke more fluently and with a better accent. Above all, he saw that Jack was as single-minded and determined as he was himself: 'The perfect complement to this scheming. Cold, calculating, not reckless but able to estimate the chances to the outermost limit of daring.' Jack would do, he decided, and so they became partners, and friends.

Unlike Alastair, Jack was a professional soldier, a graduate of

Sandhurst stationed in Egypt before the war. As handsome as any movie star, with impeccable manners and a pencil-thin moustache, he was the epitome of the dashing young cavalry officer, the type often played by Errol Flynn and David Niven. That's what he had always dreamed of when growing up around Boston, Massachusetts, where he attended Belmont Hill, an elite prep school. From there he went to Harvard, though he didn't stay long. He wanted to play polo and be part of the Empire. He claimed it was in his blood, and it's true that although he was born in Chicago to an American mother, his father was the eldest son of Sir John Pringle, a Mackenzie from the Outer Hebrides. After earning a medical degree, his grand-father, Sir John, had moved to Jamaica, married Amy Levy, and started buying land. By the time of his death in 1923, he had amassed more than 150,000 acres. Within a generation, it was all gone.

As a young lieutenant with a string of ponies and a passion for polo, Jack soon found his own fortunes waning. He knew he had to get away from the temptations of Cairo and asked to be seconded to the West African Frontier Force in Nigeria. For an ambitious young officer, his timing couldn't have been worse. He left the day war broke out and, until Italy entered nine months later, fretted that he would miss everything. Reassigned to a newly formed armoured car regiment, he fought all the way from Kenya to Addis Ababa, winning an MC for his leadership and bravery. He then returned to Egypt to rejoin the 8th Hussars. Crusader was just about to be launched and it wasn't long before he found himself in the middle of the fighting at Sidi Rezegh. That's where he was captured, on the same day and place as Alastair. Their paths didn't cross, though, until Padula.

Up till then, Jack was in the 'small and very pretty palazzo' of Rezzanello in northern Italy. When he learned he was to be moved south, and that the train would pass close to Rome, he decided it was time to escape. With a staged brawl for a diversion, he jumped from the window and immediately changed into women's clothing. He then walked nonchalantly back past the train, which had quickly stopped. The guards ran right by him in a panic. Everything seemed to be going fine. Then suddenly, one of his trouser legs fell down, and he was back in custody once again.

Alastair and Jack worked well together. They never argued or fought, and were obsessed with the same burning desire to escape. They hardly rested, each continually pushing the other. They were systematic, analytical, thorough, sceptical and forever optimistic. They explored every possibility, certain that a fourteenth-century monastery must be filled with hidden doors and secret passageways, and at least one escape route reserved for emergencies. 'The monastery was bound to have exits not yet spotted by the Italians,' wrote Jack. And they were determined to find them:

> We began to go over the place yard by yard. We looked out of every window, tapped all walls, identified sewage systems, noted guard routine, kept watch on the fields surrounding the monastery so as to observe moves of the peasants who farmed them, and generally familiarized ourselves as well as we could with the movements of everyone we could see, and with the architectural lay-out. We talked to guards with the object of finding out what happened in the adjacent part of the buildings where the Italian guard company lived, and where all the

administrative offices were. Gradually we built up our picture of the place, and we kept our knowledge strictly to ourselves.

Most of the other prisoners thought they were mad. Encased in barbed wire and watched from every angle by guards with floodlights and machine guns, the monastery seemed completely escape proof. And if making a break from the cloister was going to be difficult, getting out of Italy would be all but impossible. Only six men had managed to do so by September 1943 when the Armistice was signed. Surrounded by water on three sides and huge mountains on the other, an escaper faced much greater challenges than in Germany. It wasn't simply the geography. Everyone agreed that the Italians were simply more observant. They made better guards inside prisons, and more alert and dangerous civilians outside. Eric Newby, who escaped after the Armistice, was impressed, if not intimidated, by the incredible astuteness of the general population:

It was very difficult to travel in Italy if you did get out. The Italians are fascinated by minutiae of dress and the behaviour of their fellow men, perhaps to a greater degree than almost any other race in Europe, and the ingenious subterfuges and disguises which escaping prisoners of war habitually resorted to and which were often enough to take in the Germans . . . were hardly ever sufficiently genuine looking to fool even the most myopic Italian . . . The kind of going over to which an escaping Anglo-Saxon was subjected by other travellers was usually enough to finish him off unless he was a professional actor or spoke fluent Italian.

In the end they decided to try Jack's original idea. For some time, workers from the village had been repairing a wall in one of the smaller inner courtyards. If Alastair and Jack could make it to the other side, they should be able to climb over a second outer wall to freedom. While a guard was posted nearby, the workers promptly broke for lunch at noon every day. Leaving their buckets and tools behind, they walked straight through the adjacent kitchen which was staffed by British orderlies. The plan called for Jack and Alastair to dress up like the masons and enter the small courtyard just before the real ones returned from lunch. Once they cleared the first wall, a raucous work party would create a diversion, giving them time to get over the second. From there, they would simply look like two Italian workers on their way home.

It was the first escape from Padula and Ken Fraser, the SBO, made sure they were supplied with adequate money and documents. They already had a good supply of food, much of it bartered with Red Cross cigarettes they didn't need. When the day finally came and the tension built up as they sat waiting for noon to arrive, they sized one another up. 'I think we were each wondering,' said Jack, 'how the other would behave. I needed have no fear. Alastair was absolutely steady, and we both began to enjoy ourselves as we hid up in the kitchen after the masons had gone off to lunch.' Then, just as they were about to go, one of the cooks kindly dusted them with flour, a nice touch for two hardworking masons. The guard was nearly asleep and paid little attention as they picked up their trowels and moved to the other side of the wall. They could hear the diversion as they quickly crossed the courtyard and hid behind the bulging trunk of an ancient tree. Over the wall in seconds, they were barely visible as they walked through several acres of corn to the southern edge of the monastery's property, then out through an open wooden gate and onto a road that would circle back through the town. They confidently babbled away in Italian as they came across a small road crew that stopped to stare at them as they approached. The foreman, who knew every worker, was immediately suspicious; not because he thought they might be British officers escaping from the monastery, but because of their big packs which marked them as members of the black market. George Millar claimed it was their boots that gave them away. Everything else was in order, except for their footwear, which the foreman seemed to find peculiar. Whether it was the boots or their packs, they were arrested and searched, and back in the monastery by nightfall.

The commandant was a pompous Tuscan named Gori. Overweight and bald, he usually appeared in an absurd blonde wig. It clearly made him feel more attractive to the young women he regularly brought back for his wild, saturnalian parties. Of course, the prisoners knew nothing of this. The *colonnello* they saw was simply pretentious and unpredictable; unctuous and ingratiating one moment, and then suddenly losing all control the next. When 'the abominable Cram', as he called him, was returned to the monastery, he became so apoplectic in addressing the prisoners that his wig flew off. This really brought down the house. As for Alastair and Jack, they were given a week in the cells while their case was reviewed by the central authorities.

The 'cooler' was much more comfortable than the draughty second-floor corridor where Alastair had been living. Initially serving as the monastery's reception area, it was well lit with a desk and chairs and enough space for each bed to have a modicum of privacy. Best of all were the two barred windows at either end. The front one was strategically placed so that anyone entering the building through the main door to the right could be seen. It also had a perfect view of the guardroom and sleeping quarters directly across the hall. A week's worth of careful monitoring proved invaluable, especially when combined with the information they were able to extract from friendly guards.

They began preparing for their next escape the minute they got out. There was an added urgency now as the commandant had just announced that a new punishment camp was about to be opened in a town called Gavi, not far from Genoa. Unlike Aquila, this would be a true 'hell camp' where prisoners would live in underground caves and never see the light of day. Or so the Italians claimed, believing that such threats would dissuade anyone from even thinking about escape. Alastair and Jack were naturally at the top of the list of those they intended to send. They would have to work quickly, as it was rumoured that the first group was to leave within a week. While the information they had gathered from their time in the cells had brought them closer to forming a plan, too many questions still remained. Alastair, it was decided, would have to reconnoitre and find a way through the labyrinth of courtyards and church buildings on the Italian side.

The point of entry was the sacristy, a long, narrow room lined with wooden cabinets for the priests' robes and other objects. Located fifteen feet off the ground at the centre of the rear wall was an unlocked oval window. Jack and another officer lifted Alastair high enough to grab the scrollwork beneath it. From there, he easily pulled himself through and carefully dropped into the corridor on the other side. He would return at exactly 6 a.m., when there was an hour-long gap between the guard patrols. Should he be trapped and fail to appear, the roll calls would be fixed for at least forty-eight hours. After that, he would either give himself up or make good his escape.

His rubber shoes were completely silent as he walked down the hall, past the sleeping quarters of the guards and officers. Amused by the sound of their snoring, he resisted the 'impish' temptation to look in on Father Volpe, the camp translator behind much of the black market activity. At the end of the corridor, in front of the cell where he and Jack had recently been held, he turned right and hid inside the Prior's courtyard. As expected, a group of cara-binieri marched by on their way to the cloister. He waited a while before continuing on through the guards' mess, surprised to see scraps of food and bread left on the table. Climbing a short flight of stairs, he came to a window that overlooked the field they had crossed during their first escape. He wiped away the cobwebs, sure that it hadn't been opened in years. Then as quietly as possible, he jiggled the frame until it finally came loose. They could use it if they had a good rope, he thought. However, they'd also have to climb the fifteen-foot wall that lay just beyond. Retracing his steps, Alastair found the main entrance to the outer courtyard open and unguarded. The searchlights were poorly placed and easy to avoid. He moved inside the shadows, and less than half-way down discovered a wicket gate off to the right. They'd still need a ladder for the final wall, but he preferred this to the window: 'The route was made.'

It was only 1 a.m. by the time he reached the monastery gar-dens. It was a warm May night with just a sliver of a moon in the sky. He lay on his back with his hands behind his head and looked up at the stars. Then he noticed the fireflies which were suddenly everywhere, and the overpowering smell of roses and other spring blossoms. It was a transcendent moment he would never forget:

> I lay relaxed, sleeping in the immense quietness and peace of that ancient and lovely place. In retrospect it is that hour I remember best. Cleansed, content I lay in motionless meditation in a state bordering on adoration of the harmony of that perfect night. Fortunate is he who carries in his spirit such a recollection from the annoyance and pettiness of prisoner of war life.

Jack was there to grab his legs as he lowered himself through the oval window. After hearing Alastair's report, they both agreed to leave as soon as possible. They had originally planned to put it off until July, when the harvest would be ready and they could live off the land. But the clock was ticking and there were only a few days left before they were to be sent north to Gavi.

The waiting was excruciating, much worse, Alastair always claimed, than the actual doing:

> I reached a high pitch of nervous excitement. More I think than ever again. The venture was one of my own heart. I felt it was one suited to my capabilities but my mind shied at the risks, which always seem greater in anticipation than in practice. Sitting in the hot sun with Jack in discussion I would at one time exult in the project and yet feel a prickly chill, a nervous sweat would lie near the surface, ready to break as on a racehorse. Jack too suffered. Our mentality was different from the others quietly living, studying, talking. We some-

times envied them, occupied with the very real discomforts of food shortage, bad accommodation, fuel and water shortage, small arguments and disagreements. We seemed to live at a higher, a more vibrant pitch than they. Never is living so valuable, so meaningful as to those who undertake hazard.

With only forty-eight hours to go before departing for the new camp, they made their move. While an Australian forger put the last touches on their documents, they packed their knapsacks and arranged for two orderlies to sleep in their beds. Finally, just before going, Alastair gave Colonel Fraser a detailed map of the route he had worked out. Should they succeed, three other officers would escape the same way the following night. Then, without anyone noticing, they quietly disappeared into a storeroom where they would wait for nearly two hours before they began. Sitting in the softly lit space, surrounded by old mattresses and bales of confiscated uniforms, it was Alastair's turn to size his partner up: 'I could feel Jack's nerves tightening like violin strings to the correct pitch but I knew they were nowhere near being tested. With a curious vibration becoming less in space but more in time he came up to calm. His mind cleared as a rippled pool stills.' It was time to go.

They silently dropped into the corridor, where they were surprised to find a twelve-foot ladder conveniently lying against the wall. Alastair knew it would be hard to manage but Jack wanted to take it and so they did. By midnight, they were safely hidden in the rose bushes in the Prior's courtyard when the Carabinieri patrol passed by like clockwork. Manoeuvring the ladder around the corner and into the Italians' mess was awkward, especially with their packs tied on. Jack claims they carried it behind the backs of two guards who were seated, staring out the window. Alastair remembers a different close call when a guard surprised them as they were scaling a wall. He was sitting on top with Jack halfway up the ladder handing him their packs. A door suddenly opened and a sentry walked in. As Jack melted into the shadows, Alastair rolled over like a gymnast, holding on to the wall by his calf alone. If the guard saw anything, he chose to ignore it.

At last they reached the wicket gate, which was as far as Alastair had come. Once through, they headed in opposite directions to reconnoitre. That's when a howling dog appeared and Alastair was sure they were done for. It barked and growled for what seemed like hours. Every light came on as he sat waiting for the inevitable attack. Still nothing happened. He cooed and whispered in Italian, and began to sense a less aggressive, more uncertain bark. Finally, he found a piece of wood and tossed it over the wall, and with one last 'woof', the brute disappeared. Fifteen minutes later Jack showed up. He had found a way out. They crossed the same field they had before, climbed the perimeter wall and hid the ladder in a row of corn. It was nearly 3 a.m. Two more hours and it would be light. Their plan was to walk north to Potenza and, via Rome, go by train to Lake Maggiore. From there, they'd enter Switzerland by foot.

They quickly circled around the monastery and, with the village on their left, headed for the Maddalena Mountains to the east. They followed a mule track at first but left it when farmers with their animals started to appear. The scrub was thick and in places very steep. For Jack, who had never climbed before, it wasn't easy, especially when they crossed a buttress with a gorge 500 feet below. Although Alastair gave him some advice, Jack says he was nearly impossible to keep up with:

54

He told me to keep my knees slightly bent. This, he said, took a lot of the strain out of climbing. But he set off at such a pace that, bent knees or not, I had great trouble in keeping up with him. He rolled about in front of me like a small boat in a heavy sea, and scorned any idea of resting.

It was late morning by the time Alastair finally relented and took a break. After eating some chocolate, they leaned against their packs and enjoyed the strong Italian sun. Spring was about to give way to summer, and everywhere they looked wild flowers were in bloom – roses and bluebells and poppies and thistles, and little yellow flowers they'd seen but couldn't name. There were lots of lizards too, darting about their feet, and in the distance, sitting like a matchbox on the valley floor, the Certosa di San Lorenzo glimpsed for one last time. Or so they hoped.

They followed bridle paths along the northern slope until lack of sleep finally did them in. Fuelled by the adrenalin of escape, they'd been going non-stop for nearly thirty-six hours and were about to collapse. They found a secluded spot in a stand of pines and took turns sleeping and keeping watch. Not long after setting out again, they met a shepherd whose flock of sheep had blocked their path. Although suspicious at first, he seemed to believe their story about being workers – Jack an Italian from Savona in the north and Alastair a German posted to a new airfield. They shared bread and cheese and talked about the road ahead and what to expect. It was dark by the time they approached the next village, and after searching in vain for a place to spend the night, fell asleep inside a vineyard.

They should have done the same the next evening when they reached Marsico, a small farming community not unlike Padula.

Whether they were over confident or simply didn't think anyone would be out that late at night, it was soon clear they were in trouble. Everywhere they turned, they found people staring at them in the streets. Getting away proved even worse as each twist and turn dragged them deeper into an endless labyrinth of winding ways and cul-de-sacs. One moment they were passing through a courtyard filled with laundry and the next a pump house followed by a dairy. Dogs barked, lights went on, windows opened. When at last they made it back to the main road, they found three plainclothes policemen standing in their way. They quickly turned round and headed down the nearest alley, only to arrive at a dead end. A man came out and offered help. Jack asked directions to a different town. A torrent of history and place names followed. He was concerned they might get lost and insisted on escorting them back to the main road. What could they do? The policemen were still there and instantly approached. '*Stranieri!*' they screamed. 'Foreigners.'

They told their stories once again, two workers newly transferred to the area. Their papers needed more inspection. Would they please accompany them to a nearby wine shop where they could talk? Once inside, the three became aggressive. Alastair's picture wasn't quite right, and were they aware that the British were dropping agents to blow up bridges and dams? That was it. Alastair turned to Jack and, putting his pack down, said in German, 'We have to make a run for it.' The police edged towards the door while the frightened shop girls hid behind the wooden barrels. Then Alastair shouted, 'I am a German, and I will not be treated this way by Italians,' and, waving his hands, pushed his way out onto the street. One policeman tried to grab him but he easily shook free. Jack quickly planted himself in front of the entrance, preventing anyone else from leaving. It was an act of pure self-sacrifice that allowed Alastair to get away.

An alarm went up with calls of 'Parachutists! Enemies! Beware, beware.' He could hear the mob right behind him as he entered the maze of streets and courtyards once again. He jumped a hedge and crawled inside a field of grain. Circling around, he headed down the valley, free, he thought, until he met an armed patrol. Then back across the river, climbing through the woods and scrub all night. More patrols came by, rattling guns and screaming. One forced him back inside the brush, where he lay concealed for the rest of the day.

Jack, meanwhile, was taken to a police station for interrogation. Convinced he was a British commando, they handcuffed him to a stool, demanding that he confess. 'You're a spy,' they yelled, and then with each question, beat him. 'Where are the others?' 'How many are there?' 'What was your mission?' Their suspicions were aroused by Britain's first airborne raid, which had taken place nearby in February 1941. Code-named Operation Colossus, thirty-eight men had been dropped at Calitri, north of Padula, in order to blow up an aqueduct. Despite their success, every member of the operation was captured, many of them ultimately becoming fellow prisoners of Alastair and Jack. In the meantime, southern Italy remained on high alert with special units watching for any hostile activity.

After several hours of violent questioning, they brought out a rope and dragged Jack up to the roof. 'Tell us who you are,' they threatened, 'or we'll throw you off right now.' He knew it wouldn't help Alastair to lie any longer, so he admitted he was a British officer from the prison camp in Padula.

As for Alastair, he waited till dusk to set off again. With all his food back in the wine shop, hunger and exhaustion started to set in. He began to see strange beings emerging from the woods as he often did when pushed to such extremes; only this time, it led to an accident as well:

I remember walking over a high col, through ancient and spectral woods where trees were ghosts in the moonlight, of circling a fairy tale town of towers and fantastic mediaeval stonework clustering on a pointed hill above a broad torrent bed, of struggling with increasing weakness through endless vineyards in the dark, each a row of vines, a hedge supported on wires, a ledge on a stone terrace. I jumped from one terrace to a strip of grass a foot wide. But it was a deep drainage ditch fronded over with grasses. One leg plunged deeply in. I fell forward. There was a dull crack, an agonizing pain in my knee. I hung there, my leg trapped in the ditch, my body hung face downwards over a stone terrace unable to move until I figured out a way climbing back on my hands. My leg was not broken but movement of the knee joint was excruciatingly painful. For two months I could only hobble and eight months were to pass before my leg felt was as strong as before.

Limping over more terraces, then scrambling down a hillside, he came to a stagnant stream with wild cherries growing beside it. Eating several handfuls, he lay back and instantly fell asleep. He awoke well past daybreak, surprised to find himself in a field of potatoes and wheat. He took bites of each, which left him with an unpleasant taste of acid and grit.

That evening he got entangled in the streets of yet another town. As in Marsico, the more he struggled to get out, the further entrapped he became. He finally escaped across an iron pipe with a raging river more than a hundred feet below. Heading north, he entered a pine forest, eerie and dark like the setting for a ghost story. The brambles and cobwebs were so thick that he had to place his hands beside his face and use them as antennae. He rubbed his eyes as billows of dark grey smoke appeared, twisting and turning like a genie. What was this place, he wondered. Then he stumbled on a huge crater: he was in a charcoal burners' encampment. He found their hut nearby and easily broke in. There was bread and cheese inside as well as pasta. He also found a shotgun and rifle, and boxes filled with ammo. But he had no use for firearms and took only the food. The workers, who were busy cutting wood, soon discovered they'd been robbed. Shrieks, a search party and even a shot or two followed, then silence.

By that time, Alastair was safely hidden in a cave. Yet he knew that once the theft was reported, it wouldn't take long before others came to find him. A ring of search parties with dogs was already closing in, all looking for the fugitive from Padula. If he was to have any chance of remaining free, he would have to move and soon. This wouldn't be easy, as his knee was now completely stiff and swollen. Sitting like a yogi in his cave, he thought back on the past week since he and Jack escaped:

Night and day were meaningless to me now, mere alternations of heat and cold. I remember finding a burnt out clearing with acres of large sweet wild strawberries, where I ate until I could eat no more, slept, and ate again. I recollect one evening from a promontory ridge looking back on the hill slope when a curtain of unbelievably rich purple fell between. A little south facing alp on a rock pinnacle on the north edge of the Basilicata Plateau where high above woods and meadows the sound of cowbells rang. I sat amid little yellow, red and blue alpine flowers, gentian, primula and rosacea and gazed out over fold after fold of dove grey hills. An hour of detached contemplative happiness, which alone was worth it all.

That afternoon a soldier standing on top of a hay cart spotted him hiding in a bush. A dog was sent in, and no matter how hard Alastair tried, he couldn't shake him off. Then a sergeant got down on one knee and, sticking his rifle in the hedge, threatened to shoot unless he came out at once. Twenty-four hours later he was back in Padula, sharing a cell with Jack. They served a month for their first escape, giving them plenty of time to plan for the next. It would be a train jump, somewhere between Genoa and Rome, but only after putting all the guards to sleep.

They left for Gavi in the middle of July, when it was far too hot to ride in a train without all the windows open. Because of his knee, Alastair had convinced the doctors that he needed pills to sleep, and by now had a bottle full of them. At some point after Rome, Alastair dissolved the tablets in a nice Chianti, though he also had lemonade should the guards prefer. They chose the wine, and everyone sat back with their packs on their laps and waited. It was just before Livorno when the two guards finally nodded off. They let a burly South African fighter pilot named Lorentz go first. Alastair followed right after, and was halfway out of the window when suddenly a change of guard appeared. They pulled him back, and with a rifle butt, knocked him to the ground. It looked as though the Baron would be going to Gavi after all.

# 3

# The Escape Academy

Alastair was a lawyer. He knew the articles of the Geneva Convention. Thirty days of consecutive solitary confinement was the limit, and he had just served a full term at Padula. If two sentences were to be run back to back, a prisoner was entitled to at least three days of freedom in between. But Giuseppe Moscatelli was indifferent. He shoved them into the small cell, screaming, '*Non siete ufficiale, siete malevolo criminale.*' 'You're not officers, you're depraved criminals.' Alastair never forgot the commandant's brutality, nor his unpredictable swings of mood. Some said it was Moscatelli's shrill voice during these frequent tantrums that led to his nickname, 'The Bat', though a more likely reason was the giant cloak he wore as part of his black Carabinieri uniform. Tall and muscular with the unmistakable bearing of a professional soldier, Moscatelli – also known as Joe Grapes – received his first commission in 1908, the year before Alastair was born. Now fifty-eight and a full colonel, he was the picture of arrogance as he strode through the castle immaculately dressed with shiny riding boots and a chest full of ribbons. Several were from the Libya campaign of 1911, with others from the Great War when he was wounded more than once. An ardent fascist, it was Moscatelli who had overseen the conversion of the fortress into its present incarnation as Campo 5.

Alastair's welcome to Gavi was forty straight days in the cells, thirty for his most recent escape and another ten tacked on for insults contained within his letters. While all correspondence was censored, certain statements were considered actionable. In fact, Peter Joscelyne, a captain with the Royal Tanks, was sent to Gavi for refusing to retract a statement made in one of his letters. For Alastair, it was a case of referring to Italian officers as behaving in 'an ungentlemanly manner', a claim readily confirmed by the reception he received from Colonel Moscatelli.

The punishment cells were wedged into the furthest corner of the upper courtyard, with two small windows well beyond the reach of any light. A huge ramp formed an arch just above, rendering them even more dungeon-like than they already were. Like much of the fortress, the rooms were carved directly into the rock. In summer they were stiflingly hot and in winter so cold that their occupants were often forced to stay in bed most of the day. Mould was ever present, with a dark green seepage climbing down the walls like a tapestry. While the cells may have been designed for solitary confinement, they were usually occupied by two or more prisoners. In fact, there was only one day in the history of Gavi – Christmas 1942 – when the two punishment cells were empty. Struck by the holiday spirit, Moscatelli declared an amnesty. That night the officers dined on rabbit, although when the meat course was served the SBO stood up and said, 'Gentlemen, please don't suck the bones. We're going to use them for soup.' Moscatelli even provided an extra ration of wine, which may have contributed to the riot that followed. In the end, the guardhouse was called out and by the next day the cells were once again filled to capacity.

The Red Cross, which filed regular reports on every camp, referred to these cells rather euphemistically as 'the place of seclusion', while Alastair called them 'a little stone cloister with two windows'. For most of the prisoners, however, they were simply the 'cooler'. For the first three days, neither Alastair nor Jack was let out at all. After that, the doors were opened for an hour each morning, allowing them to wash, shave and eat their breakfast. Any remaining time could be used to walk up and down the length of the upper courtyard. In the afternoon they were let out once again for another hour of exercise. Of course, Alastair continued to do his Müllers throughout. Fortunately, the food, brought to them by orderlies, remained the same as that served to the prisoners in the mess below. But the toll on their bodies was severe. When he was finally released after seventy days of close confinement, Alastair felt like 'a damp fly emerging from a chrysalis'. His senses were numbed if not impaired. It was a while before his hearing returned to normal. His eyes, too, needed to readjust to the light and colour so absent from the endless dusk in which he'd been living. Even his distance vision took time to recover fully.

For the first time he could appreciate the extraordinary set-ting of the fortress with its expansive views of the Lemme valley and beyond. On the other side of the river and to the west was the point where the Apennines joined with the Maritime Alps. The village itself sat directly below, a compact, medieval town that had changed little in its 1,000-year history. Its walls and city gates were still visible, and rising from its centre was the grace-ful bell tower of San Giacomo, a Romanesque church built in the twelfth century. At street level the town was grey and cheerless, but from above, its red tiled roofs gave it a warm and inviting quality. He was close enough to see schoolchildren and mothers going about their daily lives. And in the fields that reached to the edge of the village, farmers could be seen tending their crops and vineyards while animals calmly grazed beside the river. It was an idyllic scene, like a Bruegel painting, a tableau vivant which the prisoners watched with both envy and disbelief. How could such a peaceful world exist when a war raged on not far away?

Alastair sat on the wall that lined the flagstoned ramp connecting the upper and lower compounds. The summer sun penetrated his body, bringing his muscles and spirit back to life. He had a fleeting sense of freedom after being confined for such a long time. Suddenly, the prison seemed spacious. It wouldn't last, of course, but Alastair let himself relax for one of the few times during the three and a half years he spent as a prisoner. The next scheme, with its obsessive preparations and furtive planning, would overtake him soon enough. Yet, for the moment, he did what most POWs did: read, study and play sports.

Since Gavi had only two small courtyards, it wasn't always easy to get exercise. Many prisoners spent the day rushing up and down the steep hundred-yard ramp that ran between the two levels. Others, like Alastair, performed their own physical fitness routines. A cellmate named Dan Riddiford recalls the way Alastair 'used to get up before anyone else, take off his pyjamas and then stand out in the open stark naked, and massage his body all over with a circular motion of the flat of his hand. It was somewhat startling in the early morning to see Alastair's pink, thickset figure engaged in these exertions.'

There was also a continuous basketball game that filled the twenty-five by sixty-foot lower courtyard while a non-stop volleyball game occupied the smaller courtyard above. To ensure that everyone got a turn, two Scottish officers and crack athletes, Tommy Macpherson and John Muir, were put in charge. Each day they created a rotation guaranteeing every prisoner who wanted it a place in one of the competitions. Still, more space was clearly needed and the Swiss 'Protecting Power' filed a complaint pressuring the Italians to provide it. Although Moscatelli responded with a promise to create a field outside the fortress, he never did.

He also limited the heavily guarded walks to two or three a week. With only twelve to fourteen prisoners allowed on each, it was a long wait before one's turn came around. Even so, a South African fighter pilot named Rex Reynolds used it as an opportunity to try to escape. The party, which regularly followed the same route, always stopped to rest on a stone bridge high above a dry gorge. In the middle of the bridge, which widened into a bay, road workers had left canvas sacks filled with rocks. Reynolds recognized the sacks as the same ones found in the camp. With some practice, he was soon able to get into one in a matter of seconds. He also knew that the guards never recounted the prisoners after their stop. If properly shielded, he would be able to get into the sack and simply be left behind. On the day of the escape, everything went like clockwork. The party reached the bridge where each man played his part in creating a human wall. In just seconds, Reynolds was transformed into a sack of rocks. The break over, the prisoners lazily got up to leave. The guards hadn't a clue. In fact, they may have been too relaxed. As the last guard walked past the sacks, he casually gave one a kick. To his horror, it was alive. Just as he was about to bayonet it, another prisoner rushed up to stop him. Reynolds was rescued. But his escape failed.

As in every camp, cards and gambling were an important part of many prisoners' lives. Bridge, which held no interest for Alastair, became the obsession of many, with tournaments and competitions frequently arranged. Just as popular were the ongoing poker games in which large sums regularly changed hands. These took place in a lower compound room known as the Casino. Every night, in a raucous, smoke-filled space, roulette, faro, and baccarat were played alongside endless games of poker and any other form of betting one could conjure. Debts were settled with camp-issued *buoni*, and when those funds were exhausted, with cheques drawn on one's bank at home. Some prisoners were known to send back large sums of money, in one case £1,200 in a single year. Of course, the reverse was also true and a number of men found themselves in serious debt.

Officers were paid according to their rank, at first in lire and then in a special camp currency called *buoni*. The exchange rate was the same for both, seventy-two to the pound, with the funds simply deducted from the men's army pay back home. A lieutenant like Alastair received as little as 750 lire a month out of which he had to buy food, wine, firewood and anything else he might wish to purchase from the canteen or elsewhere. Most officers, for example, had been forced to buy chairs, which they often carried with them as they moved about the castle. Even the orderlies who took care of the rooms had to be paid. Making do on the equivalent of just over £10 a month wasn't easy, which is why the better-paid senior officers were able to sell their surplus lire to the junior ones, who bought them with pounds drawn from their home banks.

An important supplement for everyone was the supply of Red Cross parcels. Depending on their country of origin – and many believed the Canadian ones to be the best – a parcel might contain tea, cocoa, powdered milk, sugar, chocolate, dried eggs, porridge, margarine, cheese, a tin of meat, sardines, vegetables, biscuits, jam, dried fruit, pudding, a bar of soap and fifty cigarettes. Unlike some camps, such as Colditz, where prisoners cooked for themselves in small groups, at Gavi everyone messed together. As a result, two-thirds of every parcel went into a common pool which the cooks used to prepare the meals. They were served in a long, narrow room running the length of the lower courtyard. At one time, when Gavi was a civil prison, it had been a warren of small cells. Now it was a single, wood-beamed space that sat above two floors of enlisted men's rooms. With windows along both sides, it offered good views of the village and mountains as well as the guards' quarters on the bastion known as the Mezzaluna just below. It was also the only common space where all 170-plus officers could comfortably gather.

They remained there, lingering after dinner until eight. It was during this time that a nightly news report was prepared and read by Tommy Macpherson. One of the youngest officers in the camp, Macpherson was a commando captured in Libya while reconnoitring for the attempted assassination of Rommel, a raid which failed miserably since the field marshal was in Rome celebrating his birthday. As for Macpherson, the submarine that was to pick him up never appeared. After two nights of waiting in the ocean in a small, collapsible folbot, he set off through the desert where he was eventually captured. Provided with daily copies of *Corriere della Sera* and *La Stampa*, Macpherson did his best to read between the lines and present a more accurate, if favourable and heartening, view of the war. But in summer 1942, when Alastair arrived, this was not an easy thing to do. Tobruk had just fallen with 35,000 men captured, a number of them already in Gavi. Now Rommel was on the verge of taking Egypt with El Alamein alone to stop him. The Red Army was in retreat and the Germans were on the banks of the Volga about to surround Stalingrad. The Japanese too continued to expand in Asia and the Pacific. For the prisoners in Gavi, it was a bleak picture with unknown years of captivity ahead. If Alastair was tempted to relax, the hopeless state of the war certainly encouraged it. Besides, Gavi really did seem impossible to escape from.

Across from the mess and up a short flight of stairs was a wood-covered balcony onto which opened the officers' cells in the lower compound. To many, it 'looked exactly like a slum'. A random assortment of clothes hung over the railing with flies everywhere. Directly below were storage rooms for the vegetables and Red Cross parcels. It was also the location of the constantly malfunctioning latrines. The stench was horrible and huge rats, as every Gavi inmate recalls, were a regular presence. Alastair's cell was at the end, nearest the bath house which had been converted from the original chapel. It was, in his words, 'a dismal, damp, and utterly frugal' space. Although it faced south, almost no breeze or sun ever penetrated its two heavily barred windows. It was a barrel-vaulted room, about twenty feet by twenty-five, with a depressing double door; the inner one made of steel bars like a common jail and the outer of heavy wood with a peep hole through which guards could peer.

Unlike the ambulatory at Padula, where 132 men shared one gigantic room, the Gavi cell was claustrophobic and airless with hardly any space to move between its six beds. Alastair had never lived in such close quarters with a group of people before. He was, after all, an only child, brought up without the intimacy of brothers and sisters. Yes, he had been to a public school but he had been a day student and never experienced the fraternity of young men living together as a surrogate family. And yes, he was an athlete but he was never attracted to team sports. He was a distance runner and above all a mountaineer. Solitude and the world of mountains was the compass by which he set his course. Now for the first time, he experienced a level of intimacy he had never known. And rather than reject it, he marvelled at the ability of his comrades to get along, to tolerate and support one another, to lift each other's spirits and, in the end, to transcend what for most would have been an unbearable nightmare. He appreciated that their lives, so different from his own, had taught them the skills that would make this possible. And with his very logical mind, he dissected the process, analysing the various qualities required for such a peaceful coexistence:

Men in such close confinement might well be expected to have moments of disagreement but, never did one meet with such sympathy, charity and self abnegation . . . I was blessedly fortunate in these companions. The first essential of a companion is that he is quiet. Dispassionate discussion yes but emotional argument no, pleasant banter at meals but continuing chatter never, generosity but never selfishness, self denial never self assertion, quiet steady movements but at no time pacing in the cell; humming, snoring, knocking over stools, stumbling, tapping, scraping wear thin the sweetest temper. Didactic talking, professorial superiority, parade of book learning, dwelling on personal experience, riding hobby horses, repetitive remarks, or dwelling on smut, in fact the many facets of the bore become in a short time intolerable. These officers schooled in the art of living in groups of men in confined quarters in the iron self discipline of public schools, Dartmouth, Woolwich and Sandhurst, and graduates of wardrooms and messes had all cant burned from them in submarines and tanks, cockpits, parachute regiments, naval ships in action and regiments in battle. As a civilian I was surprised at this new culture and attitude to learning and the arts . . . I owe these men and many others I was still to meet an unending debt of gratitude in the study of the art of living.

In addition to Jack, his roommates included two naval officers, a tank commander, and a captain from New Zealand. All had advanced degrees in escape which had earned them places at Gavi. And other than Daniel Riddiford, the New Zealander, they were all regular officers for whom escape was not simply a duty but a professional necessity. Wartime service was the quickest road to promotion, and while they were idly sitting in a prison camp, their fellow officers were advancing. The most senior among them was Peter Medd, a lieutenant commander who had joined the navy in 1930 as a seventeen-year-old cadet. As Riddiford noted: 'But for his being captured, he would have had a brilliant war career; as it was, there was nothing left for him but to become the model POW.'

A member of the Fleet Air Arm, Medd had been shot down in July 1940 while flying a Swordfish on a reconnaissance flight over Tobruk. Along the way he attacked a submarine and was hit by ground fire, coming down twenty miles out to sea. He made it into his inflatable raft and with his two crewmates drifted to shore, only to be picked up and imprisoned. He had already made two escape attempts before being sent to Padula, where the night after Alastair and Jack's escape, he followed the same route with two others. But they waited too long for the guard to change and were easily picked up in the open soon after.

Now in Gavi, Medd was the senior officer in the lower compound. Five foot eight and solidly built, Medd had a soft face with clear blue eyes and light, receding hair. There were few officers more respected. He had an easy style of leadership, with a generosity and warmth not always associated with the military. Alastair especially admired him, claiming he 'was the most integrated personality' he met in captivity. He was surprised, in fact, to find that professional soldiers could be so well rounded. Yet Medd was indeed the perfect scholar athlete. He was an accomplished musician, spoke fluent French, Italian and German, was an expert with the sabre and equally well versed in poetry, philosophy and history. But it was his charitable nature and skills with people that seemed to impress Alastair the most.

The second naval officer in Alastair's room was Michael Pope, affectionately known as Poppet. Three years younger than Medd, and coming from a distinguished naval family, he too became a cadet at seventeen. But Poppet had gone into 'the trade', as the submarine service was commonly known. On 1 August 1940 he was serving as the third officer on the HMS *Oswald*, patrolling the Mediterranean near the Straits of Messina. Around midnight, while the submarine sat on the surface recharging its batteries, the Italian destroyer *Ugolino Vivaldi* suddenly appeared and tried to ram them. The captain, whose name was David Fraser, may have thought the damage was more serious than it was. In any case, he quickly gave the order to abandon ship. Poppet, who was below, saw that the boat was still sound and could easily have waged a fight, but there was nothing to be done beyond seeing that all the men got out. They scuttled the sub and swam for over two hours until the *Ugolino Vivaldi* came back to rescue them. Of the fifty-five crew members, all but three were saved. For Poppet, however, it was little consolation. He never forgave the captain, who, along with the first officer, was court-martialled after the war.

They were among Italy's first prisoners, inspiring a newsreel that celebrated their capture. Local tailors even sewed the officers new uniforms, after which they travelled by first class to Venice, where they were imprisoned on the Island of Poveglia. Located in the heart of the Venetian lagoon, Poveglia had once been a lazaretto for plague victims and following that a sanatorium for the mentally ill. It was now just barely refurbished as a prison and for Poppet and his companions not all that unpleasant. When it was time to move, he along with three others hid in the rafters for several days. They hoped to steal a boat and sail to Yugoslavia. But they were soon discovered and sent on to Sulmona. A prison camp for Austrians during the First World War, Sulmona was located in the Abruzzi Mountains in central Italy. Now Poppet turned his hand to tunnelling and might have succeeded too, if a donkey hadn't collapsed it. But he did succeed in climbing over the fence with two companions. It was midwinter and deep snow covered the ground. For five days they struggled over the mountains only to be caught on the Adriatic coast while searching for a boat. He was then sent to Padula, where he teamed up with Peter Medd and a wiry little sapper named Gerry Daly. They used the same route that Alastair had found but, as already noted, left too late and were caught.

Poppet was tall and thin and very good looking. In fact, Alastair said 'he was as handsome a man as one could wish to see'. And although he had a good sense of humour, he was thought to be somewhat severe and stern. Towards those he disapproved of, he could be bitterly caustic. He was especially good with his hands, the person one called on when something needed to be fixed or mended. With little effort, he soon became an expert at picking locks. He perfected his Italian by reading Dante's entire trilogy in the original. He liked to keep busy and volunteered for different camp jobs. At Sulmona he ran the canteen, and at Gavi kept the mess accounts where he was 'initiated into the mysteries of double entry'. He was meticulous and intensely practical. Alastair wondered if he had the freedom of mind 'necessary for true mystical experience'. It was ironic, he thought, for a person who had spent so much time at sea to be so 'earthbound'. Whatever the case, Poppet was a man one could depend on.

Alastair's other two cellmates were captured at Sidi Rezegh, just as he and Jack had been. One of them, John Cruttwell, a captain in the Royal Tanks, was among the first prisoners to make an escape. He did so while still at Tarhuna, their first prison camp in Libya. Along with a pilot from the RAF, he had crawled through the wire and disappeared into the desert. They walked over a hundred miles, living for more than two weeks with different groups of Arabs, the last of which betrayed them. Eventually, he ended up in Padula, where he joined twelve others in digging a tunnel. It was started by Alan Hurst-Brown and two friends, who found a hollow space beneath the corridor of one of the ground-floor cells. All thirteen got away, though it wasn't long before they were recaptured and en route to Gavi.

Of all his cellmates, Dan Riddiford would appear to have had the most in common with Alastair. He too was a lawyer who had joined the artillery at the beginning of the war. He was also captured just days before him during the early part of the same battle. After that, their histories quickly diverged. Born in 1914, Riddiford came from one of New Zealand's oldest families. His great-grandfather, who bore the same name, had helped found the city of Wellington and by the time of his death had accumulated 56,000 acres with livestock and properties to match. His son, appropriately nicknamed 'King', continued to expand their holdings. A forceful and combative man who liked to drink and gamble, King was as comfortable speaking Maori and sleeping outdoors as he was at a society event. He was a character straight out of Edna Ferber's novel *Giant*. Yet instead of Texas, the Riddifords were the lords of the Wairarapa. Adding to his legend, King died in the arms of one of his mistresses with whom he had fathered a child. He also left six others, including Dan's father, who was a bit more conventional. He played polo, served with the Grenadier Guards in the First World War and built what was claimed to be the largest private residence in New Zealand. Named Longwood, after Napoleon's final home on St Helena, it was where Dan Riddiford grew up, at least until he was sent off to prep school in England. He remained there for university, attending New College at Oxford, where he obtained a BA with honours in the Modern Greats – Philosophy, Politics and Economics. This was quickly followed with a second degree in jurisprudence, also with honours, and then another year in chambers in London's Inner Temple.

Years later, a close friend and colleague wrote that Riddiford's 'background and upbringing was as remote from ordinary people as, in New Zealand, it was possible to be'. Yet he remained a humble and unassuming man, so scholarly and reserved that 'at first sight it was easy to under-rate him'. This was more than the simple ease and self-assurance with which the upper class so often wear their privilege. Dan was a genuinely modest and private man, and while his manner may have seemed stand-offish and aloof, he was by no means arrogant or a snob. In fact, it is doubtful that any of his companions at Gavi even knew of his rarefied upbringing. What mattered was that he had earned a place in Gavi, passing his entry exam with honours. He had also prepared for it since childhood, reading all the escape books he could from the First World War – *The Tunnellers of Holzminden, Within Four Walls, The Escaping Club* – and deciding even then that were he ever to be taken prisoner, he would escape. He already knew that the best chance of escape was as soon after capture as possible. While most new prisoners were usually too stunned and demoralized to attempt it, those guarding them were equally tired and undermanned with little experience as jailers. And so on his first night of captivity, he picked up a shovel and slipped away. Later that night, he thought he had reached Allied lines only to walk straight into the arms of a group of Germans from the Afrika Korps. 'During the whole war,' he wrote, 'I never experienced a more cruel piece of bad luck.'

Handed over to the Italians, Riddiford was sent to a new camp just outside Poppi, an ancient Tuscan village where Dante wrote part of the *Inferno*. It was housed in an attractive multi-storey stone building that once served as a retreat for Florentine nuns, hence its uplifting name, Villa Ascensione. It now became the exclusive home of officers from New Zealand, as the Italians preferred to organize their camps by nationalities rather than branches of the service, as was the German policy. Unlike Gavi, the camp was busily organized around numerous activities, most of them academic, which is little surprise given that so many of these young officers would have been at university had there not been a war. Naturally, Riddiford became part of the 'Law Faculty'. But his real focus remained escape, and when he heard that his brother had been captured and was a prisoner at Modena, just north of Bologna, he asked to be transferred, though his intention was to jump from the train along the way. In the end, the entire camp was moved and Riddiford made his leap – one of the most dangerous forms of escape – as the train slowed inside a tunnel. Spotted by the guards, he was wounded before getting very far. But he had the pleasure of terrifying the local populace who watched with hysteria as this dangerous character was carried through town on a stretcher: 'I was enjoying the sensation I was causing and taking ironical pleasure that I, feeling not at all like a desperado, should be regarded by a crowd of Italians as a highly sensational, not to say, criminal character.'

For New Zealand's future Attorney-General and Minister of Justice, who probably never broke the law in his life, it was one of the delicious by-products of escape: to transgress and break the law with impunity, to dissemble, forge, lock-pick, destroy property, jump trains and assume false identities – key elements in every escaper's kit bag – and to have them considered virtues rather than crimes. For law-abiding citizens and officers of the

Crown like Dan Riddiford, escape provided an intoxicating range of emotions, many of them never experienced before. Yes, there was talk of honour and an officer's duty to escape, and the military costs exacted in diverting troops to recapture fugitive prisoners, but the truth for most escapers, particularly those like Alastair and his cellmates, was much more complicated. As Riddiford confided:

> Such thoughts weighed with me but what influenced me too was escaping for the sake of escaping. Before I was ever captured I had been caught by the fascination of the thing. I had made one attempt immediately after being captured and I had become bitten with it. Once an escaper, always an escaper, and it was due to this fact that the Italians established Campo 5 to guard more securely the incorrigible escapers. It is a most exciting activity and I can honestly say that I have never found anything to pass it . . .
>
> The thrill, the mad delirium of being free is beyond description . . . and I shall always remember it as a magic moment. Even if, by a sudden turn of fortune, I had been immediately recaptured, I would still have considered it an intoxicating achievement, a triumph in itself to be outside the barbed wire.

The exhilarating rush that almost every escaper experienced upon achieving freedom, no matter how short lived, went well beyond the giddy prankishness of college-aged men breaking the rules. There was an electrifying high, a jolt of endorphins, a 'magic moment' that few had ever known before or since. One escaper described it as a 'wave of exaltation' and another as 'the

77

truest time of my life', while Tex Ash, a pilot who escaped several times from camps in Germany, claimed that he had 'never felt more alive'. He even wondered if there might be an 'escaping gene', a 'Houdini Syndrome' compelling one to escape over and over again. 'Escaping,' he wrote, 'is quite addictive and, like all addictive drugs, extremely dangerous.' And it was danger, coupled with the possibility of death, that provided the secret ingredient that made escape 'the greatest sport of all'.

Of course many escapers never got clear of the wire, and those attempting to escape at all were a distinct minority. One estimate from the officers' camp at Chieti, near the Adriatic, is that of 900 men not more than forty were actively engaged in escape activities and many of those were only interested in providing support rather than escaping themselves. Padula was no different. In fact, George Millar was amazed that in such a large camp only thirty men could be found to use a tunnel that had already been dug. Most were more concerned with maintaining a normal routine and not risking any of the privileges which an escape might threaten. Some accused the escapers of 'selfishness', claiming that their futile actions only hurt the other prisoners. Millar, who lived well at Padula, where he ran a lucrative black market, left the camp with a feeling of contempt. He was distressed by the complacency and even more by the lack of respect shown to escapers, in particular to Alastair: 'The would-be escaper at Padula was disliked by the majority of his fellow-prisoners . . . The Baron, who made two brilliant attempts at escape from Padula, was certainly no hero in the camp. He was regarded rather as a nuisance, as someone who interfered with the comfort of others.'

They found a very different world at Gavi. Here almost

everyone was dedicated to escape, and if they hadn't made an attempt already, they had been identified as '*pericolosi*', dangerous men who were either commandos or repeatedly insubordinate. They had a focus, a drive that not only united them but helped overcome what is every prisoner's greatest enemy: lethargy and the lack of purpose. Everyone felt it. People were confident and upbeat. The energy was contagious. Every prisoner who passed through Gavi said the same thing: it was the best camp they were in during the war.

Colin Armstrong, a captain from New Zealand who had escaped from Poppi, where he had been part of the 'Law Faculty' with Dan Riddiford, immediately saw that 'there was a different atmosphere in Camp 5. We all felt that we had, in some measure, outwitted the gaolers, despite their advantages, that we had justified ourselves and our rank, and that, even if we failed in the future, we could come out at the end of the war and say to our friends and families, "Yes, we did escape."' Not only had the men at Gavi 'banded together' around a common ideal, they were specially selected and 'by virtue of their being in this camp, probably the brightest spirits and best types among the prisoners of war in Italy. Indeed, apart from the important consideration that the castle seemed almost impossible to escape from, most of the inmates agreed that they would rather be there than in any other camp they had heard of.'

Michael Pope said the same thing: 'The spirit of the camp was better than in any other I have been in – perhaps because we had difficulties to face all the time. Anyway, we knew what we wanted, which was to be as much of a nuisance as possible, and, camp conditions apart, this was the best camp I was in.'

Dan Riddiford recalled the camp as having a 'certain gaiety', where no one took themselves too seriously and escapes were talked about in an almost light-hearted and flippant manner. 'This was one of the secrets of the good morale – no one indulged in self-pity but with a certain conscious recklessness that gave way to exaggerated optimism.' Like Armstrong, he recognized that the camp was unified by a shared value system that prized ingenuity and escape above all. 'The camp developed a magnificent *esprit de corps* of its own to which each man gladly subordinated himself, but still the essentially individual character of an escape was always recognized. In different walks of life, different values are honoured, but in Campo 5 the usual standards by which a man is judged were completely eclipsed by his escaping reputation.'

The selflessness and consideration that Alastair described among his cellmates was hardly restricted to his group alone. There was an extraordinary chemistry at Gavi which clearly infected everyone in the camp. While being a prisoner of war was often isolating and demoralizing, the spirit among these men helped replace such feelings with optimism and purpose. Despite the harshness of the conditions, the pettiness and brutality of the guards and the lack of amenities that so many other camps possessed, such as a theatre, a library and ample exercise space, Gavi remained a positive environment where one's pride, if ever lost, was soon restored. As George Millar conceded: 'It should have been the worst . . . And for all that it was the best.' In fact, it reformed Millar, who had been criticized earlier for profiteering on the black market:

> Whereas at Padula I was able to sin against the community by running a black market, I would have died of starvation rather

than do such a thing at Gavi. There was no corruption there. The junior officer was protected by his seniors. There was an easy equality and a fairness of outlook that dissolved the worst of prison bonds. Although prison conditions were much more severe than at Padula, I noticed at once that the Gavi officers were better dressed, cleaner, and more upstanding. They had more *amour-propre*. They were a community . . .

The hardness of life at Gavi bound all these men into a bond of fellowship so deep that it is difficult to write of it. I am proud to have been a prisoner there.

All these descriptions, sounding a bit like those of a beloved alma mater, recall that of another, more famous prison: Colditz. Also meant to be escape-proof, Colditz too was located in a turn-of-the-millennium castle, and was the Germans' *Straflager* or 'punishment camp', set up to house serial escapers and other intractable prisoners. However, unlike Gavi, which operated for a mere sixteen months, Colditz existed over the course of the entire war. It also housed many more prisoners, up to 700 at one time. Less intimate and homogeneous than Gavi, there were large contingents of British, French, Belgian, Dutch and Polish, each with their own quarters. And with hundreds of hidden rooms and passages, Colditz offered many more opportunities for escape, nearly all of them cleverly exploited by the end of the war. In fact, some estimate that over 170 attempts were made with at least thirty-two men making it back home.

Despite these differences, the camps had a similar ethos. Jack Pringle, one of just two men to be imprisoned in both, wrote: 'The principal resemblance between the two lay in their exceptional morale. This morale derived from the calibre of the officers – all men of adventurous character and possessed of optimistic initiative.' But it is Colditz that has provided the model for the irrepressible and resourceful escaper, always one step ahead of his jailer with the constant good cheer of a frat brother. And it is the prison itself that has entered the British lexicon as a term for any sinister and impenetrable institution. So dominant has this image become that the historian S. P. Mackenzie questioned whether it has distorted the reality of the prisoner-of-war experience, replacing the grinding tedium and daily challenges most prisoners faced with that of a collection of light-hearted and fearless escapers who bounded from one adventure to the next.

Labelling this the 'Colditz Myth', Mackenzie explores the cottage industry that has produced this image, one that has included nearly a hundred books, a commercial film, a successful television series, numerous documentaries, even a board game and a model aeroplane, and now, finally, the ability to stay at Colditz itself in a newly constructed youth hostel. Whether or not the 'Colditz Myth' has masked the unglamorous experience of most POWs, the truth remains that a unique spirit of solidarity and resistance was forged at both camps. And while each was established to make escape as challenging as possible, all agree that Gavi was the more difficult of the two. As Pringle, who knew them both, concluded, at Gavi 'there was no possibility of escape. We were virtually in a stone box with no exits.' Alastair, who never saw Colditz, agreed:

> There was nothing in the aspect of Gavi to encourage the idea of escape. Presumably all the usual routes had been exploited during the last war. No pains had been spared in the use of

barbed wire and strategic sentry posts. Out of doors there were in fact only two places, one a small triangle of the Upper Courtyard and the other the upper tunnel in the ramp where one was not visible to one or more sentry posts. At no point were we allowed to an outer wall. Very little indeed of the outer wall could be seen for recce purposes. We were locked in to the lower compound at night while those in the upper compound were actually locked into their rooms. A Carabinieri patrol continually searched the buildings and at night there was a double inspection of individual beds by the orderly officer by torchlight. Searchlights covered the whole escape area and some 400 troops, 30 Carabinieri and some 20 officers guarded about 170 commissioned officers and 50 other ranks. Nevertheless attempts were made.

# 4

# The Cistern Tunnel

Call it a provocation. The claim that Gavi was escape-proof only incited greater levels of creativity and daring. No one for a moment really believed that some blind spot, some hidden passage or bricked-up wall couldn't be found through which to make an exit. It was, after all, a 1,000-year-old castle encased in a seventeenth-century fortress. The engineers, and there were several, could see beneath the skin of stone and mortar, and imagine the labyrinth of pipes and drains that wound their way below. And though these men had not grown up in castles, with the exception of one or two, they were Europeans, familiar with the eccentricities of ancient structures built by accretion. Of course, there were many ways to make an escape, and going under with a tunnel was but one. There was also going over and going through.

Rex Reynolds had gone through in his own strange way, walking out the front gate and then transforming himself into a sack of stones. Two other South Africans, Peter Griffiths and Frank Vlok, dressed up as Italian guards and made it through two gates before being stopped at the third and final one. A more promising attempt was that of 'Boggie' Howson, a captain with the 2nd Bengal Lancers. He tonsured the top of his head and with

a dyed blanket disguised himself as a monk. As he piously shuf-
fled along, the guards quickly waved him through. But just
outside, a young soldier approached him with a pressing spiritual
question. Unfortunately, Boggie didn't speak a word of Italian
and the game was up.

It helped, of course, if you were going to bluff your way out,
to speak the language, and to speak it well. Aubrey Whitby was
a good example. He had grown up in a villa on the Etruscan
coast near Pisa. His father, employed there by Whitehead Tor-
pedo, a subsidiary of Vickers, the huge armaments firm, had
married an Italian. They raised five children, though only
Aubrey and one other were sent to school in England. When
war came, he joined the Royal Artillery, while his brother Ric-
cardo went into the Italian navy. Captured at Tobruk, he soon
found himself at Chieti, where he quickly made use of his linguistic skills. With the help of some actors, he fashioned a
Balbo-style beard and an Italian uniform, transforming himself
into the spitting image of the camp interpreter. Then, accompanied by two companions dressed as orderlies, he arrogantly
marched out of the front gate, jabbering away the entire time.
Of course, the 'orderlies' didn't know any Italian but simply
nodded as they trudged along behind. Once out, they headed for
the coast, where five days later they were arrested trying to steal
a boat for Yugoslavia. All three were sent to Gavi, where, not
long after, Aubrey received a visit from an Italian naval officer
– his brother.

More dangerous perhaps than impersonating a guard, interpreter, or priest was scaling a wall or wire. With watchtowers
and searchlights covering every possible angle, it was a good
way to get shot. It's little surprise that some of the war's most

dramatic escapes were made this way. At Colditz, Pierre Mairesse-Lebrun had a friend cup his hands and catapult him over the wire, while in Greece, another prisoner used a hand-made pole to vault over. An even larger escape took place at Oflag VIB in Warburg, Germany. After cutting the power to extinguish the lights, prisoners stormed the fence with specially constructed ladders. Forty-one escaped, with three of them making it home. At Sulmona, Michael Pope had also used a ladder; but that too was over barbed wire. Gavi would be much harder. Here the stone walls had sheer drops of a hundred feet or more, and even then, it was nearly impossible for the prisoners to get close to them. As Alastair noted, hardly any of the outer walls could be inspected. Their periodic walks outside proved just as frustrating as the Italians cleverly prevented them from gaining views of the far sides of the fortress.

Even so, Alastair saw a way. It was over the cell roof and onto a western wall and then down fifty feet to a small terrace and with the aid of a rope, over the parapet to freedom. It wasn't easy, but it was possible. One was vulnerable the whole way, with guard towers and searchlights covering the entire route. 'The party that undertook this would have to climb like cats, and as silent. It would be a desperate game as we knew that the sentries had been promised 2000 lire and a month's leave if they succeeded in shooting a British officer escaping.' Unfortunately, three other officers had also figured it out and staked their claim first. They debated whether to let Alastair join them but agreed that a fourth man would increase the risk by too much.

Among the group was a young army lieutenant named Nugent Kearns, an excellent artist and, like Poppet, good with his hands. It was Kearns who naturally volunteered to make the rope. He was already underway when a guard spotted him cutting a piece of soap stone from an outcrop in order to make a sculpture. It had nothing to do with the escape but the Italians were suspicious and carried out a search of his belongings. They found a nine-inch piece of rope, a test sample perhaps, made from strips of an old sheet. Not very much, but enough to put the guards on alert, and Kearns on their radar.

The preparations continued and, once ready, the trio waited for a stormy night when the rains would reduce visibility and keep the guards inside. They tried twice; the second time on a night so rough that bridges and roads were washed away. Even the searchlights failed, which in turn caused the Italians to double the guard. Meanwhile, Kearns and his companions were pinned down on a ledge, cold and wet as the rain beat down on them throughout the night. Just before dawn they reappeared, half paralysed and frozen. They had made it back but had left the rope behind. A sentry soon found it, and with no other proof than the nine-inch length they had found before, arrested Kearns. He was put in the cells and fined 2,500 lire for the five sheets the Italians estimated he used to make the rope. It was an outrageous amount, as was the court-martial that followed. He was taken under guard to Turin where he was accused of destroying military property. In the end, he served nearly three months in solitary. As for the fine, the men in the camp took up a collection and paid it.

Before making any escape attempt, one needed approval from a committee. By this time, such committees were a fixture in nearly every camp, and while their structures differed from place to place, their functions were broadly similar. They were the clearing houses where ideas and schemes were vetted. If a proposal was considered too reckless or dangerous, the committee might forbid it. Or if another escape was already planned and about to take place, the committee would ask that the request be put on hold. Escapes inevitably brought more vigilance and reprisals and had to be coordinated accordingly. Of course, escape committees would also offer suggestions to improve the chance of success; or perhaps even tinker with the composition of the group, asking that someone more valuable to the war effort be included. But the main function of the committee, other than serving as a patent office for registering schemes and controlling traffic, was in the logistical support needed to maximize their success. They were repositories of camp knowledge, making it available as need be. They also provided forged documents and passes, maps, compasses, train schedules and even food, clothing and money, and where possible, contacts on the outside.

In a large camp, such as Stalag Luft III, escape committees might have different departments, each with its own area of expertise. But in a smaller camp like Gavi, there was no need. Here, each branch of the service had its own representative with proposals directed to the appropriate officer. Nugent Kearns, for example, would have approached Tag Pritchard, a major with the Royal Welsh Fusiliers, who would in turn have taken the idea to the rest of the committee. Or Poppet would have brought his to Bruno Brown, a commander in the Royal Navy.

The three committee members were all quite senior and lived in a set of rooms that had originally been built to house the fortress chapel. In the late nineteenth century, when Gavi became a civil prison, this space was renovated in order to serve as offices and living quarters for the warden and other officials. It was the most modern part of Gavi, dry and well ventilated with high wooden ceilings and dramatic views. In fact, it was considered quite pleasant. Colin Armstrong, who lived in a less desirable cell directly across the courtyard, claimed that 'they were the only accommodation in the camp which could be deemed within the Geneva Conventions and, as they housed only thirty odd officers of the final total of 176, the shadow of content they cast was relatively small. They merely served to remind the balance of the camp what foul and unhealthy hovels they were living in.'

Inside were several interconnecting rooms, all reserved for the camp's most senior officers. And since they sat at the southern edge of the upper compound with a sheer drop of a hundred feet or more to the stones below, the windows were the only ones in the fortress without bars. One could sit and enjoy an unimpeded view of the majestic Apennines and perhaps forget for just a moment that one was in a prison. But such amnesia didn't last long, and as George Clifton stared out at the small, sloping roof below, the idea for an escape was born.

Clifton was the senior ranking officer in the camp, a brigadier from New Zealand who had commanded the 6th Infantry Brigade. Captured near El Alamein, he immediately escaped and walked six days through the desert, only to be recaptured by a group of Germans out hunting. It was a feat admired by Rommel, with whom he had a chat before being packed off to Italy. At forty-five, he was the oldest prisoner in the camp, and to many who were only in their mid-twenties he seemed positively ancient. But no one doubted his courage. He already had a chest full of medals, the first of which he won while serving in Waziristan near the Afghan border in 1920. He had also made several escapes, including his most recent one from Viano, where he climbed out of a window and made it all the way to the Swiss border. George Millar irreverently described Clifton as 'a bald, lobsterish man with freckles all over his muscle-rounded back and a devilish twinkle in his forget-me-not-blue eyes, [who] always preferred dash to caution'. And it's true that the escape he now proposed was quite hair-raising if not fool-hardy.

The room Clifton shared with Ken Fraser overlooked an ancient bell tower that stood between the entrance to the upper compound and the stone ramp that led to it. If one could reach the tower's small, canted roof, it would be possible to climb onto the much larger one that ran the length of the courtyard, and from there reach the camp's westernmost rampart and descend. When open, the large shutter on his window reached the tower's roof line. Clifton believed he could use it like a ladder, swinging over the abyss below as he clung on. Of course, there were a number of unknowns: no one had ever seen this part of the fortress nor knew how high the outer wall would be. There was also barbed wire and searchlights to negotiate before even getting off the roof. But the escape committee approved and helped Clifton assemble his gear, including a huge, 120-foot rope to negotiate the still unknown descent.

He waited for a dense foggy night when the guards would find it hard to see. It came at the end of April 1943. He slid open his window, pushed out the left shutter to block the guards' view, and then very carefully climbed onto the other. The search beams, which were everywhere, seemed even brighter in the fog, and as Ken Fraser got ready to swing the shutter out, he asked, in his understated way, 'Would you not be better to wait till daylight, when it is a little darker?' But over he went, clinging to the shutter, and then up and onto the tower roof. From there he scrambled up to the larger one above but was hardly on it before bullets began to fly. Some say he was betrayed by all the gear he carried and the ruckus he made getting on the roof while others claim that the lights had picked him up as soon as he left his room.

Suddenly the camp was mobilized as if an invasion had just occurred. Sentries fired madly as Sergeant Maffei, the camp interpreter, ran up and down screaming, 'Kill him! Kill him! Shoot him with your revolver.' As bullets whizzed by, Clifton found safety in a slight depression in the roof. Alastair, in the hospital at the time with a pair of broken ribs, had a perfect view and recalls Clifton 'sitting nonchalantly behind a chimney stack in the full glare of all the searchlights'. In fact, the most nervous person was a sentry in the direct line of fire on the other side. Fearing for his life, he screamed over and over for them to stop shooting. Finally, some poor private was forced to go up and get Clifton. Some claim they used a bayonet to prod him. He was terrified – and who wouldn't be? It was dark and the fog had made the roof tiles slippery; any misstep would mean a fall of a hundred feet and certain death. And then there was the desperate *Inglese*. Would he wrestle him to the ground and throw him off the roof? Clifton also knew the soldier would be nervous and was quite afraid he might be shot. So he called out: '"Feriti!" – "Wounded" – and that,' he says, 'gave him sufficient courage not to shoot. Still equally frightened, we slid very gingerly down the roof and clambered back through the window, not much worse for wear.' Marched off to the cells, he did his thirty days. But even worse was the change he found upon his release. His windows now had bars, and his lovely view was ruined.

Clifton's escape was one that Alastair could appreciate, and would even have tried himself, had he been given the chance. He had no fear of heights and 'going over' was certainly his preferred method. He had already gone over the church wall at Castelvetrano and then twice more at Padula. He had also tried crawling through the wire at his first camp in Libya and made two more attempts while travelling by train. What didn't appeal to him were tunnels, the endless calculations and pawing in the dirt or worse with inadequate tools for months on end. 'The whole method of escape lay quite contrary to my line which was bluff, disguise and understanding the weak spot in the enemy defences. But this had all been exploited at Gavi.'

It's little surprise, therefore, that tunnelling became Gavi's primary industry. Of course, tunnelling was favoured at many camps where hundreds of prisoners contributed in some small way to the enormous efforts demanded by any tunnel, whether it be digging, creating diversions, stooging (as standing watch was known), sand dispersal, or any number of other forms of support. But Gavi was special. It was more than the near impossibility of contemplating any other form of escape. It was the certainty that the key to Gavi's secret lay hidden deep inside the mysteries of its subterranean past. Unlike a hutted camp where a tunnel might be sunk directly into the dirt beneath a barrack, at Gavi it was far more complex. Tunnelling here was more akin to prospecting, with each tunnel like the shaft of an oil rig, hoping to reach paydirt. During its 1,000-year history, the fortress had added one layer after another, engulfing countless chambers and passageways unknown even to its current jailers. Tunnels usually began with the hope of reaching one of these hidden routes. Even when they did, success was not guaranteed. As Colin Armstrong noted, 'Some tunnels were successful in their immediate object but as they led only into dungeons and other cul-de-sacs, they had to be abandoned.' Nevertheless, the search went on for that 'magical escape route' which everyone believed existed: the secret passage leading from the fortress all the way to the village of Gavi itself. Such tunnels were common features in medieval castles, a way of guaranteeing safe passage to a ruler and his family once a siege was about to end and further defence hopeless.

It wasn't long before Gavi became a honeycomb of activity, with tunnels worming their way through every corner of the castle. Aubrey Whitby alone was working on three separate ones. The first escape attempt to be discovered was also a tunnel, begun only weeks after the earliest prisoners arrived. It was started by Jack Mantle, one of four sergeants living together in the lower compound. They were in charge of the Other Ranks – privates and corporals from the three services brought in to work as servants for the officers in the camp. This was a task usually assigned to batmen in the British army. Yet these were soldiers who had signed up to fight and not to serve as orderlies shining shoes, making beds, and fetching water. Nor were they in Gavi as a result of any previous experience as butlers; like the officers they served, they were there because of their records as escapers. A number of officers were made uncomfortable by this, wondering why they needed such help since so little else was now required of them. Even more common was the resentment of the enlisted men forced into their new role as servants. In Colditz tensions grew so great that the orderlies declared a strike. In Gavi, however, they seem to have been infected with the same spirit as everyone else, 'working and playing on the team', to paraphrase George Clifton. Even more important were their continued efforts to escape.

Jack Mantle's idea was to tunnel into the drainage system and from there to find a way out. The Italians discovered it well before it was finished, and whether it was the shock of uncovering the first escape attempt or the fact that its author was a sergeant rather than an officer, the reaction was unusually violent. As Moscatelli hysterically shouted insults and curses, Mantle was hauled off to the punishment cells. He was then chained to the bars and beaten with a wooden cane. It was wielded by a short, burly sergeant named Mazza, a member of the Carabinieri who would soon become one of the most hated men in the camp. Middle-aged, with reddish hair and a moustache to match, Mazza was from a town not far from Gavi. He was also a dedicated fascist. To Alastair, he was a sadistic psychopath:

> He was a typical turnkey, cruel, boastful and arrogant. His attitude was that Gavi was not a PW camp but a criminal prison as the prisoners had forfeited their privileges by repeated attempts to escape. Although Mazza was encouraged in his brutalities by his officers, he went beyond their instructions and took a pleasure in inflicting punishments. Later, he had to be restrained from taking reprisals by more moderate Italian officers . . . No normal man would have behaved as he did.

As for Jack Mantle, he was left bleeding and chained for three days, and after that spent twenty-seven more in solitary. Of course, being in the cells didn't always stop prisoners from trying to escape. Even after Clifton's terrifying experiences on the roof, he found a way to remove the hinges on the huge door of his cell. His plan, hastily conceived, was to wait for an air raid when the camp lights were switched off. He would then make his way to a point between the two courtyards where he believed the drop from the wall was no more than fifteen feet. A length of rope was smuggled into his cell and Clifton sat down to wait for the next Allied attack. But it never came, at least not for the next sixteen days, by which time his sentence was up. Such was the problem with any escape from solitary – one only had a limited time before one's sentence was over and it was time to go.

One prisoner who discovered this in an even more frustrating way was James Craig. A captain with the New Zealand infantry, Craig's journey to Gavi was more circuitous than most. Nearly six feet tall and solidly built, Craig was an excellent athlete who had rowed as well as played competitive rugby. He had also trained to be an accountant, an odd preparation perhaps for what the coming years would bring. But like so many others of his generation, the war would transform Craig, making use of his 'restless energy'. He was captured during the airborne invasion of Crete when thousands of German paratroopers overwhelmed the island in May 1941. More than 17,000 Allied troops were taken prisoner, 2,180 of them from New Zealand, the largest number in any battle during the war. Sent to Nea Kokkinia near Athens, Craig made the first escape from the camp, crawling under the wire and then over a wall. Waiting for him was the camp's garbage collector, who whisked him off to a safe house where he was provided with clothes and false papers. Craig eventually found a boat and with five other escapers sailed all the way to Egypt. He was awarded a Military Cross and asked to join MI9, the British intelligence unit set up to work with forces behind enemy lines, whether escapers, evaders, or the resistance.

Just weeks after, Craig was back in Greece arranging for the evacuation of other escaped prisoners. Two months later, he was recaptured when the submarine he and twenty-three others were waiting for failed to appear. Eventually, after some rough treatment, a bout of scabies and several nasty prisons, he ended up at Padula. By now Craig was part of 'A' Force, a special division of MI9 organized to help with escape and evasion throughout the Middle East and Mediterranean. It made sense, therefore, that when Hurst-Brown's tunnel broke in September 1942, Craig was included in the group selected to use it. With another man from 'A' Force, he headed for the Adriatic, hoping to cross to Yugoslavia and then south back to Athens. But after eight days on the run they were arrested by two carabinieri as they turned a corner on a hillside road.

If it seemed inevitable that Jim Craig would end up in Gavi, he was now on his way. It was also inevitable that, once there, he would end up spending time in solitary. No one recalls how he earned his first thirty-day sentence, no doubt for some minor infraction, but once in the cells he went straight to work. He broke into an old chimney and from there found his way into a closed-up passage. He then began tunnelling through the outer wall which was no less than fifteen feet thick. Progress was slow, and to make things worse, he learned that Moscatelli had short-ened his sentence by three days. He quickly concealed the tunnel entrance beneath his bed, determined to get resentenced as soon as possible. This proved more difficult than he predicted.

He became confrontational, insulting guards and acting erratically. When that didn't work, he pretended to be drunk and abusive, delaying the prisoners from returning to the upper compound. 'Oh, there goes Capitano Craig again,' they must have thought. In any case, it only earned him a 'measly five days', hardly enough to complete the tunnel. He tried to return once more but before he could, someone else opened it up and was discovered. Undeterred, Craig recruited George Millar and four others in a new scheme. Using an air shaft to enter a series of dungeons where Austrian prisoners had been held in the First World War, they started digging a tunnel on the side furthest from the village. It was a direction no one had yet tried. They were sure the hidden passage lay just beyond and that it would take them to that elusive yellow brick road to Oz and home.

But the most important tunnel wasn't from the upper courtyard. It was one that started from an orderlies' room just below the mess hall. It would take eight months in all to construct and, when done, finally put an end to Gavi's 1,000-year distinction as escape-proof. It was without doubt one of the war's greatest efforts. In fact, George Millar claimed: 'It was one of the most remarkable achievements in all the history of escape from prison.' To Clifton it was simply 'The Escape.' It is little surprise, therefore, that several people laid claim to its ownership. What is known for certain is that the entrance to the cistern tunnel, as it is commonly called, was discovered quite by accident.

A trooper named Hedley was sleeping on top of a three-tiered bunk when he rolled over and banged his head against the wall. To his surprise, it sounded hollow. He alerted his friend, Seaman

McCrae, in the bunk below, and together they decided to investigate. They cut a small hole, barely large enough to stick their heads through. What they found was a dark, seemingly bottomless shaft. They dropped a stone and seconds later heard a distant splash. Was it simply a dungeon that had filled with water? Or perhaps a much larger reservoir, or even an underground river opening to the outside. What they knew for certain was that they had made an enormous discovery. They quickly concealed the opening, which was high up, well beyond the view of any guards. Besides, the Italians were much less vigilant when it came to patrolling the orderlies' rooms.

What happened next is a little unclear. Hedley was a member of the 8th Hussars, the same regiment as Jack Pringle. McCrae, on the other hand, was from the Fleet Air Arm and one of Peter Medd's crew when his plane was shot down near Tobruk in 1940. Their cell was directly opposite the one that Jack and Peter shared with Alastair. According to Jack, Hedley came to him with news of the discovery, and following that, he was the one who first explored the shaft and set the tunnel in motion. Clifton claims that Hedley and McCrae went straight to the escape committee, who in turn created a six-man team which Jack and Alastair were made part of. But Alastair remembers it quite differently, saying that the orderlies sought out Buck Palm and Bob Paterson, two South Africans who in turn brought in Allen Pole and Charles Wuth. He also recalls that the first one down the shaft was Buck Palm, who in his own account claims that he was the one who actually discovered the escape route. And while this might not be entirely true, there's little doubt that the real leader of the cistern tunnel was Captain Ralph Buckley Palm.

His actual name was Reefus Pölm, but he anglicized it in rejection of his Afrikaner past, a past filled with bigotry and abuse. He was the youngest of nine siblings, brought up on a farm in the middle of the Transvaal. His mother, Anne Buckley, who was English, died while he was quite young, leaving him to be brought up by his siblings and a stern father whom the children all despised. One by one they left the farm, most disappearing in the middle of the night, until Buck and a half-brother by an African mother were the only two left. Then, at about sixteen, Buck too ran off. For the next decade and a half he travelled across southern Africa, drifting from job to job. For a while he worked in the mines around Johannesburg and then struck out on his own to prospect for gold. He also made a living as a hunter and at some point was even a professional wrestler, though no one knows exactly where or for how long. Eventually, he moved to Bechuanaland, where he joined a sister in the Okavango Delta, and after that to South-West Africa, where he lived with another sister who was married to a settler. When war came, he was running a garage on Kloof Street in Cape Town.

He wanted to be a fighter pilot but knew that, at thirty-one, he would never be taken. So he lied about his age, claiming that he was born in 1915 rather than 1908. Over the years, he would forget what he put down and either write the wrong date or give an age that didn't quite compute. But he was accepted, and despite anxieties about his lack of education and the required written exams, he passed and was commissioned as a lieutenant. Eight months later he was flying Hurricanes over Libya and the Middle East. He was a good pilot too, a night fighter shooting down at least two planes. Then, in late November 1941, only days after Alastair's capture, he came under attack while strafing around Tobruk. He managed to bail out and, though shot through the hip, walked for two days across the desert before an Italian patrol picked him up. By the time he arrived in Gavi ten months later, he had already dug four tunnels, all of them discovered.

In a camp filled with unusual characters, Buck stood out as one of the most extraordinary. He had lived a life far different from most of his companions, and with his thick Afrikaner accent was an excellent raconteur. Punctuated by his ever-present harmonica, he spun endless tales about his life with the Kalahari Bushmen, hunting wild game, and any number of other death-defying adventures. Dan Riddiford, whose own upbringing couldn't have been further from Buck's, was typical in his admiration and awe of him:

> Buck was a born escaper. It was the natural expression of his personality, and what a personality! . . . He was a genuine pioneer, one of the rare modern examples of the type which used to be found on all the expanding frontiers of the Empire and the United States. His conversation, generally a monologue, was so full of interesting experiences and shrewd comments on life that he held his audiences spellbound.

Just as impressive were Buck's many feats of strength, all of which earned him an almost superhuman reputation. Six foot tall and 185 pounds, Buck was pure muscle with the thick neck and broad shoulders of a rugby forward. Clifton called it a 'Homeric build, comparable to Johnny Weissmuller,' while Millar referred to Buck as a 'South African Hercules,' a man who 'could quickly kill anyone with his bare hands'. His presence, so genuine and unaffected, was unlike that of anyone else in the camp. Striding about shirtless with what some recall as a leopard-skin bottom and others a loin cloth, Buck could have walked straight out of a movie set. When he wasn't underground tunnel-ling, he was often seen leading a nearly impossible set of exercises of his own design. Alastair, who was second to none in the demands of his own fitness regimen, enjoyed watching Buck lead his class:

Buck's mean appearance struck terror in the hearts of his cap-tors. He had devoted much of his time to physical culture and with his massive chest, great muscles and long black heavy hair hanging down 6 inches long, as he often wore it with a big loin cloth, he was deemed the equal of Tarzan of the Apes. He carried on a PT class at 7 a.m. in the lower courtyard and his rigorous snorts and violent movements attracted so much attention that the Orderly officer and guard turned out to see if we were preparing a riot. He had no mercy in his class. I well remember Jack belly down on his blanket, contorted into a horrible arc, one of Buck's great hands clasping his knee, the other on his thorax exerting great pressure. Jack's brown eyes were glazed and resigned like a spaniel's. As Buck walked among his directees they redoubled their efforts lest they should fall into his hands.

Combine his mining background and the four tunnels he had already dug with the fact that he was utterly fearless, completely dedicated to escape, and the strongest man in the camp, and it's little surprise that Buck was selected to lead the new tunnel. So one morning after roll call, Buck and two of his friends slipped into the orderlies' room. The bed was moved and a scaffold arranged so that Buck, lying on it with his arms together above his head, could be lifted up and horizontally thrust through the opening like a spear. Inside was a steel bar stretched across the shaft. He grabbed it, swinging his body below. Hanging like an acrobat, his feet just reached another bar seven feet further down. Once on that, he carefully crouched, grabbed the bar, and dropped by his hands once again. Swinging on to a narrow ledge, he reached the top of an ancient ladder. It descended sixty feet into a pool of water that came up to his chest. He was in the centre of a huge cistern.

The original castle had two cisterns, both relatively small, though large enough to guarantee a steady supply of water. With Gavi's transformation into a Genovese fortress in the early seventeenth century, a much larger one was needed. It was constructed under the *cittadella* or 'citadel', as the lower part of the fort was originally known. Two large caverns connected by a set of arches, the cistern measured 120 by 60 feet and was as high as it was wide. It was fed by a series of channels carved into the fortress walls, and when full could hold two million litres of water, an underground reservoir capable of withstanding any siege. But the stones in the original construction were too porous and leaked. So the walls were covered up to a height of forty feet with special bricks baked with iron, and then on top of that was an additional layer of lime mortar. After 300 years, the bricks and concrete were as hard as the stone and just as difficult to penetrate. What Buck and his companions didn't know was whether the Italians were aware of the size and location of the cistern. One thing was certain: they had no idea that it was accessible through a shaft on the other side of a thin wall in the orderlies' room.

Buck carefully walked along each wall searching for any openings. In the pitch black, airtight and completely still interior, the dim light from his oil lamp didn't flicker at all. He could tell that the cistern ran the length of the lower courtyard, which meant that a tunnel might lead into 'the honeycomb of ancient cellars, dungeons and passages' that had inspired so many of Gavi's schemes. But this one would have special advantages. No matter how loud the sound of their work, nothing could be heard through the cistern's massive subterranean walls. Just as important was the issue of dispersal, the scourge of every tunnel. Here, any rock and dirt could simply be thrown into the water. And finally, there was the tunnel entrance itself. True, the Italians might discover it at any time, but they were less vigilant with the orderlies, and even then, less likely to look for a tunnel entrance high up on a wall, the view of which was already partially obscured.

Getting out of the cistern was even harder than getting in, though adrenalin probably helped. Buck knew straight away that he had found the best chance so far of breaking out of Gavi. Still, as excited as he was, he nonchalantly ambled back to his cell with his 'long, slanting, hen-toed strides'. Once there, he huddled with his co-conspirators, Paterson, Pole, and Wuth, describing in great detail everything he'd seen. They spoke for hours before finally settling on a plan. The tunnel would start just above the water line and be driven through the cistern's eastern face. This was where most prisoners believed the secret route into the village lay, and once intersecting with it they would be home free. They would work in teams of two, each digging for two hours before coming up for relief. With Hedley and McCrae, the orderlies who had discovered the shaft, joining

103

them, they would be able to get in three shifts, or six hours a day. But they would need at least two more people to run the above-ground operations: the security and scrounging, all the details that would have to be worked out to protect and outfit the tunnel, not to mention the false papers, clothes, maps, money and food that each escaper would need once the tunnel broke. They immediately settled on Alastair and Jack. While neither was a tunneller, they were two of the most respected escapers in the camp. They also spoke fluent Italian and knew exactly what needed to be done. Needless to say, they leapt at the chance.

The South Africans shared a cell at the opposite end of the corridor from that of Alastair and Jack. And while identical in size, the space couldn't have been more different. Unlike the orderly world overseen by their naval companions, Peter Medd and Michael Pope, Buck and his friends lived in a sea of chaos with clothes, papers and Red Cross parcels strewn everywhere. And in the centre of this great unruly mess sat a Yugoslavian officer named Slobodan Drašcović, a former professor from Belgrade who was a model of composure and concentration as he calmly worked on a scholarly tome about Serbian identity.

The South Africans, six in all, were an irreverent, rowdy, fun-loving bunch. The ringleader in this was Bob Paterson, a fighter pilot captured the day before Buck, though in very different circumstances. He had been flying a mission at Sidi Rezegh when a member of his group was shot down. The pilot was Hendrik Liebenberg, the grandson of the South African prime minister, Jan Smuts. Against all orders, Paterson landed beside him to attempt a rescue. But Lieby, as they called him, struggled to get out of his plane, and by the time they took off, it was too late. They were barely in the air before being shot down and captured. For Paterson, it was the second such attempt and it earned him the nickname 'Pick-Up-Pat'. Of course, no one knew that his actual Christian name was Swithun, a saint's name which he utterly detested.

Tall and thin with a ready smile, Paterson grew up near Cape Town in a large family with ten brothers and sisters. Like many escapers, he was extremely athletic, a fine swimmer and runner as well as a boxer who had won several lightweight titles. When it came to work, however, he chose book-keeping, and at the outbreak of the war was employed in a bank. Becoming a fighter pilot certainly revealed another, wilder side. As a prisoner, he was just as irrepressible. He made two escapes while still in Libya and then another from Poppi. At Gavi, he became the chief 'goon-baiter', a relentless tormentor of guards and enemy officers. Many thought of goon-baiting as a form of resistance while others saw it as simply childish and annoying. For Paterson it was a way of striking back, however small. It also relieved the tedium of prison life. His favourite prank was to empty a bucket of water on a guard as he passed beneath the balcony outside his cell. The response was invariably violent, with the Italians rushing in, machine guns at the ready, demanding to know who had tossed the water. Eventually, someone would be hauled off to sleep with the rats in one of the storage rooms below. It didn't bother Paterson though. He was soon back at it, thinking up yet another way to drive the Italians crazy.

The other two South Africans in the tunnel scheme, if slightly more restrained, brought their own skills to the group, rounding it out to make an ideal team. Although ten years younger than Buck, it was Chas Wuth who had the most in common with him. He too had lost his mother at an early age, and after struggling at home, also ran away before finishing secondary education. For a while he made a living as a professional boxer, and then at eighteen joined the naval reserves as a telegraph operator. When war came, he transferred to the Signal Corps, received a commission, and travelled the length of Africa on a Harley Davidson laying down communications. Like so many at Gavi, he was captured at Sidi Rezegh, sent to Tarhuna, and from there made his first escape. He made his second from Modena, enough to earn him a trip to Gavi. Wuth was tough with very slender hips, good qualities for someone who had to work in tight spaces. When he wasn't tunnelling, he could usually be found in the Casino room with a cigarette in his mouth, playing blackjack or poker. He had a mischievous little smile with a sweet twinkle in his eye. He was hard not to like.

Wuth and Allen Pole were close friends, and during their years in prison never far apart. They were also quite different, complementing each other in interesting ways. Where one liked to gamble, the other preferred bridge and chess. And while, like Buck Palm, Wuth had left school prematurely, Pole was studious, completing several engineering and university courses even as a prisoner. Pole was also married. In fact, he was the only one in the group who was. But then Allen Pole was the responsible type. His father had died in the flu epidemic of 1918 when Allen was just two. He grew up fast, supporting his family from an early age. Little surprise that a pre-war friend referred to him as 'an old soul'. In the camps, they called him 'Pops', in part because of his careful rationing of Red Cross parcels, but also for the way he looked after other prisoners in need.

As a young man, Pole was an avid Boy Scout, eventually becoming a patrol leader. Beyond instilling a love for the outdoors, it taught him many of the skills he would later put to use as a prisoner. Alastair claimed that it was this type of knowledge that often made soldiers from the Dominions and Colonies the most successful escapers. They had grown up in different, less industrialized environments, developing what he called 'woodcraft', a deep awareness of the natural world and how to survive in it. For men on the run, living in forests and mountains, avoiding any contact for days if not weeks on end, such skills were essential. But Allen Pole had an even more important skill. He was a trained mining surveyor.

He had gone to work for Gold Fields, the huge mining consortium, straight out of school. It was there that he learned the art of mapping the world below ground. It often brought him into small mines called stopes, and when necessary into collapsed tunnels to rescue trapped workers. Like Chas Wuth, he joined the reserves, and with the start of the war was sent to military college for officer training. He passed with high marks, impressing his superiors. 'Good personality,' wrote his commanding officer on the final report. 'Capable, keen and self-reliant. A young officer with excellent prospects, knows his work well and is definite – watch for promotion.'

Not everyone was pleased, however. Pole's mother, who depended on her son for support, was terrified that he would be sent off and killed. She wrote a heart-rending letter to Jan Smuts, begging the prime minister to assign him to a training or recruiting position in order to keep him in South Africa. Her youngest son was already in Kenya. 'I feel I cannot part with both my sons to be sent so far away,' she pleaded.

Pole might have ended up like George Bailey, the dutiful son in Capra's *It's a Wonderful Life*, who stays home while his younger brother goes off to war and glory. But he refused to stay as the terse response from one of Smuts' aids made clear:

> With reference to your minute, I have the honour to report that I have made inquiries and also interviewed the above named officer. Lieut. Pole's wish is to remain with the 1 RB [Regt. Botha], and definitely states that he has no desire to serve in any home service unit. He seems very determined about it and is looking forward to the time when he can be sent north.

As it turns out, he was lucky not to be killed. Soon after receiving his commission, Pole was transferred to the 1st South African Irish and was with them at Sidi Rezegh when German forces destroyed the regiment. He was one of a handful to escape only to be captured ten days later during a scouting mission with three other men. En route to Benghazi he broke away from the column and made it all the way to a beach near Tobruk. The city was still in British hands, so when a German patrol spotted him, he leapt into the ocean and tried to swim to it. Machine gun fire forced him back to shore, where he was captured once again. When he arrived at Gavi eight months later, he had an oil compass and a tape measure. No one knew where he had got them but they would prove invaluable, as would his training in the mines.

It made sense that the first ones down to start the tunnel were Buck Palm and Allen Pole. They were as comfortable below ground as above and their combined experience gave everyone confidence that this tunnel would succeed. It was mid-September when, oil lamp in hand, they slid into the shaft and carefully entered the cistern. The water was still only four to five feet high, making it possible to walk the thirty yards necessary in order to reach the easternmost wall. They discussed the pros and cons of where to start, and after agreeing on the best spot, drew a two-foot square that would serve as the entrance. Their tools were simple, the main one being the leg from a metal bed. Clifton claims they found an axle from a donkey cart, so heavy that only Buck was able to wield it alone. Such a tool, if it did exist, would only have helped hollow out the entrance. Beyond that, it would have been too large, but at this stage any help at all would have been welcome. The cement and brick alone were two feet thick and as hard as the South African gold mines where Buck and Pole had both cut their teeth.

Up above, Alastair and Jack, not long out of solitary, were quickly putting security measures into place. Men were posted at strategic points throughout the courtyard so that signals could be relayed when guards entered the compound or neared the room where the shaft was located. Someone sat on the top of Hedley's bed at all times, holding a huge rattle filled with stones to alert the tunnellers below if an alarm was raised. One problem was the roll calls, two a day, with extra ones sprung at any time. Once the bugle sounded, prisoners were expected to assemble in as little as five minutes, though they deliberately straggled in, causing as much disruption as possible. 'It was rare,' said Tommy Macpherson, 'that there was a roll call without the Italians losing their tempers and certainly losing their count'.

All movements in and out of the orderlies' room also had to be carefully orchestrated. Alastair called this the 'vanishing trick', as the guards would easily notice any increase in traffic.

They had to be invisible. Just as important were the many precautions taken to conceal any traces of the tunnellers' efforts as they emerged from the cistern. The Italians were sharp and would easily spot any signs of soiled clothes, muddy boots, or even a dirty fingerprint on the wall. That's the way tunnels were discovered, so the orderlies made sure that nothing in the room would give them away, starting with the shaft entrance, carefully hidden beneath a false cover nearly impossible to detect.

Progress was steady, if slow. Some estimated that the walls might be as thick as thirty feet. By the end of October they had dug nearly twenty. It was backbreaking, difficult work but they were optimistic. The Italians showed no signs of suspicion and the passageways they sought couldn't be much further. Then disaster struck; torrential rains, day after day, steadily driving up the water level in the cistern. By the end, it was a flood, the water rising to a height of twenty feet, totally submerging the tunnel. Six weeks of work were completely lost, along with the tools which no amount of diving was able to retrieve. But it didn't stop them. It just made the next phase that much harder. As Alastair wrote:

> Buck was not a man to be lightly discouraged. His whole life in the back veld of South Africa had been one of extemporizing means to overcome a harsh environment. He was not to be intimidated by a race of men whom he despised from the bottom of his straight dealing, square shooting nature. Dealing with rhino, lions, wild bushmen, and finally, Messerschmitt 109's had hardened his courage. But at the same time he was as wily as a leopard and as dangerous as a snake.

The new tunnel would start a full twenty feet above the existing water line. There was a thin, eighteen-inch ledge there which ran the entire length of the cistern. It also marked the limit of the mortar and bricks that covered the stone. To reach it, a beam was lowered down the shaft and a bridge created by placing one end on a rung of the ladder and the other on the ledge. Chas Wuth and Allen Pole were in charge of this delicate operation, cautiously working their way across the bridge and along the narrow ledge to the south-west corner. Once there, they dropped a rope onto which a plank was tied. After hauling it up, they wedged it into the corner to create a small platform. Tools and supplies were now floated across the cistern to be hauled up as well. From now on, the tunnellers would reach the platform in the same way, stripping naked, swimming thirty yards in the dark and pulling themselves up the slippery twenty-foot rope.

With the new tunnel beginning forty feet higher than the first, a decision was made to dig in a different direction. The goal now would be to tunnel straight through the outer wall, exiting directly above the ridge line of the carabinieri's living quarters. It was one of several structures found on the fortress's southernmost and lowest bastion. Known as the *mezzaluna* or 'half moon', this was the original gateway to Gavi. In fact, the carabinieri's quarters sat directly on top of the first guard post that any visitors or troops would have had to pass. From there, they would march along the hundred-foot wall to an even more imposing entrance, this one protected by a drawbridge. In the middle of this triangular space was a squat stone building that had served as the original powder house. Despite being built by a well-known Swiss military architect, it was too damp and never functioned properly. Now it served as the chapel for the Italian troops who were housed in three wooden huts that sat parallel to it. And at the outermost point of this congested space was a tower with a searchlight and armed guard.

All of this was clearly visible from the barred windows of the prisoners' mess high above. They could see that, once on the carabinieri's roof, it would be possible to drop down to another, smaller roof just below and from there reach the top of a sloping parapet from which they could easily make it to the ground. After crossing in front of the watchtower, they would need to slip by the guards' huts in order to reach the other side. The drop was much shorter from the eastern wall and, just as import-ant, there was an olive tree on which to tie a rope and descend. 'It was a grim looking route,' said Alastair, 'exposed, chancy, but Gavi was a grim fortress and demanded desperate means and risks.' It also demanded incredible precision.

Coming out exactly two feet above the peak of the carabini-eri's roof would be a remarkable engineering feat. Fortunately, they had an excellent mining surveyor. To make the calculations, they arranged for Allen Pole to spend a night hidden inside the mess. Once the fortress was asleep, he pulled out his plumb bob and lowered it down the south wall, making all the meas-urements and estimates necessary. From their platform in the south-west corner of the cistern, they would dig east, carving a six-foot-long shaft, horizontal with the outer wall. At that point they would make a chamber, four feet square and five feet high. Now the main tunnel would begin, with a right turn and then straight south to their destination.

By now it was November 1942, a year since Alastair and his companions had been taken prisoner at Sidi Rezegh. News had

1. Alastair with his parents, Duncan and Annie,
on an outing in the Highlands, mid-1920s.

2. Alastair, about to turn 19, at the start of
an expedition in the Cairngorms, 1928.

3. Alastair climbing on Aonach Dubh
buttress, Glencoe, Scotland, 1928.

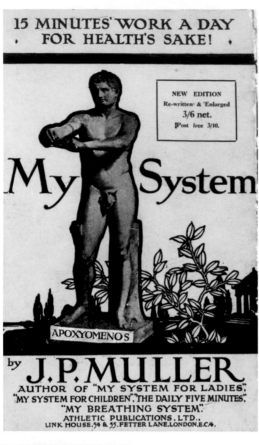

4. The cover of J. P. Müller's *My System* featuring a Greek statue of Apoxyomenos, the 'Scraper', an athlete using a strigil to remove dirt and sweat from his body.

5. Baron Gottfried von Cramm greeting Adolf Hitler at the Deutsches Stadion, Grunewald, Berlin, 1933.

6. *Left*. Lieutenant Alastair
Lorimer Cram, R.A., 1940.

7. *Right*. Captain Jack Pringle,
8th Hussars.

8. The Great Staircase
at the Certosa di San Lorenzo,
Padula, converted into P.G. 35
during the war.

ertosa di Padula (SA) - Lo Scalone ellittico del Vanvitelli

9. Padula staff. Bottom row r–l: Major Luigi Grimaldi, Lt. Col. Gori, camp commandant, unidentified visiting general. Middle, far right: Tinivella Vescoco, Monsignor of Taggia. Capt. Francesco Cariello, the camp medical officer and Grimaldi's brother-in-law, is standing behind the general. Rear, second from left: Father Volpe, a Capuchin monk and camp interpreter.

10. A 1932 postcard view of Gavi, showing the castle with the town and Lemme River below.

11. Aerial view of Gavi. The *mezzaluna* is in the foreground. On its left is the roof the cistern tunnel opened on to and on the right the tree used to tie the rope.

12. Lower courtyard, Gavi, 1940. Alastair's cell was the last one on the right balcony. The door at the top of the stairs on the left balcony led to the mess hall while the doors below were to the orderlies' rooms. The cistern tunnel started from the last one on the left.

13. *Opposite page.* Tunnellers,
clockwise from top left:
Buck Palm, Chas Wuth,
Michael Pope, Allen Pole,
Bob Paterson, Peter Medd.

14. George Clifton, left, speaking
with Major General Lindsay
Meritt Inglis, Egypt, 1942.

15. The window Clifton used
to get onto the roof in a failed
escape attempt, as viewed
from the lower courtyard.

16. Colin Armstrong and Tommy Macpherson, centre left and right, upon their arrival in Sweden in October 1943. They are flanked by Jim Hutson and John Glancy, the privates who accompanied them on their escape from Poland.

17. *Above, left*. Garth Ledgard with fellow escapees after crossing into Switzerland in October 1943. Ledgard is standing top left with Lieut. A. Kam next to him. Seated in front, l–r, are Lieut. Col. J. M. Lee and Lieut. Col. N. E. Tyndale-Biscoe.
18. *Above, right*. Buck Palm and Fernande Chakour honeymooning in Egypt, May 1944.

just arrived of the first significant Allied victory at El Alamein. Rommel and his Afrika Korps had been repulsed in their advance on Egypt and the Suez Canal. A week later, Tobruk, the port city Alastair had been captured trying to relieve, was back in British hands. Just as important, the Americans had landed in Algeria and Morocco. The Germans and Italians would soon be trapped in a pincer movement as the Allies advanced from both directions. Even the Russians were starting to turn the tide as the German Sixth Army was surrounded at Stalingrad. Churchill had reason to celebrate when he declared in one of his most memorable speeches that: 'Now we have a new experience, we have victory – a remarkable and definite victory.' But he also tempered his exuberance with a cautionary warning, saying that: 'This is not the end. No, it is not even the beginning of the end. But it is, perhaps, the end of the beginning.'

For those in Gavi, however, the end suddenly seemed wonderfully near. With the Axis forces in retreat in North Africa, they knew the invasion of Sicily couldn't be far off. 'It won't be long now' became the official new greeting. As Colin Armstrong notes, fortunes were won and lost betting on every possible date and outcome:

There is no breeding ground for wishful thinking more prolific than a Prisoner of War camp. The slightest suspicion of good news is magnified into impressive significance and rumour circulates as freely as alcohol on Armistice Day. Extraordinary prophecies would be made as to the end of the war, the fall of Italy, the invasion of Sicily and so forth and opinions would be backed by considerable sums. Much money was won and lost by betting on any wished-for event. I used to bet against any success on principle because if I lost it was worth paying for a step nearer the end, and if I won, which usually happened, the monetary gain was some panacea to the disappointment of having to face a few more months of captivity.

Of course, none of this affected the determination of Alastair and the others. And why should it? There was no guarantee that Italy would be invaded nor any schedule for when it might occur. And even if it happened, the prisoners were uncertain whether they would be set free, especially the *pericolosi* at Campo 5. No, the only thing to do was to go on tunnelling in the hope of getting out. On the other hand, they were quick to use these changes to their own advantage. After cheering the news of El Alamein and other victories, the prisoners began a subtle but well-orchestrated campaign to convince the guards that they were giving up on escape. With the end now in sight and Gavi completely unbreachable, they appeared only too happy to await their liberation. Why take unnecessary risks when they were so close to returning to their families and loved ones? It was the message the Italians had been preaching all along which may explain why they were so susceptible to the ploy now being used. At least, it seemed to work.

Prisoners experienced a slight shift in attitude. Colin Armstrong went so far as to say: 'From being autocratic and domineering, the Italian officers and men became friendly and sympathetic.' Searches became somewhat less frequent and vigilance a little more relaxed. Even the guard at the outermost point of the *mezzaluna* was removed, an enormous incentive to those working in the cistern. While Alastair appreciated how important this was, he thought that the reason might lie elsewhere: 'This perhaps explains the hopelessness of the area from the escape point of view of the Italian. The removal of the sentry at one stroke converted the route from a desperate venture to a reasonable risk that men who chose to dare a little might like with some equanimity and prospect of success.'

Of course, some guards only became worse. There were the die-hard fascists who were determined to make the prisoners' lives as miserable as possible right to the end. Some of these were transferred or volunteered for combat. Sergeant Mazza, the former prison warden, wasn't one of them. His hatred for the British was well known and he continued to take a sadistic pleasure in tormenting them, especially Alastair:

Our mutual dislike was strong. When I encountered him his neck would swell above his collar and his face suffuse with colour. If no one was in sight he would tap his pistol significantly or go through the movements of adjusting the hangman's noose. I had and have still the strongest possible intuition that we are going to meet again and that this time on equal terms.

By now Alastair and Jack were setting up their black market and intelligence network, carefully selecting the guards they would approach. Developing a reliable contact took time and patience. 'Before one can receive,' said Alastair, 'one must give. Many hundreds of cigarettes went merely to establish an acquaintanceship and during cold winter evenings, I would go out to the sentry in the lower compound with cups of hot coffee and cocoa asking nothing in return.' Trust was slowly built up with long conversations about family and home, food shortages, the difficulties of rationing, the unfairness of one's superiors, and the brutality of the government. One had to show real empathy before confidence could be established. This wasn't always easy, especially when one's true feelings were quite different. For Alastair, it was a morally compromising process. While he accepted it as part of the overall deception demanded by any escape, he had no illusions about the men he would need to seduce in what he called 'the quest for the traitor':

The morally weak man, present in every garrison who is prepared for reward or promises of reward to sell his honour, and betray his country for gold, paper money, or even tobacco, clothing, soap or valuables. This is degrading work for both parties. One has to associate for long hours over a lengthy period of time with low, stupid and sometimes vicious men to enter into the mental processes to set one's words, expressions and morality at their level, never revealing one's disgust or true intention. A man who plays this game places his life in jeopardy and hence he is usually a stupid or ignorant man who cannot see the meshes of the net spread for him in the pit dug before his feet. At the same time he must not be a fool otherwise his words and actions may lead not only to his own downfall but that of the provoker.

Inducing a guard to cross the threshold between simple conversation and active collaboration was a delicate dance requiring tremendous skill. After all, the contact had a lot more to lose and, given the risks, not that much to gain. Few got involved out of any deep anti-fascist sympathies and were easily scared off by a wrong word or glance. Once hooked, they had to be reeled in slowly. The first requests were nearly imperceptible, but a friendly chat about a recent visit home could provide useful information about trains, buses and other forms of local transportation. It also supplied details about shortages and what the contact and his family needed most. 'Coffee and soap?' asked Alastair. 'I think I can help.' The exchange of items increased little by little. Beginning with lamp oil, wine and other small objects, it soon escalated to hacksaw blades, wire cutters and anything else needed by the tunnellers. Requests now became demands backed by threats, all the more important once sensitive items such as civilian clothing, train schedules and travel passes were required.

While Alastair may have expressed discomfort with the seamier aspects of this process, he was much more amused by the subterfuge involved in the actual handoff of items. Creating hides, eluding guards, disappearing into the shadows – this was the more imaginative and athletic part of the cloak-and-dagger game. His favourite drop was in the bath house where a hole, well hidden by a roof tile, had been made above one of the urinals. If a guard had a delivery, he would simply go in to pee, leaving the package behind. Alastair would soon follow, remove the object and head toward the ramp where Jack, Poppet or Peter Medd would be waiting to take it. He would then return, free of any incriminating evidence, while they continued on to the upper compound, delivering it to Wing Commander Barney Keily, head of the escape committee. Keily would hide the articles in the senior officers' quarters until Alastair and the others needed them.

Other exchanges were made through a barred window high up in the back of Alastair's cell. The outside, which was hidden from view, could be reached by standing on top of a nearby ledge. Clothing, wine, food and other contraband items were left while cigarettes, coffee and even cash were picked up. Some handoffs were more difficult, requiring quick thinking and improvisation. On one occasion, Alastair's most reliable contact, a small, funny-looking, toothless peasant nicknamed 'Jack the Little Monster', arrived with several felt hats tucked beneath his uniform. Posted in the open within clear view of his superiors, he couldn't figure out how to dispose of them. Alastair could see that he was becoming agitated so casually walked by, telling him under his breath to throw the package into a nearby garbage bin. It took some time to manage, but once done, an orderly came by, picked up the bin and safely emptied it. Jack the Little Monster was impressed and his confidence in Alastair reinforced.

In addition to collecting material for their escape, Alastair and Jack were also involved in a coordinated attempt to gather as much intelligence as possible. This became even more pressing with the turn of events in North Africa. Every piece of information, no matter how small, provided an important clue to not only the course of the war but also the fate of those imprisoned in Italy. When the British took Tripoli in late January, this effort intensified even further. A core group of five officers – Alastair, Jack, Aubrey Whitby, Ian Howie and Tommy Macpherson – was now entrusted with extracting every conceivable scrap of information. In biweekly meetings, attended by the two senior officers as well as Barney Keily from the escape committee, they 'compared and correlated' everything they had discovered. They also used these meetings to formulate their own propaganda campaign by which they hoped to undermine the loyalty and morale of those stationed at Gavi.

Part of this campaign was to continue persuading the Italians that they had resigned themselves to await the arrival of the Allies and to forgo any future attempts at escape. In the winter of 1942–43, this wasn't hard to do. Conditions were brutally cold, with large amounts of snow filling the courtyard. Who would possibly want to escape? Even Alastair recalls that 'during the hours that I didn't spend in bed or exercising, my feet were continuously cold that winter'. And yet, to the amazement of everyone, the tunnel continued to progress. On some days, a thin layer of ice covered the water in the cistern. But even that didn't prevent Buck and his companions from stripping naked and swimming the thirty yards in total darkness to the rope that led up to the platform. If nothing else, it seemed incredible that they hadn't caught pneumonia. It took its toll though, as Alastair and others could see:

> The strain bore heavily on them and they often looked pale, thin and weary and suffered from slight chills. Once or twice the sheer magnitude of the labour gave them a feeling of hopelessness. There was in particular one great stone that took nearly three weeks' labour to loosen and pry out before being heaved into the sullen depth of the tank.

Alastair and Jack made tepid offers to help but the South Africans rejected them. They were much more valuable above ground. Besides, it was unlikely that they could make any serious contribution. In fact, Jack claims that when they finally went down 'the work [they] did was only marginally useful and wasted a shift'. Cutting through solid rock in a two-foot-square tunnel with primitive tools was tough work, demanding the type of experience that Buck and Pole, in particular, had brought with them from South Africa. Some of their techniques, like heating the rock and then splashing it with cold water to create a fissure, were especially effective. Although all six of the tunnellers gave everything they had, it was Buck, with his extraordinary strength and utter fearlessness, who became a legend among the prisoners. George Millar expressed a common view when he wrote:

> To me it is one of the fine pictures of the war; the grim, wintry fortress up above, with lesser mortals shivering in their beds, and down in the bowels Buck, a great, muscled devil, dripping with icy water, *burning* and boring his way through solid rock. Burning in fact, for in order to split the rock he smuggled down quantities of wood and built large fires against the face. Then, when the stone was hot, he flung bucketfuls of cold water against it to crack it. Then he smashed into it with his great crowbar. What a man! What a noble monster of a man!

By the end of February, with snow still thick on the ground, they reached the outside wall. That same evening, Buck re-entered the thirty-foot long tunnel and removed the last three stones. There was a cool blast of night air, a sky full of stars, the sounds of conversation and music coming from the guards' quarters on the spit of land below, and best of all, the sight of the carabinieri's ridge pole directly underneath. After six months of digging, they had come within inches of their desired goal. Right in front, however, was a huge tangle of barbed wire, placed there to prevent prisoners dropping down from the mess hall more than sixty feet above. After carefully replacing the stones, Buck rushed back to deliver the news.

Discussions immediately began as to when the actual breakout should occur. Alastair, who had been delegated the official weatherman, thought that they should wait till the middle of April, the earliest date in which the Alpine passes could be crossed without special equipment. He knew this area well, much better in fact than anyone else in the camp. He had climbed it throughout the 1930s, often at night, and on one occasion even been arrested by an Italian border patrol. But it seemed too long to wait and an earlier date at the end of March was selected. Alastair had studied the patterns and predicted that soon after the spring equinox there would be a short period of bad weather followed by a sudden change for the better. They would need a stormy evening if they were to have any hope of getting off the roof and crossing the terrace undetected. Everyone agreed: the escape would take place on the first rainy night after the equinox.

The next decision was the make-up of the group. The four South Africans along with Alastair and Jack were naturally included. But there was some debate about Hedley and McCrae, the two orderlies who had discovered the entrance to the cistern and then went down every day to tunnel. For Hedley, who could barely swim, it was a remarkable feat. Everyone wanted them to go but the escape committee, who had the final say, hesitated. They wondered if they were the most valuable assets to the war effort. Wouldn't a pilot or submariner be more important to get home? In the end, they relented and, to the relief of all, both were included. Still, the two men, selfless to the end, insisted on going last.

This left two spaces, as it was determined that the maximum number was to be ten. Any more would be impossible to get off the roof and past the guards' huts without being seen. Even then, the risk was high. It was decided that Peter Medd, the soft-spoken Fleet Air Arm pilot who had been a prisoner for nearly three years, should go. Gerry Daly, the pint-sized explosives expert, was also selected. He and Peter had escaped together before and would do so again. Poppet too was included, but for a much more thankless task. He would manage traffic and reseal the tunnel once everyone was out. If they succeeded in getting away unseen and were able to remove the rope, he would lead a later party by the same route.

Then, just when everything was set, a new prisoner arrived in the camp. It was David Stirling, founder of the SAS and a major catch for the Italians. Slightly stooped, in compensation perhaps for his towering 6'5" size, David was already a legend among those serving in North Africa. In just over a year he had risen from a lieutenant about to be court-martialled to a highly decorated colonel. In many ways, he was a man made by war. Despite the promise and expectations that accompanied his privileged background, David had so far achieved little, floundering from one scheme to another. He had grown up in Scotland, one of six children in a large Catholic family. His father was a general; his mother the daughter of Lord Lovat, a direct descendant of Charles II. Such an aristocratic pedigree might have been enough to get him into Cambridge, but it wasn't enough to keep him there. He lasted just a year before being thrown out.

He then decided to become an artist, moving to Paris to live the Bohemian life. While he certainly had the proper temperament, at least when it came to gambling and drinking, he had little talent and was convinced by his teachers to give up. Returning to Edinburgh, he decided to take up architecture. But that didn't last long either. Then, in a moment of inspiration, he announced that he was going to be the first person to climb Mt Everest. Unlike Alastair, however, he had little experience; but he was determined and moved to Switzerland, where he hired a pair of German brothers to train him. To build up his stamina and skills, he next moved to Canada, where he planned to climb the length of the Rockies. He rode horses, became a cowboy and even competed in rodeos. When the war came, his mother cabled him to come home at once, which he did, flying first class from New York.

Like so much else in David Stirling's life, his military career got off to a slow start. He joined his father's regiment, the Scots Guards, and soon after No. 8 Commando, which brought him to the Middle East. When they disbanded, he fell into old habits, frequenting the casinos and nightclubs of Cairo. Then, on the verge of court-martial for dereliction of duty, he developed a plan for the formation of a new type of special force, one that was agile and unpredictable, operating deep behind enemy lines in small groups of four to five. To the amazement of many, the proposal was accepted and the Special Air Service, a name he was forced to adopt, was born. Within a year the SAS had become a full regiment with multiple teams attacking the Germans everywhere: airbases, fuel depots, ports, railways, roads. Two hundred and fifty planes alone were destroyed. The patrols appeared out of nowhere and then vanished back into the desert. David was dubbed the 'Phantom Major' and a 100,000 Reichsmark reward placed on his head. 'Terror was meted out to the disciples of terror and they became afraid.'

At last, David Stirling had found himself. It wasn't simply that he was a brilliant and innovative strategist, nor that he was a fearless, even reckless warrior. What the war really brought out in him were his extraordinary skills as a leader, his rare capacity to inspire men to accomplish any task, no matter how difficult or dangerous. He had an irresistible charisma which touched everyone he met. Fitzroy MacLean, one of the many talented soldiers David recruited, wrote, 'He possessed above all the ultimate quality of a leader, the gift of capturing the imagination and confidence of those he led to the extent of carrying them with him on enterprises that by any rational standards seemed certain to fail and convincing them that under his leadership they were, against all probability, bound to succeed.' Alastair, who would come to know David well, agreed, though in time he would also question his judgement. 'David,' he said, 'was one of the most forceful men I have ever met. It was impossible to work contrary to David. One could rarely if ever shake him from schemes of the utmost hazard.'

By the end of January 1943, Rommel and his forces were being squeezed into the northern tip of Tunisia. With the Americans attacking from the west and Montgomery's Eighth Army coming up from Libya, it was only a matter of time before the Germans would be pushed out of North Africa. David, who was already thinking about the future role that an expanded SAS would play in the invasion of Europe, was sent ahead to provide important intelligence and to attack various strategic points. As always, he divided his men into small teams, each with a different objective. His own group would rush through the Gabès Gap, scouting the terrain all the way to the American positions on the Algerian border. The Gap was a narrow strip of land wedged between the ocean and dense, impenetrable salt marshes to the west. David had been warned to go around, but, anxious to link up with the Americans, he decided to risk going through. With typical daring, he drove straight past a row of German tanks, the occupants of which were too stunned to react.

By then his men had been awake for two solid days and were about to collapse. Pulling off the road, they drove up a wadi to find a place to rest. Within minutes of taking off their boots, David and his companions were sound asleep. The next sound they heard were the shouts of Germans yelling at them to move. A patrol scouring the area had stumbled across them by chance. That evening, David made a run for it, and after letting out 'the most horrendous rebel yell', disappeared into the desert. He walked all night, finding a place to lie up just before dawn. After sleeping most of the day, he set off again in the late afternoon. He soon met a young Arab who offered to help him. But after walking just a short way, the Arab pulled out a gun and delivered him straight into the hands of the Italians. After fourteen months of continuous action, David Stirling was a prisoner of war.

Had the Germans been able to hold on to him, David probably would have been sent straight to Colditz. But the Italians, who were delighted to show their allies up, were not about to relinquish their prize and within weeks he was on his way to Gavi. News of his arrival spread quickly with his brother Peter updating their mother in a 1 April letter from Athens:

> *My dearest Mother,*
> *. . . I got news of David today from one of the naval prisoners of war who were exchanged a few days ago, a lieut. called Brown who is flying home immediately. He was at the same camp as David – Camp 5, Post 3100, at a place called*

*Gavi near Genoa. You probably already know the address from the Vatican who have just sent it to me. David arrived at the camp about the end of February and was well and in good spirits. Brown told me he won £100 at roulette the first evening so there can't have been much the matter with him!*

*Camp 5 is the special camp for escapees or the 'molto pericoloso', David having qualified for the honours either by his reputation or because of an escape he made while still in Africa and which resulted in his recapture two days later. His present camp, though regarded as a hopeless proposition to escapees, is supposed to be one of the most agreeable and Brown told me all the best people graduated there in the end!*

*Your loving Peter*

David was given his own cell in the lower compound, a unique privilege, though it also enabled the Italians to keep close watch on their new celebrity prisoner. One of his first visitors was Jack Pringle, a pre-war acquaintance whom he 'liked enormously'. The two had similar sensibilities, intense and care-free at the same time. Jack soon introduced him to Alastair, a Perthshire man like David who also shared his passion for climbing. They immediately hit it off, talking about Everest, the time they had spent in the Alps, and what they each knew about certain peaks and approaches. It didn't take long before David steered the conversation towards escape. Alastair and Jack didn't give away much as he tried to convince them of his need to return to the front as soon as possible. He outlined the current state of the war in North Africa and the important role that the SAS had in it. He made it clear that the invasion of Europe wouldn't be far off and that he intended to participate in it as the head of a newly constituted brigade. He needed to meet with Churchill to strategize and plan. It almost seemed as if the success of the war depended on it. By the time he was finished, they had decided that David should be included in the tunnel. 'Jack and I were convinced,' Alastair said, 'that the most valuable service we could render would be to return David to England.' They wouldn't simply make him a member of the escape; they would go with him to make sure he got back.

Of course, the final decision wasn't theirs to make. It would be up to Colonel Fraser, the SBO. Jack didn't waste any time in seeing him. He was sensitive to the fact that the South Africans had done most of the heavy work and might resent the inclusion of someone who had just arrived weeks before. Even so, he laid out the reasons for including David and let Fraser know that he would be on his way to see him soon. As always, David used a combination of charm and logic to persuade the colonel of the urgency of his position. By the end of their meeting, Fraser no doubt felt that it would be unpatriotic to prevent him from going. And so it was agreed. David would be the eleventh man.

Towards the middle of March, Buck went down into the tunnel to cut through the coils of barbed wire bunched around the exit. As soon as he began sparks flew out and he was knocked unconscious. The wires were electrified. Clifton claimed it was unintentional, the result of lighting leads blowing against them. But Alastair disagreed. 'There can be no doubt,' he said 'that this was a deliberate trap. Ferrari and the Maresciallo had continually hinted that if we tried descending on a rope from the mess windows we should receive a painful surprise. And this was an obvious route.'

It wasn't easy getting Buck out of the cistern and back into the compound. He had gotten a good jolt and was pretty shaken. The original wire cutters they had worked so hard to get would have to be replaced with a high-quality insulated pair. Alastair approached Jack the Little Monster, offering him a full year's pay if he could provide them. He would do it but asked for something else as well. He wanted Kermeth Warr, the camp's South African dentist, to pull out his few remaining teeth. Then he would file for a medical discharge and return home to his small village. Alastair agreed and, as promised, the Little Monster produced the wire cutters. He also had all his teeth removed, received a discharge and said goodbye to Gavi for ever. Before he did, he thanked Alastair, extending an invitation to visit him at any time.

Buck was soon down in the tunnel again with the new clippers. And although he received a fair number of shocks, he was able to clear a passage onto the roof. At one point he even fell, breaking some of the tiles, but neither this nor the sound of his cutting were enough to alert the carabinieri. The new passageway was well concealed by the many coils of wire that were still connected above. The South Africans now began taking turns lying at the tunnel exit, recording the nightly movements of the occupants on the *mezzaluna* below. By eleven it became so quiet that one could hear the smallest sound; even two neighbours in the village saying goodnight to one another were as audible as if they had been in the fortress itself. Any escape from the tunnel would have to wait till midnight; and it could only be done during a storm.

While the South Africans took turns in the tunnel, the others were occupied above, carefully observing the path they would

128

need to follow. 'We spent hours studying our route from the mess room windows,' said Alastair, 'so that we knew every tile, every stone on the roof. Once off the exposed roof and broken wall edge we felt we would have overcome 80% of the difficulties.' Alastair was also busy assembling the twenty-pound packs that each man would carry. With his many years of experience in the back country, there was no one better to work out exactly how many calories per day would be needed and the most efficient way of providing them: thirteen pounds per person with meat, cocoa, sugar, biscuits, and oat and cornmeal all cooked into dense cakes that could last for three weeks at ten ounces per day. The packs also contained extra civilian clothing along with maps, compasses, documents and gloves.

Alastair and Jack had originally intended to travel to the Swiss border by train but now that David Stirling was accompanying them they would need to alter their plan. With his enormous height and lack of any Italian, it would simply be too risky. Instead, they would have to walk. For Alastair and David this was fine, though it did make Jack somewhat nervous. They decided on a route up the Ligurian Alps and across the headwaters of the Po to the Aosta valley. From there they would climb to nearly 12,000 feet, crossing into Switzerland by the Matterjoch Pass in the shadow of the Matterhorn. Alastair was confident that this was the best route, even for a climber as inexperienced as Jack:

I had repeatedly crossed and recrossed this area sometimes in darkness and often in bad weather and was perfectly certain it offered no difficulties in late spring or early summer to a party such as ours, provided we were not too reduced through lack of food when we arrived at the foot of the Pass. I selected the

Matterjoch in preference to the easier Theodule as I felt sure that the latter would be closely watched, whereas it would be extremely difficult to guard the more distant ice traversed Matterjoch, especially by night.

Worried that they might be interned by the Swiss before they could reach Bern, Alastair wrote to a girl he knew in Zermatt asking her to prepare for their arrival. Needless to say, the letter was extremely discreet with all the references well disguised. It was enough, however, for her to discern the route in order to explore it on her own. She sent back an equally coded message suggesting an alternative through the Aiguilles Dorées and L'Évêque, claiming that it would be less frequently patrolled. Alastair agreed that it was an excellent route, though her letter didn't arrive till well after the escape.

The only thing left now was to choose the date they would go. They had already agreed on the tunnel order. Buck, of course, would open it and be the first one out. Bob Paterson, who planned to go on his own, would be next, followed by Chas Wuth and Allen Pole. They drew lots to decide the other positions. Alastair won, which meant that he would go fifth, followed by David and Jack. Peter Medd and Gerry Daly, who were escaping together, would be next, with McCrae and Hedley, as agreed, going last. Everyone's packs and clothing were stored in the tunnel as they sat down to wait for the right conditions. But they didn't come. A storm would seem to be mounting and then simply fizzle out. Spring was a little too nice. They knew that the longer they waited, the greater was the risk of discovery. It had happened so many times, a tunnel just about to break when the guards, through luck or suspicion, found the entrance, spoiling months of hard work and planning. By now, too, everyone in the camp knew exactly what was going on. And while no one suspected that anyone would willingly give it away, such excitement was worse than a spy. Jailers could sense when the tension in a prison rose just before an escape.

At David's urging, they finally agreed to go on the next windy night. When a storm kicked up on a late afternoon at the end of March, word quickly spread that the escape was on. Arrangements had already been made for a group of orderlies to sleep in the beds of the officers who were escaping. The evening guards only glanced at the rooms of the Other Ranks, so dummies left in their place would be enough to fool them. The switch began after dinner. One by one, the escapers slipped into the orderlies' rooms and prepared to enter the cistern. They were all in place by eleven with Poppet serving as conductor. The only problem was the weather. The storm that had seemed to be brewing in the afternoon suddenly disappeared. With not even the hint of a breeze, it was completely still once again. By now the moon was up, the searchlights on, and two machine gun turrets had a clear view of the roof, all a perfect recipe for disaster.

Buck lay at the tunnel face waiting for direction. 'Do we go or not?'

'No,' came the answer. 'It's off for tonight.' So they made their way back up the shaft and were safely in bed by 2.30 when the carabinieri came by to check.

Now the wait began again, only this time they wouldn't go until there was a truly torrential downpour. Periods like these were hard. As calm as one tried to remain, there was always anxiety and concern before attempting anything so dangerous.

By now Alastair had been through it any number of times. For him the wait was an opportunity to analyse the emotions that prevented one from performing at one's best, to take a scalpel to that part of one's brain where fear and doubt reside. He had done this for years while climbing peaks, and escaping from prison was no different. It was where Alastair's hyper-rationalist legal mind merged with the mystic, that part of him which saw the possibility of transcendence in every act. The freedom he sought in escape was always linked to an inner quest. 'Not mere freedom of the body from the cruelty of the wire, but the freedom of the mind and of the spirit.' For Alastair, confronting death and danger in acts of extreme physicality provided one of life's greatest lessons:

In the month that followed before our next attempt, I completed the lesson that 94% of fear is attachment to life. The more one is attached to possessions, to an individual, to ambitions, to the world the less one wants to die. By a process of stripping away these mental attachments one gradually achieves a state of mind in which fear, risk and danger cease to have a hampering effect. They have instead a stimulating effect. So long as one is hampered by the sensations arising out of danger one cannot act with the precision, speed, and judgement requisite to meet the situation of risk. My first escape had a feeling of light hearted adventure and in the next one of exhilaration from risk met and overcome. At Gavi if I felt no excitement also there was no exhilaration, merely coolness. Like every venture escape is worse to look forward to than to do. Once the business has begun, it goes far more easily than anticipated and one has even the tiniest sensation of disappointment, instantly repressed as tempting fortune that nothing untoward has happened.

It wasn't until 20 April, the Tuesday before Easter, that the storm they had been waiting for finally arrived. Huge torrents of water gushed out of the drainpipes and overran the gutters as the fortress was shrouded in a deep mist. Visibility was reduced to a few feet, which is exactly what they wanted. No one needed to be told. They knew immediately that this was the night. Once again, the orderlies switched beds and the eleven escapers, as they had done in the dress rehearsal weeks before, lined up to enter the cistern. Alastair was in the tunnel by midnight wriggling along just behind Allen Pole. Buck had widened the opening in the barbed wire and getting onto the roof 'seemed ridiculously easy'. From there he scrambled down the wet tiles and dropped onto the broken wall that descended to within feet of the ground. He was surprised by the lights and music coming from the guards' huts. Perhaps it was part of a Holy Week celebration, or maybe for Adolf Hitler, whose birthday was the same day.

Alastair caught up with the South Africans and wondered why there was still no sign of David and Jack. Then a door opened and an Italian stepped out and looked straight at them. Had he seen them, or were his eyes not yet adjusted to the dark? Alastair hid beneath the hut as the others crept to the far side of the terrace and the olive tree that would anchor the rope. Still no sign of David and Jack. He stood and made his way to the tree as well. The rain had picked up and even when a group of guards came out of the nearest hut, they still didn't see him. He couldn't wait any longer. Buck and the others had already climbed over the wall and disappeared. Now Alastair grabbed the rope and began to lower himself down. But no sooner had he started than it broke. He fell thirty feet, landing face down on an outcrop of rocks, his twenty-pound pack crashing on top of him seconds later.

Alastair knew straight away that he was hurt. He had been knocked unconscious, though he had no idea for how long. When he came to there were sirens blaring, a bugle sounding and searchlights waving in every direction. He started down the mud-covered hillside, half running, half sliding, looking for any footholds he could find. Behind him were the sounds of men screaming and rifles being fired. Were they shooting at him? Only later would he find out what had happened.

David, with his enormous body, had been slow getting through the tunnel and had even more trouble when he got tangled in the wire. By the time he climbed off the roof, Alastair and the South Africans were already on the other side. This may have made him feel that he needed to hurry. He shouldn't have. Jack says David was 'ahead striding rapidly toward the sapling and the rope'. He had no chance to react when a group of Italians burst out of one of the huts drinking and singing. Miraculously, they walked straight past him as they bowed their heads against the heavy rain. David wasn't so lucky when a dozen more came out just seconds later. They spotted him running toward the wall and soon had him surrounded. That's when the alarm went off and shots were fired. David broke through the cordon, shoving the guards out of the way. The huts emptied and the entire triangle became a mass of confusion. The last escapers were just getting off the roof when David was finally trapped, flailing his arms and racing along the rampart.

Jack, who hadn't been seen, kept his cool and quietly made his way to the tree, grabbed what was left of the rope, and fell thirty feet. Unlike Alastair, however, he was able to roll upon impact and walk away unhurt. Peter Medd also took advantage of the chaos and, although he couldn't make it to the other side, slipped beneath one of the barracks where he hid for several hours. By then, Moscatelli had arrived. Always volatile, he walked straight up to David and struck him in the face. Everyone claimed he was lucky that the guards were holding David so tightly. If not, they were sure that David would have killed him. For his part, Moscatelli said that David had tried to throw one of the guards over the wall, which is why he claimed he slapped him. But he wasn't the only one struck. Hedley was beaten with a rifle butt and when Medd, the last to be discovered, was finally pulled out from under the hut, his face was smashed with a revolver.

They had agreed to meet at a ford just south of the village along the Lemme River. Alastair wasn't surprised when no one came and decided to head towards a monastery perched on an isolated hilltop on the other side. Crossing the river was easy, but once he started to climb the pain above his left lung became unbearable. Breathing was difficult and he could hardly raise his arms to grab a branch to pull himself up. He hadn't gone far when he sat down to look back at the fortress. If one didn't know what was happening, it might have almost seemed beautiful. Beams of light bathed the ancient castle in a warm if frenetic glow. Of course, one could also hear the sound of sirens and even the screams of the guards. He knew by now that he had at least two broken ribs and probably a concussion as well. He thought

135

about the rope and was angry with himself for not having checked it. During the entire preparation, it was the only item he hadn't personally examined. Ginger Hamilton, a cheery South African with a face full of freckles, had made it. But what did an infantryman from the Transvaal know about making rope? They should have asked Poppet.

His mind wandered, and suddenly he realized that he was sitting next to a lilac bush. The fragrance was overwhelming. In fact, everything was in bloom and he was overcome by the smells of spring, the lemon blossoms, the wild roses, the scent of the earth just opened for planting. 'And then it occurred to me,' he said, 'that in Gavi there was a complete absence of these perfumes. I revelled in these sensations and cursed the hurt that took the pleasure out of the night.' Perhaps if he took off the rubber shoes he'd been wearing since leaving the tunnel, he'd feel better. They were completely soaked, and yet bending down to remove them was impossible. He looked for a tree with a low enough fork to wedge his foot into, then laid back and prised them off. He had a pair of dry boots in his pack though getting them on and laced was equally difficult.

For most of the night Alastair wandered through the heavy rain, recalling little beyond the physical pain in his chest as he slipped and climbed over the many obstacles in his path. Just before dawn he found a small hayloft which he crawled into and quickly fell asleep. It seemed like only minutes before he was awakened by the sound of a pitchfork jabbing deep into the hay. Fortunately he was well hidden, but several hours later the farmer was back for more. He returned once again at the end of the day, although now the pitchfork was coming dangerously close to Alastair's face. And then finally, they were staring right at one another. The farmer was quite old and Alastair worried that he might have a heart attack. Instead, he flew down the ladder and was gone in an instant. By the time Alastair appeared, the entire family had assembled, several generations of them, all in threadbare clothes, some without shoes. He could tell from their faces that he was a terrifying presence: 'A horrible apparition I must have been, deformed, lopsided with torn clothes thickly covered to the hip in half dried mud and blood smeared hands and face, with a great pack and a heavy stick, and probably a rather disturbing expression.'

And then to their surprise, the apparition spoke, wishing them a good afternoon and asking in a very calm and polite voice if he might have a glass of milk. A young girl of no more than twelve raced off, returning moments later with a huge wooden mug that might have held mead in another century. They watched, silent and transfixed, as Alastair slowly drank. No sooner had he wiped away the white moustache from his upper lip than the old man he had seen in the hayloft spoke. 'Hurry, go quickly. Please, do not stay here, we beg you.'

It made no sense to pretend that he was someone else, a German deserter perhaps, as he had done with the *contadini* he had met in Sicily. Everyone knew that there had been an escape and that British officers were wandering around the area. The penalty for harbouring one was death, a risk Alastair had no intention of imposing. Instead, he walked down toward the river, searching for a secluded spot to bathe. It was that magical time of day with late-afternoon light reaching through the branches and insects busily moving from one blossom to another, and up above, the sounds of birds, doves, a woodpecker, even a kingfisher skimming along the surface of the water.

Alastair washed and shaved and laid his clothes out on the rocks to dry. It was hard for him to think about the Alps. The pain had increased and he wondered if he had punctured a lung. He knew that climbing would be impossible, that the effort it would take would only make his symptoms worse.

As the sun went down, a light rain started to fall. He now began the difficult routine of putting on his clothes and pack. If not for the terrible pain, it might have seemed comical, lying on his back and squirming on the ground. He then headed upriver, following the shoreline as it entered into a deep gorge. There was light from the moon reflecting off the water. Alastair was always comfortable travelling at night. To him, it was the best time to experience the natural world, when sounds and smells were most intense and animals likely to be found. 'The great symphony of night' he called it, that special hour he regularly sought throughout his life. He continued along the river as it twisted and turned, often seeming to lead him back to where he started. When a fortress appeared at dawn, he worried that he had come full circle and was back at Gavi. But it was a different castle built to defend another mountain. Exhausted, he climbed up to a ledge beneath a sandstone overhang, struggled out of his pack, and fell asleep for the rest the day.

When it was dark, he set off again, following the river as it headed north. By midnight, the rain was back. It was hard to imagine what the conditions would be like in the mountain passes should he make it that far. He was cold and feverish, and yet he felt his strength returning. Daylight found him in the middle of a wide expanse in the river with fields and vineyards stretching out in all directions. He needed to get away from the water and up into the hills where he could hide. It didn't take long before he came across a tool shed, unlocked and dry, a perfect place to lie up for the day. There was even a pile of empty sacks to make a bed. He had only slept a short time before the owner came in and woke him. Unlike the family from the hayloft, this farmer was welcoming. In fact, he urged Alastair to stay. 'I know you are from Gavi,' he said, 'but we don't like to think of you shut up in there. I am Piemontese, not a Fascist. I fought in the last war and your troops were quartered here in this village. Everybody liked them and they left a fine lot of good children behind, I can tell you. Come to my house and I will give you food.'

Alastair was willing to trust him but thought that entering his home in broad daylight was too dangerous. Perhaps he should have. As soon as he left the shed, it was as if a spotlight was shining on him. The hillside offered little protection and was filled with families walking to their fields. A small boy ran up to him screaming 'You are an English officer. You are from Gavi.' Alastair denied it, claiming that he was an Italian from a village near Venice.

'No, no,' the boy cried, 'Inglese, Inglese.' He tried to take Alastair's hand and it was all he could do to scare him off. But by now he could see that troops were coming up from the river to get him:

I doubled and redoubled amid the vine terraces but the heavy mudslide had made the road soft and obliterated all other footprints and I was leaving an obvious trail. At last I found a road on an embankment. I left tracks at the roadside then walked on the hard rock surface till the mud left my boots, then turned back for 400 yards, dropped down the embankment, crawled along a terrace into a small hide of dense bushes.

I was absolutely done. I buried my maps, papers, identity card and money in the earth. The landscape was now dotted with 3 man patrols going at a trot. I saw a patrol with an officer coming down the road hot on my trail and pass out of sight. Three hours passed. The patrols were now all behind me heading up the south end. Felt a return of confidence. The excitement had shown me that my ribs were going to be usable on easier ground. I ate a little. Then the patrols started coming back beating every bush on the hillside. It was maddening. Had I been fit I could have made a run for it. The hills were near enough. It ended with a patrol covering my hide with their carbines. A young lieutenant pushed an automatic through the leaves. They dug up the ground and found my papers. The young officer was quite apologetic.

His captors were part of an Alpini unit, special mountain troops identified by their olive felt hats with black raven feathers sticking up. Two full companies of them had been called out to track down the escapers. They were kind to Alastair and even carried his pack as they returned to their barracks. A doctor examined him, after which a bottle of wine was opened. Talk soon turned to climbing and for a moment it was easy to forget that they were enemies. Alastair joked about the last time he'd been arrested by Alpini, at Gressoney-La-Trinité in 1936 when he crossed into Italy illegally. And sure enough, a major was present who had been stationed there at the time. Everyone laughed. And then Alastair was put on a truck and driven back to Gavi.

His reception there was far less cordial. Moscatelli, usually so animated and confident, was slumped in his chair, a broken man. For several minutes he mumbled something in a low whisper which Alastair could hardly understand. While he neither gloated nor felt sorry for him, Alastair was still surprised. The colonel was a person who always loved to shout and his new demeanour came as something of a shock. Sergeant Mazza, on the other hand, kept shifting his weight from one foot to the next. He was clearly agitated and couldn't wait to take Alastair away. Along with another carabiniere, he escorted him to an empty cell where he was stripped. Then, while the other soldier held him, Mazza punched him in the face over and over again. When they finally let Alastair drop to the floor, Mazza began kicking him in his broken ribs. It was only when the sergeant threatened to throw Alastair over a wall that the other soldier panicked and ran for help. Mazza had to be restrained, while Alastair was left naked and bleeding on the ground. He might have frozen too if a guard hadn't disobeyed orders and given him a blanket. Eventually, he was taken to the hospital where he spent the next three weeks, barely able to move.

The day after Alastair's return, Bob Paterson appeared. He had abandoned his plan to take a train and decided to walk instead. He hadn't gone far when a dog discovered him while sleeping in a ditch. Then two days later, Buck, Pole and Wuth were brought in. They had travelled together, dressed in outfits sewn by another prisoner. Like Alastair, they were going to travel west before turning north to the Swiss border. But instead of climbing through a mountain pass, they intended to cross at Lake Maggiore near Locarno. Despite the heavy rains, they made good time, walking at night and hiding during the day. It was bad luck when a Carabinieri patrol out looking for parachutists happened to find them. That left only Jack, and as the days passed, everyone began to hope that he had made it.

When Jack fell from the wall, he suffered nothing more than the loss of his pack containing all his food and documents. Like Alastair, he ran and slid down the hillside, stopping only when he reached the ford where they had planned to meet. The two were no doubt close to one another and yet, in the rain and dark, it was impossible to see. Shouting was too dangerous, and so, after waiting a short time, he decided to strike out on his own. He quickly dismissed the idea of hiking to the Alpine passes which Alastair and David had proposed and instead decided to revert to their original plan of travelling by train. He still had his money and his Italian was nearly flawless. But he wouldn't move for twenty-four hours in order to avoid the search parties that would be scouring the area.

He found a nice thicket of trees along the river in which to hide. When some girls tending geese came too close, he simply slid into the water and disappeared. 'I was wet and cold,' said Jack, 'but I was happy.' The next night he set off, heading southwest for Genoa. It was a smart move since he knew that the escapers would be expected to go north toward Switzerland. He walked over the mountains for two days, pretending to be a German deserter whose mother was Italian. The peasants he met were sympathetic, offering him wine and food. They even invited him to play a game of bocce. He completed the journey by train and was glad to return to a city he had known before the war.

Jack liked Genoa. He felt anonymous and safe there, wandering about its busy streets. He went down to the red-light district near the port, stole a sweater from a clothesline, helped some German soldiers order food in a restaurant, spent time at a cinema, took a nap in the cathedral, and walked and walked, assessing the damage from the previous year's shelling. He now pretended to be a Croat, an Axis ally speaking a language which no one was likely to understand. He even bought a German newspaper, the *Völkischer Beobachter*, carrying it under his arm to complement his disguise.

When he returned to the station at the end of the day, it was teeming with holiday traffic. He had decided to cross into Switzerland near Pallanza, a small village on Lake Maggiore which he had once passed through. He was concerned that buying a ticket to the border would arouse suspicion, so instead he purchased a round trip to Milan. Once there, he would take a local the rest of the way. He left the next morning after a breakfast of sardines and grappa. It was Easter and the train was packed. His greatest fear was being caught without papers and, sure enough, no sooner had they left the mountains than he heard the police asking for them. He kept his head, though, and as the train slowed for the next stop, he got off, walked several cars back, and reboarded at a point they had already examined.

He needed even more guile for the next leg of the journey. Once again he decided not to buy a ticket all the way to Pallanza but to a somewhat larger lake town called Stresa. From there he would board another train. He sat beside a young woman, a milliner's assistant on her way to deliver a hat to a client. Jack, who had lost none of his charm, quickly engaged her, and by the time the police came by to check papers, they were poring over a fashion magazine, deep in conversation. He leaned especially close as if in a lover's embrace and the police, with an Italian respect for romance, simply walked by rather than interrupt.

143

That left only one short ride, the train to Pallanza, which he spent locked in the bathroom. He arrived at sunset, optimistic that he was finally going to make it. The lights from Locarno were actually visible but he still had twenty-five miles to walk. He followed the road along the shore and was relieved to find that there was no one on it. As he passed through Intra he recalled *A Farewell to Arms* and Hemingway's description of the lovers' flight across the lake. By dawn he was within five miles of the border. He was exhausted from more than a week on the move, light-headed and desperate for sleep. He decided to rest and cross later that day. Along the water, he found a thick stand of rhododendrons, the perfect place to hide. He burrowed in and was asleep within minutes. Eight hours later he was awakened by two carabinieri tugging on his shoulder.

His hiding place, as it turned out, was almost too perfect. There had been an alarm out for an escaped smuggler from Milan and the police had been checking the rhododendrons for days. 'What I had done – slept for nearly one whole day – was so awful that I could not bear to think of it,' he said. 'I was numb with disappointment.' Equally upset were Gavi's other prisoners, who watched as Jack was led up to the cells just as he and Alastair had been when they first arrived from Padula less than a year before. Except for Alastair, who was still in the hospital, everyone was there. Jack couldn't recall a time when friends were so unhappy to see him. And yet there was solace in knowing that they had been the first prisoners ever to escape from Gavi. True, they hadn't made it home, but they hadn't been caught either. It was a strange mix of emotions which Colin Armstrong summed up best when he wrote: 'Disappointing though it was that no one had succeeded in getting clean away, we felt that our pride had been saved and that we had scored over our captors. For all their boasts of the castle's impregnability, for all the wire, the rock, the countless sentries, and the eternal vigilance, we had beaten them at last.'

# Last Days of Gavi

August 1943 was especially hot, and even worse for those trapped in an airless stone fortress baking in the summer sun. It was the second birthday Alastair had spent in prison and, he hoped, the last. The reports from Italy were good, and for families with sons and husbands imprisoned there, it seemed only a matter of time before they'd be free. Alastair's father certainly felt that way as he sat down to write his only child a newsy letter just one week after the fall of Sicily:

*24 August 1943*

*My Dear Son,*

*I send you birthday greetings and hope you will spend your next birthday at home. Great events are taking place all over and we are living from day to day in great hope that you will soon be home. Part of your kit has arrived in this country and I have written to the W.O. [War Office] asking if it is the kit from Cooks or the Continental Hotel. They won't forward it here unless with your authority. They asked if I had a letter from you containing this authority and I replied I was writing you for same and would let them know as soon as I received it. I sent you ½ lb of Capstan Navy Cut today through Rattray.*

*They said you might bring it back with you! Robert has had
word from Alex. He is well but wearying to get home. We
would have gone up this week end (Monday being our holiday)
but Mother promised Stella Norman to go to Portobello, so we
will go there on Friday afternoon till Monday night. The court
is up. Val is off to Fearnan for the fishing. He got 2–3 salmon
in Loch Tay last year and hopes to repeat that feat. We are both
well and do hope you are the same. Mother is busy making
jam. We took down some plums last night. She has got six 2lb
jars filled and sterilized and jam will follow later. I have to lock
the gate at night to keep out the fruit stealers.*

*People are still asking for you. All say 'he will soon be home'.
Douglas is off somewhere and they are awaiting news. Tom
Ferguson is home for good I hear. Carruth is on holiday so I
am alone. He will be finished this week. Mother and I would
like another week in Aviemore but have not decided when. We
will no doubt see great change among the Pines.*

*Love from Father*

Three months earlier the Axis forces had surrendered in
Tunisia. The jaws of the trap so carefully set had finally slammed
shut, putting an end to the battle for North Africa. More than
a quarter of a million prisoners were taken, though Rommel
wasn't one of them. He had left weeks before, returning to Germany in a state of physical collapse. By now, the Allies had
established their superiority in men and materials. The Italians
knew what was coming next and had already begun to manoeuvre for a separate peace. Sicily, less than a hundred miles
from what was once Carthage, would be an easy target for an
army anxious to gain a foothold on the continent. The Americans

resisted, preferring an invasion of France, but Churchill prevailed and on 10 July 1943 American, British and Canadian forces landed. Within five weeks it was over, but not before Mussolini, in power since 1922, had been deposed. King Victor Emmanuel and the Grand Council of Fascism had finally had enough. Mussolini, in a state of shock, was bundled off to a secret location in the Gran Sasso, a part of Italy so remote that it was known as 'Little Tibet'.

All this was followed closely among the prisoners. A loudspeaker set up in the courtyard blared the news from Italian radio, while Tommy Macpherson continued reading his evening reports. When Mussolini fell, they cheered and hugged. They knew that Italy was quickly dissolving into chaos. Riots had occurred in several cities and for the first time in years there were strikes and demonstrations. At the same time, German troops were observed passing through the Lemme valley, a scene re-enacted throughout northern Italy as fresh divisions began to pour into the country. And yet, most prisoners continued to believe that they were safe and that liberation was imminent. The Germans, they argued, would never try to defend Italy. Instead, they would set up a defensive line along the Po and, if need be, fall back to the Brenner Pass. Besides, removing so many prisoners would be a logistical nightmare undermining their military goals.

Alastair thought that this was wishful thinking and became something of a Cassandra as he took a different position. 'I found myself,' he said, 'in a minority of one. Every man in the camp had of course entertained the belief from time to time that we might be transported to Germany but now at this critical stage it was astonishing to find how many were governed in their beliefs by what they most hoped for.' Even when two German officers visited the castle in mid-August, no one took it as a sign for concern. Alastair himself chatted with them in the mess and was later embarrassed by how easily they seduced him. 'I remember telling Jack how favourably impressed I had been by their smartness and efficiency compared to the Ities. I was yet to learn how politeness can be an assumed veneer and the ends of efficiency might be terror and brutality, for the war in the desert had been fought in a fairly gentlemanly fashion.'

At the end of the month, another group of Germans arrived, a colonel with his entire staff. This time, the prisoners watched with growing alarm as Moscatelli led them on an exhaustive tour of the fortress's various features. When questioned about this, Moscatelli dismissed its significance, treating it as little more than a social call, like old friends who just happened to be in the neighbourhood. He swore on his honour as an officer and a gentleman that if the Germans should threaten Gavi, he would not only give everyone fair warning but help them as well. This promise was reaffirmed on 8 September when a Red Cross delegation visited on one of its periodic inspections. Upon leaving, they issued a joint statement with Moscatelli guaranteeing that under no circumstances would the prisoners be sent to Germany. They even posted a printed copy of it on the mess hall bulletin board.

That evening, as dinner was being served and several officers were standing around reading the Red Cross statement, a tremendous cheer erupted from the Italian quarters below. Everyone rushed to the windows to see what was happening. The guards and carabinieri had poured out of their huts and were on the terrace throwing their hats in the air and celebrating. The scene in the village was no different. The squares and streets filled with people weeping as they embraced and kissed. The blackout curtains that had covered the windows of their homes for years were torn off and, like the set of an opera, women were leaning out of every one of them, waving their arms, shouting and singing. The armistice had just been announced.

Before the news had even sunk in, two Italian officers, both anti-fascist and friendly with the prisoners, entered the mess to shake hands and celebrate with men who only an hour earlier had been their enemies. 'Now we are allies,' they declared as they set down their guns. The irony that the Italians were elated rather than dejected over their defeat wasn't lost on anyone. To them the armistice wasn't a symbol of failure but of a victory over both the Fascists and the Germans. What any of this would mean to the men in Gavi wasn't immediately clear. Already, rumours were circulating that the Allies had landed in La Spezia and Ancona, even Genoa just thirty miles away. Clifton, the senior officer, demanded to speak to Moscatelli at once. But Joe Grapes, as he was commonly known, refused, sending word that he wouldn't be available until morning. A plan had long been in place for just this moment when the prisoners would rise up, disarm the guards and take over the fortress. Everyone knew his part and was simply awaiting the order. But it never came.

Although he was considered 'dashing and fearless' by his men, Clifton hesitated, making one of several tactical errors that he would come to regret. As he later confessed: 'There were no signs of any amphibious or air-borne operation within sight, and I frankly got cold feet and refused to play.' Instead, the men eased into a long evening of celebration, drinking wine and singing. At turns raucous and sentimental, every group offered a national song: 'Zulu Warrior', 'Waltzing Matilda', 'It's a Long Way to Tipperary' and, finally, 'The Maori Farewell', whose lyrics more than any other captured the sadness and longing of men who, in many cases, hadn't seen their families in years:

> Now is the hour when we must say goodbye,
> Soon you'll be sailing far across the sea.
> While you're away, oh please remember me,
> When you return, you'll find me waiting here.

They were awakened the next morning at 6 a.m. by the sound of gunfire. No sooner had Alastair and his cellmates pulled on their clothes and stepped into the courtyard than a party of Italians came rushing through the gate, two wounded companions in tow. Part of a group sent down to the village every morning to gather provisions, they had somehow got into a firefight with a German unit that had appeared in Gavi several days earlier. George Millar claims that it began as a lark when one of the Italians, pointing his rifle in jest and with a broad smile, imitated the sound of bullets being fired. Evidently the Germans failed to see the humour and shot the poor man dead. By the time the patrol got back to the castle, two others had been killed and several more wounded.

The armistice agreement, announced the evening before, had called on all Italians to resist the Germans and to join the Allies in liberating their country. Now Gavi was preparing to do just that. The machine guns that had been facing in towards the prisoners were suddenly turned around. Arms and ammunition were issued to the guards who were positioned along the ramparts. To the inmates, who had never taken the Italians very seriously as soldiers, it looked as though they were actually going to put up a fight. But it was only an illusion. A few dozen Germans firing several rounds and lobbing a single smoke bomb were enough to crush any resistance. The gate was hurriedly opened and the second in command, 'a miserable and decrepit old colonel', was sent out with a white flag.

It was a pitiful scene: 230 men, easily reinforced by a like number of prisoners, turning over an impregnable fortress to thirty lightly armed Germans without firing a single shot. George Millar summed up everyone's disgust when he quipped that 'Gavi had not sullied its centuries-old record of instant surrender'. Compounding the humiliation was the fact that the conquerors were a rearguard veterinary unit composed of overage Bavarian farmers and blacksmiths in horse-drawn wagons. Their leader was a simple farrier sergeant with dung-covered boots who knew nothing at all about guarding prisoners. Going from one sentry post to the next, he replaced the Italians with his own soldiers. When he had finished and the entire garrison had been disarmed, he dismissed most of the guards, who were more than happy to go home. Two prisoners, seeing an opportunity, quickly dressed as Italians and tried to go with them; but they were spotted and hauled away. By noon, the fortress was entirely in German hands. As one officer from New Zealand said: 'We realized we had fallen from the fat to the fire.'

'The siege of Gavi' was a microcosm of what was taking place throughout Italy and the Mediterranean. Everywhere from Rhodes to Elba, heavily armed and well-manned Italian garrisons were surrendering to smaller German forces without so much as a fight. For most soldiers, it seemed a safe ticket home.

At least that was the promise, but 600,000 of them were put on trains and shipped directly to Germany, where they were forced into slave labour. In the few instances where real resistance was mounted, such as Cephalonia off the coast of Greece, the Nazis unleashed their signature brutality. There, the commander and his staff along with 5,000 prisoners were slaughtered in cold blood.

Nor was any help forthcoming from the leaders of the newly formed government, whose only concern seemed to be saving their own skins. When Mussolini was arrested at the end of July, King Victor Emmanuel replaced him with Pietro Badoglio, a seventy-two-year-old field marshal best known for his use of poison gas against the Ethiopians in 1936. A political opportunist closely associated with the fascists, he was a poor choice for prime minister, a position demanding independence and initiative. Throughout the summer Badoglio haggled with the Allies over the terms of the armistice. Although it was finally signed on 3 September, he insisted that they wait five days until the eve of the Allied landings at Salerno to announce it. Part of the agreement, as devised by Eisenhower, was to send the 82nd Airborne Division to Rome and, in coordination with Italian troops, quickly take over the city. But Badoglio sat on his hands and when the moment came for the Americans to land, they found that no preparations had been made. In frustration, Eisenhower called it off and one of the war's great opportunities was lost. The Germans soon occupied the city and the war in Italy was prolonged by months.

As for Badoglio, he couldn't get out of Rome fast enough. The morning after he announced the armistice, he fled with the royal family and several of his ministers, going to Brindisi where

Montgomery's Eighth Army would protect him. His lack of leadership and courage, at the precise moment when it was needed most, cost the country dearly. With no warning of the peace agreement nor instructions on how to proceed, the Italian army simply collapsed. Badoglio also failed to hand over Mussolini as he had promised. Instead, a group of German commandos rescued him – again without firing a shot – and whisked Il Duce off to Germany, where Hitler made him head of the new Italian Social Republic. It was a puppet state, of course, in which Mussolini had no real power. Yet it legitimated the German presence in Italy, giving them a platform from which to plunge the country into a civil war.

There was one area, however, in which Badoglio, in a rare act of defiance, stood up to the Germans. In mid-August, they demanded that all prisoners of war be turned over to them. The British, foreseeing such a possibility, had already threatened Badoglio with severe consequences should he do so. Given the choice, he refused the German demand and guaranteed in the armistice that all prisoners would be protected or set free. In fact, two days before the agreement was announced, he sent an order to every camp commandant to this effect:

### British POWs

Prevent them falling into German hands. In the event that it is not possible to defend efficiently all the camps, set at liberty all the white prisoners but keep the blacks in prison. Facilitate their escape either to Switzerland or along the Adriatic coast to southern Italy. Labour units in civilian clothes may also be helped, providing they are away from the German line of retreat. At the opportune moment the freed prisoners should be given reserve rations and directions as to which route they should follow.

Whether the commandants in all seventy-two prisoner-of-war camps received this message is unclear. If so, its implementation was certainly uneven. Many commandants, like Colonel Moscatelli, were committed fascists who, even if they had seen the order, would have ignored it. But an even greater problem was the contradictory role played by the British command itself.

By August 1943 there were 80,000 prisoners of war in Italy, over 85 per cent of whom were either British or Commonwealth-related. Churchill, who had gained his first taste of fame when he escaped from a prison camp in South Africa during the Boer War, was especially concerned with the fate of these men. He insisted that the peace agreement contain a strongly worded guarantee of their release and instructed his staff to do everything it could to rescue them. His intentions were soon subverted, however, by a secret order sent to the senior officers of every camp. Known as the 'Stand-fast' or 'Stay Put' order, it instructed those in charge to prevent prisoners from leaving the camps once the armistice was declared. Although MI9, the special unit set up to work with prisoners and resistance forces, was credited with sending it, most attribute its origin to General Montgomery, who was concerned that thousands of ex-prisoners wandering about the countryside would impede his military operation. Besides, he believed that the Italian campaign would be relatively short and the prisoners quickly liberated. The order, therefore, prohibited any mass escapes and held the senior officers responsible for its enforcement. Sent through concealed radios and coded letters, the order stated that: 'In the event of an Allied invasion of Italy, Officers Commanding prison camps will ensure that prisoners-of-war remain within camp. Authority is granted to all Officers Commanding to take necessary disciplinary action to prevent individual prisoners-of-war attempting to rejoin their units.'

The interpretation of this order varied widely. At the Castello di Vincigliata near Florence, where the most high-ranking officers such as Generals O'Connor and Neame were held, it was simply ignored. Of course, it helped that the commandant took them to the train station and personally sent them on their way. At Chieti, a much larger camp near the Adriatic, the situation was far different. There, the Italians just laid down their arms and left. But Lieutenant Colonel Marshall, the British officer in charge, forbade anyone to leave the camp. When officers began to complain, insisting that they be allowed to make their own way south, Marshall posted guards, threatening anyone who escaped with court-martial. After ten days, the Germans finally arrived and took over the camp. While forty or so prisoners had disobeyed orders and escaped, 1,600 others were put on trains to Germany, where they spent twenty more months in captivity.

At Modena, another large camp filled with South Africans and New Zealanders, the senior officer initially believed that the Italians would defend them. When he realized that this wasn't realistic he told his men that anyone who wished to could leave. But fewer than 200 chose to do so, leaving 1,000 others to share the same fate as those in Chieti. Here the men weren't compelled to 'stay put', but did so out of the insidious 'inertia' that infected so many prisoners of war. As Adrian Gilbert noted:

Unlike the true escaper – who was mentally and physically prepared for the ordeal ahead – these men found the idea of marching hundreds of miles in a foreign and potentially hostile country daunting, if not overwhelming . . . While the Stay Put order played its part in encouraging such displays of timidity, it would have taken a rigorous shake-up of the entire camp system in the weeks, perhaps months, leading up to the armistice to have retrained the sedentary prisoners in the attitudes of an escaper.

The type of change in prison culture called for by Gilbert occurred at Fontanellato, just twelve miles north of Parma. Located in an attractive, four-storey orphanage, the camp housed 540 men, all of whom were well prepared for the events of the armistice. Under the exceptional leadership of Lieutenant Colonel Hugo De Burgh, they were organized into five companies, each broken into smaller platoons with various military skills spread among them. They were ready to fight and would certainly resist any German attempt to move them. Fortunately, De Burgh had excellent relations with the commandant, a colonel who had served in the First World War and was known to be pro-British. The commandant promised that he would warn the prisoners if the Germans threatened to take over and, unlike Moscatelli, he kept his word. He even posted scouts along the roads so that any troop movements could be spotted well in advance. It didn't take long. The morning after the armistice, Germans were seen approaching. De Burgh quickly assembled his five companies and, in perfect order, marched them through a large hole in the wire which the Italians had conveniently cut. A half-hour later, the Germans arrived. Furious at finding the camp empty, they ransacked the orphanage and arrested the commandant.

After hiding along a riverbank for two days, the men from Fontanellato began to disperse, heading off in small groups, some south towards the Allied lines, some towards Switzerland, and some simply finding a place to lie up until the front lines came to them. A number were recaptured and sent to Germany but many more got through. One of them was Garth Ledgard, Alastair's commanding officer at Sidi Rezegh. Unlike Alastair, he had not made any attempts to escape, dedicating himself instead to setting up a banking system by which prisoners could convert *buoni* into sterling. Now, with his bank records in hand, he travelled by train to Lake Maggiore, following a route similar to that of Jack Pringle several months before. Along with three companions, he stayed in a hotel at Baveno which had been converted into a German hospital. They then went on to Intra where the camp's interpreter had arranged for a guide to meet them. Thirty-six hours later, after a gruelling climb over Monte Gridone, they crossed the border into Switzerland.

Although as many as 50,000 prisoners escaped after the armistice, nearly half of them were recaptured. By the end of the year, 4,000 had crossed into Switzerland with another 6,500 reaching Allied troops in the south. This left thousands more still unaccounted for. Many of these settled into Italian households, some eventually taking wives and starting families of their own. Others joined the partisans or even formed their own guerrilla units. For all of them, the danger of betrayal was constant. Rewards of several thousand lire were posted everywhere, some of them promising extra food and tobacco. Even more serious were the consequences for those found harbouring prisoners. If they weren't executed, their homes were burned and their entire family sent to Germany as slave labourers. And yet, thousands of Italians still risked their lives, sharing what little they had. It was usually the poorest who did so, the *contadini* or peasants who barely had enough to feed their own families. Escapers knew that these poor farmers and shepherds were more likely to help and that their politics were less compromised. As one prisoner from Fontanellato recalled: 'Some escapers graded farms according to the number of haystacks in the yard. Five meant the family was too well-to-do and might be fascist in outlook. One indicated the family was too poor, though probably friendly. Two haystacks were about right.' In the end, it was a 'strange alliance', just as Roger Absalom said, one that redeemed the Italians in the eyes of those who had been their enemies and began the healing process.

It's little surprise that in Gavi, the 'Stay Put' order was simply ignored. The men there had spent their entire time in captivity trying to escape, and now that they had been turned over to the Germans only hours after the armistice, they were more determined than ever to avoid spending untold additional years in prison. Clifton dismissed it outright, calling it 'a damned silly order from someone who had no clues on the internal state of Italy, and a dangerous order too which caused much grief'. Unlike Fontanellato, however, where the Italians aided the prisoners in escaping, or Chieti, where the guards simply disappeared, Gavi remained sealed tight, an impenetrable mystery which the cistern tunnel alone had been able to figure out. The only solution would be to use the knowledge of so many false starts to hide inside the fortress itself with the hope that when the Germans withdrew, they would be left behind.

Realizing that not everyone would be able to hide, it was a relief when a new possibility suddenly arose. As the Germans were disarming the Italians and marching them off, a carabiniere pulled a Greek officer named George Tsoucas aside. Tapping the wall behind him, he signalled that this was where the secret tunnel, the object of everyone's dreams, began. If it was true, then perhaps there was a way for the entire camp to escape. Clifton quickly assembled a three-man team to investigate. Heading it was a major from the Royal Engineers named Roy Wadeson. Affectionately known as 'Waddy,' at forty-five, he was the same age as Clifton, making him one of the oldest officers in the camp.

When the First World War broke out, Wadeson had just turned sixteen, which didn't prevent him from lying about his age to enlist. Eventually he joined the newly formed Tank Corps, where 'landships', as they were called, were just being introduced. Six weeks before the armistice, he made a daring attempt to rescue a trapped crew under his command. Crawling through machine-gun fire with poison gas exploding around him, he tried in vain to save them, an act that earned him a Military Cross. Leaving the army as a captain in 1920, Wadeson returned to school to become a mining engineer. Once out, he had little trouble finding work, mainly in Africa – Tanganyika, Rhodesia, Uganda, Kenya, the Congo – but also in Europe, especially after his son was born in 1936. Two years in Austria helped him perfect his German. After that, he moved across the border to Slovenia to manage a zinc mine, which is where the war found him in 1940.

Of course, there was no expectation of him serving. By now he was well beyond draft age with a family to support and a profession that would easily exempt him. But he couldn't stay out of it. After taking his wife and son to Zagreb, where they caught a train to Marseille and a boat to England, he returned to flood the mine so the Germans couldn't use it. He then made his way to North Africa to join the Eighth Army, going on to fight throughout the Middle East, Greece and Crete. Like Alastair, he was eventually captured at Sidi Rezegh in November, 1941. A short, balding man with a slight but muscular build, Wadeson looked somewhat older than his years. Some even grumbled that Clifton should have chosen a younger person for the demanding job of opening the tunnel. But no one in the fortress had more experience underground than Wadeson. Nor was anyone more determined.

The tunnel's entrance was in the north-east corner of the upper courtyard, an area from which the prisoners had always been restricted. The Germans had also posted a guard there, forcing Wadeson and his accomplices to intersect the tunnel by first cutting through a cell wall in order to gain access to an ancient latrine. From there another hole was made allowing them to finally enter at a point just below the sentry post. It was delicate work as the guards were never far off and could even be seen patrolling just feet away through the steel bars of a window well. Once inside the tunnel, they found two secure metal grilles blocking their path. Getting to this point had taken a full day. It would take two more with rusty hacksaws, files, and metal cutters to break through the grilles and enter the tunnel proper. More obstacles awaited them. The tunnel, which descended at a steep incline, had been filled with rubble; even worse was the raw sewage emptying into it from an overflow valve connected to the latrines above.

While Wadeson and his companions continued to work at a steady pace, the rest of the prisoners were growing increasingly anxious. They knew that every day brought them a step closer to Germany and wondered if relying on Wadeson and his crew to get through to the outside was realistic. No doubt Clifton thought he would improve everyone's mood when he announced the order by which the entire camp would exit. But if he imagined it would boost morale by indicating that the escape was imminent, it may have backfired. Prisoners would leave in groups of twenty with half-hour intervals in between. The order itself was based not on seniority but on escape experience and importance to the war effort. As Clifton admits, 'Only the first thirty felt happy over the placings.'

More encouraging perhaps was the assurance that the tunnel did indeed have an exit at the base of the outer ramparts. This information was provided by the local Catholic priest, an ageing Friar Tuck-like figure who had flown as a pilot in the First World War and whose British sympathies were well known. In fact, according to Riddiford:

> His sole duty, as he now saw it, was to help as many prisoners as possible escape. Every day he came to the compound on the pretext of religious duties and gave full reports of the attitude of the Italians outside . . . He also gave full information about the secret passage and exactly where it came out, which he had been able to glean in the village.

As reassuring as this news was, many still continued to work on alternative schemes should the order to move come before the tunnel broke. Some, like Ken Fraser, didn't wait, and with two other New Zealanders and a good supply of food had himself bricked up in a small cleft at the top of the ramp connecting the compounds. George Millar started preparing the dungeon from which he and James Craig had been tunnelling for a much longer stay. Similar work was also underway in at least two other tunnels. And in the lower compound, the irrepressible Buck Palm had torn the seat off a toilet to descend into the labyrinth of passageways below. Alastair's room-mates, John Cruttwell and Dan Riddiford, opted for another strategy. Convinced that the Germans would only move the officers when the time came, they switched identities with two willing orderlies and began shining boots and hauling water. This feverish activity was made a good deal easier by the lack of experience of the new German guards. By now the original veterinary unit had been replaced by a group of young reserve troops, some only in their teens, who had been brought from Russia by way of France. They knew nothing about guarding prisoners and even less about the intricacies of a 1,000-year-old Italian fortress. The lack of roll calls and the mysterious disappearance of the camp's records made it even easier for the prisoners to carry on with their doomsday planning.

By now, others had joined Wadeson in clearing the debris from the tunnel. Even Alastair, who was never fond of tunnelling, had been enlisted to help. After working at the face for several hours, he liked it even less. 'I was obliged,' he said, 'to signal back to cease using the upper compound latrines to prevent a drowning accident. After half an hour the gruesome thing ceased to discharge onto our caked and plastered bodies. The scent was indescribable. I had now come to roots and was confident we were nearly out when our shift came to an end.' It was late Sunday afternoon, and Poppet was waiting at the tunnel entrance to replace him. Suddenly the sound of machine-gun fire echoed through the fortress. Alastair, who was still underground, wondered if the tunnel had been discovered. But the shooting, which came in several bursts, had nothing to do with it.

Two orderlies were outside the castle on a rubbish detail while a bored guard looked on. One of them offered the German a cigarette, carefully manoeuvring until the guard's back faced the other orderly. Then, when he was completely absorbed in their conversation, the other man, a sailor named Jack Tooes, took off for the trees like a lightning bolt. He was thirty yards off by the time the guard spotted him and three times that before he got his gun to work and started shooting. By then the sentries in the post above were also firing. But it was too late. Tooes had reached the woods and disappeared. One week later, he crossed the border into Switzerland, the first person to successfully escape from Gavi.

While one might have expected Clifton to rejoice, he reacted instead with anger. He had forbidden any individual escapes, fearing that they might arouse the guards' suspicions and jeopardize the tunnel. He even threatened to court-martial Tooes, should he be recaptured. Others were more sympathetic, especially given Tooes' difficult history as a prisoner of war. A strong, burly sailor whose companions called him 'Twinkle' Tooes, he was a member of Poppet's submarine crew captured in August 1940. He made his first of several escapes by trying to swim to Venice from the island where they were initially held. It was there too that he got into a shouting match with David Fraser, the commander of the *Oswald*, whose leadership many of the crew questioned. Some believed it was part of a mutiny; and whether it was or not, Tooes entered into a spiral of emotionally crushing situations. During one of his many spells in solitary, he even tried to kill himself, for which the Italians increased his sentence. As he later testified during Fraser's own court-martial after the war:

> I was pretty well punished by everybody when I was a prisoner. I myself used to get punishment pretty nearly every week . . . I was one of the best prisoners the Italians had. They were always giving me cells. I think I had the record for doing solitary confinement when I was in Italy.

Within an hour of Tooes's escape, the Germans, who had by now found a provisional prisoner list, held their first roll call. Soon after, Clifton paid a visit to Oberleutnant von Schroeder, the young cavalry officer in charge of the boys' brigade. He not only wanted to calm the agitated officer down but also wanted to read the tea leaves. That afternoon, just before the shooting began, the priest had revealed the location of a second secret tunnel, 'the marvellous one leading all the way downhill to the village'. Starting from a bricked-up alcove at the back of the Italian storeroom, it was guaranteed to be free of any obstructions. A simple gate with a rusty lock was the most they would have to contend with. Poppet and another officer had been sent to reconnoitre and confirmed that it would take only a couple of hours to break through. But Clifton needed to know how much longer they had before the Germans moved them.

There were two tunnels now, each on the verge of being opened for what would certainly be one of the greatest escapes of the war. Wadeson had only a foot or two left to go, and whoever didn't escape with him could take the easier route through the storeroom passage directly into town. Not a single prisoner would be left behind. Of course, an escape like this would be best done under cover of darkness; but Clifton worried that the Germans were still on edge after the excitement of the day's events. Would they hold a snap roll call or check on the prisoners in the middle of the night? His sources indicated that they still had forty-eight hours before their departure. No, he would let the dust settle and wait till morning to open the tunnels. He went to bed that night feeling confident that it would be their last in Gavi.

Monday, 13 September, only five days since the armistice was announced, though it seemed like weeks. The mess hall was filled with smoke as the men pulled out their cigarettes and pipes after an especially large breakfast. The joint statement promising that the prisoners would not be sent to Germany was still pinned to the notice board. Then, just a few minutes after nine, someone rushed in with the news that the Germans had issued an order to evacuate the entire camp within the hour. 'Bad luck again,' said Clifton, 'or a bad appreciation anyway.' Once more, he had erred on the side of caution, and lost. The night had been absolutely quiet; perfect, in fact, for a mass escape. Now, in an attempt to salvage whatever he could, he rushed to see von Schroeder to plead for more time. After nearly an hour of arguing, he was able to wrest one more.

The fortress quickly dissolved into total pandemonium. Although they had days to prepare, the suddenness of the order caught them by surprise. It was 'like a disturbed hive of bees', recalls Alastair, as they all desperately rushed off to grab their gear either to go into hiding or to leave the camp. Everyone seemed to collide with one another and spaces that were long promised were suddenly occupied by immovable squatters. Others who had planned to hide had second thoughts upon entering the dark and airless spaces that had been set aside for them. Packs handed down were just as quickly passed back.

Within two hours nearly a third of all the prisoners in Gavi had disappeared. At least ten descended into the unsavoury dungeon where George Millar was acting as concierge. Four more were lifted into a crawl space above a ceiling in the upper compound. It was hard to say whose hide was most uncomfortable. Perhaps the South African pilot who wedged himself into a chimney or the two commandos who had themselves walled into an area beneath a stairwell so small they could neither stand nor lie down and needed removable rubber tubing to both feed and evacuate. Then there were the four men who hid themselves in plain sight, burrowing into a woodpile in the middle of the courtyard. As for Alastair, he grabbed Jack and David, determined to get into the storeroom to open the new tunnel. But Poppet, perhaps the tidiest man in the camp, had misplaced the key. When they couldn't work the lock themselves, they decided to join Buck's group, and literally went down the toilet where seventeen others were already hiding.

At eleven sharp, the remaining prisoners were marched through the long, windowless passage through which they had entered Gavi well over a year before. Loaded onto trucks and buses, some wondered, with a twinge of envy, whether they had made the right decision not to hide. It appeared as though the Germans had been fooled and were about to leave them behind. But the engines never turned on and they simply sat and waited. 'Where was der

General?' von Schroeder wanted to know. He had organized an honorary salute for him as well as reserving a special seat in the front of one of the trucks. The SBO was simply nowhere to be found. Von Schroeder finally ordered everyone out for a roll call. There were fifty-six prisoners missing. Clifton had also decided to hide, joining Wadeson and seven others in the secret tunnel.

If Clifton had been too cautious in not seizing the castle on the evening of the armistice or in opening the tunnel after Jack Tooes's escape, his decision to hide from the Germans was seen by many as reckless, if not foolhardy. Even the person respons-ible for sealing him into the tunnel pleaded with Clifton not to hide, insisting that the Germans would never leave without their 'prize prisoner'. More than fifty years later, survivors from Gavi still remember that moment with bitterness. As Tommy Macpherson recalled in 2007: 'The idiocy of Clifton gave it all away. It was absurd. Clifton and his adjutant had done all the communication with the Germans and for him not to appear at the final transport . . . well, any idiot would have smelled a rat.' Others were more generous, believing that the absence of a third of the prisoners was simply too hard to conceal. Or as Colin Armstrong put it, 'Even the dumbest Jerry would know that we were not all present.'

Clifton saw it differently as well. Rather than jeopardize the chances of those in hiding, he believed he could lure the blood-hounds away from them. Of course, this depended on Wadeson opening the tunnel and having the Germans discover it empty; at which point, they would assume that all the missing men had successfully escaped. At least, that was the plan. But to Clifton's disappointment, instead of finding a large exit hole with the feet of the last man disappearing through it, 'they were all sitting around, quiet as mice, waiting'. They had decided, somewhat mysteriously, that it was too dangerous to start digging and preferred to wait till things calmed down.

Von Schroeder, who had been so enraged after Tooes's escape, responded to these new developments with surprising calm. Dan Riddiford, recalling von Schroeder as 'a charming young fellow who had been at school in England and spoke perfect English', claimed that he 'took it all in a very matter of fact way'. He simply divided his troops in half, sending one group to escort the trucks and buses to the railhead while the other remained with him to search for the missing men. One can only imagine what his orders were to the group that stayed behind. They descended upon the officers' rooms like wild dogs, tearing apart everything they found. Mattresses were slit open, furniture smashed and thrown out of windows, packs ripped apart, clothing urinated and defecated upon, papers and photographs shredded and burned, and every piece of food they found consumed. They ate so many tins of butter, they began to stagger and vomit. It was an orgy of looting and destruction. And through it all, they shouted and sang. Was it a rehearsal for terror or a simple repetition of what they had learned in Russia?

Not until they finished their 'wild stampede', as Alastair put it, did they begin to search for the hidden prisoners. They broke through walls using grenades and bullets, completely indifferent to the safety of those they were looking for. Perhaps they thought the prisoners had armed themselves or that their violent shrieks and gunfire would scare them out. The first group was found around 3.30 p.m. when several Germans snapped the locks on the main gate to the secret tunnel, entering with pistols and grenades in hand. Clifton and company 'knew the game was up', so someone calmly called, 'It's OK, Sergeant. The General is here and we shall come out quietly.' The men in the ceiling crawl space were next to be found, and then soon after, to everyone's amazement, Fraser and his two companions were disinterred. After bats were spotted leaving their small cave, several shots and the threat of a grenade were enough to winkle them out.

Although Alastair's group was in total darkness in the crypt beneath the toilets, they could hear the gunfire and explosions above them. There were also two grates near the ceiling of an adjoining crypt where they listened for news of the search. At one point English-speakers were heard in the courtyard, but it was difficult to tell who had been caught. More distinct were the loud German threats to blow up the entire fortress unless all the prisoners were found. Sitting in the pitch black in complete silence with his back resting against that of another man, Alastair struggled to contain his fear. He wondered how a person could relish the dangers of a challenging peak yet be so unsettled by the prospect of wriggling through a tunnel under the earth. He tried to reassure himself that 'healthy men do not suffer from claustrophobia'. And while he conceded that he might never feel comfortable inhabiting a dark, underground space, he did see a positive side to the situation, claiming, 'The experience proved an excellent tonic for the nerves and steadied me to meet the trials and tribulations of the next few months.'

The air was foul-smelling and filled with so much dust that some had to cover their heads with blankets for fear their coughs might give them away. Alastair joked that he would

never again hide with anyone who had hay fever. Around midnight the entire crypt began to shake with the sound of
hammering on the floor above. Everyone knew what this meant.
And then suddenly it stopped, but that was just to give the Germans a chance to step back as they pulled the pins on their
grenades. The men below moved back as well, and it was lucky
that they did, as a huge hole opened up with smoke and debris
filling the chamber. A light was lowered and then a German
waving a Luger jumped down, at which point, 'Jack stepped
forward and said in even tones, "Don't shoot. We are quite
unarmed."'

Rather than climb through the hole that had just been
opened, they showed the German a bricked up door leading to
the lower courtyard. He banged on it, and within moments,
picks and hammers had broken through from the other side.
The *pericolosi* were then marched out between two rows of heavily armed guards. As disappointed as they were, the cool, night
air was like a powerful drug as it entered their lungs. Although
the Germans had no idea how many prisoners had been hidden
inside the crypt, they took no chances that some might have
been left behind. After all, finding hidden men and women,
whether soldiers or civilians, was what these troops did best.
Several were sent back in, and sure enough, squirrelled away
beneath a pile of rubble, they discovered Buck Palm. They also
found Ginger Hamilton, the South African rope maker, who
had wedged himself inside a drain pipe. Several shots ricochet-
ing around his feet coaxed him out. And though they looked for
a while longer, that made twenty.

The next day, to everyone's disgust, Joe Grapes returned. A
number of men were still missing and von Schroeder needed

help. Moscatelli, a loyal fascist to the end, brought a plan of the castle and guided the Germans to every possible hiding place. Within twenty-four hours, all but two had been found. Then Moscatelli spotted the woodpile in the centre of the courtyard, the most obvious place of all. 'Had it been checked?' 'No?' 'Well, then pull it apart,' he ordered. And to von Schroeder's utter delight, not two men but four were discovered. The original count had been incorrect and instead of fifty-six missing officers, there were fifty-eight.

Perhaps it was the bonus of the two extra men or the fact that von Schroeder had simply considered the entire exercise an amusing game of hide and seek played with live ammunition and grenades. In any case, he was once again the 'good, cheerful and pleasant Oberleutnant' whom Poppet and others had initially admired. Of course, he took no chances of losing anyone else and forced them all to sleep in the heavily guarded orderlies' rooms. During the day, he allowed them to return to their quarters in order to salvage whatever they could. He first warned: 'You will find your things in rather a mess. I had to permit my men to enjoy themselves so that they would not get too angry with you.'

Despite having heard the rampaging troops from the safety of their hiding places, they were still amazed at the level of destruction. After sorting through the torn remains of their belongings, where they found little of use, Alastair and Jack were able to convince their guards to let them visit the Italian storeroom. The young Germans were inexperienced and made no attempt to stop Alastair from taking a brand-new civilian suit, perfect for escaping. Heading further into the storeroom, Alastair found something else even more valuable: the entrance to the long-sought tunnel to freedom. The Germans had also discovered it, using it as a way to enter the castle from the town. Alastair stood motionless, staring at it for a long time. But it was too late, 'the siege of Gavi was over'.

# 6

# The Train

Now the real thugs arrived. Not the boys' brigade, who disappeared along with their affable commander, but large, menacing troops with submachine guns and jackboots and oversized gorgets around their necks stamped with the word *Feldgendarmerie*, field police. The prisoners in Gavi, captured in either North Africa or the Mediterranean, had never seen Germans like these before. 'American film gangster types,' one quipped. And while they dubbed them the 'Breastplates' and joked about their theatrical posturing, they had no illusions as to who they were. These were real killers who had already spent years in Russia and Poland redefining the meaning of barbarism and terror. 'Grim, with hard, calloused faces,' recalled Clifton. 'They looked, and were, just efficient ruthless butchers, who had killed so often that human life meant no more than fowl or pigs . . . A bloody, evil crew.'

They had been brought to Gavi to avoid the disaster of the first transport when the trains leaked prisoners all the way to Austria. Even before they reached the railhead at Acqui, two men had leapt from the trucks and disappeared. Peter Medd, the soft-spoken pilot who had been a prisoner for more than three years, was the next to escape. Within moments of leaving the station, he was on the roof of the train, climbing down to the buffers from which he made a perfect jump. Forty-eight days and 700 miles later, he passed through Allied lines and returned home. He was soon flying once again, but on a foggy afternoon in August 1944, less than a year after his escape, he crashed into a Northumberland hillside and was killed.

When Peter Medd leapt from the train, he made a flawless ten-point landing, without so much as a scratch or even rolling over. Others weren't so lucky. Of all the forms of escape, few were as dangerous as train jumping. Any misstep could result in being dragged under the wheels of a carriage. Doing it at night to minimize detection also meant that visibility was limited and a flying body could easily inect a telegraph pole, switch box or concrete pile. Even if these obstacles were avoided, the sharp gravel along the railbed was enough to tear one's skin to shreds. The greatest danger, however, remained that of being shot, as well-armed guards were strategically placed along the train, ready to fire at anyone trying to get away.

The best moment to jump was on a long incline or immediately before entering a station, when the train was forced to slow down. Aubrey Whitby and five companions waited until they approached Cremona. It was just before dawn when they leapt, and Whitby was fortunate only to sprain his ankle. Once again, as in his first escape, he pretended to be an Italian officer, and headed to Pisa, where relatives provided him with food, clothing and money. Only when his ankle was better did he set off again, reaching the Allies a month later. Within two years he was back in Tuscany, serving as a military governor in the region where he grew up.

Of course, landing safely was only part of the challenge. The first step was to find a way out of the boxcar. The trains were the same '40 and 8's that had ferried troops to the front in the First World War: 40 men or 8 horses, little cabins on wheels with a sliding door on either side and a brakeman's booth at the end where two armed guards could keep watch. Some were steel but most were made of wood. James Craig, the New Zealander from MI9 who had tried to tunnel out of solitary, came prepared with a pocket knife and a length of rope. Others had simple table knives, good enough to break through the roof in several hours. The moon was full, much brighter than they would have preferred, and with nowhere to hide, it wasn't long before the first three to climb out were spotted. The train was still travelling at forty miles an hour when Bishop, the young Kiwi captain in front, made a suicidal leap from the top of the car. By now every guard was firing as Craig, graceful as an acrobat, used the sliding door rail to swing down the side of the train and jump. The last in line, a naval officer named Bateman, now under even more intense fire, kept his cool and did the same.

Those waiting to follow quickly retreated into the shadows of the wagon, completely shaken by what had happened. They were convinced that all three were dead, especially Bishop, who had taken such a wild leap. And he nearly was, with bullets through his wrist and knee, and his face and limbs skinned to the bone. He spent two days in a culvert before an Italian peasant came to his aid. A long recovery followed, after which he joined the partisans, eventually making it through to the Allied lines and home. Bateman, who was barely twenty, was not so lucky, and died on the spot of multiple wounds.

As for Craig, both his leg and collarbone were broken, and although he counted five bullet holes in his uniform, somehow none had touched him. After crawling for the better part of three miles, he lay in a vineyard until a young and very terrified boy found him. The boy brought a priest, who in turn brought a doctor. It was three months before Craig was able to move again, which is when he headed for the Swiss border. He crossed it too, but became disoriented and walked back into Italy, where he was captured yet again. Taken to Milan, he was put on another train to Germany. Once more, he escaped; only this time, he wasn't hurt and decided to stay in Italy. Along with two South Africans, he organized a band of partisans. They blew up bridges, attacked convoys and helped escaped prisoners rejoin the Allies. In December 1944, sixteen months after leaving Gavi, Craig decided to cross through the lines as well.

By the time the train arrived at the transit camp in Spittal, Austria, only 80 of the original 120 who set out from Gavi were left. Four days later, when they were moved to permanent camps in Germany, the number was down to 60. One of those who escaped from Spittal was Dan Riddiford, Alastair's former cell-mate. Once again, he switched identities with an NCO and then several days later left the camp disguised as a Frenchman going out on a work detail. Along with two South Africans from Gavi, he crossed back into Italy and from there to Yugoslavia, where, with the aid, and sometimes obstruction, of various partisans, he helped lead a group of sixty escaped prisoners all the way back to the British forces on the other side of the Adriatic.

Tommy Macpherson and Colin Armstrong had the same idea as Riddiford, and along with another New Zealander also left the camp disguised as French workers. They climbed over three Alpine ranges in freezing conditions only to be caught walking through a small Italian village at night. Locked in a cattle car, they began a long journey that eventually ended at Stalag XXA in Thorn, Poland. With the help of the Polish underground, they were able to escape and stow away on a freighter carrying coal to Sweden. Macpherson, who was back in Scotland two years to the day after his capture in North Africa, didn't stay home for long. Recruited by the Special Operations Executive (SOE) to be part of the newly formed Jedburghs, he was dropped into France forty-eight hours after D-Day with vague instructions to organize resistance and disrupt German movement in any way possible. With his Cameron Highlander's kilt and 'enough explosive to blow up half of southern France', it wasn't long before he had a 300,000-franc reward on his head. But he wasn't caught, and after completing a similar mission in northern Italy, returned home with a chest full of medals.

With the memory of imprisonment still fresh in his mind, Macpherson's companion, Colin Armstrong, sat down and wrote one of the first accounts of the prisoner-of-war experience. He called it *Life Without Ladies*, and spoke about Gavi with a special reverence wherein every individual shared a higher, common purpose whose realization would somehow expunge the humiliation of captivity. Being part of Gavi set them apart from other POWs, and although they might not have escaped from the castle itself, their remarkable rate of success during the train ride to Austria and beyond was a vindication of what for many were years of perseverance. As Armstrong wrote, with a bit of bravado:

Gavi has every reason to be proud of its record especially as we were never released on the Armistice, as were so many prisoner-of-war camps, and every escape was from a standing start requiring ingenuity and in many cases considerable

178

daring. Five, alas, were killed and several others wounded but we felt that we had lived up to the name the Italians had given us – *'Pericolosi'* or 'Dangerous Persons'.

The second group, made up of the fifty-eight who had hidden as well as the medical staff and prisoners in sickbay, left on a bright autumn afternoon, just three days after the first transport had departed. Their escort took no chances, making it clear they would be only too happy to shoot anyone attempting to escape. Two sat in the back of each bus with nasty little Schmeissers resting on their laps while another, equally well armed, sat up front opposite the driver. The three buses, along with their understandably none-too-happy drivers, were commandeered off the streets, their passengers having been dumped by the roadside to fend for themselves. Completing this small convoy were three motorcycles with sidecars, in one of which rode a very unpleasant and hungry-looking Doberman. Once under-way, the motorcycles continuously wove in and out of the buses as if spinning a chrysalis from which nothing could escape.

As Alastair looked back, he thought that Gavi itself was on fire. The Germans, in a final act of vandalism, had placed every-thing they could, broken or not, onto two huge pyres which they then doused with fuel and lit. The enormous plumes of smoke rising from the courtyards seemed to engulf the castle, a medieval tableau created by a pillaging army in retreat. Soon the townspeople would arrive to pick through the embers, salvaging anything that was left.

By nightfall the buses had reached Piacenza, where the pris-oners spent the night in a recently abandoned military barracks noteworthy for its large marble sinks and sumptuous fixtures. It took another full day to cover the sixty-five miles to Mantua, where the main rail line was located. Along the way Ginger Hamilton made an elegant dive out the window. Although he timed it perfectly as the bus swerved left around a curve, he landed on an airfield without a shred of cover. His bad luck could have been a lot worse if the clip from the guard's pistol hadn't fallen out as he was about to shoot.

After a cold night sleeping on a football pitch, they were marched off to the train, a distance of several miles made considerably longer by being taken to the wrong station. Along the way they were showered with cheers as well as fruit and cigarettes, a surprising reception for soldiers who had been enemies only ten days before. At least one prisoner, a crafty South African named Peter Griffiths, whom Alastair had joined on one of his first escapes in Libya, tried to disappear into the crowd but was quickly spotted and herded back.

The train, when they finally found it, was enormous, nearly fifty cattle cars interspersed with the occasional flatbed on which machine guns had already been mounted. All but five of the cars had been stuffed with more than 2,000 Italian soldiers being sent to Germany as slave labour. It was a pathetic scene, with their wives and families lining the embankment weeping and screaming. German troops, with rifles raised, held them back, adding to their desperation, while officious Blackshirts with swastikas on their sleeves marched up and down giving the Nazi salute. Then the SS officer in charge arrived to harangue them about the terms of their passage:

Because so many British officers attempted to escape from carriages and were shot escaping [he let that sink in for a bit], officers will travel in cattle trucks, with the exception of your general and his colonels. Your sick and doctors will be in one truck, the others divided between three. That is very considerate. You will notice these are French trucks, which can carry forty men or eight horses.' He waved a hand towards the rear of the train. 'We have forty Italian cattle in each truck there, but they are permitted to open the doors a little.' He paused and then added – 'I demand full cooperation. Any officer attempting to escape is a criminal sabotaging the comfort and security of his fellow-officers. He is an active enemy of the Reich, and will be shot immediately!'

Once on board and with the doors still open, Jack called across in Italian to ask some men if they would walk along the train to spot the gun emplacements. But they were too afraid and none would do it. Then an attractive blonde in her forties pushed her way through the crowd, shoving aside a guard who tried to stop her. After learning what Jack needed, she moved down the train, returning several minutes later. 'There is a machine gun mounted on the front and back of the roof of every cattle truck,' she told him, 'but I don't think their field of fire is good close to the trucks. Good luck to all of you.' Then, pushing the guard aside once more, she wandered into the crowd and vanished.

Like so much else that day, the image of the woman bravely making her way up to the train could have been included in a Rossellini film, and her part played, blonde hair notwithstanding, by the fiery Italian actress Anna Magnani. It was this type of strong, independent woman who seemed to be emerging throughout Italy to hold together not only families but also the honour of the nation. They were Italian equivalents of the French Marianne, ready to rally a population broken by war and humiliated by defeat in the rebirth of a new republic. Alastair certainly saw this, noting in his journal, 'Crisis found the men in Italy a sorry lot. The women, however, stood out in courage, outspokenness and helpfulness. They elbowed their way past the Germans and cursed them magnificently and scornfully in a language they did not understand but the sentiment was clear enough.'

The train didn't leave till dusk, which was fortunate as it gave them the entire night to escape before reaching Trento and the South Tyrol beyond. As soon as the doors closed, everyone went into a frenzy, 'like terriers after rats', searching for the best way out. Nearly all had concealed some implement for cutting through the walls – pocket knives, sharpened spoons, hacksaw blades and even a set of dentist drills. But these were useless in Alastair's car, which, unlike the others, was made of steel rather than wood. This didn't stop Buck Palm, who stripped down to his little leopard-skin underwear and with superhuman strength began to bend and break the door to allow them access to the outside latch that secured it. By the time they approached Verona four hours later, they were nearly out.

It was a slow trip with many delays caused by damaged rail lines and the priority given to troop carriers passing through. This explained why they sat in the enormous marshalling yard at Verona for such a long time. At one point they were let out in small groups to defecate along the tracks. The stench was awful, other transports having clearly done the same many times before. They called to one another between the cars, sharing information in Hindi and Urdu, Maori, Swahili and even Xhosa so that the Germans couldn't understand. 'How close are you to getting out?' 'Have you seen the loose couplings hanging under the cars?' 'Should we go at the same time to reduce the risk?' 'There's a flat-truck just behind us with two machine guns on it.' 'Be careful.' 'Good luck.'

They had barely left Verona when the first and most unlikely escape took place. The hospital car, containing a handful of patients along with two doctors, a dentist and a trio of orderlies, was much less secure than any of the others. Unlike every other carriage, the ventilators in the upper corner were free of barbed wire and there were no Germans guarding it. Climbing out through the twelve-by-twenty-four-inch opening and then down onto the buffers would not be difficult, at least if one's health was good enough to do so. In fact, two of those determined to try – Ronnie Herbert and Percy Pike – were strongly advised against it. Herbert, who had a blood clot in his thigh, was even warned that after only a hundred yards of walking, he might well drop dead. As it turned out, he walked over 600 miles.

A boyish looking thirty-year-old, Herbert had left England in 1938 in order to work for the Royal Insurance Company in South Africa. When war came, he tried returning home but was refused passage, so enlisted in the Kaffrarian Rifles. By the time he left for the front, he was married with a child on the way, one he wouldn't meet until the war had ended. He was already an experienced train jumper, having successfully leapt from the carriage taking him to his first camp after his capture at Tobruk. Now he was instructing the others on how to jump, 'stressing the absolute necessity of rolling away from the line as soon as they hit the ground'. But first he had to help Percy Pike, an RAF pilot with a bushy red moustache, cut the cast off his fractured ankle.

Herbert and Pike made the jump with little difficulty, after which they headed into the mountains where, sheltered by farmers, they spent over two months recovering from their injuries. Then, deciding that it was safer to travel alone, they split up and began the long walk south to the Allied forces. Although Switzerland was closer, and the preferred destination of many, it meant internment for the rest of the war. Their goal was to get back into action. Pike, who waited two days after Herbert's departure, had little luck and was recaptured almost immediately. Herbert fared much better. Aided by farmers and priests, he walked up to thirty miles a day for the entire month of December. On the 27th, malnourished and with holes in the bottom of his boots, he reached Aquila, just behind the German lines on the Sangro River. The next evening, as he tried to cross, searchlights picked him up and within days he was on another train heading for Germany.

In the end, nearly everyone who could escaped from the hospital car. When the doctors' turn came, they tossed a coin to see which one would have to stay. Doc Vaughan, a little Welshman with the Indian Army, lost. By then, one of the other cars was emptying out as well. Led by a tall tank commander named Stump Gibbon, all sixteen of its occupants slipped through a hole they'd cut in the front and jumped. At least one was killed as he rolled under the wheels while another was hit by the machine gun fire now raking the train. In Alastair's car, they had drawn lots to decide the order by which they would go and were already lined up by the half-open door. David Stirling, an expert in making dangerous jumps, had cut up his rucksack, from which he Alastair and Jack made pads for their elbows, knees and heads.

Now the moon came up, suddenly illuminating the train like a spotlight. The men shook hands and wished one another luck and then waited in painful silence, listening to the clacking of the wheels, suspended between elation and fear, the tension relieved only slightly by jokes that weren't funny, the sort of forced humour that men are expected to engage in at such times. To Alastair, the scene conjured another, powerful image: 'Muffled and trapped our company stood like initiates before some esoteric initiation ceremony and the door at which we stood might well have proved the doorway to eternity.' It was a transcendent moment for him, filled with kinship and the feeling of oneness he often experienced with nature but rarely with other men. 'Linked momentarily in a common enterprise,' he imagined everyone, in all the cattle cars in Italy, joined together in one great brotherhood:

I never realized more clearly that we were not sharply divided peoples – New Zealanders, South Africans, Australians, English and Scots and Irish – but one common stock. The universalism has never left me since. It was the most valuable thing I learned that night and probably the same thought occurred to the thousands and thousands of British and Dominion troops that rumbled northwards in those hectic days and nights. Even tempered, openly harmonious, seizing every opportunity. Resisting, stubborn, unwilling, they tore up floorboards and let themselves fall upon the tracks, under the revolving wheels. They cut holes in the walls, balancing on the jolting buffers, and leapt for freedom into the windy dark. They cut holes in the roofs and dying they were caught in the hail of machine gun bullets till their torn bodies rolled off turning hideously on the ballast. They opened doors and jumped in pairs, in mobs and made a dead run for it, targets for 20 guns. They were hunted like beasts and shot in cold blood. Guards were everywhere, barbed wire nailed over windows. Stranger than any Hollywood scene was that moonlit valley backed clearly by the bizarre peaks of the Dolomites. The long lumbering trains, unlit, packed as one knew with men rolling up from Italy towards the Brenner and Germany.

It was well before dawn when they stopped at a small station along the Adige River. Hearing shouts of 'Halt!' they rushed to the windows to see two Italians standing with their hands up. They had climbed out through the grilles just as the train had come to a stop and calmly walked away. '*Italienisch?*' the Germans asked. '*Si, si,*' they responded. And then, without warning, several bursts of fire left them crumpled on the ground. '*Mamma Mia!*' screamed one as he held his stomach, blood gushing through his fingers. '*Aiuto! Aiuto!*' Then the young, blond lieutenant in charge came up and casually shot both of them in the head. Even then, one was still alive and went on twitching as they threw the bodies on the train.

It was all so brutal and deliberate, leaving everyone shaken and stunned. 'We were prepared to be shot on the run,' said Jack, 'but not to be murdered after capture. We decided that we would not try to escape – not now anyway.' For others, the moment had simply come and gone. As the moonlight grew stronger and the train picked up speed, the random machine-gun fire became more and more frequent. 'There was just no point in jumping any longer,' recalls Poppet. They had made the escaper's greatest mistake – doing nothing while waiting for a 'better opportunity', the second chance which soon turns to never. By the time they reached Trento at 8 a.m., it was too late.

As they opened the doors, the Feldgendarmerie saw the extent of their evening's losses – one car completely empty and another, the hospital car, almost so. Although the journey was far from over, Clifton was clearly heartened. 'If the main body had been as lucky,' he said, 'then Gavi's reputation was still high.' Now women in spotless Italian Red Cross uniforms, pushing hand-carts filled with bread, fruit and cigarettes appeared. The Germans had provided them with nothing since leaving Gavi, and while many had brought their own food parcels, the sight of these generous women could not have been more welcome. As they reached through the doors to receive their bounty, Alastair and Jack asked about local conditions and the sympathies of the surrounding population. 'This is the last Italian town,' one said. 'Above this there are more Austrians than Italians. The Germans have armed the civilians with weapons. They are shooting Italians.'

Four hours later, they were in Bolzano, only fifty miles from the Brenner Pass, ancient gateway between the Mediterranean and northern Europe. At one time part of Austria, Bolzano – or Bozen, as the Germans called it – was now the capital of South Tyrol, known by the Italians as Alto Adige. A single political entity for over six centuries, the Tyrol was sliced in half in 1919 with Italy annexing the southern part as reward for its participation in the First World War. Until then there were no Italians in South Tyrol but an aggressive policy of colonization soon changed that. The 'Italianization' of the region accelerated even further when the Fascists came to power in 1922. German schools and newspapers were shut down with the minority language of Italian becoming the only one accepted in courts and other government transactions. Place names were also changed and even the use of German on tombstones was forbidden. The climax came in 1939 when Hitler and Mussolini signed a pact authorizing the resettlement of the German-speaking population in the newly conquered territories. By 1943 at least 75,000 Tyrolese had relocated in what Himmler euphemistically called 'human resource reallocation'. Now that Germany had occupied Italy, South Tyrol had been turned into a special operations zone. Suddenly the shoe was on the other foot, and the German-speaking Tyrolese were out for payback.

Alastair knew this history only too well from his many visits to the area while climbing in the Dolomites during the 1930s. To escape in South Tyrol would require a great deal of care. It wasn't like Lombardia or Piedmont, where most of those escaping into Switzerland had crossed. Since the armistice, the local populations there could often be depended on for help. In South Tyrol, it was altogether different. Well-armed members of a newly formed militia called the SOD (Südtiroler Ordnungs-dienste) were patrolling everywhere, arresting Jews, tracking down escaped prisoners and settling old scores from years of discrimination. As Alastair himself summed it up:

Calculatedly barbaric 20 years of Fascism undoubtedly was. I hold no brief for the Italian people but such brutalities were largely repaid during the months succeeding the Italian Armistice when the happily singing Tyrolese excelled himself and herself as harsh and heartless as anyone north of the Brenner Pass.

The rail yards at Bolzano had expanded enormously over the past two decades, much of it due to the special industrial zone created to attract Italians to the region. Now it was a target for Allied planes determined to disrupt German troop movements into Italy. Sitting in the station, waiting for hours to leave, was understandably uncomfortable. Several tracks over was another long line of cattle cars similar to their own with the words 'American Pigs' scrawled on the side. Pressed against the openings, weary and unshaven, were the first GIs anyone from Gavi had seen. Captured at Salerno, they were en route to Germany just like themselves. As Jack stood staring at them with everyone else, Alastair quietly pulled him aside. 'I think I might suffer from an appendicitis,' he said. By the time Jack managed to summon Doc Vaughan, the case had become acute and Alastair was doubled over, groaning in pain.

Loaded onto a stretcher, Alastair was carried off to the hospital car, where an examination took place. Had he been vomiting, Doc Vaughan asked. Was he running a fever? Did it hurt when he tried to stand up? 'How does this feel when I press here?' he said, placing his cupped hands on Alastair's lower right abdomen. And of course, Alastair shrieked convincingly, begging him to stop. In fact, he knew the right answer to every question; for if chance favours the prepared mind, then Alastair's sudden attack of appendicitis was a carefully chosen ruse based on his own traumatic encounter with the condition. Even though it had occurred over fifteen years earlier, the memory of his childhood friend, Edward Machonochie, almost dying was still vivid. They had been climbing in Glen Sligachan on Skye when Machono-chie suddenly had a terrible attack. After helping him along for ten miles, they arrived at a farmhouse where, by chance, there was a doctor who operated on him on the kitchen table.

The examination over, Doc Vaughan now turned to the SS officer who had been hovering over him the whole time. 'This man is seriously ill,' he said. 'He must be admitted to a hospital at once.' But the German sergeant major accompanying the officer wasn't buying it. 'That be damned for a story,' he blurted out. 'I had appendicitis and I wasn't like that.' Vaughan warned of the danger should the appendix burst and, after considering the options, the officer sent the sergeant major off for an ambulance. As Alastair was driven away howling, he was the envy of all; the last one to leave the train in Italy with a beautifully improvised escape. Put simply by George Millar: 'The wily Baron had decided that he had gone far enough towards Germany.'

A short drive away was a military hospital, where Alastair was immediately seen by an efficient, though not inconsiderate, German doctor who spoke excellent English. The examination was nearly identical to that conducted by Doc Vaughan, although they also stretched back his leg and banged on his heel, to which Alastair responded with the appropriate screams. Well rehearsed by now, he had little difficulty in convincing them of the serious-ness of his condition. In fact, he may have been too convincing as the doctor concluded by announcing, 'Operation in half an hour.'

Alastair's mind now began to race. He certainly didn't want to be cut open for no reason. On the other hand, it would be too suspicious to declare that he had suddenly recovered. He berated himself for having been so specific about his symptoms, and any joy over the success of his deception quickly vanished. And then, just as he was imagining the worst, 'the miracle', as he called it, happened. A German soldier, crushed between a truck and a wall, was rolled in on a stretcher in critical condition. The wounded man was naturally taken straight into the operating room, granting Alastair an eleventh-hour reprieve. By late afternoon he'd let the doctors know that he was feeling somewhat better and that the attack seemed to have passed.

He was now moved to a ward with around twenty German soldiers. That evening a group of young women wearing folk costumes that would make any Bavarian happy arrived to hand out food and perform. Along with everyone else, Alastair was given grapes, cigarettes and flowers. As the dancing began, he turned to the girl standing next to his bed. He was surprised to learn that she was Italian, and clearly sympathetic when he told her that he was a British officer. He asked her 'Why then are you here entertaining the Germans?' '*Perché, tenente*,' she answered. 'We are Italian and afraid that if we don't come, they will kill us.' She knew that he was going to escape and leaned over and whispered that he must be careful as the mountains were filled with armed militia. And then, when everyone was absorbed in the music and dancing, she leaned even closer, and they kissed.

No sooner had they gone than an orderly came by to swipe his cigarettes and grapes. But he left the delicate blue gentians, a mountain flower that was Alastair's favourite. Once the guard and orderlies were asleep, he slipped out of his bed and began to reconnoitre. He found a door that led to the basement, and on a landing along the way yet another. It was heavy with glass panels and a bar across it, yet with a little effort he was able to open it. The street outside was quiet and deserted, the perfect route for his planned escape. He then returned to bed, his absence unnoticed.

The next morning his clothes and shoes were taken away. Now that he was better, he suspected this would happen. Fortunately, he had hidden an extra set of civilian clothes and pair of boots beneath the covers. He spent a comfortable day, resting and eating. He even chatted for a while with the middle-aged Westphalian in the bed next to him. As the afternoon wore on, he was surprised at how calm he felt. He was excited, of course, but it was the type of excitement he often experienced before a climb, different from the tension that preceded an escape. Once again, he waited until well past two for everyone to fall asleep. It didn't take long for him to retrace his steps and disappear into the street. Although no one saw him, he felt a pang of remorse. Escaping from a hospital might make it harder in the future for a prisoner in real need to receive help. But in the end, freedom always trumped guilt.

Even for Alastair, who had perfected the art of walking without making a sound, it was difficult to conceal the rattle of his footsteps as he moved through the city's ancient arcades and stone balconies. He headed north toward San Genesio and within a short time reached a steep path leading up into the mountains. It was a crisp autumn evening with a sky full of stars, a perfect night for climbing. The higher he went, the quicker his pace became and he soon felt as though his body was coming alive once again: 'After the experience of the train the freedom of the mountainside crowned by the great fantastic spires of the

Funffinger Spitze was wine to the spirit.' With each step, he became more confident and more determined. This time, he was sure he would succeed.

By dawn he had reached the crest and found a small cave beneath an overhang where he would spend the day. Directly below was the Adige River, which he would have to cross if he were to travel west to Switzerland. He regretted the loss of his hand-drawn maps, lent to Peter Medd the morning of his departure from Gavi. But he knew these mountains and would set his course for Mount Ortler, the region's highest peak. Once there, the Swiss border was not far beyond.

That evening he worked his way down to the vineyards, where he gorged himself on grapes. He ate the lower ones right from the vine without even bothering to break them off. At every house he passed, chained dogs barked violently. One farmer came out with a shotgun and lantern, ready to shoot. Alastair dropped down into a furrow until he went back inside. When he got up to leave, the dog began to howl and strain again, nearly breaking its chain. Once more, the door swung open and the farmer came out and, cursing loudly, beat the dog.

It was pitch black and overcast by the time Alastair reached the railway tracks near the valley floor. Until then, he hadn't really engaged in any sabotage, which was odd given his mischievous nature. Now he wondered if he could derail one of the many trains travelling south from the Brenner Pass. He found some steel spikes which he placed on the tracks and then climbed up a bit and waited. It wasn't long before a train came roaring through, not affected in the least by Alastair's efforts. Further on, he burned a bundle of military phone cables which he discovered while crossing a culvert.

He eventually arrived at a large railway bridge that spanned the river. Seeing guards at both ends, Alastair quickly decided to use the same trick he'd perfected during his student days when he secretly climbed the Forth Bridge. Crawling within thirty yards of the sentry, he waited for a train to pass and then, using it as a shield, sprinted alongside. Because the bridge was so long and there was a second guard at the other end, he had to drop down in the middle and wait for another train to come. As he lay between the two sets of tracks, he contemplated the rushing water below, preparing himself to jump should he be discovered. Fortunately, another train came within a short time, and hopping up and running, he got safely past the second guard as well.

Heading into the mountains once again, he soon found himself in the middle of a large orchard filled with ripe apples. He ate until he was nearly sick and then stuffed his pockets with a half dozen more. The sound of gunfire echoed throughout the night and many of the houses he passed were burned out and abandoned. 'At one there was the smell of death in the woods.' Passing through a vineyard, a door suddenly opened and a man and woman stood framed in the light, his arm comfortably wrapped around her waist. He watched them silently from the safety of the darkness wondering what strange phantom they imagined would come.

As he climbed higher, a light rain began to fall and the terrain became increasingly difficult. The ground was already covered with a crust of snow and filled with thickets and crags. He was soon in a cold sweat as he fought to keep his footing on the wet stone. At one point his path was blocked by a huge overhang which he struggled to climb around. Pulling himself over crevices with a deep ravine opening up below, he lifted himself onto an immense slab, where he collapsed in exhaustion. Even in broad daylight with clear skies he wouldn't have attempted some of the things he did. But once again, 'the power of escape', as he called it, ignited a special force and energy.

After resting for a while, and far too cold to sit still, he headed towards a gully which led up to the crest of a ridge. Once on top, he found a path which he hiked on till dawn, when he spotted a small cave in which he would spend the day. From then on, he travelled only at night, carefully skirting any villages he came to. Although he saw no one, he often heard the sound of gunfire and saw the remains of buildings still smouldering. He felt as though he were passing through a local war zone and dubbed it 'the Valley of Terror'. Always a fast walker, his pace was even quicker as he had no pack or other weight to carry. For food, he picked grapes and apples, with half-ripened corn providing the bulk. After four days 'King Ortler', as the Tyroleans called the peak, was clearly in sight. He was getting close.

On his fifth day out, perhaps because of the excitement of approaching Mount Ortler, which was now just south of him, Alastair broke one of his own rules and began walking before it was completely dark. On a steep slope, he saw a farmhouse with two men working in the garden. It was still dusk, so he snaked along below, well out of view. He hadn't seen the young boy herding goats nearby, and when he did, it was too late. Just as startled as he was, the boy began to scream for help:

The two men were on to me like lightning, one had a shotgun, the other a revolver. They hailed me in German–Austrian Tyrolese. I maintained I was a Croat, speaking to them in Italian which they understood. 'Papers.' 'No, none.' 'He is an enemy. Shoot him,' said the younger man, a German, a big unpleasant looking fellow. The other demurred. 'There has been enough bloodshed.' The former raised his gun, cocked it pointing the barrels at my chest. The little group of people who came out of the house scattered from my vicinity. An old woman, apparently the man's mother, ran to me and flung her arms round me. The man permitted himself to be hustled away. The business had gone far enough.

The tension dissolved even further when Alastair told them that he was a British officer and prisoner of war. Now the older woman who had saved his life sent someone for a bottle of wine and some bread. The party didn't last long as the two men from the garden returned dressed in makeshift uniforms with SOD armbands on. Prodding Alastair with their guns, they set off like two hunters anxious to show off the magnificent specimen they had just caught. They marched for hours through the dark in a depressing drizzle, talking in turns of their feelings about Italy and the war. They were Germans, they said, and loyal to Hitler. They would never accept being second-class citizens in a foreign country again. 'So much,' thought Alastair, 'for the sentimental view of Tyroleans with their winter sports, folk costumes, and yodelling.'

It was well past midnight by the time they entered a small village and delivered Alastair to the local police. Placed in a windowless cell, he had barely begun to decompress when he heard a German soldier screaming: 'Where is he? I'm going to kill the English bastard! I'll cut his bloody throat! Let me in!' Then the door swung open and in flew a rabid brute – big, burly and very drunk. He grabbed Alastair by the throat and started

196

hitting him over and over again on the head. It was much worse than the pounding he had received from Sergeant Mazza at Gavi. This soldier was twice his size and even more violent. It was claimed his rage was the result of an Allied air raid that had wiped out his entire family. True or not, everyone else was much too afraid of him to intervene. When it was finally over, Alastair sat slumped against the wall, blood streaming down his face. Eventually, a young soldier came in with hot water and bandages for his head. Later on he brought bread and meat paste as well. He apologized for what had happened, after which they sat and talked for a long while.

The next day he was jammed into the back of a Fiat and driven to Bolzano, which had just been attacked by a dozen planes. Entering the city to a backdrop of sirens, they passed in front of a burning police station where carabinieri in torn uniforms were wandering about dazed. Railway lines and a bridge along with a power station had also been hit. Small squads of SOD were running all over, crisscrossing paths like actors in a bizarre pageant. The energy was explosive. 'Everyone was jumpy, expectant,' said Alastair. 'Fear was everywhere. Fear of the Germans of the Fascists of the Tyrolese of the Allied Air Force, of the future. Tomorrow seemed a vague probability. Today was hard, glittery, tense.'

After several stops, Alastair was taken to a railway siding, where a long row of cattle trucks sat waiting. Following another lengthy discussion, the door to one of them was unlocked and slid open. There wasn't an inch of room inside, but that didn't matter. They simply picked him up and shoved him in. At first Alastair couldn't figure out who his strange new companions were, nor even what language they were speaking. Of course,

Alastair, dressed in filthy civilian clothing and what looked like a swami's turban, was the strangest of all. Then he heard the familiar voice of an English private. 'They're Serbs,' he said. 'Some have been prisoners for years.' There were fifty-seven in all, with five more British soldiers who had been recaptured after escaping following the armistice.

They waited for six hours before the train finally departed. By then, Alastair, along with two others, was already hard at work removing planks from the side wall. They were discovered, however, at a stop near the Brenner Pass and moved to another car. This one contained only twenty prisoners, all Italians who had been part of the mass surrender on Elba. There was room to lie down and one of the Italians kindly lent him a blanket. As he closed his eyes, his head throbbed horribly from the beating he'd received just two days before. For a brief moment he felt better as he recalled the night when he and the mountain girl in the hospital kissed. Then the headache quickly returned, and with it the sense of failure. No matter how hard he had tried, he was going to Germany.

# 7

# The Forest

After the claustrophobia of Gavi, Moosburg was like a huge, cosmopolitan city with prisoners from every corner of the globe. Built on the site of an old fertilizer factory, Stalag VIIA, as it was officially known, was one of the first prison camps established by the Germans. Located twenty-five miles north-east of Munich on a marshy plain near the Isar River, it was an ugly, unhealthy place. Even the medical team sent to survey it advised against placing it there. Their reservations were ignored, however, as more powerful interests took over. Constructed to house 10,000 prisoners, its population eventually swelled to ten times that number, and during the last days of the war a good deal more. It was the largest of Germany's many prisoner-of-war camps and certainly the most diverse. The French formed the biggest group followed by the Russians and British. But every allied country was represented, along with their colonial forces. According to one source there were soldiers from seventy-two nations, among them Algerians, Moroccans, Tunisians, Egyptians, Malayans, Indians, Senegalese, Sudanese, Indochinese, Haitians, Martinicans and even a group of Cubans.

Shaped like a lopsided hexagon, the camp had a paved, kilometre-long main street running down its centre, with more than a dozen smaller compounds set off on either side. Each had its own gate tower and was surrounded by two fourteen-foot-high barbed-wire fences with coils of razor-sharp concertina wire filling the eight-foot space in between. Inside were four or five wooden huts with a simple washroom dividing them down the middle. Attached to the end of every barracks was a small stone structure containing a crude latrine. With doors on each side, they consisted of four metal troughs that emptied into a dry, open hole. The stench was horrible as a continuous line of gagging men filed through. The smell inside the huts wasn't much better. Triple-decker bunks covered with fleas and bedbugs were shoved together, forcing as many as 400 prisoners into each hut.

The compounds were organized by nationality although smaller groups were naturally bundled together. However, when fifty Italians were placed in a hut with British officers who had just arrived from the south, the Germans were advised in no uncertain terms that if their former enemies weren't removed immediately, they couldn't be responsible for what happened to them. The Italians insisted: 'We are here because we refused to fight for the Germans against you. We were given the choice.' But their pleas were ignored and the Germans wisely moved them. As Alastair noted with some sympathy, 'The Italians were nobody's baby and despised by all. But this did not depress the spirits of the Italian troops who walked about quite happily, no more ragtag and bobtail than they had been in service.'

Although it was forbidden to move between the different compounds, prisoners found various ways of doing so. They bribed guards, slipped away from work details or simply climbed over the double fence. The Russians were particularly adept at the latter, fearlessly bounding over the barbed wire as the

German sentries fired at them. Without the protection of the Geneva Convention, which Russia never signed, nor any support from their own government, they lived in a state of constant desperation. Many of the 15,000 at Moosburg had arrived after a three-week journey in sealed cattle cars. To survive, some had resorted to cannibalism. Despite their ill treatment and appalling conditions – many did not even have shoes – they were universally admired for their remarkable resilience and spirit. The Germans thought them wild and savage, and were somewhat afraid of them. One popular story told of a fight one night in the Russian barracks. Rather than entering, the guards opened the door and quickly let two of their vicious Alsatians loose inside. Shortly after, the door swung open and two bundles were tossed out. They were the skins of the dogs with the bones wrapped inside. Pinned to one was a note that read, 'Thank you. Please send more.'

As a camp for Other Ranks and enlisted men, large work parties were constantly passing through the gates. Some worked on local farms or at the marshalling yards or in factories, or even in small craft shops, where they were often the only men. Contributing to this constant movement was the large population in transit, officers and others, like the thousands arriving from Italy who would soon be sent to different permanent camps. The circulation of so many prisoners also helped fuel Moosburg's elaborate black market, where it was possible, with enough capital and cigarettes, to purchase almost anything one could want. All these elements taken together created a sort of controlled chaos which a smart prisoner could easily exploit. In fact, compared to Gavi, escaping from Moosburg would only be slightly harder than checking out of a large hotel – that is, if you had the experience of an expert like the Baron. Perhaps this is why Alastair was smiling as he stood in a long queue to enter the camp. He knew immediately it was a place he was going to like.

The sound of a familiar voice calling his name startled him. As he turned, he saw Poppet coming from the opposite direction. Walking along with a small party of naval officers, he was about to leave for a camp near Bremen in northern Germany. Unlike the Italians, whose camps were organized by nationality, the Germans separated their prisoners according to the branch of service they were in. They also assigned responsibility for running each camp to members of the corresponding force. At Marlag, for example, the camp where Poppet was being sent, not only were all the prisoners naval officers, the guards and administrative staff were from the navy as well.

Assembled on the other side of the large entryway just inside the main gate was a much bigger group about to be searched before their departure to another camp. Among them were many of the army officers who had travelled with Alastair from Gavi. Needless to say, they were both disappointed and surprised to see him. Everyone had been certain that, once loose in the mountains, nothing would stop him. Instead, he was standing with his head wrapped in a blood-soaked bandage, waiting to be admitted to Moosburg. And yet, despite the obvious letdown of recapture, he radiated an energy and optimism that infected everyone who saw him. George Millar summed up the feeling well when he wrote:

Cram stood ahead of us, his head swathed in bandages . . . They had beaten the Baron shamefully, and had nearly murdered him. The greatest thing about Cram (and he was a very

202

exceptional man) was the philosophic way in which he took his failures. He was smiling and enjoying a conversation with one of the German guards who handed us out our travelling rations, sour bread and a kind of sausage.

Churchill too might well have been speaking of Alastair when he said that 'Success is the ability to move from failure to failure with no loss of enthusiasm.' In fact, Alastair didn't skip a beat upon arriving at Moosburg. While he could have slipped away from the column that marched from the train station, he decided to escape into the camp itself. Still recovering from his beating and without the proper papers and provisions he would need, he quickly calculated that it would be better to enter Stalag VIIA as a ghost. If the Germans didn't know he was there, getting out would be that much easier. And so, with long columns intersecting in the depressing downpour that had started to fall, he joined a group of prisoners that had already been processed and walked into the camp without registering.

He soon took on the identity of an American sergeant, although during roll calls he also appeared as a Frenchman or Serb and even an Italian. He wasn't alone in becoming a Yank either. Buck Palm was happily parading about as a big, harmonica-playing Texan as well. He had teamed up with George Tsoucas, the Greek stockbroker who had helped discover the hidden tunnel at Gavi. Urbane and confident, Tsoucas was a forty-four-year-old intelligence officer who had mastered most of the languages of continental Europe. Together they had exchanged identities with two Americans who were now on their way to a different camp with the rest of the Gavi contingent. And there was even one more newly minted American – Richard Carr, a member of the famous family of biscuit-makers of the same name. Now a commando who had won an MC at Dunkirk, he, like the other veterans of Gavi, planned to enlist the help of the French in figuring a way out.

For Alastair, preparing for an escape was a lot like getting ready for a climbing expedition. Physical conditioning, sharpening one's language skills, acquiring the necessary provisions and maps, deciding on a route and, finally, figuring out the best way to get there were common to both experiences, and for Alastair, equally exciting. His most immediate concern at the moment, though, was regaining his strength. He was still weak from the long train ride as well as his time in the Dolomites and subsequent mistreatment. Red Cross parcels and even the camp soups, much heartier than in Italy, soon revived him. He also returned to his daily Müller routine. While his fellow inmates at Padula and Gavi had grown accustomed to the sight of Alastair stripped naked at dawn furiously contorting and rubbing himself, for the men of the 36th Texas Division it was an eye-popping experience. But their wisecracks and odd looks never bothered him. When doing his Müllers, Alastair entered a state of concentration which no distraction could disrupt.

Following his exercises, he got dressed and went to school, which is just what Moosburg was like for Alastair – a vast network of information on everything he would need to know if he were to escape successfully. The question was, which direction should he take? He was nearly giddy with the number of options:

Where should one choose to go? The choice was embarrassing. Through Poland into Russia? Down the Danube to the

Black Sea? By Vienna and Buda Pesth to Turkey, through Austria and Italy to the British line, north through Stettin to Sweden, west over the Rhine to Alsace and France, north west into Belgium or Holland, south west over the Silvretta Alps into Switzerland? The choice was dazzling, for information poured in on all routes. Friends, contacts, relatives, trains, patrol guards. I talked and listened every day until, worn out, I fell asleep exhausted at night. I learned more about the inside of Europe in a few weeks than I had done in many years of reading. For one got the essential feel of each country from a multitude of angles, above all on the internal state of Germany, for these men working in the country and in contact with a great net of foreign workers knew the very last detail.

With each day he felt stronger and more confident. He roamed the camp as if he were a goodwill ambassador, delighting in its international character. He swapped stories with the Poles, dined with the French, drank moonshine with the Russians, and even visited with former guards from Gavi who were now his fellow prisoners. And with each stop, he traded. A good army compass cost him a tin of powdered milk and some bully beef. With sixty cigarettes and several tins of food he acquired a pair of boots, which he in turn exchanged for a large-scale set of maps of Europe. He also purchased money, 120 marks, along with some Serbian, Hungarian, French and Italian currency. And for 50 marks, he hired a Russian to provide him with the perfect rucksack made of camouflage material. He also bribed some guards, though he confessed that it was as much to practise his German as anything. It was, as he recalls, 'as amusing a period as I had ever spent. For I felt fit and keen and my plans were going ahead like wildfire.'

October arrived and the weather started to change. As the days grew shorter and the evenings colder, he knew that it was time to leave. The first step in his plan was to switch identities once again, transforming himself from a GI into a French corporal. Alastair enjoyed this subterfuge, and for a shy person, inhibited in many ways, the ability to inhabit another personality so thoroughly was clearly liberating:

> When in disguise it is necessary to think oneself into the disguise. If a German one must think in German so that one's instinctive reaction to a question is in German. If a Frenchman then one must learn to walk as a Frenchman, to behave towards Germans as one. One must be careful not to mix the two languages in certain circumstances, especially in conjunctions and exclamations. A carelessly dropped German word may well prejudice one in the eyes of a friendly Frenchman etc. . . . A disguise is not merely clothes but must be thought and lived at all times. It is not enough to pretend to be another. One must be another.

There were more than 40,000 French prisoners at Moosburg, many having arrived soon after the camp was opened. In fact, they had built most of it, and while it certainly wasn't Paris, they exhibited that special air of Gallic disdain for anyone who visited. They ran most of the kitchens and infirmaries, the theatre and the work parties, and certainly had the best contacts on the outside. If one was to escape, it paid to have their help. Alastair, whose French was excellent, had little difficulty in befriending a burly sergeant from Lyon who was willing to assist. This man had already aided a number of prisoners and the plan he proposed was quite simple. Accompanied by three French soldiers, Alastair was marched right through the main gate and into the German compound. Once there he was shut inside a lavatory at the back of one of the huts. His rucksack, along with a set of civilian clothes and all his gear, had already been stored in the roof. At around 2 a.m. he let himself out and, avoiding the searchlights and guard tower, scaled the fence and escaped.

The countryside around Moosburg was flat with little cover, making it easy for Germans to spot escapers as they scrambled to get away. Civilians were on constant alert, with Hitler Youth roaming about like packs of dogs ready to run down any suspicious stranger. Alastair knew this as he headed north through fields that had been harvested weeks before. His plan was to follow the Isar, eventually crossing it and, using the forest for cover, walk a hundred miles east to Passau and the Danube. From there he would board a boat and, with luck, travel all the way to Turkey, or perhaps join the partisans in Yugoslavia like a number of others from Gavi before him.

After several hours of walking, and certain that he was being pursued, he spotted a hunter's blind thirty feet up a tree. He hid in it until just before dawn, when he climbed down and found a thicket of bushes beside a stream in which to spend the day. He had learned his lesson about setting off too early, and even though the October dusk seemed to last forever, he waited and was patient. Soon after dark he rejoined the path along the river, only to discover a series of locks. Although protected by small houses for the operators, Alastair easily bypassed them by climbing across the beams of the gates. After passing at least four of these, he arrived at a large lake more than three miles long and a mile wide. There was an overturned boat on the shore but as soon as he set it in the water, it started to sink. Frustrated that the lake wasn't on his map, he had no choice other than to detour around it.

Now he headed east and after crossing a stone bridge found himself in a marshy swamp intersected by shallow streams. He needed a pole to navigate and, even then, almost lost his boots in the mud more than once. He was relieved when he finally arrived in open country, though his path was soon blocked once again by another branch of the Isar. Searching for a place to cross, he waded in using his pole for support. Twenty yards from shore, the sand gave way and he quickly sank to his hips. Then a strap on his rucksack broke and bending to grab it, he found the water rushing past his shoulders. The current was stronger than he expected, and by the time he crawled out on the other side, he was shivering and exhausted. It was bright now as the moon was nearly full. Across the ploughed fields, he could see a line of hills and knew that was where the forest he was heading for began.

Entering the woods was like passing through a door to another universe, where Alastair would remain for the next eighteen days. His descriptions of what happened during this period often sound more like a person on a vision quest than that of an escaping British officer. And there's no doubt that his solitary adventures in the hidden nocturnal world of the Bavarian forest induced what can only be thought of as a mind-altering experience. Alastair recognized this, admitting, 'I travelled farther than the mere distance my feet trod.' He was also his typically analytical self, carefully observing what happened in his brain as days of isolation with little sleep or food produced dramatic changes in perception.

There were the occasional humans who trespassed upon his solitude – lovers out for a secret tryst, children running and laughing and, most dangerous of all, the determined mushroom hunters, who penetrated further than anyone else. But once evening came, they disappeared, frightened by the spirits of the forest. For Alastair, this was when 'the great symphony of night' began and he learned how to listen once again. Long 'dormant instincts' needed to be reawakened, which a life of hill walking and mountaineering had prepared him to do. Eventually, his senses became so acute he could hear the distant sound of cobwebs tearing, an important announcement that someone or something was coming. If animals weren't seen, they were certainly heard, their messages filled with critical life-or-death information. As Alastair immersed himself further and further in the green world of the forest, its language became as clear as any other:

In this state one need not strain for sounds of peril for these strike on the attuned ear like a misplayed note in a concerto. The 'thump thump thump' of rabbit sentries, the 'squawk' of jays, the snorting whistle of sheep, the snort and stamp of deer, the vixen's scream wailing like a 'babe in the woods'. The distant snuffle of hunting dogs. The far away pad pad pad of human feet, the slap of pigeon's wings, the gaggle and warble of water fowl, the check in the stream's chuckle caused by something fording or drinking even far away. Intuition of danger is very often an unrealized picking up of one or more unusual notes in the great outdoor song cycles of night and day. How much more meaningful must these be to the creatures continuously tuned in.

His sense of smell too became equally developed and within a short time he could discern the scent of humans, houses, animals and dogs at a considerable distance. Later, he would caution other escapers against smoking, lest it impair this vital ability. On some nights when Alastair was struggling through impenetrable thickets, and the forest was particularly still, it seemed that smell alone was guiding him: 'Only one's nose was receiving sense data, the keen fresh smell of moss, the acridness of fungi, the pungency of fox and deer scents and the warm still dusty smell of pools of trapped warm air left over from the day.'

Every night he moved further east, although at times he became so disoriented that he found himself walking in circles. The woods were thick and dark, with only the occasional moss-covered path barely visible. Most of these went in the wrong direction, forcing Alastair to continue through the dense brush where spiky branches tore at his clothes and skin. He used a stick to push them aside, or like an antenna to probe ahead. When he stumbled across a road, which he sometimes did, the sky would suddenly open up, making him feel as though he had 'stepped back into this world after some journey in the underworld'. Just before dawn was the worst time of all, when, exhausted and anxious, he rushed to find a place to hide for the day. A stand of young pines was best, no more than six feet tall with lots of undergrowth and brambles for protection. Before sleeping, he would eat a biscuit with some meat or cheese, two ounces at most, with slivers of turnip and sugar beet and one or two potatoes. 'I grew thinner,' he said, 'but remained wiry and hard.'

On the tenth day, as he slept like Puck, 'that merry wanderer of the night', with his back resting against a tree, he was awakened by the sound of a snarling wolf just feet away. As they stared at one another, it was clear to Alastair that the animal was much more frightened than him. And then, in what seemed like a well-rehearsed ritual, the grey wolf circled the tree three times and disappeared. That evening he was pursued by a tall man in a long coat and hat. No matter how fast he ran, the figure kept up, until finally Alastair realized that it was a post on the horizon. He was starting to hallucinate. Branches were turning into winged phantoms and the mist on pools of water soldiers with rifles and bayonets. The strain of being alone in the forest at night with little sleep and the constant fear of detection was starting to take its toll. Along with his heightened sensitivities came a disquieting uncertainty about what was real. As Alastair acknowledged:

A man walking alone and hunted is conditioned imperceptibly into a peculiar state of mind. His perceptions become keener and his senses acute but he tends to suffer from delusions. The impact of repeated nervous shocks, no less the steady pressure of events, will detach him from the normal and the usual and bear him away into a new mental state as the debris and current of a flooded river plucks at a bush grown on the banks and eventually whisks it away in its stream.

If Alastair was unsettled by the appearance of fleeting apparitions, it certainly didn't undermine his resolve. He remained focused and utterly confident that he would succeed. Years of experience in the woods convinced him that he could be much more cunning than any animal when hunted by his own kind. He knew how to hide. He had also trained himself to walk without making a sound, 'a learned art' requiring the proper roll of the foot as it softly landed with the weight shifted to the back one. When necessary, he could outrun most pursuers. For this, too, he had numerous tricks: doubling back in a figure 9, feigning injury and tumbling over a crest, then quickly sprinting at a right angle, and even the use of light and shadow to disappear in an open space. But most of all, he entered into another state of consciousness. He called it 'the beast, that lower part of the mind', which others have identified as part of the limbic system, the raw fight-or-flight remnant of the reptilian brain. He felt its power emerge as 'the middle self of normality faded' and the mystic, higher one became less palpable. His description of this intense transformation is like a gateway into a newly discovered world of deep, primal instincts:

I know now how a beast approaches a human habitation by night for I have been one. Mingled in with the wood perfumes comes something alien, the stale odour of decaying human food, the sour sweet smell of human bodies, the foul acrid stink of dogs and the ammoniac pungency of domestic beasts. Instantly is caution. The hearing is consciously focused forward. In silence tense and expectant the beast goes upward through the woods for it needs sweet water and food. Then past midnight and the house glimmers quiet in the clearing but the beast stands two or three rows inside the protecting woodland. Then readies and crawls into the open and lies still for many moments. Eyes four inches above the earth it can hear all, see all and is invisible. One ear is focused forward and one backward. Slowly it circles the clearing, moving so balanced that a clicking sound freezes it with one foot lifted backward so that a twig underfoot is felt before pressure is put upon it, balanced so that the feather light setting of each foot is soundless on stone or gravel. The circles narrow. Inside are the chomp and stamp of beasts, a child whispers in its sleep or some person groans aloud. Dogs bark at sound not scent it seems. Domesticated, they sleep soundly, so dulled are they that no message goes from nose to brain in sleep but the tiniest sound, two stones together, a scrunch on earth and they are on their feet growling softly and yet with a puzzlement for they smell a strange beast, a beast they instantly know is aware of them, a beast which since it smells like man ought to make a noise like man but does not. The beast closes on the steading. It drinks from the plashing water trough. The dairy smelling sweetly of cream is locked, but the maize store is not and there are heaping beet and potatoes. The house is electric with the sensation of living beings and every gregarious instinct in the outlaw beast longs for warmth and peace and comfort but it cannot be. There is the smell of cheese, and bread and cooked meats behind the shutters. And then the house lies behind in the clearing, the beast lies again in the open. Is it pursued? Are the woodlands free? When it has its answer it drifts like a shadow into its darkness. The faintly growling dog with an anxious whine lies down again to sleep and the human body whimpers.

After nearly three weeks of walking, Alastair reached a railway line, which he immediately decided to sabotage. First he found a sharp bend where he used spikes to wedge in three railroad ties. He didn't wait to see if it worked but was satisfied with the improvement on his earlier efforts in Italy. Soon after, he began to smell the river and, as a thick fog rolled in, he found himself in a swampy forest filled with juniper and yew. It was an eerie, sinister landscape, and although he knew he was getting close, he still checked his compass every hundred yards. For a while he walked beside a deep stream which suddenly plunged over a gorge. Working his way around the rim was tough going, though he finally reached a spot where it was possible to descend. After struggling down 500 feet of loose rock and mud, he landed in a bramble patch directly above a railway line on which a long goods train was travelling. Just beyond the tracks on the other side was the Danube, quietly flowing. His calculations had been perfect.

As he walked south along the tracks, he looked for a place to climb down to the river. It had been days since he'd washed and he was covered with mud and small scratches everywhere. When he finally reached the water, he tore off what remained of his shirt and sank it with several large stones. Then he bathed and shaved and put on a fresh set of clothes and walked the last three miles to Passau. By now it was nearly light, forcing him to hurry if he was to find a place to hide for the day. He discovered one just as he reached the outskirts of the city, an empty cart shed with a loft filled with hay. That evening he went down to the docks, hoping to find a barge heading for Romania. But there were only a few paddle steamers, all flying Nazi flags. He did board one, although when challenged made a quick retreat. In the end, he decided to take the evening off and enjoy Passau, a city that he had always wanted to visit.

After a month of constant pressure, he was ready to relax and was surprised at how easy it was to fit in as a tourist. No one seemed to notice him as he walked along the Danube to the point where it merged with the Inn and the Ilz. Nor were any of the soldiers interested in anything except their lovers with whom they casually promenaded arm in arm. It was the same in the huge plaza in front of St Stephen's where crowds admired the cathedral's impressive onion-shaped domes. He was just as happy as well to be swept into the church to marvel at the world's largest organ. Once outside, he wandered along the city's narrow streets which reminded him in many ways of Perth – two ancient cities defined by rivers of nearly identical size and age. He wished, in fact, that he could send a postcard to his parents telling them of their many similarities.

Eventually, he ended up at the train station, surprised by how bright it was, given the blackout restrictions. Posted just inside was a detailed map of the area which Alastair carefully studied. Having failed to locate a barge, he decided to explore the rail yards in the hope of jumping a goods train. While there were many rushing in all directions, it was more difficult than he had imagined; they were either heading north, had too many guards or were simply travelling too fast. After trying for some time, he found an empty carriage from the local City and Suburban line, into which he crawled and fell asleep.

It was almost daylight when he was suddenly awakened by the abrupt movement of the train. Quickly gathering up his things, he waited until it was out of the station before leaping onto the street. From there he returned to the river, where he found another hut loaded with hay. It was a foul-smelling place which locals clearly used as an outhouse. In fact, it wasn't long before an old man came in and dropped his trousers only to see Alastair staring straight at him. He hardly waited to pull them up as he made a comic retreat, tripping more than once as he went. Soon after, Alastair walked down to the water to see if there were any new barges. The only activity he found was an ancient paddle steamer hauling stone from a quarry just across the river in Austria. There was, however, a young boy in leather shorts aboard a canvas sailboat. It was the best thing Alastair had seen so far. If he could steal it, he could easily take it all the way down the Danube.

Unfortunately, the boy became suspicious and after Alastair went back to his hiding place, quietly disappeared, leaving a friend to watch the boat. When he returned, he was joined by two men, both carrying rifles. They went straight to the hayloft, ordering him to come out. After stashing his gear in a corner, he assured them that he was unarmed and was simply a foreign worker taking a nap. The boy, who was convinced he'd caught a major criminal, shouted, 'Liar! He was trying to steal my boat.' As for the two men, who might have been a father and son, they hardly spoke at all but simply grunted in a language that they alone seemed to understand. A slight prod with one of their guns was enough to tell Alastair to start walking behind the boy, who gleefully led the way to the local police station, where he was locked up.

No sooner had they left than he was let out of his cell and given a bowl of potato soup with a thick slice of bread. It was brought to him by a rather large woman with several feet of braids wrapped around her head. This was the jailer's wife, who had been left in charge in his absence, though Alastair suspected she was in charge in his presence as well. As he mopped up the

last bits of soup, he began to tell her that he was a French foreign worker assigned to a farm just outside the city. He had
come to Passau early that morning on an errand and was simply
taking a nap before his return. If he wasn't back by nightfall, he
was sure to be beaten as the owners were cruel and often hit
him. 'See,' he said, pointing to the fresh scars from the beating
he had just received in Italy. 'They often strike me, and I'm sure
that one day I'll be killed.' And then, in an Oscar-winning performance, he began to whine and plead.

The jailer's wife simply stood there with her arms folded, her
face absolutely still as if waiting for an encore. Then, in a voice
loud enough to startle him, she screamed, 'Heinz!' And in came
a skeletal figure with deep-set eyes holding a broom. 'Get your
bike,' she ordered, 'and take this Frenchman back to his farm.'

'*Merci, merci beaucoup, madame*,' cried Alastair as he waved
goodbye to the woman, who stood in the doorway of the station
to see them off. Then, turning his attention to his companion,
he began to give directions to his imaginary farm. By now, he
knew the area well enough to manoeuvre himself into a position
to escape. All he needed was a path with a steep incline on one
side and a sharp drop on the other. Then, exactly as he had done
in Sicily, he would shove the unsuspecting guard over and
disappear up the hill. But when the time came, Alastair didn't
have the heart to do it. Not only was the man unarmed, he was
also in no physical condition to chase Alastair up a mountain.
Besides, they had been genuinely kind to him at the police station. And so, when the moment arrived and they found themselves walking next to a steep enough slope, Alastair simply
turned and, like a billy goat, ran straight up it.

The man, whom he may have underestimated, jumped on his

bike and pedalled off as fast he could for help. He knew where to find it too, as Alastair was still catching his breath when he heard the sound of two armed groups of Hitler Youth on their way to find him. The search went on for hours, with Alastair making use of every trick he knew. Only at dusk did he feel it safe enough to return to the hayloft to pick up his belongings. It was clearly time to leave Passau.

He decided to go to Vienna, where he hoped to make contact with the underground. While taking a train would be fastest, he worried that by now the police would be watching the station. Instead, he would cycle to Linz and from there catch a train the rest of the way. It wasn't hard to steal a bike, although he was careful not take any that were simply leaning against a kerb or wall. The safest way was on a busy street, waiting till he saw a person dismount and then following him to see where he went. Unfortunately, the first two he stole had mechanical problems, so he dumped them both in the river. The third, however, was nearly new and very well maintained. It had a lock on its rear wheel, which Alastair easily broke with a kick.

The evening was overcast and cool, although after half an hour of pedalling he felt surprisingly comfortable and relaxed. It also helped that the road, which followed the Danube, was fairly flat and simple to navigate. In fact, he soon decided that, if he were recaptured, cycling would be the method of choice for future escapes. Few if any people were on the road at night and even if they were, one was quickly past them and out of sight before their suspicions could be aroused. It was also easy to pass through small villages undetected and best of all were the great distances that could be covered. By morning, Alastair had already arrived in Linz, more than fifty miles away. He considered visiting the port – much larger than Passau – but after his recent experience thought it safer to blend in with the early morning traffic to Vienna. Dropping off his bike in front of the station, he purchased a ticket on a local train and within several hours was walking down Mariahilfer Strasse into the heart of the city.

Alastair had always liked Vienna. He had visited it several times before the war and even knew a number of climbers who lived there. The city he found in October 1943, however, was far different from the sparkling capital he remembered. Everywhere felt run-down and depressing: wrought-iron gates rusting, paint and stucco chipping, shop windows empty or closed, and the streets filled with litter that swirled in the wind like small tornadoes. The parks too were untended and the orchestras that played in the bandstands were like the widows who listened, both ancient and sad. 'The whole atmosphere,' said Alastair, 'was one of decay, melancholy and heavy with approaching ruin.'

Other than the decrepit streetcars, the only traffic was military. The pavements, on the other hand, were filled with a mix of nationalities – Czechs, Serbs, Hungarians, French, Italians – all of them giving Alastair confidence that his accented German was the norm rather than the exception. The main thing was to walk with an air of purpose. Anything else made one 'stand out like a sore thumb', whereas the person who strode along with authority wore what he called 'a mantle of invisibility'. He didn't hesitate for a second as he marched past the main police station on his way to the fruit market in the eastern part of the city. The small beer cellars that surrounded it would be the most likely place to find French workers who could help him. That afternoon he visited one after another, drinking beer and eating vegetable pie as he went. Most were filled with middle-aged men playing cards and dominoes. When he did find some Frenchmen, they were much too afraid to help him.

As the sun was going down, he decided to visit the port 'to prospect for barges'. There were a couple tied up along with several paddle steamers similar to those he had seen in Passau. None of them looked very promising, which led him to give up on the idea once and for all. From there he headed back into Vienna to catch an evening movie. He had thought about it all day, especially since his foot was bothering him and he needed a place to rest. The main feature, which could have been directed by Ernst Lubitsch, was a romantic comedy in which well-groomed soldiers competed for the hand of a beautiful aristocrat. Based in an Austrian castle, the suitors also spent a good deal of time racing their cars along Alpine roads which Alastair recognized from before the war.

Much more interesting than the film was the newsreel that accompanied it. German troops were shown on two fronts valiantly resisting the Allied onslaught that threatened the victories of the last several years. Footage of the new defensive line along the Dnieper was meant to reassure viewers that the Bolshevik menace had been contained. But the reality was different, as the Russians had just retaken Smolensk and Lenino and were advancing little by little throughout the Ukraine. The second story was about Italy, where truckloads of confident soldiers were shown arriving at the Gustav Line that stretched across the width of the country from a point midway between Rome and Naples. Here, the Allies had been contained, upending their initial optimism about a quick campaign. In fact, no one had expected Hitler to commit so many of his resources to the defence of the entire country. The images of combat in difficult muddy and mountainous conditions were sobering, leaving no doubt that it would be a long struggle. All of this was watched through a thick haze of tobacco smoke by a surprisingly apathetic audience.

After the movie, Alastair returned to a large park he had passed earlier in the day. Ignoring the various warning notices against being there at night, he walked in, found a thick stand of bushes to crawl behind, and went to sleep. Other than an air raid, which he spent in a beer cellar, the next two days were much the same as the first. Establishing contact with the underground was proving impossible. His right foot had also got much worse from the endless hours of walking on hard pavement. It was time to leave Vienna and, after studying the maps conveniently posted in the railway station, he decided to go to Budapest. From there, he would continue by train to Romania and Bulgaria, and then on to Turkey. Unlike Switzerland, where escaped prisoners were interned, those who made it to Turkey were quickly dispatched to the Middle East.

Alastair loved maps, and it may be that he studied the one on the wall far too long; or perhaps it was his body language or his clothes and odd rucksack, or maybe he was simply overheard asking directions. In any case, someone followed him as he left the station. He knew it immediately, although he crossed the street once or twice to make sure. It made no sense to try to lose him; if it was the police, they probably would have stopped him right away. After several blocks he found an empty bench and sat down. Moments later, the man came up and joined him. He was neatly dressed with a jacket and tie and a stylish fedora. In fact, he looked as though he might have been a lawyer.

'You're English aren't you? I can tell.'

'No, you're wrong,' answered Alastair. 'I'm from France. I'm here as a foreign worker.'

To which he responded with a smile, 'My French is much better than yours and I'm Czech.'

'What do you want?' asked Alastair, trying to conceal his irritation.

'To help you. We're allies.' He then went on to speak about his time as a medical student in London and his affection for the British. He had continued his studies in Prague but the Nazis had shut down the universities after protests against the occupation. Many had been shot or sent to concentration camps. He too had been part of the resistance, though after Heydrich's assassination, there was little left of it. That's why he had come to Vienna, where he had an uncle who had found him work.

Alastair, surprised at how open the young man was, took a moment to reply. He believed his story, and confided that he was indeed a British officer – Scottish, not English – who had escaped from a prisoner-of-war camp in Germany. He related his plan to go to Budapest.

The Czech, who said his name was Peter, advised against it. Why not go to Yugoslavia, he asked? The partisans were already at the border and would be easy to join. He even had a friend in Maribor whose address he'd happily provide. If he travelled overnight, there would be little risk of capture. This had been one of the options that Alastair had considered. Now with Peter's help, he would do it.

That night he took a train halfway to Yugoslavia, getting out at dawn to spend the day before continuing the following evening. Just as Peter had predicted, no one stopped him, and by 8 a.m. he had crossed the border and was at the contact's house in Maribor. Unfortunately, the partisans had withdrawn and a twenty-mile no-man's land had been created. It was far too wide to cross in a single night and anyone found inside was shot at once. Alastair's new host strongly advised against it, adding that the partisans were nothing more than rabble. No, the best thing to do would be to return to Vienna and look for Peter.

With little alternative, Alastair retraced his steps and went back to Austria. To avoid travelling during the day, he again planned to break his trip midway, this time stopping in Brück. For a while, he chatted with the young woman sitting next to him and then, like nearly everyone else, fell sound asleep. Only at the last minute did she awaken him with the news that they'd arrived at his stop. By the time he got off he was nearly alone on the platform, a perfect target for the station police. Where were his papers? 'Oh, you have none? Let's go into the office and talk.' Of course, he claimed he was a French foreign worker, beaten and abused and desperate to get home. They seemed to believe him too, when all of a sudden the door opened and in came a French-speaking German from Strasbourg. The game was up.

Once he confessed to being a British officer, the mood changed and his captors became almost apologetic. One gave him a week's worth of butter rations and another coupons for bread. He dined at the station restaurant, where the other patrons craned their necks as if a movie star had appeared. Even the waiter whispered in his ear: 'I am sorry to see you like this. I had the pleasure of serving many English people before the war. I hope it will not be long before the English are back again.'

'Don't worry,' replied Alastair. 'They soon will be.'

From the restaurant, they took him to the local army barracks, where he was held in the main office. He sat there all day except for a visit to the laundry room, from which he easily escaped. But he was weak and exhausted and was picked up within a hundred yards. For the first time, he was handcuffed. It almost didn't matter:

> I was in a peculiar state of mind. Capture had seemed so imminent for so long that now that it was a reality I felt curiously little disappointment, only a sensation of relief from strain. My legs were sinewy but stick like, ribs projected like a picture of famine and I had a waistline like a Victorian debutante.

Around 4 p.m., two Austrian soldiers came to take him away. They were a curiously mismatched pair – one tall, one short, yet both remarkably calm. Alastair called them 'placid'. They took the train to Klagenfurt where they found a first-class carriage to spend the night. The guards were asleep in minutes, their rifles left within easy reach. While part of him preferred to rest as well, it seemed almost irresponsible not to escape. The door was open, the guards snoring, all he had to do was leave. Across the river was a low range of Alps and beyond that, Italy. Of course, he knew that he was in no condition to climb. He was 'as weak as a new born puppy dog'. And yet, he couldn't resist.

Once outside the station, he grabbed a bike. Only this time, the owner was standing nearby and started to shout. A crowd quickly formed and might have turned violent if the two guards hadn't arrived to save him. More embarrassed than angry, they agreed to say nothing for fear of being punished for negligence. Their next stop was Spittal, the same camp near the Italian border from which many of the first group from Gavi had escaped. Now Alastair had to struggle to get in. He hadn't a shred of evidence to prove who he was – no papers, no identity disc, nothing.

'Then perhaps I can just leave,' he said.

'*Ja, ja, ja*,' smiled the commandant, as if he'd heard this joke a million times. 'We'll let you in.' And off he went to solitary.

Alastair was at Spittal for a week, most of it spent eating, thanks to an Australian sergeant major who brought him large quantities of food every day. This was never a problem as the prisoners, who worked on surrounding farms and in the forest, returned with a daily haul of dairy, meat and other products. There was even an excellent brewery, run by a select group known as the Haggis Busters. By the time he left, he felt strong and healthy once again. His rucksack, miraculously returned with his compass and maps intact, was also stuffed to the brim with an assortment of delicacies. Among the guards who came to get him was a middle-aged sergeant captured at the Somme during the First World War. Held as a prisoner near Glasgow, he spoke English with a Scottish accent and didn't stop talking all the way to Moosburg.

Getting back into that camp was even harder than at Spittal, especially when he refused to tell the Germans how he had escaped. By now he'd had so many identities that no one was quite sure who he was. He convinced them, though, and after a week in a gloomy punishment block was wandering about the compounds once again. He found many new prisoners from Italy, including more than 1,000 from Chieti. Among them were a number of old friends who told the pathetic story of how their own men had been posted as guards after the armistice to prevent their escape. Three people he didn't find were Buck Palm, George Tsoucas and Richard Carr, all of whom were long gone. From the bush telegraph, he learned that the first two were already in Paris. As for Carr, Alastair would meet up with him later and hear the details of what occurred.

Like Alastair, Palm and Tsoucas had assumed American identities to avoid being transferred to another camp. Turned back on their first attempt to get out as part of a Russian work detail, they arranged, with the help of the French, to hang on to the bottom of a trailer that was carrying food parcels to be loaded onto a train. Once at the railhead they dropped down, crawled across the track beneath a goods wagon and began walking to Munich. Towards evening they were stopped by a German officer on a bike. They claimed they were French workers on their way back to a farm but the German demanded that they return to the camp to check their identities. At that moment, two privates appeared. They were clearly dressed for a night on the town, and were understandably upset when the officer ordered them to escort the prisoners back to Moosburg. Along the way they met yet another officer on a bike. He agreed to take them off the privates' hands, and foolishly walking ahead, lectured them on the dangers of being out after curfew. Then, as they passed beside a somewhat muddy pond, Buck picked him up and tossed him in. They ran off as fast as they could with the sound of gunfire behind them. Four days later they were in Munich, having eaten nothing but raw potatoes, cabbage and beets they dug up along the way.

Exhausted and hungry, they headed for the Café Rouge, where they had been told to look for a Frenchman named Phillipot. He was there as promised and took them to a labour camp where the foreign railway workers lived. Given blue overalls and passes, they spent nearly three weeks waiting for a train to stow away on. At one point Buck even tried to steal a plane but found an Alsatian guard dog sitting in the cockpit. By now Richard Carr, who had climbed over the same fence as Alastair, had also arrived. At last, word came: a goods train was being loaded for Strasbourg. They were to be at the rail yards at 8 p.m. and hidden inside wooden beer casks. Once locked in, with no food and little water, the train sat for over thirty hours; it was two more days after that before it finally reached its destination.

From Strasbourg they walked north-west along the Marne canal with the hope of stowing away on a barge. Buck and Tsoucas went ahead with Carr to follow thirty minutes later. He missed the rendezvous in Vendenheim, however, when he went to the wrong hotel. Striking out on his own, Carr walked another two days before the police arrested him. As for Palm and Tsoucas, they couldn't find a boat and simply kept on walking. Three days later they crossed the border into France. On the outskirts of Lunéville, they stopped at a farm to ask for help and were told that the head of the local gendarmerie was the man they needed to see. He had helped others before and welcomed them as well. After several comfortable days at the police station, they were taken, with new false papers and clothes, to the first stop on the Marie-Claire escape line.

There were various organizations throughout Europe run like the Underground Railroad with agents and safe-houses, creating a secret highway along which refugees, downed airmen and escaped prisoners were passed. Some had support from governments-in-exile or the intelligence services in London while others were small family affairs operating within limited areas. Whether large or small, they were all extremely vulnerable to infiltration by spies and traitors, and more often than not had a short lifespan. Capture for the courageous men and women who ran them meant almost certain torture and death. Of all the lines, none was more famous than Marie-Claire, as much for its effectiveness, perhaps, as for its colourful leader, the Comtesse de Milleville.

English by birth, Mary Lindell was a decorated nurse with the Red Cross during the First World War and remained in France after marrying a count. With the help of her two teenage sons, she began ferrying British soldiers into the Unoccupied Zone as soon as France surrendered in June 1940. Her group, christened the Marie-Claire line, grew quickly, as did her legend. 'Dedicated', 'fearless', 'imperious' and 'impossible' were all adjectives used to describe her. Always dressed in her Red Cross uniform, with her British medals prominently displayed, she seemed to advertise rather than hide her presence. Inevitably she was arrested and held in solitary by the Gestapo for nine months. Upon her release, she used her own line to flee to England, where she was recruited by MI9 and sent back to rebuild her organization. Her headquarters were in Ruffec, a small town west of Limoges that conveniently straddled the demarcation line.

The person responsible for escorting escapers and others from eastern France was a viscountess and, like Mary, tall, middle-aged, and domineering. It was the Vicomtesse Pauline Barré de Saint Venant, alias Madame Laroche, who picked up Palm and Tsoucas in Nancy and brought them to Paris. First, however, she made them change their outfits, which simply wouldn't do. On 3 November she took them to Ruffec, where four other airmen were also waiting to cross into Spain. Three of them were evaders, meaning that they'd never been captured after their planes were shot down. One, a Kenyan Spitfire pilot named Mike Cooper, had been on the run since August while the other two were Canadians from the same bomber crew. The fourth was an Australian pilot named Allan McSweyn who had successfully escaped from Germany on his sixth attempt. Like Buck, he was in great physical shape and incredibly tough.

Several days after their arrival, ten of them climbed into an old truck and headed for a train station twenty-five miles south of Limoges. If stopped, Mary planned to say that she was a nurse taking a group of 'bombed-out refugees, deaf, dumb and shell-shocked, to a resort in the south'. The trip was a disaster. The truck's rear axle broke; they missed their connection to Toulouse; they stayed in a hotel where they were nearly discovered by the Germans; and they learned just short of their rendezvous in Foix that they'd been betrayed and a trap had been set for them. They were lucky to get back to Ruffec in one piece.

They arrived in a terrible state, everyone on edge with tensions running high. Mary and Pauline, similar in so many ways, had often been at one another's throats. Now they were yelling at full throttle. Pauline was sick of Mary's arrogance and hated the condescending way she spoke to the French. Mary, in turn, accused Pauline of trying to take over her organization. There could be only one leader and she was it. And what was this she heard about her and Tsoucas having an affair? Didn't she know that was strictly forbidden? She would have him arrested, although under what authority wasn't clear. It became so violent they had to be pulled apart. The next morning Pauline left for Paris and George Tsoucas with her.

Mary, with the help of her husband and son, quickly established an alternative route across the Pyrenees. Instead of going from Foix to Andorra, they would now start much further west, at Pau. They took a train there on 12 November and, led by the first of several guides, boarded an ancient wood-burning bus for Tardets-Sorholus, where their journey by foot began. After stopping at a cafe for beer they continued on to the home of 'a small, wiry Frenchman,' whose wife had prepared them a meal. He and a Spaniard, who was already there, would take them over the mountains to Spain. It was less than ten miles and, with any luck, they should be there the next day.

They set off around 1 a.m. in a freezing rain, walking all night to avoid German patrols and to cross a key footbridge by dawn. They were just approaching it when one of the Canadians was discovered on the ground. His heart had given out and his face was turning blue. They carried him across the river and into a house, where he was slightly revived. But the next stage was straight uphill and much harder. It wasn't long before the Canadian's heart acted up once again. Even though he begged them to go on without him, Buck and McSweyn made it clear that no one was getting left behind. They pushed and pulled him all the way up to a razor sharp peak. It was just the beginning. Two ridges later, the rain had turned to snow, which was soon up to their knees. They were in the middle of a huge blizzard.

Now Cooper, the Kenyan pilot, started to fall behind. He had eaten too much snow and was suffering from hypothermia. It wasn't long before he was nearly delirious. While McSweyn and the French guide took turns helping the Canadian, Buck put

Cooper's arm around his shoulder and started to carry him. Even he couldn't keep it up for long and had to switch to other tactics: kicking, cursing, hitting, bullying and shoving, all of which Cooper gratefully admits saved his life. For part of the way, the trail was so narrow and the drop so deadly that everyone had to cross on all fours. Finally, they stumbled upon a small shack where they were able to take temporary shelter, even though large parts of the walls were exposed. It wasn't long after they started again that the guides confessed they were lost and were going home. Buck and McSweyn threatened to kill them if they dared.

The French guide, who had lost a shoe and was exhausted from helping the Canadian, started to fall further and further behind. Once they realized that he had disappeared completely, Buck and McSweyn went back to find him. Half-buried in the snow and nearly invisible in the white-out conditions of the blizzard, they discovered his dead body, face down and frozen. Soon after, they reached the crest marking the Spanish frontier. The descent was much easier, even though the snow and ice made it hard to find footholds. Cooper, half-crazy by then, rolled a good deal of the way down, eventually crashing into a wooden hut. It was a shepherd's cottage used in the summer while grazing sheep and cattle. When they couldn't break the lock, Buck and McSweyn used a log as a battering ram to force their way in. It was dark by the time they got a fire started and stripped off their clothes. Several had frostbite, and they knew that, if they hadn't found the cottage, they probably would have died.

By morning the storm had ended. With huge drifts blocking the door, it was as hard to get out as it had been to get in. Making progress through the snow, which was at least four feet deep, was nearly impossible. And then, out of nowhere, a phantom herd of horses appeared and, walking in single file down the mountain, beat a perfect path for them to follow. By noon, they had reached the valley floor, where they found other trails that were clear. Two hours later, they were in the village of Uztárroz, free and safe in Spain.

It was still several weeks before they were allowed to travel to Gibraltar, where the British quickly flew them home. After a raucous celebration in London, Buck was given a well-deserved leave and headed straight to Egypt. What no one had seemed to know was that Buck was engaged. Nine years younger and from one of Alexandria's most prominent families, Fernande Chakour had met him at a dance the year before he was shot down. After being promoted to major and reposted to the Middle East Command, Buck and Fernande were married in April 1944. He remained in Egypt after the war, taking a job with the newly formed Iranian Airways. In September 1950 he went to Tehran to pick up a spare engine and fly it to Jeddah. Improperly secured, it shifted on take-off and the plane went down in flames. Buck Palm, the teenage runaway who had made good, was dead at forty-one.

Mary Lindell, meanwhile, who always knew she was living on borrowed time, was arrested in Pau within two weeks of Buck's departure. Shot twice in the head as she tried to escape, she was operated on by a Luftwaffe surgeon and miraculously saved. Upon recovery, she spent eight months in solitary, and after that was moved to Ravensbrück. As a trained nurse, she was assigned to the infirmary, which explains, in part, how she survived. The Marie-Claire line continued for a while longer when Pauline stepped in to take it over. She also had her own line called Marie Odile and, with so many people passing through, it was only a matter of time before she too was betrayed. Sent to Ravensbrück, she came into contact with Mary once again. But unlike her rival, she didn't survive. As for George Tsoucas, Pauline's reputed lover, after two more false starts he finally crossed into Spain in early March with a party of thirty-four Poles.

Buck Palm and George Tsoucas had received the one gift that every successful escaper needs but can never plan for: luck. Richard Carr, who had done everything they did, was now back in a POW camp in Germany. He had the misfortune of running straight into a policeman while walking at night along the Marne canal. Palm and Tsoucas, on the other hand, stopped at a random farm outside Lunéville and were directed to a key link in the Marie-Claire escape line. If they'd stopped at the next farm, they might have found a German collaborator and been turned in. It certainly would never have occurred to them to contact the chief of police. Yet, they were lucky, and when they needed assistance, it came their way. If Alastair was ever going to escape successfully, he'd need a healthy dose of the same.

Encouraged by the news that Palm and Tsoucas had made it to Paris, Alastair considered his next move: 'I needed a new line of escape. I had fairly exploited the East and South and now my thoughts were turning to France and to the West. The ease of open travel in Germany was illuminating. Posing as a foreign worker was too simple not to be exploited.'

This time he would go out as an Italian. He spoke the language well and was able to obtain good forged documents claiming he was a foreign worker. He also found an excellent set of civilian clothes belonging to an Italian diplomat, which he exchanged for the exorbitant price of three American Red

Cross parcels. Through his French contacts, he collected several addresses in Munich where reliable railway workers could be found. While there were a number of options, he still felt the best escape route was the one he had used to get out of Moosburg the first time. Then one of the Americans he was living with suggested that he hide in a truckload of blankets they were taking to the train station the next day. It didn't take him long to say yes and get ready.

On the first trip he dressed as an American corporal, pretending to be part of the work detail. They planned to make several runs and he wanted to find the best place to slip away. After an American cut his hand on one of the bales, the German in charge insisted on returning to the camp to have it checked. When they finally began to reload the truck again, Alastair changed outfits, putting on his civilian clothes and on top of that a French uniform, overcoat and puttees. Then he hid in between the blankets and the trailer wall. Another American rode in front to take his place. His preparation was as methodical as always:

The road to the station yard was busy with French workers and Germans. Everything depended on a quick change at the utmost speed. I had spent a couple of hours the night before planning the exact order of disrobing. I would bend down, remove my puttees and thrust them into the pockets of my greatcoat, remove my shoes, pull off my breeches, put on my shoes, remove the greatcoat, roll the garments together, put on my felt hat and be a civilian.

He had selected an empty carriage, half-hidden behind a shed, for his changing room. As the truck neared the spot, he stepped onto the back running board. One of the Americans sitting in front leaned forward to light a cigarette, blocking the rear-view mirror. The road curved around. Alastair dropped off. He walked along behind a cart pulled by a horse, another French soldier in an oversized coat. No one looked back, and no one noticed as he entered the carriage. Three minutes later a well-dressed civilian emerged on his way to Moosburg.

Alastair knew his disguise was good when he passed the camp interpreter heading in the opposite direction. Despite having spoken to one another several times, the man simply glanced at him and continued walking. Once in Moosburg, he waited outside a restaurant until a customer went in and left his bike. Confident that they wouldn't be back for a while, he discreetly got on and pedalled away. By evening he was in Munich, looking for the address he'd been given for Arbeitskommando 2903, the French labour unit assigned to the marshalling yards. Unfortunately, they were no longer there. He then headed for the Café Rouge. He didn't find Phillipot but he did meet two other Frenchmen who invited him back to their place to stay.

Travelling around Munich in civilian clothes proved remarkably easy. With the aid of excellent street maps posted throughout the city, Alastair made a tour noting recent bomb damage as well as any relevant fortifications and camouflage. His new hosts also recommended several good cafes where French waitresses could be depended upon for help. Cinemas too were cheap and safe and good places to spend the afternoon or evening. If he was lucky, there might be a feature about mountain climbing, a favourite Nazi genre. Even the worst film helped him practise his German.

Of course, he hadn't intended to stay in Munich as long as he did. His initial plan was to travel to France locked inside a postal car, a twenty-hour journey which several escapers had already made. He soon discovered that this route was now closed. Two prisoners using it had been captured and had given up the names of those who helped them. Many French were killed or imprisoned and their network shut down. Alastair would have to wait and find another way.

He moved to a different location on Nymphenberger Strasse, where a new contact arranged a meeting with a French railway worker. It was on the same platform that Buck Palm and George Tsoucas had left from just weeks before. As they stood on the steps of a carriage for privacy, the German overseer walked by and heard them. He jumped up and grabbed Alastair just as the train began to move. Alastair tried to push him out but the German, whose grip was strong, leaned back and pulled him towards him. Then the train jerked again and the German lost his balance. It quickly turned into a tug of war as Alastair did all he could, punching and kicking, to drive the German off the steps. Then the inevitable happened and they both tumbled down onto the ground. As they separated, Alastair rolled away from the train, but the German fell the other way and was crushed beneath the wheels.

Alastair was dazed as he stood up, suffering no doubt from a slight concussion. He walked back into the station and, as he approached the gate, an elderly woman tripped in front of him, scattering a large bag of food. He instinctively bent down to help her, not noticing that the police were already on the way. She was a black marketeer they had been on the lookout for. 'And who are you?' they asked Alastair as he started to walk away. 'An Italian foreign worker? Papers, please.' The officer, who seemed predisposed to doubt, glanced at the papers quickly before ordering Alastair to follow him. Alastair knew where they were headed and as soon as the opportunity arose, shoved the policeman down a steep embankment and ran. The officer pulled out his gun and started to shout, at which point two soldiers who were right in his path grabbed Alastair and held him down. The policeman rushed up and took aim. Only the soldiers stopped him from shooting. As for the old lady, she seems to have escaped in all the confusion.

Alastair continued to maintain that he was just an innocent Italian worker. They didn't believe him, and insisted he come to the police station for further questioning. Once there, they left him alone while they went to make some calls. Within seconds he was out of the door and up the street. Unfortunately, they quickly saw that he was gone and were right behind him in pursuit. Once again, some soldiers stopped him, though this time the police arrived with truncheons and started to beat him. Finally he screamed: 'I'm a British officer! I'm a British officer!' And like some magic incantation used to break a spell, they dropped their clubs and obediently saluted.

Eventually, the Gestapo was called and Alastair was trundled off between two leather-clad thugs in the back of a Mercedes. No one said a word, which was fine with him as he wanted to rehearse the story he'd tell at his interrogation. He knew that the Germans would try to discover the names of anyone who had helped him during his escape. He was especially anxious to protect the French railway workers who were just re-establishing their underground network after their recent betrayal. Since the authorities at Moosburg would have no idea when he left, he would insist that he had just arrived in Munich and had had no time to make contact with anyone. The Gestapo seemed to buy it, and after he had been searched, photographed and fingerprinted, took him to a military prison.

There the process started all over again, thorough strip search and interrogation, conducted completely in German. In the middle of the night he was dragged from his cell and thrown into the back of a car. After a half-hour drive to the outskirts of Munich, he was placed against a wall with two machine guns pointed at him. He stood there for several minutes waiting for them to fire and then, without a word, was shoved in the car again and taken back to prison. Was this silly game really meant to soften him up? He couldn't tell, but was immediately interrogated upon his return.

In the morning he was taken to the office of an SS major to be interrogated yet again. Same questions, same threats, same traps, only this time the unctuous inquisitor held out a big carrot, surprising Alastair with an offer to broadcast to England over German radio. It would be a great benefit to his fellow prisoners and would also earn him special privileges. Of course, everything would be prerecorded so there would be no opportunity to pass along any secret messages. Or perhaps Alastair would like to join the Freikorps, a British unit in the German army recruited to fight the Russians? Alastair felt nauseous: 'The German's whole attitude and manner were abominable.'

Whether they believed his story or not, Alastair was returned to Moosburg, where he was immediately thrown into solitary. Would they actually be foolish enough to let him escape from the camp a third time? He spent the next week contemplating how he would get out as well as all the contingencies once he did. But he wasn't let back into the main camp and, when the time came for his release, was handed over to the Gestapo once again. The weather was as grim as their company – a cold white sky that promised snow. It had been over three months since he had left Gavi and it would soon be Christmas. As he squeezed into the car between the two agents, he felt the bulge of their holsters press against him. For a moment he wondered if they might really shoot him this time. One thing was certain, there would be no escape on this ride.

# 8

# Stirling's Folly

Solitary again, in a seven-by-fourteen-foot whitewashed room with a concrete floor and no heat. Just a bed and a small window well beyond reach and painted over. No toilet, no books, no writing materials, no tobacco, no wash kit, only the clothes on his back and a blanket and pillow. Guards came to take him to the bathroom; beyond that, he never left his cell. There was no exercise and just a bowl of soup with some potatoes and a slice of bread once a day. Sometimes a British sergeant brought it, lingering behind to ask Alastair about where he'd been and if there was anyone he wanted to get a message to. Alastair guessed that the man was a member of the new Freikorps he'd been invited to join after his arrest in Munich, and even if he wasn't, he had stooge written all over him.

After eight days he was woken up in the middle of the night and dragged out for interrogation. He was surprised by the questions, mostly about weaponry and ordnance, followed by a detailed discussion of the finer points of Scottish law. Was he really who he claimed to be, an officer in the Royal Artillery who had been a lawyer in Edinburgh before the war? Establishing the identity of prisoners who were caught in civilian clothes and without papers was the stated purpose of the Luckenwalde

Vernehmungsstelle, a special interrogation centre created by the Germans about thirty miles south of Berlin. Located in a separate compound within Stalag IIIA, a camp similar in size and composition to Moosburg, those brought there were suspected of much more than simply discarding their uniforms in order to effect a successful escape. These were prisoners who the Germans believed were either commandos or special agents, or, as in the case of Alastair, had had contact with the underground and even engaged in espionage.

Two nights later the interrogation was repeated, only this time Alastair was drugged with a crude truth serum that left him groggy and unable to concentrate. Back in his cell, night and day began to merge into one. Lights were left on as guards barked senseless commands about not sitting down or whistling, all calculated to create a sense of vulnerability and lack of control. Some prisoners were forced to march for hours in the snow or had all their clothes save their underwear taken away from them. Then there were the threats of beatings and the phoney firing squads which Alastair had already been subjected to.

Most of this was orchestrated by a walking parody of the brutal, sadistic Nazi. Only he was real, behind the imaginary persona he'd created as 'Captain Williams', an American officer who spoke a coarse, uneducated English. While he had lived in the United States for many years, 'Captain Williams' was actually Adolf Schaper, a lowly sergeant from Bremen who had served in Russia during the First World War. Now in his mid-forties, he was the chief interrogator at Luckenwalde. A thickset man, over six feet tall with thinning blond hair and wire-rimmed glasses that pressed against the sides of an unusually flabby face, Schaper could be extremely intimidating.

Almost everyone he questioned described him as 'a shouting, bullying, ranting type of German, constantly making threats'. When Alastair finally met him, he was no different.

Schaper, or Captain Williams as he presented himself, wore his own version of an American uniform, although it was hard for Alastair to see past the bank of bright lights that was shining in his eyes. Unlike the previous sessions, conducted by another interrogator, there were no questions about artillery or the legal profession. After a calculated pause in which he made an almost comical display of cracking his knuckles, Schaper slammed his hand on the table, screaming, 'We know everything about you, Lieutenant Cram. We know that you have been engaged in espionage and are a member of the underground. So no fairy tales, please, or you will be shot as a spy.' Alastair, who had gone through a similar grilling after his last escape from Moosburg, insisted that he hadn't received any help, much less met anyone who was a member of the resistance. He had simply walked to Munich, where he was immediately arrested upon entering the train station.

'And what about Brück?' yelled Schaper. 'Who helped you in Austria?'

Alastair feigned complete surprise at every accusation, maintaining that he had always acted alone and never even conversed with any of the local population. This only inflamed Schaper more, and while Alastair had initially watched his cartoonish tantrums with detached bemusement, he was now concerned that Schaper, who had turned bright red, might actually have a seizure and collapse. Instead, he pounded the table, shrieking that if Alastair didn't start cooperating and providing names, there would be no alternative to having him shot. But Alastair never wavered from his story, forcing Schaper to eventually throw up his hands in disgust. He did so with a stern warning that if Alastair was ever caught making another escape, it would be his last. He was now 'a marked man'.

It seems surprising that at this point he wasn't sent to Colditz, the Germans' special camp for serial escapers and other enemies of the Reich. He'd certainly passed the entrance exam, though maybe the Germans didn't give credit for classes taken in Italy. Of course, Alastair wasn't trying to get in and was much happier being sent to a camp like Moosburg from which it was relatively easy to escape. Instead, he was put on a train for Czechoslovakia or what once had been. Following the Munich Agreement in September 1938, when Hitler took his first bite out of Europe, the country was quickly dismembered. The Sudetenland, with its large German-speaking population along its borders, was the first to be annexed. Then Slovakia was encouraged to secede and become an Axis ally. Even Poland and Hungary couldn't resist and cut off generous slices for themselves. On 15 March 1939 the Germans occupied what remained, declaring it the Protectorate of Bohemia and Moravia. Czechoslovakia, which had just turned twenty, had disappeared.

Of all the Sudetenland communities, none had a higher percentage of Germans than Mährisch Trübau, an attractive market town built around an enormous stone square with a towering plague column at its centre. Known as Moravská Třebová in Czech, the concentration of artists and scholars was so great during the Renaissance that it earned the epithet 'Moravian Athens'. Now, as part of the new geography, the town was located in Germany, around seven miles inside the redrawn border. It was also the home of Oflag VIIIF, a camp dating back to the First World War when it was built to house displaced persons and, following that, refugees from the Russian Revolution. In 1935 it was turned into a military academy, one of several initiatives the Czech government took in the region in response to Germany's increasingly aggressive rhetoric. Once in German hands, it was converted into a POW camp, first for the French and then for the new wave of British and Commonwealth prisoners pouring in from Italy.

When Alastair arrived in Mährisch Trübau in late December, the ground was covered in snow and the temperatures so cold that the prisoners dubbed it 'Little Siberia'. But the camp had something that almost no other had: central heating. In fact, the most common term used to describe it was 'luxurious'. Most prisoners were housed in the modern four-storey building constructed as a residence along with classrooms for the students of the short-lived military academy. Its new occupants quickly nicknamed it the Biscuit Factory. No one was sure exactly why, although a young officer named Alan Hurst-Brown, who had just celebrated his twenty-third birthday, suggested it was because 'everything came out of there; that's where maps and other things were produced. There was a newsletter produced there and the Red Cross parcels, which contained biscuits, came out of there as well. So in that sense it was like a factory.'

For Robert Simmons, one of several army chaplains, the building conjured up an even more dramatic image: 'This huge 4-storied building, originally a Czech Military Academy resembles nothing so much as a huge liner in dock. At night when the light is on, the four banks of windows create the illusion of a ship's decks. From the point of view of a billet this is a luxury camp.'

Located on a gentle slope above the Biscuit Factory was a

double row of two-storey bungalows where the senior officers lived. Surrounded by trees and shrubs, these pleasant cottages were the former residences of the college staff and looked more like a country lane than a prison camp. There was also a hospital, a chapel, a library, a theatre, a cookhouse, two playing fields, a gym and a swimming pool that doubled as an ice-rink. The largest building after the main barracks, however, was an impressive, multiroom schoolhouse erected in the 1920s for use by the refugee community. Now it was the centre of what quickly became an informal university with courses, lectures and study groups on every conceivable subject. Bill Murray, another well-known Scottish mountaineer who was also at Mährisch Trübau, described it as a vibrant campus atmosphere:

> Among our number were several who held chairs at British and Commonwealth universities, and many lecturers. Between them, they managed to organize a curriculum of higher education embracing a great range of subjects: mathematics, engineering, physics, chemistry, biology, anatomy, medicine, psychology, history, literature in all its branches, music, philosophy, theology, comparative religion, and the languages of Europe and Asia, including a score of Indian dialects. Correspondence with universities in the UK was quickly established, so that several subjects could be studied to the standards of first professional examinations. This work had every encouragement from our German hosts. They allowed every facility in vain hope of turning our thoughts from escape.

In Murray's case, there was little need for the Germans to dissuade him from escaping. Like the great majority of prisoners, he simply settled into the routine of camp life, preferring 'the course of self improvement' to the unknown dangers of the world beyond the wire. Captured near El Alamein in June 1942, he spent more than a year in Chieti completing a book about his pre-war climbing experiences. The fact that it was written entirely on toilet paper and hidden inside his tunic led the Germans to believe that it was a coded message intended for either British intelligence or the Czech underground. As a result, it was confiscated upon his arrival at Mährisch Trübau. While initially devastated, Murray eventually decided that they had done him a favour and sat down to write a much-improved version. Published in 1947, *Mountaineering in Scotland* remains a revered classic and is credited with inspiring a whole new generation of climbers.

For Murray, being a POW was as liberating as it was confining. 'For the first time in my life,' he wrote, 'I had the leisure to think, to be still.' The irony that prison could offer a type of monastic freedom, unburdened from the demands of everyday existence, was one that a number of people appreciated. In Murray's case, this inner journey toward self-awareness was supported by a group with whom he practised meditation. He also established a mountaineering club, with the requirement that every member give at least one lecture about a climb they had made. Alastair, who had met Murray during an especially difficult ascent at Glen Coe in 1938, was one of the first to join. Although their prisoner-of-war experiences could not have been more different, Murray respected Alastair's sense of duty, extolling 'the extraordinary character of the man' it revealed. In a letter to his sister back in Scotland, he confided: 'Cram is here and quite the most remarkable man I have met in this war.'

In addition to the mountain club, Alastair began learning Czech. Despite the Gestapo's threats, he was anxious to escape again, especially since he was now surrounded by potential allies. He also discovered many old friends from Gavi who, while a minority in the camp, had no intention of letting themselves be seduced by its country club atmosphere. Their focus remained on escape just as it had been in Italy. Like Alastair, a number had arrived after lengthy detours. Richard Carr, following his arrest near Strasbourg, escaped once again from the train taking him to Mährisch Trübau. With freezing temperatures and inadequate clothing and papers, it wasn't long before he was picked up. Ronnie Herbert was also there after having walked over 600 miles only to be recaptured a stone's throw from the Allied lines. Peter Griffiths and Bob Parrott got even further. Part of the group that jumped from Stump Gibbon's car on the way north, each made it to Yugoslavia, where they joined the partisans. Unfortunately, both were recaptured after spending time fighting alongside them. Waddy Wadeson, that venerable quatrogenerian, along with Ian Howie and a charming captain from the Bengal Lancers named 'Boggie' Howson, had even less luck. They escaped from the same car as Alastair although not until the train reached Innsbruck, where it stopped for the night. Climbing out through the ventilator grilles, they disappeared in heavy rain only to be nabbed two days later while still in Austria.

Then, in the first week of January, Jack Pringle and David Stirling arrived. Everything was about to change. Like Wadeson, they had also escaped from the rail yards at Innsbruck. Crossing the Inn River, they climbed to just below the tree line and headed west for Switzerland. It was cold and wet and by the third day when they were stopped walking across a wooden bridge they almost welcomed the comfort of a warm jail. From there they were taken to Markt Pongau, a sprawling camp for Russian prisoners just south of Salzburg. They didn't stay long. When a heavy mist rolled in, they threw blankets on top of the wire and, standing on another prisoner's shoulders, scrambled over. Things got off to a bad start when Jack nearly drowned swimming across the Pongau River. Dogs soon picked up their scent and chased them high into the Alps. They had no maps, no papers, no provisions and no warm clothes. They also had no idea where they were, though they knew that if they headed east, they would eventually bump into Yugoslavia. Neither of them was very optimistic. 'We were on a sure loser,' said Jack, 'but we were free and on our own. That seemed worth while.'

The second night they came across an isolated farmhouse, where they stopped to ask for help. They claimed to be Italians on their way to join the German army. It was an unlikely story but the couple seemed to believe it and invited them in for a meal. After dinner, they sat by the fire and were so comfortable that they hardly noticed when the husband left to take care of some chores. Half an hour later he returned with four soldiers and Jack and David were on their way back to Markt Pongau once again. From there they were taken to Luckenwalde, the same interrogation centre that Alastair would soon visit. David was convinced they were about to be executed. As it turned out, they never even saw 'Captain Williams', and after several conversations with the suspect sergeants were on their way to another camp, this time in Bavaria.

Located between Nuremberg and Munich, Eichstätt was a relatively comfortable camp with many officers who had been prisoners since the fall of France in 1940. Rather than being broken and demoralized, they were remarkably defiant, engaging in constant acts of resistance. While Gavi had a certain amount of 'goon-baiting', the prisoner-of-war culture in Italy tended to be much more passive and compliant. At Eichstätt, and many other camps, German authority was undermined at every turn: officers weren't saluted, guards were mimicked and ridiculed, and roll calls became endless games of cat and mouse in which accurate counts became nearly impossible. Though some found such behaviour childish and undignified, it clearly appealed to David Stirling's subversive side, teaching him lessons he would soon use at Mährisch Trübau.

Even more instructive was the information he gleaned about escaping. Only six months earlier, Eichstätt had been the scene of one of the war's most successful mass escapes. Sixty-five prisoners had crawled out of a hundred-foot-long tunnel and disappeared undetected into the Bavarian countryside. Although none got away completely, it was a model of organization and discipline in which the entire camp focused its energy and skill on a single objective. Of equal interest was the brilliant escape which the leaders of the tunnel had executed in August 1942 in their previous camp. Known as the 'Warburg Wire Job', four teams used specially constructed ladders to scale the double set of fences surrounding the camp. Twenty-eight men got out in a matter of minutes, with three of them making it home. David was taking notes.

When Jack and David were moved to Mährisch Trübau with seventy other officers, Alastair was there to greet them. It was a warm reunion lasting well into the night. Each spoke of their various adventures since Bolzano, when Alastair had been carried off on a stretcher. Inevitably the conversation turned to escape and what the chances were of getting out of their new camp. Like Alastair, Jack immediately saw the many advantages of being surrounded by a friendly population. So did David, but he had other ideas. Over the next couple of weeks he hatched an ambitious plan in which the entire camp would be turned into one giant escape factory with every prisoner contributing to the final product: a mass breakout of 200 officers, the largest and most daring of the war.

Of course, David would be the CEO of this new factory and no escape activity would be undertaken without his approval. Although he knew it would be a tough sell, he was sure the benefits would far outweigh whatever the outcome might be. According to him, 'The place was in absolute chaos', and in desperate need of basic discipline. His goal was to get people back into the war again. He also knew that there would be no better way of raising morale than to have everyone working together towards a common end. His first stop was Colonel Waddilove, the SBO, whom David described as 'a delightful cove'. Captured on the Island of Kos only two months earlier, Waddilove welcomed the idea and quickly gave him the necessary approval. From there he visited every group in both the Biscuit Factory and the cottages to explain his plan. Using every bit of his legendary powers of persuasion, he succeeded in enlisting their support. From this point on, he would be 'the kingpin of all the escape rackets'.

It's not clear how many of the 1,581 prisoners at Mährisch Trübau actively participated in David's operation. Alastair puts the number at 400, an impressive figure given that 245 were Indian officers with very little if any engagement at all. Then there were others, and many of them, who simply wanted nothing to do with escape. In most camps, they comprised the overwhelming majority. David Walker, a key member of both the 'Warburg Wire Job' and Eichstätt tunnel, talked about this often rancorous divide:

> If you gave up escaping as an occupation, which I did for months at a time even in those earlier days, and you learned a language, or studied law, or economics, you switched totally to considering the escaper fraternity a nuisance, a disrupter of routine, a dangerous lot of maniacs who at their best caused interminable cold parades while the camp was being searched, at their worst could draw gunfire upon innocent people. One could, and did, switch one's mind from one point of view to the other overnight. In a camp of about three thousand prisoners the engrossed escapers might, at any one time, total perhaps a hundred.

David increased this number many times over, which was necessary if his plan was to succeed. Getting more than 10 per cent of the camp out would require forgers, tailors, carpenters, engineers, map makers, compass makers, tunnellers, dirt disposers, and lots and lots of security. It would also take excellent intelligence, which Jack, serving as David's second-in-command, oversaw. The recruits for this work, who included Alastair, were responsible for assembling as much information as possible about the physical conditions surrounding the camp and the adjoining countryside. They also established contact with the Czech underground and other sympathetic locals who could be counted on to help escapers or, in a worst case scenario, the camp, should the Germans decide to liquidate it.

In addition to intelligence, three other units were formed as well. The largest by far was the one charged with protecting escape activities. Stooges, as they were known, were strategically placed to give ample warning to anyone working on tunnels, documents or any other illicit behaviour. They also tracked the movements of every German who entered the camp. Internal security was the responsibility of a third group. Led by a future deputy director general of MI5, they ensured the overall secrecy of the operation, plugging any leaks where they might occur. As plans for the mass escape evolved, so did an increasingly vocal opposition. Containing this threat, along with several suspected traitors, became an important task. The final group was the news agency that David promised as a condition for the SBO's support. Based on BBC broadcasts received through a secret radio that David had built, the group posted daily summaries of the news.

By the beginning of February the organization was up and running. All the Germans saw, however, was a camp bustling with wholesome activity. The Art Club, which had just moved into its own studio, was conducting life drawing classes while Tommy Sampson, Scotland's King of Swing, was holding rehearsals for his new band. Auditions were also taking place for *Sweeney Todd* and *The School for Scandal*, both to premiere at the camp theatre. In the basement of the Biscuit Factory finishing touches were being applied to the Rum Pot, a night club featuring a powerful brew prepared by Ian Howie from raisins, plums, and sugar. Out on the ice, people were playing hockey, and in the gym, basketball, or simply doing calisthenics and running. And at the education building prisoners were constantly coming and going like students at any major university late for class. With so much movement, no one even noticed when Alastair walked past the two lookouts in front of Jack and David's room.

They had asked Alastair to drop by to discuss a mission they wanted him to take on. Would he be willing to exchange identities with one of the Other Ranks in order to explore the area outside the camp? In addition to creating valuable maps and timetables, they wanted him to contact locals and other foreign POWs who might be willing to assist the escapers. Alastair already knew from his experience at Moosburg what this would entail and that as an orderly he could join work parties that would give him access to Mährisch Trübau and the countryside beyond. It didn't take long for him to agree, at which point Jack and David asked if there was anyone he could recommend to join him. 'What about Leslie Hill? He speaks perfect German and pretty good Czech as well.'

Alastair had first met Hill on the boat from Benghazi when Skipper Palmer had tried to organize a mutiny. They had also been in Italy together, although until now Hill had shown no interest whatsoever in escaping. A studious-looking twenty-six-year-old with thick glasses and dark, wavy hair, his energy had been entirely devoted to his one great passion: language. This was little surprise, given his background. Born in Athens to a Greek mother who was raised in Germany and an English father with a family business in Istanbul, Hill grew up speaking a number of languages, including French, which was taught to him by his Russian nanny. At Cambridge, he gained a first in German and also became an avid rower. His holidays were spent in Berlin, a city he 'grew to love and feel more comfortable in than any in England'. While there, he stayed with his uncle, Adalbert Zuckschwerdt, a retired admiral and rabid Nazi.

Upon graduating from Cambridge in 1939, he returned to Greece where he coached a rowing club and worked for the British Council. It was meant to be a gap year before enrolling at either the Sorbonne or Heidelberg in order to complete a doctorate. That would only happen thirty-eight years later. When the Germans invaded Greece, he served as an army interpreter, although it wasn't until he reached Egypt that he was officially commissioned. Like Alastair, he joined the Royal Artillery and won an MC at Sidi Rezegh, where he was also captured. From there he followed a similar itinerary – Tarhuna, Castelvetrano, Capua, Padula, Moosburg, Mährisch Trübau. By the time he reached Oflag VIIIF, he had already learned five new languages, including Czech and Russian. He was also one of a handful of code-writers, using personal letters to pass along messages to the War Office. When asked if he would join Alastair as an orderly in order to gather information for the escape committee, Hill didn't hesitate. He had been ready to switch gears for some time and, besides, working with the Baron would be a pleasure.

Once their false identity cards were prepared, they moved in with the ORs and started going out on details. The sergeant major in charge was a gruff South African named Arhus who didn't like the arrangement one bit, which he made clear by assigning them difficult tasks inside the camp. When David got wind of this, he called Arhus in and gave him a dressing down. Cram and Hill, he told him, were only to be sent on work parties outside the camp, with the less supervision the better. They were soon driving a horse and cart filled with laundry to the next village and picking up turnips and potatoes at local farms. They also spent a good deal of time at the station helping with Red

Cross parcels and mail. None of it was very strenuous, but it all contributed to the bank of information they were compiling. It also helped Alastair improve his Czech, which at the end of two months was quite good. That's when the Gestapo started asking questions about him again. They were still convinced he was a saboteur and wanted the commandant to keep a special eye on him. Everyone agreed; it was time for Alastair to come in from the cold.

By now, the four tunnels David planned to use to get the 200 men out were well underway. Like the rest of the escape organization at Mährisch Trübau, these too were dominated by the Gavi brotherhood. In fact, of the four tunnels, three were directed by former inmates of the camp. One officer who was naturally involved was Waddy Wadeson, though few others of his rank and age were. Having a wife and child made him even more unusual among his fellow escapers. Most family men were happy to sit it out, but not Wadeson. It had been four years since he'd said goodbye to his son in Croatia. Now the boy was about to turn eight and Wadeson had hardly heard a word from him. A letter he wrote just before leaving Gavi expressed his frustration at being separated from the child at such a tender age:

*My Dear Tim. Haven't had a letter from you except the one more than six months ago. Still I live in hopes that you may be able to spare a little of your time to write me! How are you and how's the Kid? I get so few letters here that I'm always out of date. Do you go to a new school now and where is it? Is it a mixed school – boys and girls – and how old are they – do any of your friends go there and most important – do you like it? I wonder if you remember our last days together – all three of us in Zagreb? Someone gave you a train-guard's outfit and you directed the trains at the station where I left you both. After that I never heard any of the details of your trip to England. I wired to the hotel in Marseille but they wired back that you'd left and the next I knew was a week later – cable from the Kid in London. But those are old times – the new are coming – and soon I hope. At present I'm in solitary confinement – sounds worse than it is. Write me. Love*

*Roy*

Like the other tunnels, Wadeson's began from a building not far from the double wire that surrounded the camp. Unfortunately, the high water table combined with seepage from the melting snow completely flooded it. When the same thing happened to Bob Parrott's tunnel, they tried to exploit the loss by sending an anonymous letter to the Germans giving away their exact locations. The author claimed to be a devout – though clearly mad – Christian who wanted to prevent the loss of life that an escape would provoke. In an attempt to lower the Germans' guard, the letter also promised to inform them of any future attempts.

The ruse, if it worked at all, was soon undermined by the dramatic discovery of a third tunnel, directed by Herbert Buck. While he hadn't been in Gavi, Buck was a member of the SAS and a close associate of David's. He grew up in India and after reading German at Oxford was commissioned with the 1st Punjab Regiment. Upon arrival in North Africa he formed his own commando unit – the Special Interrogation Group or SIG. Composed mainly of German Jews trained in Palestine, the SIG used Afrika Korps uniforms and equipment to conduct daring raids far behind enemy lines. When captured during one of them, Buck managed to escape, leading nine others to freedom. The unit eventually became part of the SAS, with Buck's extraordinary exploits forming the basis of *Tobruk*, a 1967 film starring Rock Hudson. When he wasn't digging tunnels, he led a group which included Bill Murray in a spiritual practice called the Perennial Philosophy. The tunnel he oversaw at Mährisch Trübau was already beyond the wire when one of the guards crashed through it as he walked back and forth on patrol. By the time he landed, his head was barely visible above the hole.

This left just one tunnel, originating in a long, narrow building at the southern end of the camp. Used by a group of cobblers during the day, it was no more than ten yards from the wire and positioned in such a way that Jack Green, the talented young engineer in charge, could create an irrigation system to keep it from flooding. By erecting a false wall, he also created a hidden room in which dirt was stored and the actual tunnel entrance located. To enter it, Green designed a beautifully camouflaged passage that ran beneath the base of the wall. With three teams alternating shifts, it wasn't long before the tunnel had reached the wire. Lists of those who were to be given a place in the escape started to be assembled. Everyone was confident that this time they would make it. Then, as the tunnel neared its goal, the camp's security officer, Oberleutnant Haberhauer, arrived and marched straight to the building where a new team of diggers was just about to lift the trapdoor. Brushing them aside, Haberhauer directed his men to pound the floor with crowbars until they found the hollow spot and from there the tunnel. David, noticeably shaken, blamed the discovery on the leader of the group that had just taken over. The fact that the Germans seemed to know where the tunnel was as well as the exact timing of the change in shifts suggests that the blame may have lain elsewhere. Rumours of one or more camp informers were becoming difficult to ignore.

If David was upset, he certainly didn't let it derail his plans for a mass escape. After all, it was his relentless positive energy that continually seduced people into doing 'things against their better judgement'. The scheme he now proposed would certainly test this ability as even those who agreed to participate thought it both 'suicidal' and 'hare brained'. Reducing the number of escapers to 150, David devised a 'wire job' worthy of the SAS motto, 'Who Dares Wins'. He began by insisting that the Scottish prisoners needed a Highland dancing platform in order to practise their cultural traditions. The Germans, who thought the request quite reasonable, provided them with several of the large plywood containers in which Red Cross parcels were shipped. The mess hall where the platform was to be set up was so close to the twelve-foot-high perimeter fence that it could be reassembled into ten gangplanks that would stretch from the windows to the outer wire. Some of the gangplanks, which were to be twenty feet long, would be used as battering rams in order to open up more window space from which to launch them.

Although the lights would be shut down during the escape, the men scrambling across the ramps would still be in danger of being shot at from the machine gun towers on either side. To neutralize them, hoses had been smuggled in and would be used as water cannon to be trained on the sentries; at least that was the idea, which many people found implausible. There would

also be diversions, including groups dressed in German uniforms who would rush about barking commands in order to
create confusion among the guards. And at the opposite end of
the camp there would be an even larger, as yet to be determined
diversion. David orchestrated all this like a great theatre director, clearly amused that at its centre was a stage for the
performance of Highland dance.

The platform was to be employed much like the Wooden
Horse, where a vaulting apparatus had successfully concealed
the activities of the tunnellers inside. David conceived his plan
in similar ways, describing how the escapers would suddenly
emerge from below, instantly turning the platform into ten separate assault units. During the preparation, a half-dozen
Highland dancers would be on top doing jigs, reels, and flings,
particularly when any Germans were in the area. While certainly not its intention, this all appears to have provided a great
deal of entertainment, especially when the 6'5" David got up to
instruct his pupils on the finer points of a difficult step.

By mid-March, Jack's intelligence network began to pick
up rumours about important developments within the Czech
resistance. This led David to start rethinking the goals of the
escape; but not before Jack had come into contact with a South
African medical officer named Gerald van Zouco, or that's who
he claimed to be. Fluent in half a dozen languages, van Zouco
quickly made himself indispensable at the camp hospital, where
he was said to be 'in the confidence of the Germans'. In fact, he
seemed to roam about at will and was called upon whenever a
doctor was needed outside the camp. This included frequent
trips to the neighbouring town of Zwittau, where more seriously
ill patients were taken for treatment. It was clear that his contacts

and freedom of movement might be an invaluable resource to the escape committee. When asked by Jack if he wanted to help, his response was almost too enthusiastic.

'Listen,' he said. 'I can get anything from these Germans – anything! Do you want something? I get it for you. Tell me what you and Stirling want – I get it . . . Tell Stirling I want to help, and I *can* help too, believe me!'

Alastair, on the other hand, was having none of it. He'd observed van Zouco in action and was convinced that he was either a con man or, even worse, an informer. He was also sure that he wasn't South African. Not only did he avoid any contact with his 'fellow countrymen', but there was the question of his German. Alastair was familiar with the way South Africans sounded when they spoke it, and van Zouco's was that of a native. As it turned out, his father was a Berlin Jew and his mother, who gave birth to him out of wedlock, a Christian from the Baltic. He eventually confessed to having escaped en route to a concentration camp, and from there joining the South African Medical Corps. As Alastair ultimately learned, the truth was somewhat different. For the time being, he 'felt an instinctive distrust for van Zouco'. 'He was a clever opportunist,' said Alastair, 'glib and convincing in "selling himself" wherever he believed personal profit lay.'

Jack and David understood Alastair's concerns, conceding that working with van Zouco was a definite risk. At the same time, they believed that he could be used without being trusted. He would be told nothing about their plans and kept in the dark regarding the details of the escape. What mattered was that he promised to take Jack on his next trip to Zwittau, where they hoped to make contact with the Czech resistance. Since his near-fatal swim across the Pongau River, Jack's heart had been weak. Not only had he been hospitalized at Eichstätt, he also had a serious case of pneumonia upon arriving at Mährisch Trübau. Now, with van Zouco's help, he was on his way to visit a medical review board for possible repatriation.

Once there, van Zouco took charge. He advised the doctors, directed the guards, flirted with the nurses and, when needed, handed out small bribes of coffee and chocolate. He also made sure that Jack received special accommodations with his own room. It helped that he was introduced as 'Major Count Pringle, one of the biggest landowners in England'. Jack even started to bow as he assumed his new title demanded. Arranging a meeting with someone from the underground was another matter. Van Zouco, who was something of a Lothario with his thin moustache and slick wavy hair, was sleeping with a nurse whose brother had contacts in the resistance. It took a pledge of marriage and undying love before she agreed to convince her brother that he should set up a meeting between Jack and one of the leaders. After much back and forth, he announced that someone from Prague would be waiting in the church the next day at 2.30 in the afternoon.

Jack hardly slept at all that night, worrying about the various levels of betrayal that might soon await him. He had no idea if anyone could be trusted – van Zouco, the girlfriend, her brother, or the mysterious visitor from Prague. Any of them could be laying a trap, but he had gone too far to turn back. Once inside the church, it was easy to spot the person he'd come to meet. Wearing a black leather coat with a camera hanging around his neck, Kopřiva, as he introduced himself, was a handsome blond in his mid-thirties. One might even have taken him for an architect out doing a survey of Moravian churches. 'I am from the Czech underground army,' he told Jack. 'I will be glad to tell you anything I can.' He then went on to describe the make-up of his army, their pro-British sentiments, a contingency plan to liberate the camp, the best places to hide and find support in the Protectorate and, most important of all, two addresses in Prague where escaped prisoners could go for help. This was precisely the information they'd been hoping to find.

That evening, a visibly shaken van Zouco brought some disturbing news: the Gestapo had just executed a number of escaped prisoners from Stalag Luft III, an air force camp located several hours away in Silesia. It was the first information to reach them about what became known as the Great Escape, in which seventy-six British and Commonwealth officers got away through a brilliantly constructed 334-foot-long tunnel. When it was reported to Hitler the next day, he flew into a rage, demanding that every recaptured prisoner be shot. Göring and Himmler, fearing that it would be difficult to explain and lead to British retaliation, asked Hitler to reconsider; at which point, the number to be killed was set at fifty.

The executions marked an important shift in German policy towards escaped prisoners. While they were unaware of it, the Gestapo had issued an order on 4 March, three weeks before the Great Escape, decreeing that all recaptured prisoners be taken to Mauthausen concentration camp to be killed. The High Command had issued a similar order a month earlier, making a special concession for British and Americans, who would be handed over to the Gestapo, but dealt with on a case-by-case basis. Only in late July did posters go up, warning, 'The escape from prison camps is no longer a sport!' and that POWs entering newly created 'death zones' would be shot. 'In plain English,' it concluded, 'Stay in the camp where you will be safe! Breaking out of it is now a damned dangerous act. The chances of preserving your life are almost nil!'

In early April 1944, when Jack heard the news about the murdered airmen from the Great Escape, none of the changes in German policy had been made public. At the same time, Jack must have shared van Zouco's disturbing story with David and other members of the escape committee. It's curious that not a single mention of these events and their obvious implications for David's plan is to be found in any of the journals, memoirs, or books written by those who were at Mährisch Trübau. Jack is the only one, and even his statement is followed by the single terse comment: 'With a guilty conscience such as I had, there was no peace of mind after this.'

If David, whose plan was far more dangerous than the Great Escape, had any hesitation about the new hazards his men would face, he kept it to himself. In fact, he was determined to move as quickly as possible. There was, however, a significant change in the overall objective. Based on the information gathered at Zwittau, the escapers wouldn't return to neutral or Allied territory; they would join the Czech underground army as military advisers. They couldn't bear arms according to the Geneva Convention but their presence might be enough to affect the future of the country after the war; at least, that was David's theory. He worried that, just as the British had handed Czechoslovakia over to the Nazis in 1938, they would now deliver it to the Communists. 'A good-will mission,' he suggested, could be a powerful catalyst for changing this outcome. As David explained it:

I decided that to have maximum effect during what seemed probably to be the closing year of the war we should think again about our actions after the escape . . . Certainly if our escapers were to stay with the Czechs it would establish a memorable degree of British solidarity with their cause . . . To me it seemed that 150 British officers making friends with the Czechs could do an enormous power of good. Given the knowledge we had, it is quite possible we could have saved Czechoslovakia from going over to the East. Britain paid scant attention to them before the war and they were ripe for an appeal by the Communists.

As for the actual role the escaped officers would play, David said with a wink:

I was not advocating taking up arms with the resistance group against the rules of the Geneva Conventions but I dare say it would have happened to some degree; I doubt if any soldier would have been able to deny himself another crack at the Germans.

For the plan to work, advance parties would have to make arrangements with the underground in order to receive the 150 escapers. Special routes and guides, along with safe houses and addresses, would all have to be established, and the information relayed back to the camp. Those selected to go out in what became known as the 'First Flight' were mainly German-speakers who were given additional training in Czech as well as strategies for dealing with interrogation should they be caught.

When an announcement was made in early March that a

group of air force officers was to be transferred to Stalag Luft III, arrangements were quickly made for three of David's men to exchange places with them. Once on the train, they planned to overpower the guards and escape through the window. Peter Griffiths, who already had experience with the resistance in Yugoslavia, jumped first with John Forsdick, another South African from Gavi, right behind. He was almost out when one of the guards got loose and struck him in the back with his rifle. The train then returned to where Griffiths had jumped, only to find him lying on the ground with a large piece of his skull missing. The Germans refused Forsdick's request for a doctor or even a pillow. Instead, they simply threw him on a stretcher, where he died soon after.

News of his death stunned the camp, the first casualty of what many considered a reckless plan. Plus, Griffiths was well liked. Just two weeks shy of his twenty-fourth birthday, Griffiths, like many, had come of age during the war. An insurance company clerk in Johannesburg when it broke out, he joined the Botha Regiment and made captain just two years later. Short and wiry with a big crop of sandy hair, Griffiths was as serious about escape as anyone in the camp. The train jump was his eighth attempt.

Despite the grumbling, which picked up considerably after Griffiths' death, David pushed ahead with plans for the escape. It was now set for early June, although they still hadn't verified the information that Jack had received in the church at Zwittau. What exactly was the underground army? And were they really on the verge of an uprising with a plan to liberate the camp? Alastair, who had his own sources from his time as an orderly, was sceptical. In fact, he thought it was part of a campaign of rumours started by the Russians to confuse German intelligence and force them to reallocate their resources. It was true that the Czechs hated the Nazis, but after six years of brutal repression they had become compliant, and their resistance organizations had either broken up or been infiltrated. Even Heydrich's assassination, organized by the government in exile in spring 1942, seemed to have the opposite effect from the one its planners intended. The historian Vojtech Mastny pointed this out in a book subtitled *The Failure of National Resistance*:

> Although brilliantly executed, the assassination of Heydrich was a political mistake. It decimated the Czech underground to an extent hardly paralleled elsewhere in Hitler's Europe. Still more important, the living memory of the Heydrichiáda, as the people dubbed the awesome weeks following the tyrant's death, was a powerful deterrent to a revival of active opposition. By his death, Heydrich fulfilled his primary ambition – the pacification of the Protectorate.

To unravel the truth behind all this, they decided to send Ian Howie out next. He was the logical choice since he had coordinated contact with the local workers. They trusted him, as did almost everyone. Tall, soft-spoken, and very smart, Howie evoked the image of a British Jimmy Stewart. At Gavi, he'd contorted himself like a yogi to hide inside a wood pile rather than go to Germany. Now he did the same inside a laundry cart, burying himself deep beneath the soiled bedding that was being taken to the village to be cleaned. He had studied the route for days and knew the exact number of minutes it took for the cart to reach its destination. Only this time it went a different way and when he finished counting and stood up, there was a shocked German soldier standing next to him. Howie never skipped a beat and within seconds was out of the cart, racing down the street. A long pursuit followed with more and more Germans joining in. He was finally cornered in a brickyard, though not before destroying his papers along the way.

This was David's low point: four tunnels found or destroyed, one escaper dead and now Howie serving thirty days in solitary. There was also the chorus of naysayers who, emboldened by the string of failures, began to cackle even louder. Wasn't this verging on a military operation and in violation of the Geneva Convention, some of them asked. And wasn't this putting everyone's life in danger and not simply the men who would be rushing over the wire with machine guns firing at them? Even Alastair, who remained loyal to David, began to question the legitimacy of putting so many people at risk. 'The plot,' he concluded, 'was quite indefensible.' And while he had once considered it, he turned down the invitation to escape with the 'First Flight':

> The whole scheme now seemed so phoney that I told Stirling that I was no longer prepared to go out on the 'First Flight' since I had twice, within the past 6 months, been accused by the Germans of espionage and was well known to the Munchen Kripo and had been repeatedly warned that the next time would be the last but that I would act as Col. Stirling's personal interpreter when the big escape took place.

It was clear to David and Jack that they desperately needed a success to restore confidence in the escape. They found it in a scheme suggested by a young lieutenant with the Durham Light Infantry named Humphrey Moon. Captured during the fall of France in 1940, Moon had passed through all of Germany's major *Oflags*, witnessing a number of escapes. His idea, as presented to David, was to take advantage of the Russian work parties that regularly came into the camp to clean and do odd jobs. Rather than use the main gate, they entered through a much smaller one on the other side of the playing fields. With no barrier or sentry checking papers, the guard accompanying them simply took out his own key and opened the gate. If a small group dressed up as Russian prisoners with a German escort, they could do the same. Of course, they would need a key to open the lock but Moon had already worked that out as well. Since arriving at Mährisch Trübau, he had become friends with the closest thing to a professional lock picker, or at least that's how Curly Laing presented himself. According to him, there was no lock he couldn't open. With Curly, who was completely bald, joining the party, they would have someone to open the gate.

David, who at this point was ready to try anything, liked the idea. Moon and Laing, he said, could be part of the escape and head anywhere they wanted, but the other four places would be filled by his men who would be going out on a special mission. One of them would be Leslie Hill, the eccentric linguist. He would be paired with Peter Joscelyne, who had studied at Heidelberg University and spoke excellent German. The two would travel south together to Brno, where Joscelyne would head for Slovakia and Hill for Prague, each to gather information on the condition of the underground. Major Wadeson would be the group's ranking officer. In addition to speaking fluent German,

Wadeson had spent years surveying the region as a mining engineer. His partner and the last member of the group was a thirty-
one-year-old liquor salesman named Tubby Mackenzie. That's
what his friends and family called him before the war. At Mährisch
Trübau, he was simply known as Hugh.

Six foot tall and solidly built, with a loopy smile and hair
carefully slicked back with Brilliantine, Mackenzie was an
immensely likeable man. Tirelessly upbeat with the extroverted
good cheer that his profession demanded, he seemed almost
immune to the many mood swings that years of imprisonment
typically induced. 'I am well and cheery,' he wrote home. 'No
getting me down . . . only wish one had unlimited space – my
letters must sound incredibly dull but I am full of life! Yours as
ever, love galore – Tubs.'

He was born in Calcutta, where his father was a doctor with the
Royal Army Medical Corps, though after a somewhat sordid
divorce the pair rarely saw each other. When war came and it was
time to sign up, the choice was obvious. It didn't matter that he'd
never lived in Scotland. The Seaforth Highlanders was the Mackenzie regiment and he was a direct descendant of its founder,
Kenneth Mackenzie. Commissioned and sent to France, he was
part of the last stand against Rommel at St Valéry. On the run in
search of a boat for four days after the surrender, he was finally
captured on 16 June 1940. From there he began the same odyssey
across Germany as Humphrey Moon – Laufen, Tittmoning, Warburg, Eichstätt and finally, three and a half years later, Mährisch
Trübau.

Much of his time, when not playing football, was spent
studying Hindustani, the language spoken by his family in
India. Like a good salesman, he also networked, planning for

his future when the war ended. After receiving a first class pass in his brewing exam, he wrote to his mother with even better news: 'I have made arrangements for a job also, after the war; the owner of the firm is here and asked me to consider working for him. It's drink but allied to the brewing trade and from what I know the job is a good one. So you see, dearest, I am not losing time.'

Hanging out with the brewing community at the Rum Pot may have also led to his involvement in the escape. Perhaps it was Ian Howie, a fixture at the club as well as part of David's inner circle, who brought Mackenzie in on the plan. While the connection isn't certain, it could explain how someone with so little experience was given such a demanding and important role. According to Alastair, 'Mackenzie had not been outside of a camp,' and when he did make an abortive attempt at Eichstätt, his close friend John Mansel responded with disbelief:

> I got the shock of my life this morning. I was told that Hugh Mackenzie had got out of the Camp yesterday morning with a chap called – I think – Smiley or some such name, anyway I don't know him. But Hugh I know well and he might have told me he was going to have a shot. But he kept it very much to himself. What a madman. In the washing, laundry truck I was told.

Now Mackenzie was on his way to Prague to make contact with the Czech resistance and prepare for the arrival of 150 men. Before going, he sat down and wrote a letter to his mother filled with optimism and hope for the future:

*Dearest Heart,*

*Still no news from you but one from Freddie, Vi and Babs, both dated from Jan. '44. Sorry to hear Babs is ill, do hope she is alright now – glad Roses has completely recovered . . . Roses spoke about a small place – what about Elmstead Woods, Chislehurst, or even Oxford. Do you remember the house at Oxford back from the road, opposite the pub, we had a drink at – What do you think, dearest? You know I can always help with the cost – And I have a good job for afterwards, no fooling – wonderful thought – something one can call one's own piece of country – to love and improve it – the soil at least repays one for the labour – the flowers it gives us are gay, alive for a short time – but in that time what happiness they emanate – War is beyond them. And, first of all, the best gifts in life to me were free – 'you', 'Babs', the sun, sky, trees, flowers. Well, my sweet, get all you can out of life, and let us look forward to the future. Yrs as ever, Tubs*

Preparations quickly got underway for the escape. Tailors were visited for fittings, forgers created identity cards and cover stories were established and memorized. Leslie Hill, for example, would travel as a Dutch technician transferred to Prague to work for the Germans. He was also given three addresses, one of them only to be used in an emergency. This was for the camp electrician who had been helping David and the escape committee all along. He went home to Prague every weekend and would be responsible for relaying the escapers' reports back to the camp. Wadeson and Mackenzie were also given his address along with those for the resistance that Jack had got in Zwittau.

And finally, everyone was given maps, money, food, ration cards and a compass.

After several rehearsals, they were ready to go. Meeting in a ground-floor room in the Biscuit Factory, they donned their civilian clothes and then on top of that dark green overcoats with 'SU' painted in white block letters on the back; all except 'Waddy' Wadeson, who put on a goon skin, as a German uniform was called. Shuffling along, caps pulled down over their eyes, they were indistinguishable from any of the Russian work details that came and went from the camp. Wadeson, who was dressed as a sergeant, was in the back with Curly Laing leading the group in front. Like an athlete in training for a major event, Laing had spent the better part of the week opening every lock he could find. Everyone knew not to stare or to call attention to them, especially when they reached the gate and Wadeson threw Laing the key. No one worried at first when he struggled to open it. After all, Laing was the best lock picker in the camp. But seconds turned into minutes and Wadeson knew that if he didn't act quickly, the whole operation would be in danger. 'OK,' he said, as Laing finally admitted defeat. 'Let's go. About face.'

It didn't take long for Moon, who had come up with the plan in the first place, to suggest an alternative. 'What if,' he asked, 'we simply walk through when the gate is open?' No, he wasn't being silly he assured them. When the guard was changed, they opened the gate to let them in. If they timed it right, they could arrive at that exact moment and nonchalantly go through in the opposite direction. Moon had already done the recce and confirmed that the Germans always opened it at 11 a.m. on the dot. Everyone agreed; it was simple enough to work.

Several trial runs were made to figure out the timing, after which they set the date for 20 April, Hitler's birthday and the one-year anniversary of the cistern tunnel. The preparation was almost identical to the first attempt. They met again in the same room, changing into their civilian outfits with their Russian overcoats on top. Only this time Leslie Hill wore the goon skin, as it would take a perfect German speaker like him to bluff their way through. A lookout stood at the door, ready to signal when to start. Hill removed his glasses, adjusted his hat and wiped the sweat from his forehead. 'OK, you're off,' said the officer watching the door, and out they marched.

It was a short distance to the gate, although in his excitement Hill started to speed up. 'Easy does it,' said Wadeson, who was walking beside him. Timing was everything and at 11 a.m. when the gate opened they were just where they should be, several strides away. 'Let us through,' ordered Hill, never slowing down for a second. 'I need to get these men back.' No one tried to stop them and no one asked any questions. They simply walked out of the gate and didn't stop until they were a quarter of a mile away in a grove of trees well above the camp. Watching from the top floor of the Biscuit Factory, David and Jack smiled for the first time in weeks.

By nightfall, Moon and Laing were back in custody. They had planned to travel by train to Stettin, where they hoped to stow away on a ship for Sweden. But they were confused by their map and after crossing into the Protectorate were arrested by a border patrol as they re-entered the Sudetenland. Several days later Peter Joscelyne was returned. He and Hill had walked to Blansko, where they made contact with the local underground in a small inn. They continued by train to Brno and, as arranged, split up at the station. Headed for an address north of Bratislava, Joscelyne was also confused by the border, which had been redrawn three days earlier. He was arrested trying to cross it, and after a brief interrogation by the Gestapo, escorted back to Mährisch Trübau.

Once in solitary, he began to converse with Humphrey Moon in the cell next to him. He talked about Argentina, his life with the gauchos, and his plan to return there after the war. Moon, who had been studying Spanish, was intrigued. By the time of their release, they had agreed to start a farm together near Rosario. When the war ended, Moon invited Joscelyne home to help convince his parents to invest in the project. He also introduced him to his sister Ursula, whom he fell in love with and married. They never went to Argentina, though they did eventually farm tobacco together in Rhodesia.

As for the others – Wadeson, Mackenzie and Hill – there was no news at all. If they had been recaptured, no one knew about it, nor had they received any of the reconnaissance reports they'd been sent out to gather. Then the electrician who was going to transmit them disappeared. They soon learned that he'd been arrested and executed. There were other mass arrests as well, as the Czech underground, long dormant, re-emerged with a new umbrella organization – the PRNV or National Revolutionary Preparatory Committee. In addition to worrying about an uprising, the Germans were increasingly convinced that the Czechs were hatching a plan to liberate the camp. Nothing seemed to terrify them more than the thought of prisoners taking up arms in support of the local resistance movement. More guards were brought in and new defences erected. Instead of simply keeping prisoners in, the camp was turned into a fortress to keep potential attackers out.

The German presence inside the camp was also beefed up. Haberhauer tripled his security staff. Spot searches became routine and new listening devices to detect tunnelling were employed. Several valuable caches were uncovered as relations turned increasingly volatile. Goon baiting, which until then had been individual and sporadic, became a form of systematic resistance. Whereas any movement of a German in the camp was formerly monitored at a distance, they were now taunted by groups of prisoners trailing them wherever they went. Sometimes they carried banners with slogans like 'Down with the Snoopers.' One prisoner, who lacked any musical ability, liked to follow close behind with a tuba, which he regularly blasted with predictable results. Robert Simmons, who confessed some sympathy for the hapless guards, noted yet another form of subtle torture designed to demoralize them:

A list of bogus but provocative lectures are put up; 'The Punishment of War Criminals', 'The Division of Europe after the War', 'The Duties of Armies of Occupation' etc. And now a huge War Map of Europe goes up. In striking colours and with arrowheads it shows the advance and retreat of the German armies since 1939, and around the sides are appropriate quotes from Hitler.

The Commandant, a vain little man who seemed to spend a good part of every day in front of a mirror, was clearly losing control, and knew it. Many thought he was worried about being relieved and sent to the Russian front. He started shouting at prisoners with little provocation and demanded that Colonel Waddilove put an end to all the goon baiting at once. But it didn't stop and his growing hysteria only made him more vulnerable. Hoping to curb any illicit activities, he announced that in addition to the morning and evening roll calls, there would be new random ones occurring at all times of the day. The men promised to ignore them and refuse to appear. When the bugle blew signalling the first one, there was no response at all. Nor was there any when it sounded again. Everyone just went on with what they were doing.

The Commandant, who had already started to scream, called out the guard, ordering them to use any means necessary to assemble the prisoners. Several hours of cat and mouse ensued with officers being chased out of the front door only to walk around and re-enter the back. When at last they were herded into the building that served as the gym, the Commandant stepped onto a little box and began to speak. Every word was greeted with mock applause and cheers, until finally, he pulled out his revolver and, waving it about, yelled: 'The next person who moves will be shot!' This was the signal for David Stirling to walk over to the window and, climbing out, stroll past the stunned guards and return to his room. It was the last snap roll call they held.

Tensions were reaching a dangerous level. Even among the prisoners there was growing dissension. Many who had been opposed to David's plan from the start were now concerned that the goon baiting would erupt in violence. Alastair was also convinced that by now the Germans knew that a mass breakout was imminent. 'The scheme was too grandiose to keep secret,' he said, 'and it seemed that either careless talk or a "stooge" had "blown" the plot'. When the Gestapo started making regular visits to the Commandant's office, everyone knew that something was about to happen. That's also when van Zouco told David and Jack that Haberhauer knew they were at the centre of whatever was going on.

Then, with the escape only ten days away, the Germans announced that the entire camp was about to be moved. The Sudetenland was simply too exposed for 1,500 Allied officers, especially with an underground army threatening to liberate them. Even worse was the prospect of another mass breakout just weeks after the Great Escape. They were to be taken in stages to a former Luftwaffe barracks in Brunswick, hundreds of miles away in northern Germany. The buildings too would be stripped bare, with not a stick of furniture or anything else left behind. While no one mentioned bringing the Highland Dancing platform, there was a huge sigh of relief among those who had agreed to race across it. 'Saved by the gong!' cried Alan Hurst-Brown, summing up many participants' feelings.

Alastair was also relieved, as he predicted that after the escapers' initial casualties, 'a holocaust would have followed in which nearly a 100% of the remainder would have perished'. Somewhat more surprising was David's own assessment, in which he conceded that it was 'all highly improbable in retrospect'. Nevertheless, he added, 'there had to be a focal point until a better idea was formulated'. The problem now was how to contact Wadeson and Mackenzie, who were still in Prague making arrangements for the escape. They needed to be told that the camp had been moved and that anyone who had signed on to help was relieved of their obligation. If they could also find Hill, who was on his own, so much the better.

David decided that he and Jack would go themselves and, using the same strategy they had at Gavi, hide until everyone in the camp had left. Only this time, there wouldn't be fifty-eight others hidden away as well. It would be just the two of them secured inside the cavernous space created under Colonel Waddilove's room. At the same time, they knew that they had become the highest-profile prisoners in the camp and that it would be hard for Haberhauer to leave without them. As a precaution – even before the move began – they abandoned their cottage and relocated deep inside the bowels of the Biscuit Factory. While it was hard for the 6'5" David to conceal his identity, Jack took on various disguises in order to move about the camp. He shaved his signature moustache, wore thick glasses, reparted and slicked down his hair and, in the best thespian tradition, transformed his speech and gait. Not even his close friends recognized him. He also made arrangements for at least four people to use his name when checking identities on leaving the camp. Others were making it as difficult as possible for the Germans in different ways. One group raided the records office, destroying or stealing a number of identity cards. The SBO created even more confusion when he instructed everyone to give false names as they were processed. The big breakout may have been aborted, but resistance would continue until the very end.

Haberhauer meanwhile was sure there was still an underground treasure he hadn't discovered. Perhaps an informer directed him to it or his seismic equipment registered activity in the area. For whatever reason, he had homed in on the SBO's cottage and, with the help of four specialists, conducted a search as intense as any archaeological dig. Finally, on the third day of the move, they found the underground room with its enormous reserves of food and equipment. It was a devastating loss, though fortunately a second, back-up hide had been constructed behind a false wall in one of the building attics. Then, just before they were going to use it, David emerged from hiding, only to walk straight into Haberhauer and his men. He tried to run, but it was no use. Within twenty-four hours, he was on a train to Brunswick.

With David gone, Jack immediately thought of turning to Alastair, his old escaping partner, to see if he would join him in the hide. Waddilove, however, wanted Jack at the new camp and refused to let him to stay. So he asked Alastair if he would go to Prague on his own. 'I knew his form so well,' wrote Jack. 'And I had complete confidence that he would get to Prague if anyone could.' It was a death warrant, of course, but Alastair, despite his misgivings about David's plan, agreed to go. Wadeson and Mackenzie had to be found and he was the only one who could do it. And then there was Hill, who, recalling Alastair's incredible sense of duty, said simply, 'He was a very brave man.'

By the beginning of May the last prisoners were marched out of the camp and put on a train to the newly christened Oflag 79 in Brunswick. Alastair, together with a tank captain named Jim Gaze, was already sealed in the attic. It was Gaze who had built the hide and, since Jack and David weren't using it, he was given the opportunity. It was a comfortable space with cots and lanterns and enough food and water to last for two weeks. Gaze, whom Alastair barely knew, was a good companion. Filled with lively stories told in a thick Yorkshire accent punctuated with laughter, he helped the time go by quickly. On the evening of the third day, they decided that it was safe to venture out. The camp was pitch black and, as far as they could tell, completely abandoned. They were still cautious as they crawled to the fence and cut their way through three sets of wire. By eleven they were in the hills walking through a light drizzle that soon turned into heavy rain.

For three days they walked south, mainly through birch and poplar forests. The rain never let up and by the time they crossed into the Protectorate, Gaze was shaking with fever. Alastair knew he couldn't go on and finally sought help in the small village of Sulíkov. A hilltop community set on a long slope with an attractive onion-domed church rising above its centre, Sulíkov was self-contained and quiet; the perfect place to hide. There was only a handful of extended families, each with its own farmhouse to which a number of smaller buildings were attached for crops and animals. Most had fruit trees in front and on the side large smokehouses with firewood stacked up the length of the property.

Only the dogs were out when Alastair and Gaze arrived at dusk and selected one of the smaller homes set back from the road. An older couple answered and, after hearing they were escaped British officers, invited them in. A young boy was sent to fetch the local priest, and it wasn't until he arrived that the Hruškas – their hosts – began to breathe again. They stayed four days and in the end were begged not to leave. Gaze, who had recovered by then, agreed to meet Alastair in Sulíkov in two weeks. In case he couldn't come, Alastair would send word through the priest where to find him in Prague. In the mean-time Gaze would discover what he could about the underground along the Bohemia–Moravia border. As for Alastair, he walked another two days before boarding a train for Prague.

He timed his arrival, as best he could, for the weekly rendez-vous that had been prearranged with Wadeson and Mackenzie on the steps of the National Museum. It was a short walk from the station, and with several hours to kill he took a tour of the city. Signs of the Nazi occupation were everywhere with banners, posters, flags and, of course, lots of troops, many of them SS and Gestapo. Even worse was the fear he felt in nearly everyone he passed. Hunched over, faces down, with no eye contact whatsoever, it was the body language of years of oppression. By 5 p.m., he was ready to get back to the museum, where he was disappointed not to find either Wadeson or Mackenzie. After waiting more than an hour, he decided to try the addresses that Kopřiva had given Jack in the church at Zwittau. Perhaps they would know what happened to the two escapers.

He tried to find a train to take him to the first address, yet no one seemed to know where it was. Finally someone confirmed that neither the street nor the neighbourhood even existed. It was the same with the second location. Was Kopřiva a double agent? And had Wadeson and Mackenzie been set up? Alastair began to suspect the worst. That night he slept outside, just as he had in Vienna. He spent the next day walking and then went back to the museum once again in the hope they might appear. He was about to give up when a middle-aged couple who had been observing him approached and started to speak. 'You look lost,' said the man in Czech. 'Is there some way we can help you?'

'No,' answered Alastair curtly. 'I'm waiting for a friend.'

'Your Czech is quite good,' he said, clearly surprised. 'But your accent is very English. Is that where you're from?'

It was pointless denying who he was and, besides, these people seemed quite genuine and sincere. As it turned out, they were also Communists with ties to the underground. Eventually they invited him home and, after sharing an excellent meal, showed him to his room. He was out in seconds, exhausted from days of walking and sleeping rough. Then, in the middle of the night, he was suddenly awakened by the sound of people screaming and banging on the door. The Gestapo had come to arrest the couple. In an instant he was under the bed, pulling whatever he could find in front of him. The Germans, who only came for the husband and wife, never suspected that anyone else might be in the house, and after a cursory look round, left.

Alastair couldn't go back to sleep after the raid and instead spent the rest of the night weighing his options. There was no reason to remain in Prague any longer. Wadeson and Mackenzie had disappeared, the contacts he was given didn't exist and the one couple he had met with connections to the resistance had been arrested and put in prison. No, he would return to Sulíkov, and whether he would 'spread Pro-British propaganda', as his instructions indicated, or escape to Switzerland or Italy would depend on what Gaze had discovered.

As soon as it was light, he headed for the station. He planned to retrace his steps to Moravia, first taking a train and then walking the rest of the way. After buying a ticket, he took his place in the long queue waiting to pass through the barrier, where two policemen were checking identity cards. He was confident his papers would withstand scrutiny and also happy to be returning to his friends in Sulíkov. The queue was slow, and as he waited he began to admire the cathedral-like dome of Prague's historic station. He even craned his neck a bit to get a

better view of the huge ring of allegorical figures that surrounded the space. It was at that precise moment that two
Gestapo agents surprised him. 'Come with us,' they ordered,
pulling him out of the line.

As they led him off to be interrogated, Alastair bent over,
clutching his stomach in pain. 'I'm going to be sick,' he cried. 'I
have to get to a toilet.' And then with the Germans blankly
staring at him, he began to retch violently. This was enough to
convince them that a visit to the bathroom was necessary. With
the Gestapo standing on the other side of the door, listening to
the terrible sounds of vomiting, Alastair shredded the incriminating documents he was carrying and flushed them down the
toilet. Now he was ready.

Back in Sulíkov, Jim Gaze was anxiously awaiting Alastair's
return. When he didn't appear, Gaze promoted himself to major
and began circulating the pro-British, anti-German message
from one village to the next. At first he lived in a small lean-to
in the forest and then, when it became too cold, with various
families willing to take him in. Making contact with the partisans proved more difficult, and when he eventually did, he found
that in place of an underground army were random acts of sabotage and revenge. Then, at the beginning of 1945, Russian
commandos began parachuting in to organize their own units.
Despite the language barrier and a good deal of suspicion, Gaze
joined the Labunsky Group; an ironic twist as it was two-thirds
Russian and clearly fighting for Uncle Joe. But they were inflict-
ing serious damage on the Germans and Gaze wanted to be part
of it. In mid-April, after blowing up a railway bridge, he was
accidentally shot in the leg by another partisan. He would have

died too, if not for a twenty-five-year-old factory worker named Jarmila Stejskalova, who nursed him back to health. They had met soon after his escape and been close for nearly a year.

Gaze didn't return to England until June 1945, a full month after the German surrender. He stayed just long enough to file for a divorce and then went back to Czechoslovakia as the British vice-consul in Bratislava. On weekends, he would drive up to see Jarmila, though sometimes she took the bus down to see him. As soon as the divorce came through, they married and went on to have five children. In May 1950 they were expelled from the country, accused of being part of a conspiracy to build an underground army to overthrow the government.

# 9

# Crazy to Get Home

No one asked Alastair if he was feeling any better as they made the short trip to Gestapo headquarters just two blocks from where he had waited for Wadeson and Mackenzie to appear. He had seen the building as soon as he arrived and, like most Czechs, crossed the street whenever he had to pass it. It was a huge four-storey structure with a granite base and smooth limestone walls above. There was also an attic full of dormers tucked inside a copper mansard roof with a decorative railing capped by globes and urns. All of this had been part of the Petschek and Company Bank, founded by three brothers in 1920. With extensive holdings in coal mines and chemical plants, the Petscheks had become one of Prague's wealthiest families. But they were also Jewish, and knew as soon as the Munich Agreement was signed that they would have to leave the country. The bank was sold to the government and sat empty for nearly a year until the Gestapo took it over. What was once the Petschek Palace soon became known as the Palace of Death, or simply, the Pečkárna.

The bureaucracy of terror was complex and no fewer than 1,000 people worked in the building every day. Secretaries, translators, clerks, typists, stenographers, printers, janitors, all joined the SS and Gestapo on the various floors where special units had been set up. The first was dedicated to Jewish affairs, the second to Gestapo administration and the third to communists and left-wing groups. The most feared space, however, was the basement, where private vaults for the bank's wealthiest clients had been converted into small, windowless cells. It was entered through an unmarked door at the far end of an inner courtyard, which is where Alastair now found himself. A middle-aged German in a black uniform, overweight and sniffling with allergies, sat behind a desk like a concierge at a rundown hotel. Alastair needed to register, yet instead of a key he was issued an armband with a number on it, and warned that he was responsible for keeping it clean. It was the property of the Reich and would have to be returned before he left.

As he stood at the desk, a door directly behind it swung open. Inside was a man suspended from a steel bar by his wrists and ankles. He had clearly just been beaten and was sobbing and moaning uncontrollably. The Germans who had tortured him stared at Alastair as they left the room. They were only too happy to display their handiwork as it fitted into a carefully orchestrated process in which prisoners were destabilized by fear and helplessness well before any interrogation even began. That was the formula the masters of terror had perfected.

By now Alastair had spent so much time with the Gestapo he could almost predict the next step. Led into a room with ten wooden benches facing a bare, white wall, he was ordered to sit in silence, hands on his thighs, palms facing up. Hanging beside him was a sign warning that anyone who spoke or moved without permission would be forced to stand, face against the wall and hands behind their heads, for three days without food or water. As they sat for hours staring at what looked like a blank screen, prisoners inevitably conjured up their own terrifying scenarios of what was about to transpire. With each person producing his own private horror movie, the room was quickly dubbed 'the cinema'.

Alastair endured all this with the help of his training in what he called 'the endless patience of the prisoner, how to kill time by focusing the mind on blankness by effort of will'. If that failed, there was always the physical pain of the bench on which to focus one's attention. At the same time, he was resigned to the likelihood that he would be shot as the Gestapo had repeatedly promised. Being a prisoner of war was no longer a guarantee of protection, especially since the Germans had just murdered fifty escapers from Stalag Luft III. He knew that first they would try to extract whatever information they could. By linking him to David Stirling's plan to join the Czech underground army, they would try to confirm what they had long suspected: that he was a special agent working with the resistance and probably not even a member of the Royal Artillery at all.

The two Gestapo agents who finally questioned him were much more sinister than Luckenwalde's Sergeant Schaper, with his buffoonish impersonation of an American captain. Dressed in dark suits like undertakers, they spoke no English; and while Alastair could have demanded an interpreter, the interrogation was conducted entirely in German. Seated at a separate table was a stenographer, a young woman with pasty skin, who never looked up as she recorded every word that was uttered. To Alastair's relief, it soon became clear that they had no idea who he was, something for which he credited 'the Wehrmacht and Camp authorities who were decent enough not to send any records to Prague'. He was even more heartened when, after answering several questions, the two Germans turned to one another and said in Czech, 'Do you think he's telling the truth or is he just an idiot?' They had made the rudimentary mistake of assuming that no Scottish lieutenant from Edinburgh was going to understand such an exotic language as Czech. From then on, Alastair was at a definite advantage. Not only did his inquisitors announce their response to everything he said; they also revealed their strategy as it unfolded over the course of several days and nights of interrogation.

There was, of course, the usual dose of table-pounding and screaming, interspersed with periodic threats of torture and even execution. What did he know about the camp's escape organization, they asked repeatedly. And what was Colonel Stirling's role in it? How did they plan to connect with the Czech underground? Who was his contact? And wasn't it true that Alastair was in Prague to meet with them in order to get arms? They also claimed to know who had helped him during his escape. According to them, his co-conspirators were already in Gestapo custody. Now if Alastair would simply confirm their names, he would be returned to the safety of a prisoner-of-war camp. To every question he responded with the same combination of feigned ignorance and surprise. He even insisted that he had never heard of a Colonel Stirling. Could they describe him, or better yet, did they have a photograph?

His legal training certainly helped as he easily deflected almost any question that was asked. And while he enjoyed inciting such bullies as Sergeant Schaper and the two agents currently berating him, he knew that the most important thing was to say as little as possible and never to change one's story.

For their part, the Germans believed that relentless questioning of a sleep-deprived prisoner under bright lights would eventually lead to the confession they sought. And if this didn't work, physical torture was always available to facilitate the process. Despite the never-ending bombardment of threats and accusations, of little food and no sleep, of unbearable fatigue and the feeling of complete abandonment, Alastair never wavered. Eventually, his jailers threw up their hands in defeat. If he was a secret agent, they couldn't prove it. Once again, he had slipped through the eye of the needle.

But the Gestapo wasn't about to let Alastair go so easily. After being locked in a pitch-black cell for three days and nights, he was thrown into the back of a van and taken to the Geheime Staatspolizei Untersuchungsgefängnis, better known as Pankrác Prison. Located at the south-eastern edge of the city, Pankrác was originally built in an attempt to reform the Habsburgs' archaic penal system. Now it belonged to the Gestapo, an overcrowded, evil place with more than 2,000 inmates, many awaiting execution. In fact, if Petschek Palace produced terror as a means of maintaining power over an occupied people, Pankrác Prison produced death. With a thin veneer of legality, prisoners were dragged in front of a tribunal which usually took no more than three minutes to deliberate. Defendants had no right of appeal and were given only ninety seconds to speak before the sentence was carried out. The prosecution, on the other hand, was welcome to protest if they thought the court was being too lenient. Any call for the death penalty in particular was usually heeded by the judge.

Once condemned, the prisoner was led behind a curtain at the end of the room. Inside was a white-tiled space across which ran a heavy iron rail fitted with hooks on rollers. Resembling nothing so much as a slaughterhouse, it was where the victims were hung, their bodies moved along the rail with a long pole in order to make room for the next. At times, the macabre assembly line got so backed up that chairs had to be brought out so those waiting their turn could sit. Not all victims were hanged. There was also a guillotine whose 140-pound blade could be heard dropping throughout the prison. Even this instrument, which was used on more than 1,000 people, wasn't enough to satisfy the thirst for slaughter. Many had to be driven to Kobylisy, an old firing range north of Prague, where they were tied to posts and shot.

Those still awaiting trial, or simply languishing in their cells with no promise of release, faced a constant torrent of abuse and humiliation meted out by guards whose sole qualification seemed to be a sadistic temperament. According to Peter Demetz, a young student at the time, many of them 'were ethnic Germans from Romania who had volunteered for the SS and behaved accordingly'. Demetz, who had no idea why he was being held, called it 'the worst days of my life'. The brutality he described was similar to the experiences of most prisoners:

In the morning when the guards banged on our door, the oldest of us had to shout 'Alles gesund (All are healthy),' but that did not stop the guards from rushing in to dunk our heads in the toilet bowls or taking us out to the corridor to do special gymnastics – that is, standing for hours with raised hands at the wall or doing push-ups until we dropped or fainted, in which case we were resuscitated by being kicked or beaten. Waiting for interrogation or transport was even worse; on Wednesday mornings the names were called of prisoners who were to go to the Small Fort of Terezín, a place of fatal horrors.

Alastair was treated much the same. However, he did find the two Czechs he was put in with quite congenial; at least, when they weren't arguing. Self-proclaimed revolutionaries, they came from opposite ends of the political spectrum. While one was a communist, the other was a member of a right-wing ultra-nationalist organization. They welcomed Alastair as an inde-pendent third party with whom they could share their views. The nationalist, in particular, wanted him to know that after wiping out his group, the Germans had found their radio and were luring more agents into a trap by transmitting phoney messages to England. Alastair, he insisted, had to get word home to warn them. And while Alastair said he would gladly do so, he still had no idea if the Germans intended to carry out their threat to have him shot. As for his two cellmates, it was only a matter of time.

He had expected to find Waddy Wadeson and Hugh Macken-zie at Pankrác but there was no sign of them. Then he heard that another British officer had arrived just days earlier. For a moment, he thought it might be Leslie Hill, though after hear-ing a description, he was sure it wasn't. Said to be a dishevelled and gloomy-looking man with a ruddy complexion and bushy red hair, he was being kept in complete isolation in cell 206. It was rumoured that he had been part of a mass escape that had pushed Hitler over the edge.

After more than two weeks of listening to his room-mates bicker, the cell door swung open to let in a short, sandy-haired man with thick oval-rimmed glasses. It was 'Tojo' Wedderburn. Like 'the Baron', 'Tojo' was one of those nicknames that a soldier picks up when in the company of other men during a war. With his 5'4" stature, droopy moustache and owlish glasses, he did slightly resemble Tojo Hideki, the Japanese general and prime minister; at least, according to his comrades in the SAS. To Alastair, he was simply Sandy Wedderburn's little brother Tommy, a member of one of Edinburgh's most prominent legal families. His father, Sir Ernest, was head of the Council of Solicitors as well as the Deputy Keeper of the Seal of Scotland. He was also a scientist and inventor who earned his knighthood by working out a better way to calculate the trajectory of long-range artillery. Alastair remembered Sir Ernest best as a dignified and solitary figure walking in his black robes through the halls of Edinburgh University where he taught.

His eldest son Sandy also studied law at Edinburgh after first earning a degree at Cambridge. There he had served as president of the Mountaineering Club, and in 1932, invited Alastair to join them on an expedition to Norway. After smuggling arms for the Republic during the Spanish Civil War, he joined the Royal Scots and as a commando developed new techniques for high altitude warfare. By 1944, he was second-in-command of the Lovat Scouts, a unit specially trained in mountain combat. They spent nine straight months fighting in the Apennines, and were relieved when a holiday R&R brought them to Aquila, the same town where Alastair once gazed upon his Bambola Rossa. Christmas Eve arrived and everyone got drunk and let off steam. Then Sandy decided it would be fun to slide down the big marble banister in their ancient hotel. Going on his back was a bad idea as he sailed straight off into the abyss, landing in the stairwell several floors below. Sandy Wedderburn – soldier, lawyer, and mountaineer – was dead at thirty-two.

Like his older brother, Tommy Wedderburn also went to Cambridge, studied law, served as head of the Mountaineering Club and coxed for the crew at Trinity Hall. He was active as a night climber as well, pulling himself up drainpipes and chimneys, crossing roofs and dangling from gutters and window ledges, and finally summiting on top of the tallest spire; all without a rope and with the added risk of expulsion should he be discovered by a porter. It was a dangerous sport, made famous at Cambridge, where the conquest of fear was said to lead to self-realization. And while they couldn't have known it, for those who later became prisoners of war, it was the perfect training. Climbing the walls and traversing the roofs of ancient Gothic structures – with care to avoid detection – would be the same skills needed for those attempting to escape such castles as Gavi, Colditz, Laufen, Tittmoning, and Spangenberg.

When it came time to join up, Tommy chose the Royal Artillery like Alastair, although it didn't take long before he was seconded to a newly formed regiment of the SAS. On the day before the Italian armistice, he was dropped with twelve others hundreds of miles inside enemy territory. Splitting into pairs, they were to blow up railway tunnels, disrupting German supply lines. Five of them were quickly rounded up and shot, despite wearing uniforms. But Tommy and a corporal named 'Tanky' Challenor reached their targets and destroyed two tunnels just as trains were passing through. For the next two months they walked south, living with peasants and avoiding the enemy. Their luck finally ran out near Aquila, where they were stopped by a German patrol. 'Tanky' eventually got away dressed as a woman and five months later reached Allied lines. 'Tojo' wasn't as fortunate. After being placed in front of a mock firing squad, he was put on a train to Germany, eventually turning up at Mährisch Trübau.

He was hardly settled in before Bill Murray, the Scottish climber, asked him to join the mountaineering club. Although happy to do so, he was much more anxious to meet David Stirling. As a member of the SAS, he was soon helping with preparations for the mass escape, and would have gone over the wire as well if it hadn't been aborted. Within two months of his arrival, word came that the camp was to be evacuated. On the last day of April 1944, they were marched to the railway station once again. The prisoners, most of whom had moved a number of times, had never seen such a nervous, trigger-happy group of guards. When they were ordered to hand over their boots, belts and braces, the catcalls and complaints became increasingly voluble. Then they were handcuffed and the Germans needed their bayonets to prevent a riot. Asked why they were taking such unusual precautions, the Oberleutnant in charge claimed it was 'because British officers had been known to attack their guards'. And while it was true that Peter Griffiths and John Forsdick had purportedly done so, a more likely reason was the feared alliance with the Czech underground army.

An even greater surprise awaited them as they entered the cattle cars. Large wooden frames threaded with barbed wire had been set up, confining them to a third of the space. On the other side sat six guards commanded by a sergeant. At least one remained on duty at all times with his rifle trained on the prisoners. That didn't stop them from quickly unlocking their handcuffs, though. One group hid them in a slop bucket which the Germans unwittingly threw out; others reached agreements that they would only wear them when the train was stopped in a station. With such restricted movement and heavy surveillance, there seemed little opportunity for escape. The only opening was a twelve-by-twenty-four-inch ventilator in the uppermost corner of the car. If the barbed wire covering could be removed, Tommy Wedderburn was pretty sure he could wriggle through. Plus, he had an extra pair of boots stashed away in his pack.

By nightfall a routine had been established in which prisoners stood at regular intervals to stretch their limbs and relieve their cramps. With the tallest men in front, it was difficult for the guards to see the dark corner where the ventilator was located. After several tries, the barbed wire was torn off and the small opening ready for use. They waited until all the Germans but one were asleep, and even he was starting to doze. Then several men got up to stretch while others shook their blankets as if to clean them. Within seconds Tommy was in the air, picked up by four men who passed him, feet first and horizontal, through the opening. For a moment, his fingers could be seen holding on. And then he was gone.

Without papers or civilian clothes, or any knowledge of the language or area, it was unlikely that Tommy could get very far. It was also hard to count on the local population for support. Even Alastair, who was helped in both Sulíkov and Prague, recognized that years of harsh reprisals and countless informants had left the Czechs too 'frightened to give assistance'. In the end, Tommy was able to remain at large for only two days. Arrested just forty miles east of Prague, he sat in a local jail for more than three weeks before the Gestapo arrived to take him to Pankrác.

He was only with Alastair a short time before two well-armed guards entered their cell and told them to get ready to move. Fearing that this was the long-awaited invitation to a shooting party, Alastair calmly asked 'Where to?'

'You're to join your comrade in 206,' one of them replied. 'You'll be more comfortable there.' Alastair, who was both relieved and amused by this answer, could only surmise that he was referring to the company rather than the accommodation. At the same time, it was with real warmth that he embraced his companions of the past several weeks. He wished them luck and hoped that they might meet again under better circumstances.

Their new cellmate, Desmond Plunkett, was a short, furtive man, clearly rattled by his two months with the Gestapo. Most of it had been in solitary, although spies had periodically been sent in to see what information they could extract. He initially suspected Tommy and Alastair, and only let his guard down once he realized they knew his uncle, who was a solicitor in Edinburgh. It was Tommy as well who eventually sent a coded letter, letting Plunkett's family know that he was alive in Prague. An RAF pilot shot down over Holland, he was the thirteenth person to emerge from the tunnel in what became known as the Great Escape. He was also the last to be recaptured, a fact that saved his life. For while he wouldn't know it until much later, Hitler's quota of fifty executions had already been met by the time he and his Czech companion were finally arrested.

With his well-tended handlebar moustache and amusing persona, Plunkett was the perfect stock character that every prisoner of war movie would eventually require. Messy, forgetful and a bit eccentric, he was a popular figure in the camp. He was also a regular on the *kriegie* stage, forming half of an acrobatic team called the Royal Raviolis. Yet beneath the chaos – and his bed was known as the 'lair of the troglodyte' – was a remarkably disciplined draughtsman who became the chief mapmaker for the escape. Creating an ingenious mimeograph process that used gelatine from Red Cross parcels for ink, he led a team of a dozen men in preparing nearly 4,000 customized maps.

It was typical of Plunkett to choose the thirteenth spot in the tunnel, a position that no one else seemed to want. Together with a Czech fighter pilot named Freddie Dvorak, he travelled by both train and foot to the Protectorate, which they criss-crossed several times before deciding to head for Switzerland. His papers claimed that he was Sergei Bulanov, a worker at a Siemens factory, off on holiday. It didn't help that his ID showed a man with a huge, English-style moustache. The fact that he'd shaved it off just before the escape only added to the confusion whenever his documents were inspected. But they were excellent forgeries, getting them all the way to Klattau, where the Czech, Austrian and German borders meet. Then, on 8 April, a full two weeks after the escape, Plunkett was stopped by the police. After checking his identification card, they asked to see his travel permit. They pored over it like two holy men studying a sacred text, when at last they looked up and announced that it had expired.

By now, Dvorak, who hadn't been stopped, was a good way ahead. He could have easily gone on alone, but in an act of great selflessness went back to see if he could help. He tried to convince the police that they had simply come to Klattau to rest and visit friends. The officers, who pretended to be sympathetic, insisted that they come down to the station. It was just a formality, they said, and wouldn't take long. Plunkett had no illusions.

He knew that this was the end. Within hours, they were in Gestapo hands.

Alastair and Tommy spent nearly three weeks with Plunkett, and although they were never sure why they were put together, each felt that every day might be their last. Tommy had barely escaped being shot as a commando in Italy, while Plunkett still had a death sentence awaiting him for his role in the Great Escape. As for Alastair, it seemed like only a matter of time before the Gestapo made good on its promise to shoot him. Even Freddie Dvorak, who was in another part of the prison, was given a date with the executioner. And yet in the end, they all cheated the hangman. In mid-June, Alastair and Tommy were each handcuffed to guards nearly twice their size and put on a special prison train to Brunswick. Dvorak, after a detour or two, landed in Colditz, which is where he ended the war.

Plunkett returned to solitary, remaining in Pankrác until the beginning of December, when he was moved to Hradin military prison. Finally, at the end of January 1945, ten months to the day after his escape, he was sent to a proper POW camp in northern Germany. Stalag Luft I, located near the coastal town of Barth, was a Luftwaffe camp for downed airmen. By the time he arrived, Plunkett was a mental wreck, nervous and fragile from months of isolation, much of it spent listening to people being tortured or beheaded. To the American prisoners, who were the majority at Barth, his behaviour seemed erratic, as if he were hiding something. Many were convinced that he was an informer, placed in the camp to spy on them. Suddenly he was shunned by his own side.

Even worse was the discovery that fifty of his fellow escapers had been murdered. This news, which he had been unaware of until arriving at Barth, drove his already delicate psyche over the edge. He was seized by uncontrollable guilt, believing that details he might have leaked during his various interrogations were somehow responsible for their deaths. Although baseless, it led him to the brink of suicide and an eventual breakdown. He found some help in the camp hospital, yet as he described in his third-person memoir, it took many years to recover:

> It was not the treatment in the jails that broke him but the awful reality of the death of so many of his personal friends and colleagues. Not only did he blame himself for their deaths but in a strange way he felt guilty that he had been spared when so many of them had perished. This played on his mind and he would not be free of its destructive consequences for over twenty-five years.

Alastair also had a rough time. He'd lost thirty pounds and looked terrible. When Jack Pringle saw him, he was shocked. He claimed he looked like 'a ghost of his former self. He was thin, hollow-eyed and nervous . . . I knew Alastair pretty well,' he said, 'and could see that he was shaken.' Some even thought 'he was on the point of a nervous breakdown'. Yet everyone agreed that it was a miracle he had made it back alive. The fact that few, if any, knew exactly what had happened seemed to fire people's imaginations, increasing the legend of the Baron with each telling. Bill Murray, who treated being a POW as a cross between a writer's residency and a meditation retreat, published an account of Alastair's story, which he claimed the Baron had told him:

One morning after roll call, I heard that Alastair Cram and Tommy Wedderburn had arrived back in camp. Astounded, I went at once to see them . . . Cram told me the story.

The pair had succeeded in reaching Prague, where they had tried over many days to contact the Czech patriot forces. They were betrayed to the Gestapo, who, catching them in civilian dress, believed them spies. Their fate should have been sealed, had not Cram been able to claim so strongly in such excellent German that they were escaped British prisoners . . . The Gestapo despatched them to Dachau for full and final interrogation.

There Cram fiercely maintained that both were escaped prisoners of war. The Gestapo continued in disbelief, judging that no one of Cram's linguistic ability would have been wasted on desert fighting. He, and Wedderburn too, must be Secret Service or SOE agents. Ensnared by their own mix of incredulity and curiosity, they sent their captives' names, alleged army numbers and fingerprints to Berlin with the query: 'Are these escaped British prisoners?'

Meanwhile they were held at Dachau, interrogated day and night under bright lights, forced to watch the torture of Czech women to bring disclosure of their mensfolk's whereabouts in the patriot bands, then returned to their cells but denied sleep while Jews, screaming in the neighbouring cells, were beaten with rubber truncheons. The truncheon bearers would then visit Cram and Wedderburn and stand around menacingly, before hauling them off again to interrogation rooms. After four weeks of this hell, a written command came from Berlin. It stated that Cram and Wedderburn were indeed escaped British prisoners, ending, 'Return to Oflag

79, Braunschweig'. In the face of that direct order the Gestapo had to comply.

No other of our freedom-bidders had come back from the Gestapo alive. He escaped once more when his place of confinement was hit in an air-raid. This time he made it to the American lines. He and I never met again. I honour his memory. This man was indomitable.

It's difficult to say how Murray came up with this semi-fictional account. Alastair was never in Dachau, nor was he 'betrayed to the Gestapo'. And while he did meet up with Tommy Wedderburn in Pankrác, the two had made their breaks separately. As to the story of his final escape, it was a different matter altogether. Yet with Alastair's reluctance to speak about these traumatic events, it is Murray's description that is most commonly cited.

By now, few prisoners were still thinking about escape. After the Allied landings in Normandy, confidence was high that the war would soon be over. Only a handful of Jeremiahs remained, invoking the memory of Italy when the liberation of the camps failed to materialize. Then the British and Canadians had the door slammed in their face at Arnhem as they tried to take a shortcut into Germany through Holland. Two months later the Americans also had the brakes placed on their advance when the Germans launched a massive counteroffensive in the Belgian Ardennes. Progress ground to a sudden halt, proving the naysayers right; it was going to take a lot longer to defeat the Nazis. Eventually, supply routes too were affected and the flow of Red Cross parcels reduced to a trickle. Hunger became a reality and the currency of escape which the parcels provided was no longer available.

There was also another disincentive: the *Kugel Erlass* or 'Bullet Decree,' issued in early March 1944. As authorized by the German High Command, recaptured prisoners would no longer be protected by the Geneva Convention. Instead, they would be shot immediately, or in the case of British and Americans, handed over to the Gestapo to do with as they saw fit. The new policy was announced with posters blaming England for starting this 'non military form of gangster war!' After the murder of the fifty tunnellers from Stalag Luft III, such printed messages seemed superfluous.

Even David Stirling and Jack Pringle changed course. With liberation now in sight, they turned their energy away from escape and started to focus on Japan and the war in the Pacific. David, in particular, wanted to make sure they had a plan in place that included the SAS. Then one morning, while poring over maps, the mysterious Captain van Zouco appeared. Breathless and slightly incoherent, he had just learned that David and Jack had been tried in absentia as enemies of the Reich. It didn't surprise them to learn that they had been found guilty – after all, that was their job. The death sentence, on the other hand, definitely shook them. As David later confessed: 'The news really scared the hell out of me and I worked le bon Dieu very hard that night . . . I think I was more frightened then than I have ever been before or since.'

When the order finally came in August for them to move, they expected the worst: a stop along a quiet highway, a bullet in the back of the head, a note pinned to their coffins, 'Shot while attempting to escape.' But execution was never part of the plan, and to their relief (and surprise), they arrived safely at Colditz, which is where the end of the war found them.

Now the 'ghosts', who had been hidden since their arrival at Brunswick, decided it was time to show themselves. David had taken care of this immediately after getting off the train, first cutting a hole in the fence to make it appear as though someone had escaped and then arranging for two men to be concealed inside the camp. When an escape did occur, they would be available to make up the numbers at roll calls, buying valuable time for those who had got away. According to Alastair, they had planned to stand in for David and Jack. With their departure, there didn't appear to be any demand left for 'ghosts'. Escaping had just become too dangerous, and with the war nearly over, not worth the risk. At least, it seemed that way to almost everyone except Alastair.

The absence of a massive escape industry like the one that dominated life at Mährisch Trübau would result in a very different experience at Brunswick. Most of the men had been prisoners since North Africa or before and had little trouble in quickly resuming their routines. The cards were reshuffled and games that had lasted years picked up exactly where they left off. The Rum Pot quickly found a new home and started brewing its signature moonshine. Casting calls were posted for *Ah, Wilderness!* and *The School for Scandal*, while bands and orchestras from the Tea Room Quartet to the Philharmonic could be heard rehearsing from one end of the camp to the other. Sports teams vied for space, knocking over easels at a meeting of the art club and threatening sunbathers further down the pitch. Inside, classes on every subject were starting up once again. James Chutter, the camp's senior clergyman, claimed: 'What was virtually a university was established, and from Brunswick alone over 400 officers are believed to have sat for Public Examinations. It was in Brunswick camp that POW life found its fullest expression. Primarily it was a life of the mind and the spirit.'

Chutter might well have been speaking of Leslie Hill, who reappeared at Brunswick on D-Day, more than six weeks after his escape dressed as a German sergeant. Together with Peter Joscelyne, he had travelled to Brno, and from there gone on alone to Prague. Like Alastair, he soon discovered that the addresses he had been given were of streets and districts that didn't exist. Finally, after two frustrating days, he decided to give himself up. David Stirling, he believed, needed to know that his information was bad and that the Bohemians couldn't be relied on for help. Leaving Prague, he travelled east to the ancient mining town of Kutna Hora, where he walked into the local police station and turned himself in. His expectation of being driven straight back to Mährisch Trübau was as naive as his decision to surrender. Instead, he was taken to a Gestapo prison in Kolín, where he was held for over a month, much of it in solitary. By the time he reached Brunswick, his information was useless, leaving David and Jack to wonder if there wasn't something else to his story.

Hill's one adventure with escape proved more than enough. Free from all the cloak-and-dagger activities that had absorbed his life for months, he returned to his great passion, the study of language. He also took up meditation, and in addition to joining Herbert Buck and Bill Murray, worked with several well-trained Indian officers. 'I used to go into an attic,' he said, 'sit cross-legged, and roll myself up mentally, first the extremities, then the torso, then up to the neck and into the front part of my brain, until I was quite unconscious of my body, and felt that "I" was

19. Mährisch Trübau, Oflag VIIIF with bungalows in the foreground and the four-storey Biscuit Factory beyond.

# To all Prisoners of War!

## The escape from prison camps is no longer a sport!

Germany has always kept to the Hague Convention and only punished recaptured prisoners of war with minor disciplinary punishment. Germany will still maintain these principles of international law.

But England has besides fighting at the front in an honest manner instituted an illegal warfare in non combat zones in the form of gangster commandos, terror bandits and sabotage troops even up to the frontiers of Germany.

They say in a captured secret and confidential English military pamphlet.

### THE HANDBOOK OF MODERN IRREGULAR WARFARE:

". . . the days when we could practise the rules of sportsmanship are over. For the time being, every soldier must be a potential gangster and must be prepared to adopt their methods whenever necessary."

"The sphere of operations should always include the enemy's own country, any occupied territory, and in certain circumstances, such neutral countries as he is using as a source of supply."

*England has with these instructions opened up a non military form of gangster war!*

Germany is determined to safeguard her homeland, and especially her war industry and provisional centres for the fighting fronts. Therefore it has become necessary to create strictly forbidden zones, called death zones, in which all unauthorised trespassers will be immediately shot on sight.

Escaping prisoners of war, entering such death zones, will certainly lose their lives. They are therefore in constant danger of being mistaken for enemy agents or sabotage groups.

Urgent warning is given against making future escapes!

In plain English: Stay in the camp where you will be safe! Breaking out of it is now a damned dangerous act.

The chances of preserving your life are almost nil!

All police and military guards have been given the most strict orders to shoot on sight all suspected persons.

*Escaping from prison camps has ceased to be a sport!*

20. *Above, left*. David Stirling in North Africa in 1942. On his cap is the SAS badge with its winged Excalibur sword and the motto 'Who Dares Wins'. 21. *Above, right*. 'Escape is No Longer a Sport' poster, first circulated by the Germans in July 1944.

22. Roy Wadeson, Serbia, 1920s.

23. Hugh Mackenzie, second from right, at Oflag VIID, Tittmoning, 1941.

IL COMANDANTE
del Presidio Militare Tedesco di Livorno

NOTIFICA

Chi aiuta prigionieri di guerra inglesi
viene severamente punito.

Chi consegna questi alle truppe ger-
maniche o da informazioni tali da poterli
fermare, riceve un premio di:

**Lit. 5000**

e una assegnazione supplementare di generi
alimentari e di tabacco.

Livorno, 17 settembre 1943.

DALLMER - ZERBE
COLONNELLO E COMANDANTE

24. *Above, left.* A poster threatening to punish anyone who aids British prisoners of war and to reward those who turn them in. Aubrey Whitby collected it while on the run after the Armistice. 25. *Above, right.* Gestapo Headquarters in the former Petschek Palace, Prague.

26. *Above, left.* L. G. 'Jim' Gaze, undated wartime photo.
27. *Above, right.* Tommy 'Tojo' Wedderburn, second right, in an undated photo with fellow officers of the Royal Artillery's 57th Medium Regiment.

28. 'Train Jumpers', J. F. Watton.

29. Prisoners from Oflag IX A/Z heading east, early April 1945.
Sheets used to spell 'PW' in case of an aerial attack can be
seen draped over several officers' shoulders.

30. *Top*. The spa grounds at Bad Oeynhausen, home to both the British Army of the Rhine and the War Crimes Group.

31. *Above*. Alastair, with SAS cap badge, Bad Oeynhausen, Germany, 1946.

32. *Left*. 'No Germans Permitted', Bad Oeynhausen.

33. Gerald van Zouco, as seen in a wanted poster after the war, which also lists him as Gerald Marcel Salinger, alias Suckow, alias 'Captain' or 'Doctor' van Zouco.

34. Anthony Somerhough, at Alastair and Isobel's wedding, Nairobi, 1951.

35. Isobel Nicholson in 1946, the year she met Alastair.

36. Alastair and Isobel cutting their wedding cake with an ice axe decorating the wall behind them. Cathedral of the Highlands, Nairobi, 13 June 1951.

37. Alastair, Kenya, 1951.

38. Alastair, sailing during their honeymoon, 1951.

39. Alastair and Isobel climbing Mt Marmolada, the highest peak in the Dolomites, during their honeymoon, 1951.

only a consciousness with no physical dimensions, floating in a void, with no emotional or mental attachments.'

Finding peace at Oflag 79 wasn't always easy. Although the attractive, two-storey brick barracks built for the Luftwaffe were relatively new, there were only four of them; certainly not enough to accommodate the 2,000 men who had just arrived from Mährisch Trübau. The Red Cross called it 'absolutely insufficient', and demanded that other buildings in the complex be opened up. Many of them, however, had suffered bomb damage, which in addition to overcrowding was the camp's main problem. Sandwiched between the Braunschweig Fighter Aerodrome and the Hermann Göring Works, it was a natural target for the Allied planes that passed overhead nearly every day. Everyone knew that placing a prison camp alongside such military installations was in violation of the Geneva Convention. But the Germans, who clearly didn't care, thought their presence would reduce the possibility of being bombed. As one wag put it: 'The Luftwaffe, finding Allied bombing of Brunswick a little too hot for them, graciously turned over their barracks to us.'

Attacks seemed to increase with the unleashing of the un-manned V-2 rockets, which were rumoured to be produced in part by slave labourers in the adjacent factories. Night raids were conducted by the RAF with Mosquitoes marking the targets for the big, four-engined Lancasters that followed. Most prisoners appreciated their precision, especially when compared to the American Flying Fortresses that came over during the day. James Ratcliffe, who won the George Medal for the disposal of ninety-six unexploded bombs, wrote: 'One had the impression that, at least, the RAF tried not to bomb those of us in the camp. Their bombing runs were quite impressive really, and even though the odd stray landed inside our wire, we were thrilled. The Americans on the other hand, didn't even try. They just carpet bombed everything.'

The worst attack took place on the morning of 24 August, when a raid on the Hermann Göring Works spilled over into the camp. In just thirty minutes every building was on fire, with roof tiles stripped off and windows shattered. Prisoners stepped in to control the damage, though it was still several weeks before water and electricity were fully restored. Then there were the casualties: four dead and forty severely wounded. The trauma of the Blitz – celebrated in heroic murals of the Luftwaffe throughout the camp – had now come to Brunswick.

There were other casualties as well. At the end of June, Colonel Waddilove was summoned by the commandant. Sitting on his desk were two small urns containing the ashes of Waddy Wadeson and Tubby Mackenzie. A short, rather awkward conversation followed in which Oberst Strehlo, never known for his sensitivity, reported that they had been shot while attempting to escape. One mystery had been replaced by another. They now knew the fate of the two men, yet no one for a moment believed the story of their deaths. Alastair, aware that they would have been handcuffed and closely watched, scoffed at the explanation. 'The possibilities of such an escape,' he said, 'were unlikely. In any event, the object of Wadeson and Mackenzie would not have been to escape but to return and tell the escape organization that they had been betrayed.'

A more feasible scenario was that the Gestapo had been tipped off about their mission and were waiting for them at one of the safe houses they planned to stay at. Once in custody, they were probably tortured in order to discover what they knew about the Czech underground. Then, like the murdered officers from Stalag Luft III, they were shoved in a car and, somewhere on the road between Prague and Breslau, taken out and shot. After that, they had to be cremated to destroy any forensic evidence.

The news sent a shiver throughout the camp, reminding everyone how close they had come to storming the wire at Mährisch Trübau. As part of the 'First Flight', Wadeson and Mackenzie had given their lives for a mass escape that never happened. While everyone admired them for their courage, those who knew them best mourned their loss more deeply. When John Mansel heard about Mackenzie, he wrote, 'Hugh's death has shaken me very considerably, as he was one of the best friends I ever had.' Similar feelings were expressed about Wadeson. John Forsdick remembered him as 'a slow talking, empty pipe sucking, even tempered, good man', while another friend from Gavi claimed that 'a more kindly, gentle man one could never hope to meet'.

A collection was taken up and fifty pounds sent to each family. Then on 1 July, a funeral was held at the garrison cemetery. Afterward, Colonel Waddilove wrote letters of condolence, describing the event:

*Dear Mrs. Wadeson,*

*I am writing as the Senior British Officer of this Oflag offering on behalf of the camp and myself our sincerest sympathy in the loss of your husband.*

*He escaped from the camp on 20 April 44 and I have been told that he was shot at the end of May whilst trying to escape again after re-capture. I, with his personal friends, have just returned from his funeral which took place at the Garnison Friedhof (Garrison) Cemetery, Brunswick, Germany and was officiated at by a padre from the camp. There were two big wreaths with roses and other flowers interwoven in them. A stone is being erected and if it is possible to get a photograph of the grave I will do so and send it to you. I am so sorry to have to tell you this and please accept my very deepest sympathy in your sad loss.*

*Yours Sincerely.*

*Malcolm Waddilove*

Once again, Alastair realized how lucky he was to still be alive after his arrest in Prague. The fact that he had been searching for Wadeson and Mackenzie and yet avoided a similar fate would gnaw at him for years. Now, as he settled into Brunswick, he began working with a small group responsible for gathering intelligence. One of his tasks was to evaluate information obtained from the two dozen or so coded letter writers. He also cultivated his own sources among the guards and workmen who entered the camp every day. One of them, an Austrian sergeant, confided that there were 900 seriously disabled Germans whose repatriation had been delayed owing to the difficulty the British were having in finding prisoners to exchange. This had happened at least once before, forcing the Swiss Medical Commission 'to scrape the bottom of the barrel to make up the numbers'. It didn't take Alastair long to decide that feigning mental illness would be his next means of escape.

Working one's ticket in this way was not without its critics. Some felt it was unethical and could make it more difficult for those in real need of being sent home. Still, it was no cakewalk and usually required long periods of painstaking privation to succeed. 'Ollie' Oliver, for example, spent months in the hospital at Stalag Luft III, where he made himself throw up so often he could hardly get out of bed. A good-humoured banker from Trinidad, Oliver had also been in Gavi and, like Alastair, was determined to find a way out. When sent for X-rays, he swallowed small pieces of rolled up silver paper. The Medical Commission bought it, approving him for repatriation based on a diagnosis of chronic stomach ulcers.

The best-known case was that of Richard Pape, an RAF navigator shot down over Holland in 1941. After several failed escape attempts, he decided to apply to the Medical Commission complaining of acute kidney failure. As with any serious escape, his preparation was meticulous. He fasted for weeks, eating almost nothing but soap until his skin turned a ghoulish green. He had his ankles beaten to make them swell to the proper nephritic size. He even switched chest X-rays with that of a tubercular Pole. His *pièce de résistance*, however, was a prosthetic penis used to carry the urine of another patient into the exam. The board, horrified at the state of his health, needed less than six minutes to approve his petition.

Psychiatric cases, on the other hand, were not as easy to put over. While one could always manufacture physical evidence for conditions such as those of Oliver and Pape, psychological complaints depended on a much more subtle set of clinical observations. Besides, simply being a prisoner was depressing. Winston Churchill, who had been a POW himself, called it 'a melancholy state'. The Germans even had a word for it: *gefangenitis* or 'prisonitis', a listless torpor seasoned with irritability and the occasional fit of rage. During the First World War, it was known as 'Barbed Wire Disease', and was an accepted diagnosis for both sides. Described as 'a well-recognized form of neurasthenia caused by confinement for long periods in barbed-wire enclosures', one could present it for repatriation, though a more likely outcome was internment in a neutral country. By the Second World War no such agreement existed, and claiming mental illness in order to be sent home had become much more difficult. Still, it could be done.

Alastair, who would allege he was suffering from melancholia, began withdrawing from all of his normal activities. He spent more and more time in bed and, when he wasn't sleeping, simply stared into space. He even stopped doing his Müllers, an alarming development to those who knew him. His weight too continued to plummet as he reduced his intake to a bare minimum. All of this, including his monastic silence, might have been more difficult for anyone else to endure. Yet Alastair, who was a combination of introvert and stoic, had spent years learning how to control both his body and his mind. If anyone could play the part of the melancholic patient, it would be him. It helped that he had read Freud and Jung and had a genuine interest in psychology.

It's unclear whether he shared his plan with anyone else in the camp. Others who tried similar ploys emphasized the need for absolute secrecy. In Colditz, for example, where Frank Flinn spent a year building his case, the isolation and loneliness nearly drove him crazy. Flinn also strengthened his claim by staging a suicide attempt as well as attacking another officer. Such anti-social behaviour, endangering both himself and others, was a significant factor in his eventual repatriation.

While Alastair never resorted to such strategies, he seems to have convinced his fellow prisoners of the fragility of his mental state. Bill Murray, for one, wrote that 'Dachau had left Cram in no condition for further prison life. After a few days, the German Commandant had to send him off into the care of Brunswick's mental hospital.' Murray's recollection of the sequence of events is somewhat confused as he claims that Alastair was transferred almost immediately after arriving from Pankrác. However, it wasn't until October, four months later, that he was taken to Köthenwald, not far from Hanover. There, in an unprecedented move, he was placed in a high-security psychiatric ward of a civilian facility. The Germans, suspecting this might be another one of his schemes, were taking no chances.

Köthenwald Asylum, also known as the Klinikum Wahrendorff after the father and son who founded it, was part of a complex of buildings set out on a large plain. Like many institutions for the mentally ill, Köthenwald had struggled to maintain its integrity with the rise of the Nazis. The start of the war saw an intensification of this process as every institution was ordered to compile a diagnostic list of their patients. Known as the Aktion T4 programme, it was the preface to the Holocaust when a range of victims from the incurably ill and 'non-Aryan' to the epileptic and criminally insane were deemed 'unworthy of life' and murdered. Köthenwald, under the leadership of Dr Hans Willige, was one of a handful of organizations that refused to cooperate. Rather than provide a list, Willige falsified records to indicate that various individuals were capable of working. Undeterred, Berlin sent its own commission, which after interviewing 300 patients, took 70 of them away. Then, in a scene out of *Schindler's List*, the head nurse, Martin Fischbach, followed the group to Regensburg, where he managed to get a number of them returned.

By 1944, when Alastair arrived, the Klinikum had already lost a good deal of its space to the army. Now the government, who wanted it for convalescing soldiers, was about to seize the rest. In a risky move full of intrigue, one of Wahrendorff's sons-in-law was able to intervene. Still, many patients had to be relocated, which led to severe overcrowding. By mid-October, nerves had reached a breaking point in the asylum's cavernous communal space. Then the planes started coming over and the building began to shake. It was the area's largest bombing raid of the war. When it was over, Brunswick would be on fire for almost three days. In Köthenwald, the patients began to panic and were soon stampeding towards the locked doors. Alastair was nearly crushed and only saved himself by climbing into a window well. Others weren't so lucky. Among the three who died was a nurse who had tried to calm the herd. His head had been crushed and his brains strewn across the floor.

Soon after the bombing, the Berlin commission returned. This time they took ninety men and fifty-three women, none of whom was ever seen again. It was around then that Dr Willige came to see Alastair. His period of observation was coming to an end. While sympathetic, Willige made it clear that he thought Alastair was faking and that there was nothing wrong with his mind. What concerned him most was the conversation he'd had with the Gestapo. They had called to warn him that Alastair was a dangerous man and needed to be watched very closely. 'Be careful,' Willige told him. 'They can make you disappear.'

*

Waiting at the gate upon his return to Brunswick was the unbearably smug Oberleutnant Haberhauer, whose crisp salute and all-too jolly greeting seemed to mock Alastair's melancholic pose. As for Alastair, he barely looked up as he slowly raised his hand to return the salute. He might have lost the first round, but he certainly had no intention of abandoning his scheme. If the staff at Köthenwald wouldn't support his diagnosis, he'd find a place that would. In fact, he had already heard that the medical officers at Rotenburg, a small camp on the Fulda River, were extremely helpful to those seeking repatriation. Of course, POW camps weren't like hotels where one could check in and out depending on the quality of the accommodation. Nevertheless, prisoners did have the right to speak with the Protecting Power when they conducted their periodic inspections of the camp. Their next visit was scheduled for early December, giving Alastair several weeks to prepare his case. No one knows exactly what he said when the time came, yet whatever it was, it worked. At the end of January 1945 he boarded a train to what would be his eleventh prison camp.

An impressive five-storey brick structure that looked like the main hall of any large provincial university, Oflag IX A/Z was the former Jacob Grimm School for girls. Many also believed it was the setting for the scandalous 1931 film *Mädchen in Uniform* with its steamy lesbian scenes. Now it was a subcamp – hence the 'Z' for Zweiglager – of Oflag IX A/H at Spangenberg, just a few miles up the road. Among its 400 or so current inhabitants was a large contingent from Gavi. Chas Wuth and Allen Pole, two of the South Africans who worked on the cistern tunnel, were there. So was Gerry Daly, the wiry little commando, looking more spindly than ever. Brigadier Clifton had also come and gone after being shot jumping from a train near Munich.

The person Alastair was happiest to see was Ernest Vaughan, the doctor with the Indian Army who had diagnosed his sudden attack of appendicitis in the rail yards at Bolzano. Without his help, Alastair would never have made it off the train. He also knew that, before coming to Gavi, Doc Vaughan had successfully coached another officer in feigning insanity. At Rotenburg, he'd taken the unusual step of setting up a mock medical board to prepare those applying for repatriation. Sitting before the three-person panel, in imitation of the two Swiss and one German, they were grilled on every aspect of their ailment until they could respond with the confidence of the most overpaid medical expert.

It didn't take Doc Vaughan very long to arrange for Alastair to be sent to another asylum, hoping that at this one the results would be different. Located on the outskirts of Dresden, Alastair was packed and ready to go by the second week of February. Then the RAF and Americans started to bomb Dresden. For two days and nights waves of planes flew over the city igniting a firestorm that left more than 25,000 dead. Travelling was now becoming dangerous for prisoners of war. The commandant had already suspended parole walks outside the camp, fearing that angry citizens might attack them. Even when Alastair was caught in the middle of an air raid while switching trains at Hamm, his guards thought it much too risky to bring him to a shelter full of Germans. Instead, they locked him in a small hut on the platform, where Alastair was certain he was going to die. When the raid was over and he saw the devastation, he said, 'I'm sorry.' It was the only time he ever did.

Three weeks after the Dresden bombing, the Allies established their first bridgehead over the Rhine. Although the crossing at Remagen proved too small for the full-scale invasion of Germany, the prisoners in Rotenburg celebrated with elaborate 'Rhine Bashes'. It appeared that Alastair wouldn't have to pretend to be mad after all. On the other hand, he had lived through this once before in Italy; the rush of euphoria capsized just when liberation seemed within reach. By the time the actual crossing of the Rhine began on 22 and 23 March, many in Rotenburg doubted that the Allies would arrive in time. They knew that prison camps in the east like Stalag Luft III and IV had already been evacuated just as the Russians were approaching. Dozens had suffered frostbite and even died as they were forced to march through blizzards in sub-zero weather.

Despite questions from his staff, Hitler showed the same disregard for his resources as he had at the time of the Italian armistice. Only now, the numbers were much greater as he ordered that no POW or foreign slave labourer fall into enemy hands. Many prisoners suspected a darker purpose in this decision. Ian Reid, who had escaped several times while in Italy, expressed a common concern:

In the event of a move, the next problem which faced us was: 'Should we or should we not escape?' At this stage of the war none of us wanted to risk his life; but at the back of our minds there lurked a constant fear that we might be marched southeast into the much-boosted 'Bavarian redoubt' and there held as hostages against the lives of the war criminals. We were the last counters the Nazis still held. It seemed then a choice of two evils.

315

On 28 March 1945, with Patton's Third Army bearing down on Kassel and the Americans only eleven miles away, the order to evacuate was given. Stocks of powdered milk, cocoa and biscuits were handed out to be packed alongside each person's reserve of cigarettes, soap and chocolate. It wasn't until 2 p.m. the next day that the camp emptied out. Ian Reid, who had already made the decision to escape, described the somewhat undisciplined scene:

> It was a long, straggling, slow-moving column which eventually plodded out through the barbed-wire gates. There were guards armed with rifles about every twelve yards. Some officers, 'old lags', who had received many parcels from home, were carrying an immense amount of kit. George and I had reduced ours to a minimum. My home-made pack was filled with food – we had been given a surprisingly large bulk issue just before we left – cigarettes, a spare pair of socks and the manuscript of my book.

They marched over twelve miles the first day, reaching the farm they were to sleep at well after dark. Many of the prisoners at Rotenburg were older, a number of them in their forties and early fifties. Some had been prisoners for nearly five years, captured at Dunkirk or during the Norway campaign. Add to this a poor diet and relative inactivity and it's little surprise that a good deal of them found the march extremely difficult if not impossible. Even Alastair, who had given up his daily exercise routine in favour of long stretches in bed to prove his melancholia, was worn out after the initial day.

Their original destination was Mühlhausen, forty-five miles

to the east, where they would get on a train to Bavaria. This soon changed when news arrived that the Americans had captured the city. They now veered north, stopping in small villages with names like Windeberg, Keula, Nohra, Uthleben, Bucholz, and Dittichenrode. They mainly slept in barns, though at times were also billeted in homes. While they had expected the local population to be hostile, most welcomed them, due in large part to the belief that their presence would protect them from being attacked. Equally welcome were the coveted items they brought with them. Eggs, milk and even yogurt and sausage were eagerly traded for camp-issued soap, chocolate and, of course, cigarettes. Many who hadn't tasted such rich food in years reacted violently with bouts of diarrhoea, or, as they called it, 'the squitters'.

The greatest threat was meeting a trigger-happy group of SS who would think nothing of unleashing their wrath on a column of unarmed British prisoners. But it was the friendly fire from the ever-present Mustangs, Thunderbolts and Typhoons that concerned the slow-moving column most. Other groups, mistaken for German soldiers, had already been strafed with substantial loss of life. To prevent this, they carried white sheets that could instantly be assembled to spell 'PW'. Easily read from the air, it seems to have worked, as the evacuees from Rotenburg were never attacked.

There was, however, plenty of evidence of those less fortunate. Displayed on either side of the road as they trudged along was a showcase of the terrors of war: a smouldering home, an abandoned pram, a downed plane with its nose planted in the earth, a burned-out troop carrier filled with grotesque human remains, a rotting horse on the verge of exploding. All of these were made even gloomier by the steady drizzle that fell almost every day.

Cold, muddy, and exhausted, it was now almost two weeks since they'd set out from Rotenburg. What had begun as a march with a clear destination had quickly deteriorated into an aimless journey through a demoralized world. At every stop, it seemed as though the Americans were just hours away. And yet the commandant, Rudolf Brix, refused to give in. It didn't matter that men were slipping away at night, escaping into the woods to make their own way to the Allies. Brix, never popular in the camp, was consumed by Hitler's order to keep prisoners from being liberated at all costs. With few options left, he headed towards the Harz Mountains.

Hitler had just designated the large range as one of several *Festungen*, or fortress areas, where resistance would be carried out till the last man. While thousands of troops from the Waffen SS to the newly formed Volkssturm had already taken up positions there, the column of prisoners was too far south to be noticed. They remained in the foothills, hugging the edge of the mountains in an arc that took them east once again. On 8 April they came within five miles of Nordhausen with its concentration camps and underground rocket factories. That night, Alastair found a set of civilian clothes which he quickly stuffed inside his knapsack.

The sun finally came out the next day and, under a perfect sky, the mountains were at last visible. It was time to go. He decided to wait till dark when it would be easier to get away and safer to be out climbing alone. For now, he continued with the column, never taking his eyes off the mountains for a second. He was like a painter observing a live model, studying its shapes and contours and strategizing on the best approach to take. By evening, he could hardly contain himself. Then, as the column stopped to rest near the town of Rossla, Alastair discreetly changed into his civilian outfit, pulling his hat down over his eyes. When the order came to resume marching, he quietly started walking in the opposite direction. Apparently, he was a bit too close as the guards not only began to scream, but also lifted their rifle butts to drive him away.

It was a warm spring night, dry and perfect for climbing. He started slowly, uncertain as to whether his stamina would return. It had been ages since he'd travelled up a small path laced with switchbacks as it rose to the top of a crest and beyond. The last months had been hard – the interrogation by the Gestapo, the time spent in Pankrác Prison, the burden of trying to prove that he was suffering from melancholia. As he climbed further, he felt as though he was leaving all of this behind. It wasn't just the column on the valley floor he was escaping from. It was also the years of disappointment and failed attempts, of beatings and humiliation. The higher he went, the more these too seemed to fade away, replaced by a new optimism which Alastair could always rely on mountains to provide.

He climbed like this for two days. Some areas reminded him of the Highlands and the Cairngorms, though not as wild and much more forested. He still had a good amount of food and as long as the weather held, there was little reason to seek assistance. Then, while walking down a road, he suddenly found himself inside a clearing with a fair-sized cabin set above it. There was a group of men sitting in front, chatting and smoking. One of them signalled for Alastair to come over. They assumed he was either a deserter or a prisoner of war. Now more people came out of the house, including several women. Most were foreign labourers although there was another POW along with some mysterious refugees. All of them were simply waiting for the war to end. Alastair, they insisted, would have to stay. But it turned out to be only for a day or two as an advance unit of the US 3rd Armored Division soon overtook them. When they left, Alastair was sitting in the lead jeep. It was his twenty-first escape, and he was almost home.

# 10

# Killing by Means Unknown

After spending three and a half years doing everything he could to get back to Scotland as quickly as possible, the homecoming that awaited Alastair was far different from the celebration he had long dreamed of. He had heard almost nothing from his family since leaving Italy in 1943, and only now learned that his father, whom he loved dearly, had died three months earlier. With no interest in returning to the family firm in Perth, he instead joined the SAS, and at thirty-six began parachute training. Inspired by Jack and David's discussions at Brunswick, he hoped to be sent to the Far East before the war ended. But that never happened and in October 1945, the SAS was disbanded. Alastair, who would soon be promoted to major, was ordered back to Germany to join the War Crimes Group responsible for tracking down and prosecuting Nazi criminals. He was also awarded a Military Cross based on his 'outstanding persistency and ingenuity in repeatedly attempting to escape'. The lengthy citation ended with the unusual statement that 'eighteen officers have recorded their admiration for his efforts'.

He arrived in Germany just as the world's first major war crimes trial was getting underway. Forty-five guards and senior staff from Bergen-Belsen were being tried by a British military court for murder and other crimes. As part of the process laid out in the 1943 Moscow Declaration, only 'major' war criminals – or those 'whose offences have no particular geographical location' – were to be tried by an International Military Tribunal with judges from Britain, the US, France and the Soviet Union. All other cases, which formed the overwhelming majority, were tied to specific places – concentration camps, mental institutions, Roma encampments, village squares, the killing fields of Poland and Russia. These 'minor' war criminals, as they were euphemistically called, were to be tried in military courts set up in the occupational zones or countries in which the offences occurred. Bergen-Belsen, located in Germany's populous north, fell under the jurisdiction of Great Britain. Its troops had also liberated the camp in mid-April 1945. Now, as a horrified public looked on, eleven of the accused, including the commandant, Josef Kramer, were hanged while eighteen others received relatively light sentences and fourteen were acquitted altogether. The criticism was harsh: the judgments were too erratic and too lenient. Equally upsetting was the fact that many guards and other SS weren't charged at all.

As that trial came to a close, a very different court began to assemble in what was once the epicentre of the Third Reich: Nuremberg. Twenty-four of the leading architects of the Nazi regime were to be tried in the only deliberation of the International Military Tribunal. The year-long proceedings that followed, with its indelible images of Hermann Göring and other Nazi leaders, disdainful if not disinterested as they sat fiddling with their headsets, has remained the dominant symbol of postwar justice. But there were hundreds of other 'minor' trials that took place in each of the occupation zones as well as in the various places that had been terrorized by the Nazis. Churchill was initially opposed to this process, preferring a type of 'swift justice' in which short, extrajudicial hearings would be followed by immediate execution. Ironically, it was Stalin who argued against this, convincing him, with Roosevelt's help, that some form of trial was necessary, both to legitimize the process and to educate the public on the evils of fascism. In the end it was Churchill who drafted the Moscow Declaration in prose so distinctive that neither Stalin nor Roosevelt dared make a change. It concluded with a powerful incantation:

Let those who have hitherto not imbrued their hands with innocent blood beware lest they join the ranks of the guilty, for most assuredly the three Allied powers will pursue them to the uttermost ends of the earth and will deliver them to their accusers in order that justice may be done.

The Nuremberg Trial, which sent eleven Nazi leaders to the gallows, was barely over before rumblings about bringing the entire war crimes proceedings to an end began. The occupation was too costly, some claimed, especially for Great Britain, a nation whose economy had been devastated by the war effort. Strict food rationing was still in place and would be for almost another decade. Even Churchill was booted out of office, an indication of the country's desire to move beyond the agony of the past five years. Of course, the Germans were equally anxious to derail the whole process, arguing that the trials were less about justice and more about revenge. But the biggest force undermining the continued pursuit of Nazi war criminals was the new equation of power in Europe. The Soviet Union and its satraps had replaced Germany as the main threat to stability and peace. With the arrival of the Cold War, old enemies were about to become new friends, and the search for justice its first casualty.

Despite a chronic shortage of staff and resources, the War Crimes Group forged ahead, and while there were hundreds of criminals who were never prosecuted, they did succeed in achieving what Donald Bloxham called 'a symbolic reckoning'. By the time of the last trial in 1949, over 1,000 men and women had been indicted in 357 different cases. Of these, 249 were condemned to death and one third acquitted. Given the many obstacles placed in their way, it was an impressive accomplishment made possible in large part through the remarkable leadership of Tony Somerhough. An Oxford-trained lawyer who first joined the air force in 1927, Somerhough was now an RAF group captain, having spent the war as Deputy Judge Advocate General for the Middle East. He was a huge bear of a man with a round, bald head and a wonderful sense of humour. When he had time, he liked to fish, open a bottle of good wine and tell stories. Charismatic and charming, he knew how to put people at ease. He also knew how to fight and had a tough, fearsome intellect. Vera Atkins of the SOE claimed he had 'the quickest brain I have ever known'. For a position that required battling on two fronts – one in the courts with war criminals and another at Whitehall with government bureaucrats – there was no one better than Tony Somerhough. Alastair adored him, as did most of the men who served under him.

The staff allocated to Somerhough's group was pitifully small: just over fifty officers with three times that number of Other Ranks. By contrast, Operation Paperclip was given 3,000 men to find and recruit Germany's most important scientists and engineers before the Russians did. While they were legally forbidden to work for the Allies if they were members of criminal organizations like the SS, no one seemed to really care. Rocket scientists like Wernher von Braun, an early SS member who regularly used slave labour, made an easy transition to American missile and space programmes. The message in all of this was quite clear: the 'minor' trials were simply not a high priority for the British government. As one wag summed it up: 'Those charged with tracking down the war criminals did not have so much as an operational code name.' For Tony Somerhough, the problem was more basic. Writing to the War Office in exasperation soon after taking over, he complained, 'We have nothing, not even a typewriter.'

When new positions did open up, they were often difficult to fill. The most qualified people were anxious to leave the army and return to civilian life. Among those who stayed, few wanted to take on the grim task of pursuing war criminals. Alastair, as Somerhough quickly recognized, was the exception, the ideal candidate who could tick every box in the list of required skills. Not only was he an experienced lawyer with SAS training, he spoke German, French, Italian and Czech, and was as familiar with the region as anyone. He had also witnessed the depths to which human beings were capable of sinking.

Alastair was happy to be working again, though the load was overwhelming. There were simply too many cases and too few people to prepare them. In a letter home he confessed, 'I am so busy on trials at the moment, I have scarcely a moment to write.' Organizing evidence for indictments, arguing cases in court, locating perpetrators and witnesses, extraditing criminals from other zones, soliciting the help of the French, the Russians or the Czechs, all of it was a race against time. Prisoners who hadn't been charged were being let out by the thousands while in London, the politicians were already setting deadlines for an end to the process. Added to that was an order for the War Crimes Group to reduce their number by 20 per cent.

Its cases, as prescribed by a special Royal Warrant issued in June 1945, were to be limited to crimes against British subjects, or, if they occurred in the British zone, to citizens of Allied nations. Atrocities against Jews and other targeted minorities were not viewed as war crimes but as internal acts of violence. The Germans were to be responsible for trying them, a cynical proposition in which few had any confidence. This didn't mean that the criminal activities in concentration camps were simply ignored. However, the victims had to be British or from an Allied country. When the commandant and five others from the Natzweiler-Struthof camp in Alsace were put on trial, the charges focused on the murder of four female SOE agents who had parachuted in from England. And when nearly forty staff, guards and others were tried from the women's concentration camp at Ravensbrück, the judgment read, 'Being concerned in the ill treatment and killing of Allied Nationals interned therein.'

Most of the cases Alastair prosecuted dealt with either POWs or RAF airmen who had been attacked after bailing out. Late in the war, when German cities became increasingly vulnerable to punishing air raids, many started calling for revenge. Goebbels, the Minister of Propaganda, demanded that all captured pilots be killed like 'mad dogs', while several generals abetted the process by lifting the Geneva Convention's protections. The

German public hardly needed encouragement, as their anger was already at a boiling point. As for the so-called *Terrorflieger*, or 'terror fliers', their best hope of survival was to be picked up by members of the Luftwaffe or Wehrmacht. Even that, however, didn't guarantee a pilot's safety.

A chilling example was the fate of an RAF crew captured in mid-March 1945 near the southern city of Pforzheim. They were returning from a raid on an oil storage facility in Leipzig when flak set one of their engines on fire. Believing they had crossed the Rhine and were over friendly territory in France, the pilot gave the order to bail out. By the time he untangled himself and discovered that his parachute was ripped, the fire was extinguished, so he continued on to England alone. In the meantime, seven of the crew were arrested by an army patrol who handed them over to the Luftwaffe the next day. They were then marched through Pforzheim, or at least what was left of it after a massive attack only three weeks earlier. The minute they were spotted, people began hurling stones and cursing them. They would have suffered a lot worse if the soldiers hadn't intervened.

They continued on to a small village two miles outside of Pforzheim, where many of those displaced by the bombing were now housed. Locked inside a boiler room at the local school, the airmen, who hadn't slept for days, quickly nodded off. They weren't out for very long before an armed mob burst into the room screaming, 'English swine!' 'Murderers of women and children!' The elderly Luftwaffe guard, who tried to stop them, was simply shoved aside. Kicked and hit with rifle butts, they were forced out of the basement, certain they were about to be lynched. In the confusion, three were able to break away and escape. The other four were led to the village cemetery, where they were beaten and then shot. Two of those who escaped were eventually picked up by an army patrol and saved. The third, a much-decorated forty-year-old flight engineer of Indian descent, was not so lucky. Recaptured the following day, he was brought to the police station of a neighbouring village where another mob composed mainly of sixteen-year-old Hitler Youth broke in and, shouting racial epithets, pulled him out. No sooner had they reached the street when someone began beating him with a heavy plank. As he fell, another Hitler Youth shot him in the back of the head.

Seventeen months later to the day, twenty-two people went on trial for the five murders. Despite pretending to be a simple mob of enraged citizens, the killings were carefully orchestrated by members of the SA and Hitler Youth. Three of the leaders were hanged while others were given prison terms. Within two years, six of the Hitler Youth, including the one who shot the flight engineer, were released owing to their age when the crimes were committed.

By war's end, it was estimated that more than 800 RAF crew members had been murdered, with only a hundred fewer American fliers meeting the same fate. Each one was treated as a war crime and the culprits, wherever possible, brought to justice. While the Pforzheim killings had multiple perpetrators of varying complicity, other murders were committed by single actors with no eyewitnesses. Equally frustrating were the air-tight cases in which the suspects couldn't be located. Although a Central Registry of War Criminals and Security Suspects (CROWCASS) was established, extraditing them from one zone to another often proved difficult. It was a world of ghosts and shadows, just as Carol Reed depicted in *The Third Man*, where the characters descend further and further into the dark and sordid universe of post-war Vienna. Alastair too would find the same as he pursued his own version of Harry Lime.

Living in Germany, which he had tried so hard to escape from, aroused a strange mix of conflicting emotions. Most of the population was still in a state of shock, sitting amid the rubble of bombed-out ruins, tableaux of pain and loss, staring listlessly into space, hardly noticing the long columns of displaced persons shuffling along in front of them. And inside the courtrooms was an even grimmer reality as the atrocities of the past twelve years were relived day after day. In contrast to this was the tidy English village created out of the royal spa town of Bad Oeynhausen. Located eighty-five miles west of Brunswick, it had avoided any bomb damage during the war. Many locals claim that it was actually protected by the RAF, who, after spotting it from the air, decided it would make an excellent site for an occupying force. Built by King Frederick William IV around a network of therapeutic springs, it had long been the playground of European aristocracy. Now it would house the 5,000 men and women of the British Army of the Rhine (BAOR). With its ample hotels, villas and large administrative buildings lining carefully tended lawns, it was the perfect setting. When the local residents were ordered to leave their homes, taking no more than they could carry in a suitcase, most believed they would be back within a month. Some even left flowers and other small gifts on their dining room tables. But it would be ten years before they ever returned, a memory still recounted with some bitterness today.

Barbed wire and sentry posts were quickly erected, only these were meant to keep people out rather than in, and where signs once forbade entry to Jews and other 'undesirables', new ones now warned that Germans weren't permitted. Shops and restaurants, which listed their wares in English, were well stocked, while in the theatres, the latest movies and plays were presented. Unlike the world beyond the wire, there was no shortage of entertainment or alcohol, and even if there was a ban on fraternization, there were plenty of single women working any number of jobs. For a while Alastair was seeing a twenty-four-year-old major named Edwina Instone. A staff officer with the Women's Royal Army Corps, Edwina would eventually go on to a distinguished career that included journalism, radio, children's books, television, fashion and, finally, politics. It was under her married name, Coven, that she was to serve in the City of London government for thirty years. During that time, she and Alastair never lost touch, remaining close friends for the rest of their lives.

At the end of his first year with the War Crimes Group, Alastair was given a short leave to return to Scotland. He couldn't wait to get back to the mountains and, following a brief visit with his mother, grabbed his bike and boarded a train for Glencoe. On the valley's eastern slope, where the Glasgow and Edinburgh roads come together, was a rambling two-storey Victorian hotel called the Crianlarich. He'd stayed there before, attracted by the ease with which one could reach some of Scotland's best climbing. It was dusk by the time he arrived and the staff were busily lighting stoves and adjusting lanterns. There was only one other guest in the lobby, a tall, sensibly dressed redhead in her mid-twenties framed by the last rays of sunlight.

Alastair had the strange sensation she was expecting him and later said of their first encounter, 'her hair was like a city on fire'. She, on the other hand, had watched the staff scurrying around all day, 'talking about the captain this, the captain that. By the time the captain arrived,' she said, 'it was like a stage entrance'.

Before Alastair could say a word, she introduced herself as Isobel Nicholson, a nursing student from Surrey. She already had a good deal of experience with the VAD (Voluntary Aid Detachment) during the war and was in Scotland taking a maternity course required for colonial service. She had hitchhiked from Edinburgh the day before, and despite a sturdy new pair of boots, had never actually ventured up anything. 'I didn't even know you could climb mountains,' she claimed. 'There were none in Surrey, not even hills. The thought that you could go up them . . . well, it won my heart.' Though she hadn't spent time in the mountains, Isobel was brought up on a farm with fruit trees and animals and a father who was a veterinary surgeon. She felt at home in the outdoors and didn't mind roughing it, essential qualities for anyone thinking of being with Alastair.

The next day he took her up Buachaille Etive, the 'Shepherd of the Glen', with its dramatic views of Glencoe in one direction and the Etive valley in the other. It was her first climb and she loved it, though she loved Alastair even more: 'The moment I saw him, I knew he was the one. The problem was convincing him that I was the one for him!' Whether he admitted it or not, by the time he returned to Bad Oeynhausen, Alastair too was smitten. They couldn't stop thinking about one another, and in a series of playful letters, Alastair warned her of the dangers in falling in love with him:

I may as well disillusion you here and now. I am not terribly nice. A great many people would not even think me nice. I can be agreeable and courteous and I have read enough to carry on a conversation but there are things in my life that would blunt a pixie's ears if spoken.

I am afraid too that there have been WOMEN IN MY LIFE. I AM NOT NICE. I AM TOO NATURAL. So, no illusions, young woman or when I have lured you into some lonely mountain range (ah-ha!) you will be confronted with the REALITIES OF LIFE. You have been warned. Nature in the raw and all that. So if you are a nice sweet girl, stop writing to me.

Two weeks later, he sent an equally flirtatious letter in which he coyly confessed his feelings:

I write to you because I found a sort of bond. I assumed we were meant to meet in Glencoe. Not essentially to have an affair but people often are thrown together for a specific purpose – experience – to rub corners off – deflect from a wrong course of action and so on. I liked you because you were adventurous enough to travel so far alone – and I suppose simply because you were there and young (fairly) pretty (high standard) had nice legs (essential) were brainy (a useful but needless asset) and had beautiful red hair (k.o.)

Meanwhile, the clock was running out for the War Crimes Group. London, which had already pushed the finish line back more than once, decided that no new trials were to begin after 1 September 1948. Some protested that war criminals who

suddenly surfaced after that date would basically be granted
amnesty. But the government maintained that 'the purpose of
the trials was deterrence, not retribution, and that additional
trials would not advance this objective'. The trials were also
threatening the support of the new German government, a key
ally in an increasingly polarized Europe. Calls to 'bury the past
as soon as possible' were repeatedly voiced. Even Churchill,
who had been among the first to argue for a swift and thorough
justice, now demanded that the trials cease:

> Retributive persecution is of all policies the most pernicious.
> Our policy should henceforth be to draw a sponge across the
> crimes and horrors of the past – hard as that may be – and
> look for the sake of all our salvation, towards the future.
> There can be no revival of Europe, without the active and
> loyal aid of all the German tribes.

While the Official Secrets Act prevented Alastair from speaking about his work, it was clear he began to feel a greater urgency
to resolve certain cases. These were ones that had directly
affected both him and his friends and, in several instances cost
them their lives. Among them was an investigation and possible
indictment of Colonel Moscatelli and Sergeant Mazza. Although
Alastair was asked to help, a different War Crimes Group for the
Mediterranean was ultimately responsible. Jack and David along
with Tommy Macpherson, Michael Pope and Aubrey Whitby
all testified. Each accused Moscatelli of collaboration with the
SS, which resulted in an additional twenty months of prison in
Germany. No one, however, found him guilty of an actual war

crime. After holding the former commandant as long as they could, the British eventually had to let him go.

Sergeant Mazza, on the other hand, was still at large. He had been particularly brutal, beginning with the beating of Jack Mantle when he was chained to a wall for three days following a failed escape. His treatment of Alastair was no better, as he repeatedly kicked him in his broken ribs, sending him to the hospital for three weeks. Once again, everyone agreed that 'Mazza was a thoroughly unpleasant character'. Yet his actions, as egregious as they were, never quite rose to the level of a war crime. Even Alastair, who had suffered the most at his hands, considered it a personal affair which he hoped to settle one day:

> I encountered many bad men while a PW, but Mazza easily heads the list from the point of view of taking a vindictive pleasure in making British prisoners squirm. He was feared and despised by his own Carabinieri. I think his sadism was due to some psychopathic pressure. He had some conscious or subconscious reason for hating Englishmen. No normal man would have behaved as he did . . . All the same I have always regarded this matter as a private one between Mazza and myself.

Alastair hadn't forgotten Peter Griffiths either. It was the quiet South African who had invited him to join in his first escape. Unfortunately, they weren't able to get beyond the cookhouse in Benghazi where they were crouched for hours, searching in vain for a way past the guards. Now Alastair was looking for a Sergeant Schmidt, who was in charge of the train detail when Griffiths made his final leap on the way to Sagan. Schmidt was more than just brusque and insensitive when he found Griffiths with half of his skull torn off; he refused to call a doctor or offer the most basic care. And yet, it would be hard to convict him of a war crime; that is, if you could find him. In addition to being one of hundreds of *Feldwebels* named Schmidt, he had been transferred to the Russian front months before the end of the war.

Finding someone to indict for the murder of Waddy Wadeson and Hugh Mackenzie was proving even more difficult. Without a corpse or a suspect, it was nearly impossible to piece together exactly what had happened. But Alastair, who had now become the hunter instead of the hunted, wasn't discouraged. This was one crime he was determined to solve. The office of the Judge Advocate General (JAG) was equally committed, convinced that the murders were tied to those of the fifty officers killed after the Great Escape. The task of tracking down those responsible had been delegated to a separate unit in the RAF's Special Investigation Branch. While the British public had grown weary of the war crimes trials in general, the one exception was the fate of the fifty airmen. Every detail of their tragic executions was closely followed in the press. In addition to being included in the charges made at Nuremberg, the delay in apprehending the guilty was one of the principal reasons for postponing the end of the trials altogether. Now the JAG was encouraging Somerhough to collaborate with the RAF investigation. A confidential letter, dated 22 October 1946, made it clear that the prosecution of Wadeson and Mackenzie's killers was to be a dress rehearsal for the long anticipated trial of the Great Escape murderers:

I feel that we should be justified in assuming definitely that these two officers were shot by a similar method to that employed in the Stalag Luft III killings, somewhere on the autobahn between Prague and Breslau and probably by members of the Prague Gestapo . . . It would be extremely satisfactory if we could bring this case to a successful conclusion particularly in view of the fact that the first of the Stalag Luft III trials is due to take place soon, the similarity between the two cases being very striking. I will endeavour to find out whether these two officers were shot as a result of an order from Berlin as was the case in the Sagan Killing but I do not hold much prospect of success.

Alastair had already come to the same conclusion, and while prohibited from going to Prague himself, was sure that's where the evidence they needed was to be found. After much prodding, the Czechs finally interrogated several former Gestapo officials, though not before Alastair received a note from another member of the War Crimes Group, who testily 'pointed out that this section cannot start a search for the accused who are so far un-named'. In the end, everyone they questioned drew a blank, claiming never to have heard of either Wadeson or Mackenzie. Alastair now took a step back and tried to identify where they were arrested. He and Leslie Hill had been given the addresses of safe houses, and so too had they. One of them was a tavern in a small village, where they were instructed to enter through a basement door. Wadeson had favoured this location, making it clear that's where they would head. Given that the other addresses didn't exist, it seemed likely that this one was a trap. If Alastair could find it, they'd be that much closer to tracking down the killers. Unfortunately, no one could remember the name of the village or the tavern, except of course, for the person who had arranged it: Captain van Zouco.

Alastair's own misadventures in Prague, searching for fictitious streets and neighbourhoods, confirmed what he believed from the first moment he'd met van Zouco: that 'he was an able and accomplished liar', and probably a double agent. He remained amazed at how easily van Zouco had manipulated Jack and David. They continued to believe in him when van Zouco called on them for help from a London detention centre. He had been there since April 1945 when he arrived in England, stateless and without papers. By the time van Zouco returned to Germany eight months later, his improbable web of lies was starting to unravel and at least three countries were lining up to try him.

In the end, the only thing certain about him was that van Zouco wasn't his real name, nor was he South African or a doctor. However, he had studied medicine briefly in Berlin before being forced to drop out due to lack of funds and a Jewish parent. By then, he was already using different surnames. Sometimes he was Salinger after his father and at other times Sukow or Suckov, from his unmarried mother. To his friends, he was Gerry, a street-smart kid nearly six feet tall with curly black hair and a thin moustache. For a while he sold electrical appliances and, following that, worked as a chiropodist in various beauty salons. All this came to an abrupt end when he was arrested by the Gestapo and sent to prison. He claimed it was for affiliation with the Social Democrats, though others suspect it was for more criminal activities than that. After seventeen months he escaped while en route to a concentration camp. The war was just about to begin as he made his way to Belgium, where members of the Jewish community, whom he would later betray, helped him.

Two days after Germany invaded Poland, he enlisted as a doctor in the French Foreign Legion, eventually ending up in North Africa. He fled, however, when the Nazis came searching for German Jews. He then made his way to Oran, hoping to join de Gaulle and the Free French Forces. But he was arrested and, after being found guilty of desertion, sentenced to a year in prison. By the time the Americans landed in November 1942, he had already returned to his unit. Wounded in the stomach and taken prisoner, he first claimed to be French and then once in Italy, a Luxembourger. Not long after the armistice he began working for the Germans, going so far as to join the SS. They, in turn, sent him to Bergamo, where, disguised as an escaped POW, he infiltrated the Italian partisans who were using a certain florist as a front. It was then that the character of van Zouco was born.

According to some versions, though naturally not his own, the Germans planted him as a spy in a convoy of prisoners being sent to the Sudetenland. When he finally arrived at Mährisch Trübau, it was as Captain Gerald van Zouco of the South African Royal Army Medical Corps. Oddly enough, the Germans seem to have lost his paperwork, leaving the staff at Oflag VIIIF believing he was who he pretended to be, a South African medical officer. The position came with a good deal of freedom, which van Zouco skilfully exploited to ingratiate himself with Jack and David. By the time they decided to contact the Czech underground army, he had already become indispensable, and was the first person they approached to arrange a meeting. Of course, they had no idea that van Zouco was sharing their plans with Haberhauer and the camp staff. They were the ones who brought Kopřiva, the supposed member of the underground army. Although Alastair had already distanced himself from the escape, he warned that Kopřiva was probably a double agent working with German intelligence. But it was to no avail. The addresses he provided were as phoney as he was, except perhaps for the tavern where Wadeson and Mackenzie were most likely captured.

Despite the fact that van Zouco was an informer who spoke perfect German, Haberhauer and the commandant still believed he was a South African. To them, he was simply one of a small group of prisoners who were sympathetic enough to the Nazis to betray their own country. Many of these collaborators, such as Railton Freeman, Walter Purdy and Theodore Schürch, had been active members of Oswald Mosely's British Union of Fascists. It didn't take much to convince them to join the British Free Corps or to broadcast propaganda in English over the radio. Then there were the opportunists like Douglas Berneville-Claye, a self-styled aristocrat who claimed to be Lord Charlesworth, though his inflated tall tales quickly earned him the title of 'Lord Chuff'. More delusional than political, and more con artist than soldier, he had numerous run-ins with the law before lying about his background in order to win a commission. As an informer, he wasn't very adept, since everyone at Mährisch Trübau seemed to suspect him. Removed for his own protection, 'Lord Chuff' resurfaced once again near the end of the war when, dressed as an SS officer, he tried to rally the remnants of the British Free Corps.

While there were a number of parallels between van Zouco and the other collaborators – particularly Berneville-Claye –

there was one critical difference: van Zouco wasn't English but German, which meant that trying him for treason would be impossible. Ironically, Jack always believed that the principal motivation behind van Zouco's behaviour was his desire to get papers. As he noted in a 1946 affidavit: 'van Zouco was extremely anxious to obtain British citizenship, having had only a Nansen passport before the war. In Colonel Stirling, he recognized a man who would pay for services rendered to the escape organization with a recommendation on a high level that this citizenship should be granted.'

Following the move to Brunswick at the end of April 1944 – due in large part to information he had provided – van Zouco made contact with the Abwehr, Germany's military intelligence. Would they be interested, he wondered, in the names and addresses of safe houses used by escapers in Budapest, Strasbourg, Paris and Brussels? If so, he could furnish them. In the meantime, he informed on two separate escapes as a demonstration of his sincerity. It worked, and a counter-intelligence officer named Rudolf Kielhorn was sent from Hanover to interview him. If Kielhorn was initially sceptical, van Zouco, the ultimate con artist, was able to convince him that 'his reason for doing this was his sympathy for the German cause'. He then proposed that they go to Brussels together, where, disguised as an escaped POW, he would lead Kielhorn to the main staging area for both prisoners and evaders on the run.

They left on 6 June, a week before Alastair arrived from Prague. After stopping in Hanover to change into civilian clothes, they continued on to Brussels, where they each took a room at the Hotel Metropole. The next day, with Kielhorn and two other agents trailing close behind, van Zouco went to the safe house. Or so he claimed, as it turned out to be the house he roomed at in 1938. Run by a friend of his mother's, it had no connection whatsoever to any escape line. Yet, after speaking in private to the owner and her daughter, van Zouco reported that in two days, a group of escapers was expected at the Albert 1st Tennis Club. He then went out on the town as the local Abwehr prepared for the upcoming raid. When it finally took place, there were no downed pilots or resistance leaders lurking about like Jean Gabin; only a large group of well-heeled people dressed in white. Rounded up, racquets in hand, they were loaded onto trucks and driven off.

Van Zouco, of course, was ready with an explanation. But Kielhorn was losing patience and began to doubt that van Zouco knew anything of use. Exhausted by the steady stream of implausible stories, he finally decided to return to Hanover:

> After four days, I left Brussels while van Zouco stayed there for another two weeks, closely surveilled by the Brussels Abwehr. He spent a good deal of money, acquired a girl friend and had what is generally known as a 'good time'. He left the impression that he was a petty liar who would have liked to work for the Germans in order to enjoy life and let the Germans pay for it.

While van Zouco was running around Brussels, the commandant at Brunswick received an unusual request. The British War Office, in a message delivered via the International Red Cross, would be grateful if he could tell them who the heck this Captain van Zouco was. They had no record of him and yet his name kept appearing everywhere. Hauptmann Kielhorn, who was as dumbfounded as anyone, was brought back once again.

It didn't take him long to discover what no one, save Alastair, had been saying up to that point: that 'van Zouco' was a complete fabrication. He was neither a doctor nor a South African. In fact, he was a German Jew who had escaped from the Gestapo almost ten years earlier. When Kielhorn finally confronted him with a file-full of evidence, van Zouco still refused to confess. It didn't matter that he had obviously never been to Cape Town – his supposed home – or that he couldn't produce any documents or witnesses to support his claim. He was, he maintained, exactly who he said he was: Captain Gerald van Zouco of the South African Royal Army Medical Corps.

Kielhorn, who was 'mystified by the whole affair', continued to treat van Zouco as a prisoner of war. Or was it as a double agent and colleague? After having his uniform with the red badges returned, van Zouco was sent to Marlag und Milag Nord, a camp for naval personnel near Bremen. Whether or not he worked as an informant during his time there isn't known. However, his sudden reappearance at Brunswick on 9 April, just three days before the camp's liberation, was certainly suspicious. Two weeks later he was detained while trying to enter Britain without papers and imprisoned once again. Despite his best efforts, he was unable to get himself released and was sent back to Germany a week before Christmas 1945. He thought he was simply being deported but British authorities were waiting to arrest him at the airport. After five months in a Hamburg prison, where he was being held for possible war crimes, van Zouco made a brief three-day escape. Only then was he transferred to the main interrogation centre in Minden, a short distance from the former Oflag 79. Code-named 'Tomato', it was the last stop before charges were brought and judicial proceedings begun.

By now van Zouco had been a prisoner on and off since the mid-1930s, held in turn by the Germans, the French, the Italians, the Germans again, and the British. It was nearly two years since the war ended and he was still locked up without any charges being filed. Even his jailers were starting to sympathize with his demand for some resolution one way or the other. But there was no indication that his day in court was any closer. In fact, the War Crimes Group, increasingly doubtful whether they could try him at all, was beginning to shop around for a country that could. As a letter to the Italian War Crimes section admitted:

> Salinger [alias van Zouco] has told a different story to every person by whom he has been interrogated . . . Both at Oflag VIIIF, Mahrisch Trubau, and at Oflag 79, Brunswick, to which the camp was transferred, Salinger betrayed the escape plans of British officers to the Abwehr. Although two British officers and possibly several Czechs were murdered by the Gestapo as a result of the betrayal, apart from anything that may have happened in North Italy, it may not be possible in law to bring home a charge of War Crimes against Salinger personally or (on account of his German nationality) to charge him with treason.

After several months in Minden, van Zouco began complaining of stomach pains; the result, he said, of wounds suffered in North Africa in 1943. Owing to his earlier escape, he was watched more closely than other prisoners and his initial request for transfer to the hospital was ignored. It took a good deal of effort before they allowed him to move as the hospital security

343

was much more lax than in Tomato. Once there, he befriended another doctor, Bruno Weber. Recently captured after an intensive manhunt, Weber had been the head of the Waffen SS Hygiene Institute at Auschwitz. Located in Raisko, a couple of miles from the main camp, the institute dealt with everything from malaria and typhus to water and blood analysis. Weber, who received his PhD in the United States, was interested in the use of psychotropic drugs for interrogation. Yet his main work, for which he subjected inmates to life-threatening transfusions, involved blood types and their compatibility. In spite of these experiments, Weber claimed he was innocent of any wrongdoing. He also denied accusations that he had ever participated in the daily selection of Jews and others for the gas chambers. According to him, he was a Schindler-like figure who stood up to the Nazis in order to protect the men and women who worked in his institute. At least that's the way he portrayed himself in a rather dubious statement made soon after his arrest:

Instead of destroying lives, it was the foremost interest of my institute to help prisoners to stay alive. I always had the support of my superior authorities at Berlin when I acted on my own initiative to help Auschwitz prisoners . . . By personal interference and negotiations with the help of Berlin authorities [SS hierarchy] I was able to save the lives of more than 150 prisoners. Part of them I transferred to Raisko or I put them in dummy 'Kommandos' connected with the institute.

It wasn't long before the two began discussing the possibility of escape. Each felt enormous pressure to act quickly. Weber had good reason to believe he would hang, while van Zouco knew that his best chance of getting away was while still at the hospital. They had also been promised help by one of the doctors, a man named Wolfgang Sytwalla who was an admirer of Weber. By carrying messages back and forth, Sytwalla was able to enlist the aid of a number of Weber's friends. He also provided them with clothes, and while no one knows for sure, probably papers as well. They would have needed them, as they walked out of the hospital in broad daylight dressed in long overcoats and boots. It was a little past noon on 31 January 1947.

The two men, different in so many ways, probably split up soon after their escape. Weber, a small, somewhat frail man, had been ill for much of his life and wasn't even drafted until 1942. When he learned that he was assigned to the Waffen SS, he fled into the mountains, or so he claimed. He now threatened to kill himself rather than return to Poland to be tried. In the end he did return. Recaptured once again, he was handed over to the Poles, who, despite a wealth of evidence to the contrary, proclaimed him innocent of any crime. He died in 1956 at the age of forty-one.

With Weber back in custody, attention turned to van Zouco. Wanted posters with lurid descriptions and multiple photographs were circulated throughout Europe:

Salinger, Gerald Marcel, alias Suckow, alias Captain or Doktor van Zouco . . . May pass as quack doctor. Consorts with prostitutes. Inveterate cadger shady with money. Will probably have made for Berlin or Hamburg or may seek to find his illegitimate mother Frau Suckow once a resident in Rostock and Lubeck. Urgently wanted as important war criminal.

Teams of investigators fanned out, visiting every acquaintance of his they could find. Many had been imprisoned with him in either London or Hamburg. His mother too was tracked down to a small Berlin apartment, just blocks from Tempelhof Airport. When questioned, she complained that she hadn't seen her son since 1938. No one, in fact, had seen him. He had simply vanished. And then in June, six months after his escape, it was rumoured he was in Berlin. By now the German police had joined the search, and for two consecutive nights they raided every whorehouse, gambling parlour and black market operation in the city. Beyond a few worthless leads and several arrests for unrelated crimes, they were no closer to finding him than when they started. Then a call came from Brussels. Mlle Medjanka, van Zouco's former lover, had seen him for just a moment on the first of July. It was the last time that anybody would.

Even though the British had decided that they might not be able to prosecute him, they were still concerned with van Zouco's value on the booming spy market lit up by the Cold War. Before, he was a war criminal; now, he was a 'dangerous security suspect'. Alastair pointed this out in a letter to the Judge Advocate General's office: 'The importance [in finding him] lies in the probability that Salinger may attempt to "sell" himself as an agent to the Intelligence Service of another power as this has been his "line" in the past.' Whether he went over to the Russians or simply migrated to America under another alias, no one knows. Wherever he went, he carried with him the best chance that anyone had to solve the mystery of Wadeson and Mackenzie's murders. A year after his disappearance, the case was officially closed and the file stamped 'Killing by Means Unknown'.

*

With the end of the trials in sight, the War Crimes Group was starting to be dismantled. No proceedings were allowed to begin after 1 September 1948, which meant that some cases, like that of the final Stalag Luft III suspects, were quickly opened just before the deadline and then resumed weeks later. Arrangements also had to be made for closing Tomato, relocating prisoners, archiving papers, disposing of furniture, phones, cars and other surplus material, right down to turning off the lights. Code-named 'Fleacomb', the process was overseen by Tony Somerhough, who, with his usual humour, described it as 'a stock taking operation on a vast scale at which we propose to examine the goods and offer a great many of them at bargain prices'.

A number of those at Bad Oeynhausen had already left, either returning to civilian life or accepting other postings. For a while it appeared that Alastair was on his way to the newly formed Malaya Union, where he had been offered a position in the Colonial Legal Service. Then, at the last minute, he accepted an appointment as a magistrate in Kenya. In addition to being dotted with peaks he'd always wanted to climb, it was also a country that Isobel was interested in going to. He had a certain amount of ambivalence, though, as he confessed in a letter: 'It will break my old heart to leave the Army and if there's more trouble it's sorrowful I will be.' Two months later he was in Liverpool, boarding a ship for Africa.

The journey out was a lot like the one Alastair had made on the *Scythia* eight years earlier. This time he wasn't going to war, he was sailing away from it. He was also leaving Europe behind and, with it, part of the rebellious spirit that had always guided his life. His new destination, which he could never have tolerated in Scotland, was filled with all the trappings of domesticity, privilege and a rigid professional hierarchy, right down to the type of gown and wig one was permitted to wear. As he turned forty, a new set of responsibilities was there to greet him. And yet, he resisted taking himself too seriously, and in typical, self-deprecating fashion wrote: 'Here I am posted to this outpost of Empire, surrounded by men with long spears, elephants, lions, Victoria Nyanza and – at the moment – very heavy rain.' Perhaps Miss Pagan, the psychic who read Alastair's horoscope at birth, would be proved right when she promised that 'The best part of his life would be toward the middle and end.'

As a Resident Magistrate in the Kenya highlands, Alastair heard every type of case imaginable – smugglers, pickpockets, prostitutes, perjurers, poisoners, petty thieves, con men, and, once he became an acting judge, murderers. Writing to Isobel, he confided that:

> Being a Magistrate has its drawbacks. One has to be so beastly respectable. No more brawling or drinking or love making but endlessly punishing chaps I rather envy for doing such things. I feel it might be worth being back in prison even for the sake of breaking out again. I am happy in my few remaining years to think I broke every place I was in long enough to have time to think.

The antidote, as always, was to be found in the mountains. In fact, if one reads his correspondence alone, it's difficult to determine whether he was a mountaineer who spent his spare time sitting on the bench or a judge with a singular passion for climbing. In an April 1949 letter to Isobel, he described his feverish itinerary:

In about 12 days I cleaned up Meru 15,100, Kibo (Twice, 20,000) and had three attempts on M'wenzie, 17,500. Kibo is a flop. One walks some 40 miles in three days and climbs some 17,000 feet and finds a crater as bare as the palm of your hand with ice-bergs sitting in it. At one end is a forest of ice trees about 30 feet high on ice about 100 feet thick and all round the ground smoulders about 10 feet from the huge glaciers . . . M'wenzie however is one of the toughest mountains ever built. I doubt if it has been properly climbed. It has one fairly easy looking route. First up a rotten ridge, then a traverse above a huge precipice and finally up a couloir full of ice with two iced waterfalls. Above that are two huge rock towers of rotten rock. Down the couloir come stones – eight while I was there. We gave up below the second fall at 16,900 because we had only one axe and my companion was not very experienced. The other side of the mountain has 4,000 foot precipices as near to vertical as I have ever seen. Every where else are huge rock towers, buttresses and ridges. We did a tower or two on uncertain rock. At one col we made on the main ridge we were faced with a 2000 foot lift of narrow ridge very steep. Even at Chamonix I have never seen anything quite so deterring. The fascination is that it is all unclimbed . . . One difficulty is that everything strenuous begins at 16,000 where one is not at one's best for difficult rock. Of course I flew home in a savage temper cursing and grinding my teeth and vowing to return with rope ladders, rockets gelignite and bows and arrows. Now the rains have broken and my hopes of getting up Kenya next week have vanished.

His letters were also filled with detailed advice, as Isobel had become an avid climber since their first meeting at Glencoe. She was now – either alone or in the company of admirers – starting to 'bag' Munros, Scotland's 280-odd peaks over 3,000 feet. While Alastair frequently warned her of the dangers of climbing alone, he was equally sceptical of joining large parties. 'I am sorry to hear of this communal mountaineering,' he wrote. 'It is rather like making love in a public beer garden surrounded by the vulgar populace.' Though too discreet to admit it, he was becoming increasingly impatient with her lack of progress towards joining him in Kenya. In the end, it took two years, along with another proposal or two, before she finally arrived. Even so, it was a while longer before they were together, as Alastair was still posted in Eldoret, 200 miles north-west of Nairobi. Then, one weekend, 'half way up a thorn infested gully on Mt Kenya', Alastair proposed, asking Isobel if she would be second on his rope for life. She was tied on before he even finished speaking.

They were married on 13 June 1951 at the Cathedral of the Highlands in Nairobi. A police photographer took pictures and, although Tony Somerhough attended, the best man was the president of the Kenya Mountain Club. The next day they left on a four-month honeymoon, most of it spent hiking and camping in the Alps. Several of their climbs, including those in the Dolomites, retraced Alastair's footsteps while escaping during the war. They also visited Gavi, a pilgrimage made by a number of former inmates and their wives. For the newlyweds, it was a preview of the life they would enjoy together over the next four decades; two adventurers, unencumbered by children, roughing it as they explored every major mountain range on the planet – the Alps, the Andes, the Pyrenees, the Himalayas, the Great Dividing Range in Australia. On one trip, they drove a Silver Dawn Rolls-Royce all the way from Nairobi to India; then drove back again via Pakistan, Iraq, Syria, Turkey and London. It was on this journey that Alastair saw a Yeti, an event well covered by the press. Most nights they spent sleeping outside under the stars, just the two of them, soulmates, completely dedicated to one another.

Back in Kenya once again, they could feel the mood in the country changing. People were starting to clench their teeth, preparing for the storm to come. The Mau Mau, who had become the face of a growing insurgency, had already been outlawed for two years. But that didn't reduce the anger and alienation felt by the Kikuyu, who were the movement's main supporters. Attacks started to escalate, some against white settlers, though the vast majority against other Kikuyu loyal to the government. In October a State of Emergency was declared and, with it, a long list of anti-terrorism laws, most of them capital offences, such as taking the Mau Mau oath, consorting with someone who had, and owning weapons or explosives. A single cartridge or a forbidden pamphlet was enough to send one to the gallows and forfeit a family's property. Estimates of the number of people arrested or detained range as high as 360,000. Most were never charged, though Special Emergency Assize Courts – which condemned over 1,500 – were set up to handle the capital cases. In the end, the war against the Mau Mau was fought in the courts as much as anywhere else.

Alastair and Isobel had now moved into a small cottage on Protectorate Road with an Anglican minister next door on one side and a Presbyterian on the other. Across the street was an arboretum with a trail that farmers used to bring their produce to market. It was also the Mau Mau's main route for entering Nairobi. Neither of them ever felt threatened or afraid. In fact, Isobel's greatest fear was losing the small Beretta hidden in her bag as it would have meant a hefty fine of over fifty pounds. Alastair, on the other hand, always preferred a Luger, which he'd picked up in Germany after the war.

Alastair began hearing Mau Mau-related cases from the very start of the Emergency. Many of them, such as the Christmas Eve murders when five loyalist Kikuyu families were wiped out, were critical in establishing the popular image of the Mau Mau as bloodthirsty and savage. The most iconic of these events was the Lari Massacre which took place late at night in March 1953. After diverting the Home Guard, scores of Mau Mau descended on various hamlets around Lari, burning and hacking to death as many as a hundred Kikuyu, women and children included. A second massacre of even larger proportions immediately followed, as armed posses tracked down and killed an estimated 400 people, some guilty, others innocent. The graphic images of charred and limbless bodies that quickly circulated throughout the world were more than just a temporary PR disaster for the Mau Mau. As historian David Anderson pointed out: 'The Lari massacre became the crucial turning point in the Mau Mau war . . . At Lari, Mau Mau became something evil, to be despised and detested. This was how Mau Mau would for ever be remembered.'

In the end, 136 people were convicted for their roles in the massacre, 71 of whom were hanged. While Alastair didn't preside over any of the trials, he did serve as one of the principal investigators, helping to piece together the chain of events as well as determine who should be charged. As he interviewed one prisoner after the other, he became increasingly concerned with something he suspected was happening in other cases as well: the use of torture to extract confessions. According to Anderson:

> Again and again Cram acknowledged in his reports that suspects had been beaten or mistreated whilst in custody. With his usual scrupulous honesty Cram did his level best to establish that the statements that he then attested were freely made. But it was a dirty business.

Alastair's fears were soon borne out in what became one of the Emergency's most important and controversial cases. In mid-July 1954, a headman named Muriu Wamai reported the deaths of two Mau Mau killed during an attack on the Home Guard post he commanded at Ruthagathi, eighty-five miles north of Nairobi. What originally looked like an open-and-shut case of self-defence soon turned into an accusation of murder as police began receiving anonymous letters suggesting a dramatically different story. The two unidentified victims were neither Mau Mau nor members of the fictitious gang invented by Wamai to cover up what actually took place. Like many other innocent Kikuyu, Mathenge Wanjau and Marathe Gachohi had been picked up in one of Wamai's regular sweeps. Thrown into a crowded cell, they were beaten and tortured in an attempt to make them confess their involvement with the Mau Mau. In the end, whether guilt was admitted or not was unimportant. They were still brought before the African Court at Karatina, where forged confessions were provided and hefty fines and sentences administered. It didn't take Alastair long to figure out that it was all part of a vicious 'extortion racket'. Even more alarming was the fact that the colonial government, which had only recently created the Kikuyu Home Guard and African Courts, was now protecting them. It wasn't just a lack of oversight either. Detention centres were turning into concentration camps where Kikuyu were brutally policing and intimidating one another. 'The reign of terror,' wrote Alastair in horror, 'is well advanced.' At the end of a two-week trial, he delivered a thirty-three page decision, carefully organized into two parts; the first was an excoriating attack on the local court system, and the second, an examination of the case against Wamai and his five accomplices. His critique of the Nyeri District Court was especially severe:

Wherever we may research, among the comparative law School of Sir Henry Maine, among the analytical jurists of the Continent of Europe or in the practices described by Sir James Fraser in his 'Golden Bough' there runs through all judicial systems from the most mature to the most immature one golden thread and that is a justice seen to be done which does not offend the fairmindedness of mankind. It is this universal sense of justice, equity and fairness resident in nearly everyone's mind throughout time that is one of the most hopeful of all signs in humanity. Now I must solemnly declare that the practices of the African Court at Karatina during the whole of this year are abysmally perverted and run contrary to the most elementary canons of natural justice. It is a travesty of justice. It is a mockery even to mention justice in the same connotation. Indeed, it is not justice at all but naked oppression.

Alastair was equally contemptuous of Muriu Wamai, whom he referred to as 'a vile mind reeking with ill-will . . . The counterpart of a Gestapo man.' Wamai initially maintained his innocence, insisting that the murdered men had been released two days before the alleged attack. He even offered a poorly forged log book as proof. A number of eyewitnesses, however, testified that he was lying, including several who had seen Wamai and five other guards escort their victims from the post on the night of the murder. They then heard four shots, followed by bursts of gunfire meant to simulate a fight. The six defendants returned a few minutes later without Mathenge or Marathe.

After three days on the stand, Wamai suddenly broke down and changed his plea to guilty. Yes, he said, he had shot the two men when, after two weeks of beatings, they still refused to sign a confession. As for the other guards, they simply fired their rifles in the air as part of the deception. He then described a grim reality in which terror – much of it in the form of 'economic warfare' – was used to control the population. To defeat the Mau Mau, one had to make people too afraid to even whisper their name, no less join them. Ruthagathi wasn't simply 'a special interrogation camp where atrocities were continually committed'. It was part of a much larger strategy to sow fear and intimidate potential sympathizers. According to Wamai, the torture and murders were not his responsibility alone. He had tried to confess several times but the police and his own chief had warned him to keep quiet. In fact, at least five of his European superiors had committed perjury during the trial. 'All what I did,' he claimed in defence, 'I did because I was instructed and I concealed the facts because of orders I had received.' His five co-defendants said the same thing: 'If I did not obey orders, I would be shot.'

Alastair, who had spent two years in post-war Germany listening to the same claim repeated over and over again like a mantra, was having none of it. 'It is nauseating,' he wrote, 'to hear a plea of compulsion from mere lawless brigands.' There were other parallels to Germany as well, which no doubt fuelled the forcefulness of his decision. In writing about 'the torture chambers of Ruthagathi', his thoughts must have returned to the Petschek Palace and other Gestapo prisons where he was abused during the war. It's little surprise that he referred to Ruthagathi as the 'Kenya Nordhausen or Mauthausen'. It wasn't just his own experience either that was evoked. Mathenge and Marathe could easily have been Wadeson and Mackenzie: two innocent men tortured for weeks before being taken out and murdered in cold blood. For the defendants at Ruthagathi, there were no mitigating circumstances. Alastair sentenced Wamai to hang while his second in command was given seven years 'with hard labour'. The other four, who 'assisted in the reign of terror', were sentenced to five years each.

The Ruthagathi decision, announced just before Christmas, caused considerable alarm. Like a handful of other landmark cases that have occurred periodically – such as My Lai in Vietnam and Abu Ghraib in Iraq – it put the occupying power itself under a magnifying glass, and what it revealed was not pretty. Nearly everyone felt threatened by it – except, of course, the many innocent people who were being preyed upon by a violent and corrupt system. The Home Guard, immune from prosecution up to this point, was particularly upset, as was the Nyeri District African Court which Alastair immediately shut down. In an attempt to minimize the damage, Governor Baring announced a commission of inquiry to review the decision. Sir Hugh Holmes, a reliably conservative judge who had fought at Gallipoli and served on the bench in Egypt, would lead it. Until the commission's findings were known, Alastair's decision would remain confidential. Or at least that was the plan. Leaked to the Federal Independence Party in Britain, it was widely circulated under the title 'Kenya's Belsen.' According to one disgruntled minister, it had become 'a stick to beat the government'.

The Holmes Report was predictably critical of Alastair's decision, though surprisingly inept at analysing it. Beyond questioning a number of his assertions, it called for the immediate reopening of the African Court, albeit with increased supervision. No sooner was the document submitted than Kenya's chief justice and the president of the Court of Appeals for East Africa leapt to Alastair's defence. Their scathing point-by-point review, which dismissed the report as 'superficial, fallacious and in parts misleading', also accused it of 'verging on contempt of court'. They warned that if the government made any of it public, they would publish their own critique in response. Nor was this the end of it. Telegrams, letters and studies flew back and forth between Nairobi and London for months. Some complained of Alastair's use of 'extravagant and sensational language such as "abysmal perversion" and "oppression"', while others were angry that he 'had brought the case into the political arena'. But it always had been. As David Anderson pointed out, Alastair 'had, in effect, accused the administration of being complicit in illegal detention, torture and extortion'. He had blown the whistle on Kenya's dirty war and for the first time put the British and their policies on trial.

The governor, who was afraid of alienating the Home Guard, was no doubt equally concerned that the trail would lead back to the European officials who had perjured themselves and then some. He was determined to do what he could to discredit Alastair and bury the case. Although relieved when Wamai's five accomplices were freed on a legal technicality, it still left the ringleader in prison, awaiting execution. Then, despite Wamai's admission of guilt and the lack of any public sympathy, Baring pardoned him. It came just as the British were reducing the sentences of the war criminals still being held in Germany. By 1957, the last of those prosecuted by Alastair's War Crimes Group were let out. If he was frustrated, believing perhaps that justice had been undone, he never spoke or wrote of it. Nor did Alastair ever speak about the controversy surrounding Ruthagathi. Had he lived to witness the successful 2013 lawsuit of five former Mau Mau against the British government, he surely would have felt vindicated. Finally acknowledging the torture and abuse they had subjected the Mau Mau to, the government agreed to pay nearly £20 million, to be divided among 5,000 survivors.

By mid-1957, the fighting had all but ended and the camps were starting to empty out. It would still be another three years before the Emergency was officially lifted, and three more after that till independence. By that time, Alastair and Isobel had already moved to Nyasaland, where, in 1961, he was appointed to the High Court as a puisne judge, second only to the chief justice. Unlike other former colonies, Malawi, as it became known, invited its European officials to remain during the transition to self-rule. They stayed for seven years, when Alastair finally retired. Even then, it was hard to leave Africa, which they'd both come to love. They considered moving to Cape Town, but in the end decided it was time to return to Scotland. They found their perfect home in the Stockbridge district of Edinburgh. Built by the well-known Scottish artist Sir Henry Raeburn, it overlooked the Water of Leith and St Bernard's Well, both visible from the large windows of the elegant, first-floor sitting room.

On most days, when they weren't off climbing or travelling in their caravan, Alastair could be found working in the garden or taking long walks in the city. Few knew who he was, and even fewer had any idea of the many extraordinary things he had done. No one noticed him striding down Princes Street, just another elderly gentleman out for a constitutional. He neither gave interviews nor wrote or even talked about his adventures. Those who met him in Africa, or later in Scotland, were stunned when they read the obituaries following his death in 1994. Yes, they knew he had been a hero of some sort during the war, and that he preferred not to speak about whatever it was he had done. None of them, however, knew anything about the Baron and the daredevil escaper, the prisoner marked for death who had slipped through the hands of the Gestapo a half-dozen times, the commando who went back to Germany to find the guilty ones and make them pay, the judge who stood up and denounced his fellow countrymen when they behaved in the same way. It was all a revelation about a quiet Scotsman who preferred not to call attention to himself.

He did confide in Isobel, and in an early letter talked about courage and leadership and the nightmares these events still caused:

When I am relaxed and you say I look like a baby I think it is probably true and you are seeing down into the well. I think it must be true or otherwise I could not have come through certain experiences unscathed. There have been many times when I have had to do something from which I instinctively recoiled and I have had to go deep into myself to find steadiness and firmness. Earlier there were uncounted times on big mountains when I was leading and there was bad weather or bad conditions or I had a weak party or a party that relied on me not to get them into a mess or to get them out of trouble and without showing any uncertainty one had to make a decision and then put it into action. The same thing happened in battles and on patrols and later when a prisoner I had to place freedom above security in situations where it was reasonable to lie back and wait for the war to end. I am happy to think that I did not fail in these tests . . . There are incidents which I can only face in bed or alone on dark nights where no one can see my face or contortions when to keep alive and to keep secrets under pressure I was worn down to a hair line of steel wire and there were the long long nights of solitary and the nights awaiting execution that were both long and very short and the floggings and the walls against which one was going to be shot and the insidious promises. There were days and weeks of living a double life or a life of hideous crime or being hunted until all one's normal middle self melted and one had one's beliefs only and one's atavistic animal self, the 100 mile marches by night across frontiers, the fire from patrols and the insistent need for shelter and food and behind the sinister shadow of the Sicherheitsdienst, the Uffizio Secreto or the N.K.V.D. . . . But deep down they have not touched me. I am still the little baby in the Wordsworthian sense that 'not in entire forgetfulness and not in utter nakedness but trailing clouds of glory do we come'.

Perhaps Alastair was getting ready to start writing when he bought his first computer at the age of eighty-four. It was the middle of March, when winter was starting to give way to spring. He spent the morning walking, and in the afternoon had a friend visit for tea. At dinner, he and Isobel made half a dozen plans for the rest of the week. Then he turned on the new computer, and with the manual open beside him, played with it for an hour or so. To get to bed, he belayed himself up the big spiral staircase using ropes and hooks: his remedy for a lifetime of falls and broken bones on top of a small stroke. He never complained, and when he died that evening in his sleep, he was just as quiet and peaceful.

At the memorial service, they sang 'The Fight is O'er' and the pipers – as befitted a true Highlander – played the soldier's lament, 'Lochaber No More'. Soon after, Isobel took a bus up to Aviemore with an urn containing Alastair's ashes balanced on her lap. She was bringing him back to Glen Einich and the Cairngorms, where he'd started climbing alone at the age of fourteen and where, three years later, he would find Thomas Baird, half dead and buried in the snow. He ran six miles to Coylumbridge to call for help. When the doctor's car got stuck in a snowbank, he jumped out and ran all the way back again. By evening, he'd hiked thirty-four miles, and although Baird died and his companion wasn't found till spring, the papers hailed Alastair as a hero.

As Isobel drove up with Jimmy Gordon, the gamekeeper, they passed the very spot where Baird had first been sighted. They didn't stop until they were well above the loch. Then, getting out alone, she walked on for another half mile or so until she found the right place. It was Alastair's favourite, 'the enchanted road', with views that seemed to stretch across the entire Highlands. This is where he had wanted his remains scattered. She found a boulder to sit on, and as she looked out over the Cairngorms, she thought about all the climbs they had made together. It was a while before she stood up and tested the wind, making sure the ashes wouldn't blow the wrong way and hit her. She wept as she opened the lid and watched them fly away. All but one, which came back and brushed her cheek. And she knew that it was Alastair kissing her one last time.

# Acknowledgements

It didn't take long for a book that started out as the story of Alastair Cram to become that of countless others as well. To tell these stories required the help of many people, a number of whom were prisoners with Alastair on his long journey from North Africa to the Harz Mountains in Germany, where he finally escaped. Among them were Sir Tommy Macpherson, Allan Yeoman, Alan Hurst-Brown, Norman Blair, Geoffrey Ravenor and Mick Wagner. Their vivid recollections of their time together in Gavi and Padula have enriched this volume enormously and I am extremely grateful to them for it. I am especially grateful to Humphrey Moon, whose memory and sense of adventure remain as keen as ever at the age of ninety-seven. As the sixth man on the 'First Flight' from Mährisch Trübau, Humphrey was able to provide numerous details on the planned mass escape heretofore unknown.

I am also grateful to the many family members whose fathers and husbands, uncles and grandparents were part of this story as well. Their generosity in sharing journals and letters along with photographs and other documents reflected the same trust and selflessness displayed by their kinsmen while prisoners together. Suzanne Kyrle-Pope and Yvonne Riddiford, whose husbands,

Michael and Daniel, shared a cell with Alastair at Gavi, were particularly generous in making rare archival material available to me. No less helpful and supportive were Colin Armstrong's children, Miles and Gay Thorburn; Norman Blair's daughter, Shirley; James Craig's daughter and son-in-law, Robyn and Terry Malloy; John Forsdick's son and daughter-in-law, Charles and Elizabeth; the Gaze family, Peter, Pepi, Jari, Alena, and of course, Jarmila, and daughter, Dorothy Scholefield; Peter Joscelyne's nephew, Colonel Andrew Joscelyne; Garth Ledgard's son, Nick; Bob Paterson's daughter, Anne Owen; Allen Pole's daughter, Diana Duff; Jack Pringle's daughter and grandson, Angela Bamberg and John Portman; James Ratcliffe's son, Jim; Jack Tooes's son, Dave; Thomas Wedderburn's son and grandson, Alexander and Martin; Aubrey Whitby's daughter, Elizabeth; Charles Wuth's son, Michael; and Allan Yeoman's daughter, Judy. I owe them all a huge thanks for their continued help and support throughout this project.

Sincere thanks are also due to Ronald Herbert's three sons – Steve, Terry, and Paddy – and to Leslie Hill's wife, Jane, for granting me access to the unpublished manuscripts in their possession. 'Ronald Herbert's War' and Leslie Hill's 'A Bit of an Outsider, Really' have been inexhaustible sources of information to which I have been fortunate to be able to turn. I was also fortunate to gain access to the diary of Robert Simmons, thanks to his son Geoffrey. A chaplain at Mährisch Trübau, Simmons was a keen observer, leaving a wealth of valuable insights.

A number of other family members, such as Tim Wadeson, also made indispensable contributions. Barely seven when his father Roy disappeared in Czechoslovakia, Tim was as anxious as anyone to discover what happened and did everything he could to help. I was delighted when in 2016, after decades of prodding, the War Graves Commission finally recognized the location of Roy's burial, placing a long-overdue headstone over it. The same was also done for Tubby Mackenzie, after whom his nephew, the Australian actor Hugh Keays-Byrne, was named. Hugh and his brother Shaun had carefully preserved every letter their uncle sent home from Germany while a prisoner. It's a remarkable collection and they were extremely generous in sharing it with me. It also led to the discovery of a previously unknown aunt whose connection was as much a surprise to her as it was to Hugh and Shaun. The daughter from a subsequent marriage, Josephine Mackenzie Gawman, provided additional family information along with a fine set of photographs.

The first person I met just as I was beginning this project was Ronnie van der Weide, a big South African with a striking resemblance to his great-uncle, Buck Palm. Needless to say, Buck was a mythic figure in his household growing up where his grandmother liked to tell stories about him. Our interests in both Buck and Gavi happily converged and there's little we didn't share in our mutual searches right up to Ronnie's recent discovery of Buck's widow, Fernande, alive and well at the age of a hundred in Egypt. His enthusiasm coupled with the same dogged determination of his great-uncle have been a tremendous source of support and I am grateful to him for it.

Finding all these people wasn't always easy, and sometimes required the aid of that great Belgian sleuth, Edouard Renière. Andrew Davies, another saint of lost causes, also helped, as did Kay Stead, who tracked down important information about the Kiwis in Gavi. Many thanks are also owed Peter Green, not simply for his excellent book, *The March East, 1945: The Final*

*Days of Oflag IX A/H and A/Z,* but for his willingness to revisit his sources in order to flesh out the details of Alastair's final escape. An equally important resource was the archive of the Monte San Martino Trust, set up by Keith Kilby to repay the bravery of the many Italians who risked their lives aiding escaped prisoners following the armistice in September 1943. A prisoner of war himself, Keith was always ready to open his door and share his vast knowledge of the POW experience. He was helped in this effort by Brian Lett, to whom I am equally grateful.

Together with my wife, Kate, I felt welcomed in nearly every place we visited, and was genuinely touched by the openness we were shown. In Padula we were guided by Maria Teresa D'Alessio, the granddaughter of Major Luigi Grimaldi, who was part of the camp staff during the war. A romance novelist, there was little she didn't know about the Certosa di San Lorenzo and if there was, her co-worker Alfonso Monaco was sure to. They gave us a wonderful history lesson with rich insights into Padula's Carthusian universe.

At Gavi we were taken in hand by Graziella Rabbia, the daughter of the long-term caretaker, who was awarded his position after helping several Italian generals held there since the armistice escape. The castle, where she was born and grew up, had been her home her entire life. Our visits were enhanced considerably by the members of the Amici del Forte di Gavi Association. Led by Andrea Scotto, they did everything possible to show us not only the wonders of the castle but the beautiful Piedmont area surrounding it as well.

We received a similar welcome at the Military Secondary School and College in Moravská Třebová, formerly known as

Mährisch Trübau. Starting with the impressive new museum, the staff, led by Josef Kučera and Jaroslav Flieger, helped us uncover the many traces of its past identity as Oflag VIIIF. At the Gestapo Museum in Prague, Colonel Emil Kulfánek kindly agreed to serve as our guide while Jiri Beran from the British Council acted as translator. A member of the Czech Freedom Fighters Society, Colonel Kulfánek was only fourteen when he joined his father in the uprising against the Nazis in 1945.

There were many others who helped in this research, each one a caretaker of part of Alastair's incredible story. In Castelvetrano, it was the debonair expat Andrew Brownfoot who helped recreate Alastair's Sicilian escape, while Padre Curto and the men of Racalmuto's Società di Mutuo Soccorso showed us where he was recaptured. Dr Andrea Hoffmann provided a wealth of information about the Klinikum Wahrendorff where Alastair feigned insanity. And in the historic bath town of Bad Oeynhausen, which was home to Alastair for more than two years, Doris Koch helped recreate the presence of the British Army of the Rhine. I was also given access to the city's archives thanks to Stefanie Hillebrand. The Royal Air Force Museum Archives in Hendon also provided valuable information, especially regarding Buck Palm.

My guide through the labyrinthine world of the 'major' and 'minor' war crimes trials was Lorie Charlesworth. Relentless and good-humoured, she never failed to ask the hard questions. Nor did David Anderson, who provided similar guidance navigating the judicial war against the Mau Mau. A model of academic collegiality, Anderson invited me to Oxford University to explore his extensive collection of court records. I learned more about Alastair's time in Africa from Colin Baker, Angus

Macdonald and Peter Smith, who happily reminisced about their days together in Malawi. I am also grateful to Ian Balfour for his efforts to recreate Alastair's life in Edinburgh of the 1930s, when Alastair was apprenticed at Balfour and Manson, the Frederick Street law firm which Ian's grandfather founded. Alastair's cousins, Jean and Robert Cram, helped considerably toward this end as well.

The first lines of this book were written while a fellow at the Liguria Study Center for the Arts and Humanities in Bogliasco, Italy. Just forty miles from Gavi, it was the perfect place to start and I am thankful for their initial support. I also owe thanks to the American Philosophical Society whose Franklin Research Grant allowed me to spend the better part of a summer conducting research at the British National Archives at Kew. My own university, Tufts, was no less supportive, awarding me several travel grants, and in 2014 a Senior Research Fellowship. A year later I was invited to be a fellow at the Hawthornden Retreat for Writers on the North Esk River in Scotland. What the castle and landscape didn't provide in inspiration, my castle-mates – Kia Corthron, Ian Holding, Marianne Jungmaier, Hamish Robinson, Pauls Toutonghi, and Barry Webster – did.

I had the good fortune as well to be able to work with Georgina Morley at Macmillan who supported this project from the moment it was introduced. Always on the lookout for a good escape story, Georgina gently steered the book home with a sure hand. My agent, Andrew Gordon, was not only equally supportive but a wonderful critic whose subtle suggestions helped make this a better book in many ways.

There are some people without whom this book might never have been written. One of them is Robin Campbell, the archivist for the Scottish Mountaineering Club. Robin was the first person to register the existence of the journals, and even though he doubted I would ever be able to decipher them, still made the effort to scan and send them to me. Of course, without the indefatigable Amelia Gray, Robin's prediction might have proved true. In addition to being a talented short-story writer, Amelia turned out to be a brilliant cryptographer, capable of understanding what others couldn't. Today Alastair's journals are housed in the Manuscript Collections of the National Library of Scotland in Edinburgh.

Robin did much more than simply provide access to Alastair's journals. He answered endless questions about the world of Scottish mountaineering, and even more important, introduced me to Isobel Cram. It didn't take long for Isobel to throw herself into the project, contributing in any way she could. The fact that she was already in her mid-eighties by the time we met never seemed to matter. Consistently upbeat and sharp as a tack, she had a hysterical sense of humour and perfect recall; in short, the kind of person one liked to be around. She was a great friend and we miss her dearly.

While everyone listed here has made a real contribution, no matter how small, to telling Alastair's story, no one did more than my wife, Kate Wheeler. Despite working on her own novel and at times feeling captive to the demands of my research, she never lost faith in the project and remained its biggest booster from the very start. On every trip she was there beside me, translating, exploring, imagining what Alastair might have felt and done. She made his story her own and it is to her that this book is dedicated. She was the best companion one could have, the ideal partner should one ever need to escape.

# Notes

Unless otherwise noted, all quotes by Alastair Cram are taken from his collected journals, now in the National Library of Scotland. The collection was organized and donated to the library by Isobel Cram, whose kind permission for their use here is gratefully acknowledged.

## Preface: Finding Alastair Cram

'the Harry Houdini of the Second World War'. Personal communication from playwright and novelist Kia Corthron. The figure of twenty-one escapes is based on Alastair's own calculations although others have placed the number as high as twenty-nine. See Alastair Lorimer Cram, MI9 report, and Stewart 2009: 1.

'Alastair was a modest man . . .' and 'He was a well-known loner . . .' Letter from Isobel Cram, 13 October 2006.

'For, when you escape, you court loneliness . . .' Reid 1974.

'He was a contradiction in terms . . .' Isobel Cram, personal communication.

The pre-war years were restless ones for Alastair who found it difficult to settle down and practise law. He wandered a bit and even spent time as a member of Fraser Darlings' experimental community on Tanera in the Summer Isles. A pioneering conservationist, Darling immediately recognized the inner conflict Alastair was going through:

What an extraordinary open and innocent face for a lawyer, I had thought to myself, but soon I saw how his face could be that of the mystic and idealist he is, one moment, and the sharp, practical man of affairs the next. The dualism was in his character as well as in his face, and the warring of these two sides had brought him here, now the mystic in the ascendant. Darling 1944: 73.

## Chapter 1: The Mountain

*Operation Crusader* began on the evening of 18 November 1941, when the British Eighth Army crossed into Libya from Egypt. While fighting went on west of Tobruk until the end of December, Rommel abandoned the siege on the 4th. German and Italian combined casualties were 38,300 while British casualties were 17,700. The total number of tanks destroyed was well over 1,000. Although Alastair places his date of capture as 23 November 1941, his commanding officer, Captain Garth Ledgard, puts it a day earlier. Murphy 1961: 524.

'Most of us army types . . .' Hill, n.d.: 318.

'That SOB ruined a perfect escape'. Palmer 1981: 266.

'I felt guilty and ashamed at the terrible and utter waste of it all . . .' Ross 1997: 60.

'Mountaineering is a means to an end and that end is merely a beginning'. Alastair Cram, 'Notes on How To's of Climbing'. Unpublished paper. Courtesy Isobel Cram.

*the sensation of not being alone* . . . See, for example, Howell 1947.

## Chapter 2: Enter the Baron

*Like most Italians, he was amazed that anyone would want to leave the safety of a prison camp* . . . When a tunnel was discovered at Chieti, the bewildered commandant told the assembled prisoners, 'Gentlemen,

I cannot understand why you try and escape. After all, you have the Italian sun!' Horner 1948: np.

'Capua was about as miserable a place as could be.' Ross 1997: 78.

'We were certainly much more free . . .' Newby 1972: 44.

'lost interest in everything . . .' Millar 1946: 94.

'There are reports from thousands of men and women . . .' *The Times*, 1 November 1916.

'The undoubted excellence of our Vice-Captain . . .' *The V.A.N.*, 9 March 1933.

'At first Cram used to have an excited . . .' Millar 1946: 82.

'fanatical'. Hill n.d.: 320

'an escapologist'. Millar 1946 81.

*one of the greatest tennis matches ever played.* See Fisher 2009.

'escapers were the military elite of the POW world'. Gilbert 2006: 274.

'We felt our spirits rise as we passed inside'. Straker n.d., Pt 2: 22.

'Worn out though I was . . .' Millar 1946: 77.

'Alastair was of course another matter . . .' Sir Thomas Macpherson, personal communication, 11 December 2007.

'I had to convince him that I was serious'. Pringle 1988: 42.

'small and very pretty palazzo'. Ibid.: 32.

'The monastery was bound to have exits . . .' Pringle 1988: 42.

*Only six had managed to do so . . .* This remarkably low number of successful escapes was based on a total of 602 attempts as reported by the Italian War Ministry between December 1940 and July 1943. 'Out of a British, Imperial and Commonwealth prisoners-of-war population in excess of 60,000, this was a disappointingly small proportion: 1 in 100 tried, 1 in 10,000 succeeded.' Absalom 1994: 28.

'It was very difficult to travel in Italy . . .' Newby 1972: 30.

'I think we were each wondering . . .' Pringle 1988: 43.

*George Millar claimed it was their boots* . . . Millar 1946: 104.

'He told me to keep my knees slightly bent . . .' Pringle 1988: 50.

## Chapter 3: The Escape Academy

'Gentlemen, please don't suck the bones . . .' Interview with Sir Tommy Macpherson, 21 August 2007.

'used to get up before anyone else . . .' Riddiford 2004: 65.

*Debts were settled with camp-issued buoni* . . . Gambling was such a widespread problem that in some camps it was completely prohibited as noted by Michael Ross: 'Gambling debts, sometimes well beyond an officer's army pay, resulting in the main from card marathons, were settled by personal letters to banks at home requesting transfer of funds. At one point matters started to get so out of hand that the SBO wisely intervened and put a stop to these practices altogether.' 1997: 85.

'it looked exactly like a slum'. Riddiford 2004: 63.

'But for his being captured . . .' Ibid.: 64.

'initiated in the mysteries of double entry'. Pope n.d.: 75.

'background and upbringing was as remote . . .' Marshall 1975: 142.

'at first sight it was easy to under-rate him'. Ibid.: 141.

'During the whole war . . .' Riddiford 2004: 15.

'I was enjoying the sensation I was causing . . .' Ibid.: 51.

'Such thoughts weighed with me . . .' Ibid.: 47–48, 104.

'wave of exaltation'. Hargest 1954: 100.

'the truest time of my life'. Walker 1984: 122.

'never felt more alive'. Ash 2005: 170.

'escaping gene', 'Houdini Syndrome' and 'Escaping is quite addictive . . .'Ash 2005: 172, 237, 112.

'the greatest sport of all'. Reid 1952: 17.

*One estimate from the officers' camp at Chieti* . . . Wilson 2000: 118.

*Only thirty men could be found* . . . Millar 1946: 106.

'selfishness'. Ross 1997:100.

'The would-be escaper at Padula . . .' Millar 1946: 101–102.

'there was a different atmosphere in Camp 5 . . .' Armstrong 1947: 134.

'banded together' and 'by virtue of . . .' Ibid.: 143.

'The spirit of the camp was better . . .' Pope n.d.: 70.

'a certain gaiety', 'This was one of the secrets . . .' and 'The camp developed a magnificent *esprit de corps* . . .' Riddiford 2004: 69.

'It should have been the worst . . .' and 'Whereas at Padula I was able to sin . . .' Millar 1946: 129, 130.

*Over 170 attempts were made with at least 32 men getting back home.* See Chancellor 2001: 393.

'The principal resemblance . . .' Pringle 1988: 141.

'Colditz Myth'. Mackenzie 2004.

'there was no possibility of escape . . .' Pringle 1988: 59.

## Chapter 4: The Cistern Tunnel

*At Colditz, Pierre Mairesse-Lebrun* . . . Chancellor 2001: 51–7. Brian Jackson was thrown over the wire into a snow drift in early spring 1944 at Marlag, the German camp for naval officers. He was unfortunately recaptured on the Swiss border. Pope n.d.: 35.

*while in Greece* . . . Farran 1948: 109.

*Oflag VIB in Warburg* . . . Arkwright, 1948.

'They were the only accommodation in the camp . . .' Armstrong 1947: 138.

'a bald, lobsterish man . . .' Millar 1946: 138.

'Kill him! Kill Him! Shoot him with your revolver.' Clifton 1952: 290.

'"Feriti!" – "Wounded" – and that gave him sufficient courage . . .' Ibid.

'Some tunnels were successful in their immediate object . . .' Armstrong 1947: 149.

'magical escape route'. Clifton 1952: 282.

'working and playing on the team'. Ibid.

'He was a typical turnkey, cruel, boastful and arrogant . . .' Alastair Cram in a letter to Colonel G. Barratt, Judge Advocate General's Office, 17 September 1946. In Ill-Treatment of PsW at PG 5 (Gavi): TNA WO311/1200.

*2,180 of them from New Zealand* . . . Mason 1954: 60.

'measly five days'. James Craig papers, courtesy Robyn Molloy.

'It was one of the most remarkable achievements . . .' Millar 1946: 136.

'The Escape'. Clifton 1952: 282.

'Buck was a born escaper . . .' Riddiford 2004: 68.

'Homeric build, comparable to Johnny Weissmuller'. Clifton 1952: 282.

'South African Hercules [who] could quickly kill anyone with his bare hands'. Millar 1946: 136, 155.

*the cistern measured 120 by 60 feet and was as high as it was wide.* There is some variation on the exact size of the cistern. *The Times* (14 December 1945), Cram's journal, and Palm's MI9 Report, generally agree with the dimensions used here. Di Raimondo (2008: 156), who worked from historical sources but was never in the cistern, claims it was somewhat smaller, measuring 75 feet by 60 feet and 30 feet high.

'long, slanting, hen-toed strides'. Millar 1946: 137.

*The South Africans, six in all* . . . While there were six South Africans in Buck Palm's room only four of them, Palm, Paterson, Pole, and Wuth, worked on the cistern tunnel. The total number of South African officers at Gavi was 23, second in number only to the 122 British officers in the camp. International Red Cross Committee Report Number 5 on Prisoners of War in Camp No. 5, Inspected on September 8, 1943. Red Cross 34.

'an old soul' and 'Pops'. Diana Duff, personal communication, 11 December 2011.

*soldiers from the Dominions and Colonies the most successful escapers* . . . As Cram noted in his journal: 'The high percentage of successful escapes by officers and men recruited from the Dominions and Colonies is largely due to the advantages enjoyed by them in their home environment. Many of these to whom I spoke were quite unaware of the comparative breadth of their woodcraft. They accepted this skill as a commonplace, a natural background to their method of life.' Cram Journals.

'Good personality . . .' South African Military College Report on A. J. H. Pole, 23 October 1940.

'I feel I cannot part with both my sons to be sent so far away'. Letter from Ivy Pole to Jan Smuts, 12 August 1940. Courtesy Diana Duff.

'With reference to your minute . . .' Letter from Colonel, O. C.: Voortrekkerhoogte & Transvaal Comd. to Ivy Pole, 9 September 1940. Courtesy Diana Duff.

*an axle from a donkey cart.* Clifton 1952: 283.

'It was rare that there was a roll call without the Italians losing their tempers and certainly losing their count.' Macpherson 2010: 79.

*a well-known, Swiss military architect.* The architect was Pietro Morettini, who in addition to designing the powder house in 1718 was responsible for several other projects at Gavi. Di Raimondo 2008: 85.

'Now we have a new experience, we have victory . . .' Winston Churchill, in a speech delivered at the Mansion House, London, 10 November 1942. A full version of the speech was published in the *New York Times* the following day.

'There is no breeding ground for wishful thinking more prolific than a Prisoner of War camp . . .' Armstrong 1947: 141.

'From being autocratic and domineering, the Italian officers and men became friendly and sympathetic.' Ibid.: 142.

'the work [they] did was only marginally useful and wasted a shift'. Pringle 1988: 64.

'To me it is one of the fine pictures of the war . . .' Millar 1946: 137.

*100,000 Reichsmark reward placed on his head.* Hoe 1990.

'He possessed above all the ultimate quality of a leader . . .' MacLean 1990.

'the most horrendous rebel yell'. Hoe 1992: 223.

'My dearest Mother . . . I got news of David today . . .' Ibid.: 236. The naval officer referred to was Commander Walter 'Bruno' Brown, a Fleet Air Arm officer who was captured with Peter Medd when their Swordfish was shot down near Tobruk on 20 July 1940. In March 1943 he was one of a number of naval officers exchanged for prisoners with equivalent ranks from the Italian navy who had been interned in Saudi Arabia after the fall of Abyssinia. Michael Pope was extremely disappointed when he wasn't selected, recalling it as 'one of the most disturbing events in my time as a prisoner'. Pope n.d.: 79.

'liked enormously'. Hoe 1992: 233.

'ahead striding rapidly toward the sapling and the rope'. Pringle 1988: 72.

'I was wet and cold, but I was happy'. Ibid.: 73.

'What I had done . . .' Ibid.: 84.

'Disappointing though it was that no one had succeeded in getting clean away . . .' Armstrong 1947: 153.


## Chapter 5: The Last Days of Gavi

'My Dear Son, I send you birthday greetings . . .' Letter courtesy Isobel Cram.

*when two German officers visited the castle in mid-August*. Dan Riddiford also recalled his response to the Germans' visits and the consensus in the camp regarding possible transfer to Germany: 'The Italians told us that these visits were due to the fact that Gavi – Campo 5 – occupied a strategic position, and the Germans might later have to hold it to secure their line of retreat. But it was not contemplated by anyone, German or Italian, that the prisoners would be removed to Germany.' Riddiford 2004: 79.

'Now we are allies'. Ibid.: 80.

'dashing and fearless'. Ibid.: 78.

'There were no signs of any amphibious or air-borne operation . . .' Clifton 1952: 294.

*George Millar claims that it began as a lark* . . . Millar 1946: 143.

'a miserable and decrepit old colonel'. Ibid.

*It was a pitiful scene* . . . While the number of Italians versus Germans varies depending on the account, the sense of disbelief at the overwhelming odds in favour of the Italians is consistent. I have used Riddiford's estimate of 230 Italians against thirty Germans.

(Riddiford 2004: 81). Armstrong, on the other hand, speaks of 'the spectacle of 480 Italians handing over their arms to about 100 Germans'. Armstrong 1947: 158.

'Gavi had not sullied its centuries-old record of instant surrender.' Millar 1946: 144.

'we realized we had fallen from the fat to the fire'. Yeoman 1991: 112.

*the commander and his staff along with 5,000 prisoners were slaughtered in cold blood.* See Lamb 1993: 133. In addition to the 5,000 Italians massacred after their surrender, 1,200 were killed in combat and many others died when the three ships taking them to Greece were sunk by mines.

'British POWs: Prevent them falling into German hands . . .' Ibid.: 163. Why the Italians instructed camp commandants to free only white prisoners is unclear. As Lamb emphasizes, it contravened Allied policy and did not emanate from the British or Americans. While there may have been a handful of African-American prisoners, the main group of blacks referred to would have been soldiers from colonial Africa as well as Ethiopians from the 1935–36 Abyssinian War.

*By August 1943 there were 80,000 prisoners of war in Italy* . . . Absalom, who conducted the most thorough study of this subject, gives the following breakdown: 'British 42,194; Imperial (mainly South African) 26,126; French (Gaullist) 2,000; US 1,310; other European allies 49; Greek 1,689; Yugoslav 6,153; Russian 12.' Absalom 1994: 23.

'In the event of an Allied invasion of Italy . . .' Ibid.: 27. For additional discussions of this order and its consequences, see Foot and Langley 1979: 156–70, Gilbert 2006: 279–96, and Lamb 1993: 160–73.

*And while 40 or so prisoners disobeyed orders and escaped, 1,600 others were put on trains to Germany* . . . Absalom 1994: 218. Gilbert estimates that the final number of officers and orderlies in the camp was 1,300. Gilbert 2006: 286.

'Unlike the true escaper . . .' Ibid: 284, 286. For more on the 'moral inertia known as *gefangenitis*' as it affected prisoners' 'fitness, confidence and initiative needed to make a break', see Absalom 1994: 28 and Foot and Langley 1979: 162.

*They then went on to Intra where the camp's interpreter had arranged for a guide* . . . The principal interpreter and second-in-command at Fontanellato was Captain Mario Camino. With an English mother and wife, as well as a business in Britain, Camino's sympathies were no secret. After the armistice, he helped settle many of the prisoners in surrounding farms and also led several parties of escapers to the Swiss border, including Lieutenant Colonel De Burgh and his two staff assistants. An account of the varying experiences of the Fontanellato prisoners can be found in English, ed., 1997. See also, Davies 1975, Graham 2000, Newby 1972, and Ross 1997.

*Although as many as 50,000 prisoners escaped* . . . Absalom 1994: 11, 31–2. Absalom calls it 'the greatest mass-escape in history'. Ibid. 11. See also, Lamb 1993: 168 and Gilbert 2006: 287.

'Some escapers graded farms according to the number of haystacks'. English, ed., 1997: 44–5.

a 'strange alliance'. Absalom 1994: 11.

'A damned silly order . . .' Clifton 1952: 293.

*Clifton quickly assembled a three-man team* . . . Wadeson, who was also called 'Uncle Waddy', was born on 4 July 1898. The other members of Wadeson's team were Brian Upton, a major in the Essex Yeomanry known as Hack-in-the-Bush, and John de Filek Jago, a lieutenant commander with the Fleet Air Arm known as Don Jago.

'Only the first thirty felt happy over the placings.' Clifton 1952: 296.

'His sole duty, as he now saw it . . .' Riddiford 2004: 84. For a further appreciation of the priest, see Oliver 1998: 79.

'I was pretty well punished by everybody . . .' TNA ADM 156/272 Proceedings and Findings Court Martial for Lieutenant Commander David A. Fraser, RN, Submarine H. M. 'Oswald'. Royal Naval Barracks, Portsmouth, April 17–18, 1946: 1193, 1207. Clifton claimed Tooes was 'half-crazy with home worries' (1952: 297) while Alastair recalled him as 'a little unbalanced'.

'the marvellous one leading all the way downhill to the village'. Clifton 1952: 298.

'Bad luck again or a bad appreciation anyway.' Ibid.

'prize prisoner'. Oliver 1998: 88: 'We told him it was more than the lives of the German officers were worth to leave without him, the prize prisoner. But the more we beseeched him to join the rest of the prisoners who depended upon him for a semblance of legal protection the more adamant he became. In this sudden crisis he suddenly looked fearful and small and, stripped of his insignia he was no longer our Senior British Officer but a figure of contempt.'

'The idiocy of Clifton gave it all away . . .' Interview with Sir Tommy Macpherson, 21 August 2007.

'Even the dumbest Jerry would know that we were not all present.' Armstrong 1947: 165.

'they were all sitting around, quiet as mice, waiting.' Clifton 1952: 301.

'a charming young fellow who had been at school in England and spoke perfect English . . .' Riddiford 2004: 85. The admiration expressed by several prisoners for von Schroeder recalls the relation of von Rauffenstein and de Boeldieu in Jean Renoir's *Grand Illusion*, where class trumps nationality, especially among aristocrats.

'knew the game was up . . .' Clifton 1952: 302.

'Had it been checked?' A compilation based on the accounts of Clifton 1952: 304, Millar 1946: 150, and Riccomini 1943: 3. Among the four officers found in the woodpile were Lieutenant Dudley Schofield, Royal Fusiliers and Commandos, Lieutenant Harry Wakelin, Royal Horse Artillery and SOE, and Captain Ian Howie, Royal Armoured Corps.

the 'good, cheerful and pleasant Oberleutnant'. Pope 1992: 29.

'You will find your things in rather a mess . . .' Millar 1946: 149.

## Chapter 6: The Train

'American film gangster types'. Riccomini 1943: 4.

'Breastplates'. Pope n.d.: 91.

'Grim, with hard, calloused faces . . .' Clifton 1952: 305.

*Even before they reached the railhead at Acqui, two men had leapt from the trucks and disappeared.* The two officers were Captain Frank Simms,

Royal Warwickshire Regiment, and Lieutenant Ormsby Pitchford, Northumberland Fusiliers. Simms met up with Peter Medd soon after and together they completed the 700-mile journey to the Allied lines. Pitchford also got through to the Allies, where he rejoined his unit only to be killed four months later at Cassino.

*only 80 of the original 120 who set out from Gavi were left* . . . Riddiford 2004: 88.

*Along with two South Africans* . . . The two South Africans, whom Riddiford claimed 'always did everything together', were Flight Lieutenant Harry Currin, South African Air Force, and Captain John Forsdick, Transvaal Scottish Regiment. Ibid.: 93.

*Tommy Macpherson and Colin Armstrong [and] another New Zealander* . . . The third member of their party was Captain Allan Yeoman, 21st New Zealand Infantry Battalion. Yeoman was able to reach Yugoslavia after eluding capture in Italy. After spending two months with the partisans, however, he was arrested once again.

'enough explosive to blow up half of southern France'. Macpherson 2010: 132.

'Gavi has every reason to be proud of its record . . .' Armstrong 1947: 177.

'Because so many British officers attempted to escape . . .' Clifton 1952: 311.

'There is a machine gun mounted on the front and back of the roof of every cattle truck . . .' Pringle 1988: 90.

'Crisis found the men in Italy a sorry lot . . .' Michael Pope recorded a similar impression in his Wartime Log: 'The men were entirely apathetic waiting to see who would win, unwilling to take on the Germans themselves; the women were more courageous & told the Germans what they thought of them.' Pope n.d.: 92.

'like terriers after rats'. Millar 1946: 157.

'How close are you to getting out? . . .' Pope 1992: 29.

'stressing the absolute necessity of rolling away from the line . . .' Herbert 1962: 19. While known to everyone as 'Percy', Pike's real name was David Ivor Pike. A flight lieutenant with the 113th Squadron, he was captured 29 June 1940, when his Blenheim was shot down near Tobruk. In January 1942 he escaped from Sulmona with Michael Pope and E. Garrad-Cole but was recaptured five days later after crossing the mountains to the Adriatic.

*At least one was killed* . . . Lieutenant P. H. Watters from South Africa was the officer killed while Lieutenant Gregory Phillips of the Somerset Light Infantry, who was the last to jump, was wounded in the shoulder and recaptured soon after.

'We were prepared to be shot on the run . . .' Pringle 1988: 91.

'There was just no point in jumping any longer'. Pope 1992: 30. Peter Medd (1951: 23) made a similar observation in *The Long Walk Home*: 'The greatest bogey to spontaneous escape is apathy. A fleeting opportunity occurs; you say to yourself: "No, a better opportunity is bound to occur soon." Or you suddenly think of the danger to the others, and, thinking, the chance slips by, never to return. You know you are determined to escape, but the starting friction is terribly hard to overcome. The secret of spontaneous escape is: Don't think go.' Alastair called it 'the fatal error'.

'If the main body had been as lucky . . .' Clifton 1952: 318. Clifton states that of the second group of seventy-two prisoners only between thirty-four and thirty-nine arrived at their final destination in Moosburg, Stalag VIIA. Michael Pope puts the number who arrived at forty in his Wartime Log (n.d.: 96) and forty-five in his memoir (1992: 30). Colin Armstrong (1947: 177) makes an overall calculation that at least eighty prisoners from the combined group of 176 escaped from the trains or transit camps before arriving at a permanent camp in Germany. A number of prisoners escaped from the second train while it spent the night in Innsbruck. Among them were Jack Pringle, David Stirling, Bertie Chester-Williams, Ian Howie and Roy Wadeson.

*The 'Italianization' of the region* . . . See Steininger 2003 for a detailed discussion of this history.

*By 1943 at least 75,000 had relocated* . . . Ibid.: 1, 50. The German-speaking population of South Tyrol at this time was estimated to be 200,000.

'This man is seriously ill . . .' Clifton 1952: 316.

'The wily Baron had decided that he had gone far enough towards Germany.' Millar 1946: 160. Alastair's dramatic escape from the train was noted by everyone present. However, the placement of the event varies somewhat. Both Alastair and George Clifton say it occurred in Bolzano, which all evidence would support. Jack Pringle, writing fifty years after the event, places it at 'Mezza Coronna, just short of the Brenner Pass' (1988: 91). Yet Mezza Coronna is only 15km north of Trento and far short of the pass. George Millar, on the other hand, says it was in a small village one station beyond Mezza Coronna (1946: 160). And Michael Pope recalls it taking place in two separate locations. In his 1992 memoir he writes that Alastair was taken off the train at Coronna (sic). But in his Wartime Log, written immediately after the event, he says that 'Cram went to hospital in Bolzano' (n.d.: 96).

'the great fantastic spires of the Funffinger Spitze'. The Funffinger Spitze is part of the Langkofel group, a dramatic amphitheatre-like formation of peaks in the western Dolomites, which would have been directly north of where Alastair was heading.

*On his fifth day out . . . Alastair broke one of his own rules . . .* In the escape manual Alastair wrote immediately after the war, he emphasized: 'It is essential not to begin walking too early in the evening although the temptation may be very great due to cold and excitement and the urge to cover the ground.'

'Where is he? I'm going to kill the English bastard . . .' Clifton 1952: 322. Clifton claims that Alastair arrived at the local prison already bloody and beaten by the SOD who captured him, but Alastair makes it clear that it was a drunken German soldier who came into his cell soon after his arrival and beat him. Alastair Lorimer Cram, MI9/S/PG (G) 2988: 5.

## Chapter 7: The Forest

*Stalag VIIA:* Stalag is an abbreviation of *Stammlager* or 'central camp'. Stalags also had numerous work camps attached to them. These

*Arbeitskommando*, as they were known, supplied labour for agricultural and non-military factory work. Oflag, on the other hand, stood for *Offizierslager* or 'officers' camp'. Officers, as agreed upon by the Geneva Convention, were prohibited from working. The Roman numerals attached to each camp referred to the defence district in which it was located. Gilbert (2006: 66) puts the number of POW camps in Germany at 248.

*According to one source there were soldiers from seventy-two nations . . .* Franz, ed., 1982: 14.

*Many of the 15,000 at Moosburg . . .* Ibid.: 21. Charles Rollings (2007: 5) states that of the 5.7 million Russians taken prisoner during the Second World War 57 per cent, or 3.3 million, died.

'Thank you. Please send more.' There are a number of versions of this story including Edy 2010: 116, Hill n.d.: 328, and Millar 1946: 169. Alastair was equally appreciative of the Russian prisoners at Moosburg: 'The Russians were as daring as men could be. They would climb the wires into our compounds by day or night like cats while the Germans fired on them from the sentry towers. Firewood they brought and leather goods and an infinity of good humour. Then slipping the tins inside their padded jackets back they would go careless of shouts, dogs and bullets.'

'Cram stood ahead of us, his head swathed in bandages . . .' Millar 1946: 171. Clifton made a similar observation upon seeing Alastair at Moosburg: 'So Cram rejoined us, his head literally bloody but his spirits as high as ever. Once upon a time Robert Louis Stevenson prayed for "courage, gaiety, and the quiet mind" – Alastair had full measure of all of these qualities.' Clifton 1952: 322.

*he arrived at a large lake more than three miles long and a mile wide.* Although Alastair didn't realize it, the lake was the reservoir at Eching that formed part of the Isar river's extensive hydroelectric system.

*Heydrich's assassination . . .* Acting Protector of Bohemia and Moravia, SS Gruppenführer Reinhard Heydrich was the highest ranking German official to be assassinated during the war. Attacked by British-trained Czech commandos on 27 May 1942, he didn't die

until several days later, at which point the Germans unleashed a
reign of terror, destroying two villages and murdering and arresting
hundreds. The decision by the Czech government-in-exile to carry
out the assassination remains a controversial one to this day.

*Spittal*, whose official designation was Stalag XVIII A/Z, was a subcamp of the much larger Stalag XVIIIA in Wolfsberg, a hundred
miles to the east. Built for Other Ranks and enlisted men, it housed
prisoners from various countries who worked in the surrounding
countryside.

*Allan McSweyn*. A twenty-five-year-old bomber pilot shot down over
Bremen at the end of June 1941, McSweyn was a dedicated escaper.
After several failed attempts he exchanged identities with a private
to take advantage of work parties' reduced security. His final escape,
however, was through a tunnel at Stalag VIIIB, Lamsdorf, on 19
September 1943. Like Palm and Tsoucas, he passed through
Lunéville, where the same gendarmerie captain helped him.

The two Canadians, whose Halifax was shot down on the
evening of 16 September, 1943, were Sergeant Len Martin, wireless
operator, and Pilot Officer Harry Smith, navigator. It was the 6'4"
Smith who developed heart problems during the crossing.

'bombed-out refugees, deaf, dumb and shell-shocked, to a resort in
the south'. Clutton-Brock 2009: 143. The others in the truck in
addition to Mary, Pauline and the six escapers, were the driver,
Henriette Rejern, and Lieutenant Peyraud, a Ruffec gendarme who
at great personal risk had provided the petrol.

'a small, wiry Frenchman'. Cooper 1997: 50.

*free and safe in Spain*. For additional accounts of this remarkable jour-
ney, see Clutton-Brock 2009, Cooper 1997, McSweyn 1961,
Wynne 1961 and the MI9 reports of Richard Carr, Ralph Buckley
Palm, and George Tsoucas.

*The Freikorps*, or British Free Corps as it was officially known, was a
unit of the Waffen SS made up of volunteers from the ranks of
British and Commonwealth prisoners of war. Established in the
autumn of 1943 with the goal of recruiting soldiers to fight against
a 'common Bolshevik enemy', the Free Corps never had more than

two dozen or so members who were limited to non-combat duties. However, several of them worked for German radio, transmitting propaganda to English-speaking audiences. After the war, the founder of the British Free Corps, John Amery, was tried for treason and hanged.

'The German's whole attitude and manner were abominable.' Alastair Cram, MI9 Report 7.

## Chapter 8: Stirling's Folly

'a shouting, bullying, ranting type of German, constantly making threats.' Captain Ian Weston Smith in 'Ill-Treatment of Col. Kenyon at Luckenwalde'. TNA WO311/1021. Schaper's adopted American identity was apparently used for multiple purposes, one day pretending to be the turncoat interrogator and the next a plant trying to extract information from fellow prisoners. It's impossible to say how many people he fooled if any.

'a marked man'. Hill n.d.: 338.

'Little Siberia'. English and Moses 2006: 50.

'everything came out of there . . .' Alan Hurst-Brown, personal communication, 7 July 2012.

'This huge 4-storied building . . .' From the private diary of Robert Simmons, courtesy Geoffrey Simmons.

'Among our number were several . . .' Murray 2002: 94. The Red Cross report from 7 December 1944 states that 'Lectures are being given in approximately 45 subjects, covering about 135 periods per week. Classes range from 150 students downwards.' TNA WO224/77: 10.

'the course of self improvement'. Crawley 1985: 5.

'For the first time in my life I had the leisure to think, to be still.' Lloyd-Jones 2013: 96. For more on what Michael Burn called the 'mental escaper', see Burn 1974, Morgan 1945: 130–31 and Newby 1972: 45–6.

'the extraordinary character of the man . . .' Murray 2002: 95.

'Cram is here and quite the most remarkable man I have met in this war.' Lloyd-Jones 2013: 91.

'We were on a sure loser'. Pringle 1988: 98. David Stirling expressed the same pessimism: 'We were quite sure we were not going to make it. There was a lot of tough country ahead with not much prospect for filling the nosebag with the sort of fodder we would need. It was the most marvellous feeling though, just to be out in the countryside again and though we quickly tired no one could take away the pleasure of freedom, no matter how temporary.' Hoe 1992: 239.

*Though some found such behaviour childish and undignified, it clearly appealed to David Stirling's subversive side* . . . David recalled Eichstätt (Oflag VIIB) as 'a most unruly place and really quite jolly in many ways – the Germans were totally incapable of maintaining discipline'. Hoe 1992: 240.

Robert Simmons, on the other hand, noted the difference between POW cultures in Italy and Germany, especially after the arrival of a group at Mährisch Trübau: 'There are some 70 blokes here who arrived from Eichstätt in January. They notice a difference both in our own people and the Germans. Our people are much more passive, not at all obstreperous and very keen on planning and organization. The VIIB-ites note the absence of antagonism.' From the private diary of Robert Simmons, courtesy Geoffrey Simmons.

'Warburg Wire Job.' The escape, also called 'Operation Olympia', is commonly known by the name of the town in which the camp, Oflag VIB was located. For more on this escape, see Arkwright 1948 and Walker 1984.

'the place was in absolute chaos'. Hoe 1992: 241.

'a delightful cove'. Ibid. Colonel Malcolm Cyrus Waddilove, King George V's Own Light Infantry, Indian Army.

'the kingpin of all the escape rackets'. Herbert 1962: 43. Alan Hoe, David's biographer, claims that: 'In Mährisch Trübau prison camp Stirling achieved what was probably one of the greatest feats of persuasion and leadership of his life.' Hoe 1992: 240.

*1,581 prisoners at Mährisch Trübau.* In addition to the officers, there were also 166 Other Ranks serving as orderlies. Mason 1954: 367, fn 2 and Oflag VIIIF, later Oflag 79, TNA WO224/77.

'If you gave up escaping as an occupation . . .' Walker 1984: 82.

'grew to love and feel more comfortable in than any in England'. Hill n.d.: 65.

*He was also one of a handful of code-writers* . . . There were a total of twenty-six code-writers in the camp at different times, all of them specially trained before their capture. Although Alastair never wrote coded letters, he was listed as the intelligence officer in charge of deciding on the information that should be sent to the War Office as well as disseminating the information that was received. Secret Camp Histories Oflag 79 (VIIIF) Querum TNA WO208/3292. For more on prisoner of war code-writing, see Green 1971.

'My Dear Tim . . .' Letter from Roy Wadeson to his son Tim, dated 18 August 1943. 'The Kid' refers to his wife Ruth Jean Wadeson. Courtesy Tim Wadeson.

*David, noticeably shaken, blamed the discovery on the leader of the group* . . . The officer in charge of the shift was Robby Mason, a Gavi veteran described by Millar as 'a lawyer, solemn and deep and intensely South African in all his opinions and reactions'. He was fined 720 Deutschmarks for destruction of German property. Millar 1946: 131 and Herbert 1962: 48.

'things against their better judgement'. Hoc 1992: 24.

'suicidal' and 'hare brained'. Yeoman 1991: 169 and Hurst-Brown n.d.: 70.

*much like the Wooden Horse* . . . This ingenious tunnel escape from the east compound of Stalag Luft III took place in October 1943. By using a vaulting horse, the tunnellers were able to shorten the distance they needed to dig considerably. All three participants succeeded in reaching Sweden. For a detailed account written by one of the participants, see Williams 1949.

'in the confidence of the Germans'. Pringle 1988: 114.

'Listen,' he said. 'I can get anything from these Germans . . .' Ibid.: 115–16.

'felt an instinctive distrust for van Zouco . . .' Killing by Means
  Unknown: TNA WO309/244.
'I am from the Czech underground army . . .' Pringle 1988: 124.
*That evening, a visibly shaken van Zouco brought some disturbing news . . .*
  Van Zouco learned about the murdered escapers from Ober-
  leutnant Haberhauer, the camp security officer, who had gone to
  Zwittau in order to inform Oflag VIIIF's commandant who was
  hospitalized there.
'The escape from prison camps is no longer a sport!' Bailey 1981: 75.
  For a more detailed discussion of the *Kugel Erlass* or 'Bullet Decree',
  issued by the head of the Gestapo on 4 March 1944, see Walters
  2013: 182.
'With a guilty conscience such as I had, there was no peace of mind
  after this.' Pringle 1988: 125.
'A good-will mission'. Pringle 1988: 128.
'I decided that to have maximum effect . . .' Hoe 1992: 247–8.
'I was not advocating taking up arms . . .' Ibid.: 247.
*three of David's men to exchange places* . . . The third officer with Griffiths and Forsdick was Lieutenant Geoff Jowett, a commando
  who had been in Gavi and was well known for his self-described
  fierceness. As one fellow commando said of him: 'Geoff Jowett, a
  Canadian, was small and stocky with a nearly bald head and a
  large moustache. More Scottish than the Scots, he wore his emotions on his sleeve and prided himself on being more aggressive
  and bloodthirsty than anyone else.' Deane-Drummond 1992: 13.
'Although brilliantly executed, the assassination of Heydrich was a
  political mistake . . .' Mastny 1971: 221. One of the main architects
  of the 'Final Solution', SS Gruppenführer Reinhard Heydrich was
  acting Protector of Bohemia and Moravia when he was assassinated
  by Czech commandos in May 1942. German retribution was swift
  and brutal, resulting in the deaths of 1,331 people, with hundreds
  more arrested and the villages of Lidice and Lezaky completely
  eradicated. Ibid.: 220.
'The plot,' he concluded, 'was quite indefensible'. Killing by Means
  Unknown: TNA WO309/244.

'The whole scheme now seemed so phoney . . .' Ibid.

*Curly Laing*. Lieutenant Arthur H. Laing, Royal Tank Regiment, was captured in North Africa and held in Campo 21, Chieti, before being moved to Germany. Laing remained in the army after the war, retiring as a major in 1971.

'I am well and cheery . . .' Letter to Maud Mackenzie, 10 May 1943. Courtesy Shaun and Hugh Keays-Byrne.

'I have made arrangements for a job also, after the war . . .' Letter to Maud Mackenzie, 20 February 1943. Courtesy Shaun and Hugh Keays-Byrne.

'Mackenzie had not been outside of a camp'. Killing by Means Unknown: TNA WO309/244.

'I got the shock of my life this morning . . .' Beckwith 1977: 98.

'Dearest Heart, Still no news from you . . .' Letter to Maud Mackenzie, 2 March 1944. Courtesy Shaun and Hugh Keays-Byrne. 'Babs' was the nickname of Mackenzie's younger sister, Ruth. Vi refers to Violet Dick who lived with the Mackenzie family and Roses to one of Maud's suitors. The Mackenzie home, Crofton Hurst, was destroyed by German bombs in 1941 which explains why they were discussing finding a new one.

'What if,' he asked, 'we simply walk through when the gate is open?' Humphrey Moon, personal communication, 27 December 2013.

'Easy does it,' said Wadeson . . . Hill n.d.: 347.

'A list of bogus but provocative lectures . . .' From the private diary of Robert Simmons, courtesy Geoffrey Simmons.

'The next person who moves will be shot!' Hurst-Brown n.d.: 69.

'The scheme was too grandiose to keep secret . . .' Killing by Means Unknown: TNA WO309/244.

'Saved by the gong!' Hurst-Brown n.d.: 70.

'a holocaust would have followed . . .' Killing by Means Unknown: TNA WO309/244.

'all highly improbable in retrospect . . .' Hoe 1992: 245.

'I knew his form so well . . .' Pringle 1988: 133.

'He was a very brave man.' Hill n.d.: 338.

*Jim Gaze*. Lawrence Gordon Gaze, Royal Tank Regiment. Captured at

Tobruk, Gaze spent two months at Gavi in the summer of 1942. Following his move to Germany after the Italian armistice, he made at least two train jumps, one of them on his way to Mährisch Trübau.

'spread Pro-British propaganda'. Killing by Means Unknown: TNA WO309/244.

## Chapter 9: Crazy To Get Home

'the Wehrmacht and Camp authorities who were decent enough not to send any records to Prague'. Killing by Means Unknown: TNA WO309/244.

*There was also a guillotine* . . . Prison records indicate that 1,176 people were guillotined during its years of operation. MacDonald and Kaplan 1995: 95–6, 100.

'were ethnic Germans from Romania . . .', 'the worst days of my life' and 'In the morning when the guards banged on our door . . .' Demetz 2008: 214, 216.

*the conquest of fear was said to lead to self-realization* . . . See Whipple-snaith 2007: 219–23.

'because British officers had been known to attack their guards'. Herbert 1962: 50.

'too frightened to give assistance'. Cram MI9 Report 8. Plunkett, like many others, made a similar observation based on his own experience: 'The Czech population had been so intimidated by the Gestapo that few Czechs were able to resist the Nazis and they all lived in fear, not for themselves but also for their families.' Plunkett and Pletts 2000: 49.

'lair of the troglodyte'. Walters 2013: 104.

*preparing nearly 4,000 customized maps* . . . Gill 2002: 170. The term 'Great Escape' emerged after the war with the publication of Paul Brickhill's popular account of that name. Roger Bushell and the other participants referred to it as 'Operation 200', derived from the number of escapers they planned to get out.

'It was not the treatment in the jails . . .' Plunkett and Pletts 2000: 82.

Plunkett's escaping partner, Bedrich 'Freddie' Dvorak, also survived, and was sent to Stalag Luft I with Ivor Tonder, another Czech from the Great Escape. They were only there a short time before being moved to Colditz, where they joined seventeen other Czechs in the RAF. Since Czechoslovakia had been annexed by Germany, they were treated as traitors and sentenced to death. The executions fortunately never took place.

'a ghost of his former self . . .' Pringle 1988: 136–7.

'he was on the point of a nervous break down'. Murray 2002: 105.

'One morning after roll call . . .' This account is a composite of two nearly identical versions found in Murray 2002: 105–6 and Dutton 1995: 745–6.

'non military form of gangster war!' Bailey 1981: 75.

'The news really scared the hell out of me . . .' Hoe 1992: 249.

*According to Alastair* . . . Killing by Means Unknown: TNA WO309/244 and Herbert 1962: 54. The two 'ghosts' were Capt. Tim O'Reilly, Royal Tank Regiment, and Lieutenant Alec Ling, Rifle Brigade. Both were former Gavi inmates. Ling had won an MC 'for conspicuous courage and leadership at Sidi Rezegh'.

'What was virtually a university . . .' Chutter 1954: 131.

'I used to go into an attic . . .' Hill n.d.: 391.

*The Red Cross called it* 'absolutely insufficient'. Red Cross Report, Oflag VIIIF, later Oflag 79: TNA WO224/77.

'The Luftwaffe, finding Allied bombing of Brunswick a little too hot . . .' Horner 1948: n.p.

'One had the impression that . . .' Ratcliffe n.d.: 35.

'The possibilities of such an escape . . .' Killing by Means Unknown: TNA WO309/244.

'Hugh's death has shaken me very considerably . . .' Beckwith, ed., 1977: 121.

'a slow talking, empty pipe sucking, even tempered good man'. John Forsdick, Letter to Miles, 1998: 3. Courtesy Charles and Elizabeth Forsdick.

'a more kindly, gentle man one could never hope to meet.' Yeoman 1991: 171.

'Dear Mrs. Wadeson . . .' Courtesy Tim Wadeson. Wadeson and Mackenzie's remains were moved to a military cemetery in Hanover after the war where they were left unmarked for seventy years. In July 2016, the War Graves Commission finally provided proper headstones following the tireless efforts of Roy Wadeson's son, Tim.

'to scrape the bottom . . .' Oliver 1998: 139.

'a melancholy state'. Rollings 2007: 3.

'a well-recognized form of neurasthenia . . .' Yarnall 2011: 163.

'Dachau had left Cram . . .' Murray 2002: 107.

*Doc Vaughan had successfully coached another officer* . . . The officer was Flight Lieutenant John Leeming who tells of his experience suffering from a 'bad case of persecution mania' at the Castello di Vincigliata in his 1951 book, *The Natives Are Friendly*.

*When the raid was over and he saw the devastation* . . . Isobel Cram, personal communication.

'Rhine Bashes'. Green 2012: 45.

'In the event of a move . . .' and 'It was a long, straggling, slow-moving column . . .' Reid 1947: 282–3.

'the squitters'. Green 2012: 112.

*Other groups, mistaken for German soldiers* . . . Victor Gammon documents a number of instances of POWs being strafed by Allied planes. One of the worst cases was at Gresse on 19 April 1945, when six RAF Typhoons attacked a column of evacuees killing at least thirty-seven prisoners and six German guards, with many more seriously wounded. Gammon 1996: 240–52.


## Chapter 10: Killing by Means Unknown

*in October 1945, the SAS was disbanded.* After considerable debate, it was believed that the SAS was no longer needed, and on 8 October 1945 it was disbanded. The decision was reversed, however, and the SAS was recommissioned as 21st SAS on 1 January 1947.

*the world's first major war crimes trial* . . . Harding 2013: 195.

'whose offences have no particular geographical location'. Bloxham 2003: 92.

'Let those who have hitherto not imbrued their hands . . .' Jones 1998: 547.

*The Nuremberg Trial, which sent eleven Nazi leaders to the gallows* . . . By the time of the trial, there were only 21 defendants. In addition to those hanged, seven were given prison terms and three were acquitted. There were twelve subsequent trials in Nuremberg with 184 defendants of whom 24 were put to death. These trials of doctors, industrialists and others, were conducted by US military courts rather than the International Military Tribunal.

'a symbolic reckoning'. Bloxham 2003: 118.

*over 1,000 men and women had been indicted* . . . Jones 1998: 544 and Charlesworth 2008. These statistics are only for the British. The Americans held 489 trials with a much higher rate of conviction; 1,416 of the 1,672 tried were found guilty. By January 1946, the British had already reported 3,678 known crimes, many with multiple suspects, 1,281 of whom were in custody (Tobia 2010: 127 and Bower 1982: 205–29). For the entire Western Zone the number of defendants was 5,000, with 800 of them sentenced to death. There were many more investigations, however, that did not go to trial owing to insufficient evidence or the inability to locate the accused.

'the quickest brain I have ever known'. Charlesworth 2006: 38.

'Those charged with tracking down the war criminals . . .' Bascomb 2009: 16.

'We have nothing, not even a typewriter.' Bower 1982: 117.

'I am so busy on trials at the moment, I have scarcely a moment to write.' Letter to Isobel Cram, 19 May 1947.

*Added to that was an order for the War Crimes Group to reduce their number by 20 per cent.* War Crimes Group: TNA WO309/1673.

'Being concerned in the ill treatment and killing of Allied Nationals interned therein.' Ravensbrück Case: TNA JAG No. 225.

'English swine!' 'Murderers of women and children!' Norman James Bradley affidavit, Pforzheim: TNA WO309/125.

*it was estimated that more than 800 RAF crew members had been mur-*
   *dered . . .* Clutton-Brock 2003: 473.

'her hair was like a city on fire'. Isobel Cram, personal communication.

'I didn't even know you could climb mountains'. Isobel Cram, personal communication.

'I may as well disillusion you here and now . . .' Letter from Alastair
   to Isobel, 23 November 1946.

'I write to you because I found a sort of bond'. Letter from Alastair to
   Isobel, 16 December 1946.

'the purpose of the trials was deterrence, not retribution'. Paraphras-
   ing the Foreign Secretary, Ernest Bevin, Jones 1998: 565.

'Retributive persecution is of all policies . . .' Winston Churchill, 28
   October 1948, in Bower 1982: 239.

'Mazza was a thoroughly unpleasant character'. Letter from the Judge
   Advocate General's office, 24 October 1946 in Ill-Treatment of
   PsW at PG 5 (Gavi): TNA WO311/1200.

'I encountered many bad men while a PW . . .' Letter to Col. G.
   Barratt, 17 September 1946 in Ill-Treatment of PsW at PG 5
   (Gavi): TNA WO311/1200.

*the delay in apprehending the guilty was one of the principal reasons for*
   *postponing the end of the trials altogether.* Jones 1998: 564.

'I feel that we should be justified in assuming . . .' Letter from the
   Judge Advocate General's office, 22 October 1946 in Killing by
   Means Unknown: TNA WO309/244. After a lengthy search for
   the perpetrators of the Stalag Luft III murders, two trials took
   place – the first from 1 July to 3 September 1947 and the second
   from 28 August to 6 November 1948. Thirteen of the twenty-one
   defendants were eventually hanged. Andrews 1976 and Jones
   1998.

'pointed out that this section cannot start a search for the accused who
   are so far un-named'. Letter from Major P. M. Priestly, 4 November 1947 in Oflag VIIIF, Killing of Major Wadeson and Capt.
   Hugh McKenzie (sic): TNA WO309/1270.

'he was an able and accomplished liar'. Salinger, van Zouco: TNA
   WO309/731.

'extremely anxious to obtain British citizenship . . .' Jack Pringle affidavit, 23 January 1946, ibid. Nansen passports, which originated
after the First World War, were special documents issued to stateless people.

'After four days, I left Brussels . . .' Interrogation of PW Rudolf Kielhorn in Salinger, van Zouco: TNA WO309/731.

'mystified by the whole affair'. Hans Joachim Kalms affidavit, ibid.

'Salinger [alias van Zouco] has told a different story . . .' A synthesis
of two letters from Major A. E. Reade, the first dated 8 January
1947, was a query to the Italian War Crimes Section as to whether
the Italians wanted to extradite him, and the second, dated 10 June
1947, to the British War Crimes Liaison Officer in Paris. Both in
Killing by Means Unknown: TNA WO309/244.

'Instead of destroying lives . . .' Dr Bruno Weber Statement, 20 July
1946 in Dr Bruno Weber: TNA WO309/472.

'May pass as quack doctor . . .' Salinger, van Zouco: TNA WO309/731.

*Mlle Medjanka*, whose real name was Esther Grunspan, was born in
Mainz, Germany in 1907. Accused of both fraud and prostitution,
she had been van Zouco's lover when he lived in Brussels before the
war.

'The importance lies in the probability . . .' Alastair Cram, Letter to
Military Dept, JAG, 1 May 1947, in Salinger, van Zouco: TNA
WO309/731.

'a stock taking operation on a vast scale . . .' Group Captain Anthony
Somerhough, 1 March 1947, in War Crimes Group (NWE) Run-
down: TNA WO309/9.

'It will break my old heart to leave the Army . . .' Letter from Alastair
to Isobel, 23 January 1947.

'Here I am posted to this outpost of Empire . . .', 'Being a Magistrate
has its drawbacks . . .' and 'In about 12 days I cleaned up Meru . . .'
Letter from Alastair to Isobel, 11 April 1949.

'I am sorry to hear of this communal mountaineering . . .' Letter from
Alastair to Isobel, 10 March 1949.

*Estimates of the number of people arrested* . . . Anderson estimates that 'at
the peak of the emergency the British held more than 70,000

Kikuyu supporters of Mau Mau in detention camps', while all told, as many as 150,000 spent some time under arrest during that period. Caroline Elkins believes that number may be as high as 320,000. As to the number executed, while 1,574 were convicted and sentenced, the final number hanged was 1,090. Anderson 2005: 5–7, Elkins 2005: xiii.

'At Lari, Mau Mau became something evil . . .' Anderson 2005: 177.

'Again and again Cram acknowledged . . .' Ibid.: 137.

'The reign of terror is well advanced.' All references to the Ruthagathi case are to be found in the complete file of Her Majesty's Supreme Court of Kenya at Nyeri, Criminal Case No. 240 of 1954.

'a stick to beat the government'. Edward Windley, Minister for African Affairs, Reference (44) Her Majesty's Supreme Court of Kenya at Nyeri, Criminal Case No. 240 of 1954.

'superficial, fallacious and in parts misleading', 29 July 1955 letter in Holmes Report, Commission of Inquiry into African Courts: CO822/787.

'had, in effect, accused the administration . . .' Anderson 2005: 305.

'When I am relaxed and you say I look like a baby . . .' Letter from Alastair to Isobel, 1 January 1951.

'the enchanted road' was part of an epigraph Alastair used for the Kodak Memories album he put together for a spring 1928 trip to the Cairngorms. The entire epigraph, most likely taken from Edgar Wallace's 1910 play, was:

> *An enchanted road it softly gleams*
> *In the depths of the forest of Happy Dreams.*

# Bibliography

Absalom, Roger, *A Strange Alliance: Aspects of Escape and Survival in Italy 1943–45*. Florence: Leo S. Olschki Editore (1994).

Agar-Hamilton, J. A. I. and L. C. F. Turner, *The Sidi Rezeg Battles 1941*. London: Oxford University Press (1957).

Anderson, David, *Histories of the Hanged: The Dirty War in Kenya and the End of Empire*. New York: Norton (2005).

Andrews, Allen, *Exemplary Justice*. London: Harrap (1976).

Arkwright, A. S. B., *Return Journey: Escape from Oflag VIB*. London: Seelcy, Service & Co (1948).

Armstrong, Colin, *Life Without Ladies*. Wellington, NZ: Whitcombe & Tombs Ltd (1947).

Ash, William, *Under the Wire: The Wartime Memoir of a Spitfire Pilot, Legendary Escape Artist and 'Cooler King'*. London: Bantam Press (2005).

Avagnina, Giorgio, *Partigiani di Mondovì nel forte di Gavi*. Lecco: Editoria Grafica Colombo (1995).

Bailey, Ronald H., *Prisoners of War*. Chicago: Time-Life Books (1981).

Bascomb, Neal, *Hunting Eichmann*. Boston: Mariner (2009).

Beckwith, E. G. C., ed., *The Mansel Diaries: The Diaries of Captain John Mansel, Prisoner-of-War – Camp Forger – in Germany 1940–45*. Privately printed (1977).

Berrett, Neil, 'Every Picture Tells a Story'. *Britain at War* 85 (May): 37–42 (2014).

Blair, Norman, *There and Back – No Short Cuts, 1939–1945, A Memoir*. London: Daily Mail (2005).

Bloxham, Donald, 'British War Crimes Trial Policy in Germany 1945–1957: Implementation and Collapse'. *Journal of British Studies* 42 (1): 91–118 (2003).

Bower, Tom, *The Pledge Betrayed: America and Britain and the Denazification of Postwar Germany*. Garden City: Doubleday (1982).

Boyd, J. Morton, *Fraser Darling's Islands*. Edinburgh: Edinburgh University Press (1986).

Brickhill, Paul, *The Great Escape*. New York: Norton (1950).

Browne, Douglas G., *The Tank in Action*. Edinburgh: W. Blackwood 1920.

Burn, Michael, 'Escape! Why I didn't break out of Colditz', *Observer*, 3 November: 26–8 (1974).

Calnan, T. D., *Free as a Running Fox*. New York: Dial Press (1970).

Casanova, Giacomo, *My Escape from Venice Prison*, trans. Arthur Machen. Venice: Lineadacqua. Reprint of the 1922 edition (2009).

Challenor, Harold, with Alfred Draper, *Tanky Challenor, SAS and the Met*. London: Leo Cooper (1990).

Chancellor, Henry, *Colditz: The Definitive Story*. London: Hodder & Stoughton (2001).

Charlesworth, Lorie, '2 SAS Regiment, War Crimes Investigation and British Intelligence'. *Journal of Intelligence History* 6 (13): 13–60 (2006).

—, 'Forgotten Justice: Forgetting Law's History and Victims' Justice in British "Minor" War Crimes Trials in Germany 1945–8'. *Amicus Curiae* 74: 2–10 (2008).

Chutter, James B., *Captivity Captive*. London: Jonathan Cape (1954).

Clifton, George, *The Happy Hunted*. London: Cassell & Co (1952).

Clutton-Brock, Oliver, *Footprints on the Sands of Time: RAF Bomber Command Prisoners of War in Germany 1939–45*. London: Grub Street (2003).

—, *RAF Evaders*. London: Grub Street (2009).

Cooper, Mike, *One of the Many*. Hailsham: J & KH Publishing (1997).

Crawley, Aidan, *Escape From Germany*: New York: Dorset Press (1985).

*Daily Telegraph*, 'Obituary: Lord Campbell of Alloway'. *Daily Telegraph*, 4 July (2013).

Darling, F. Fraser, *Island Years*. London: G. Bell & Sons (1940).
—, *Island Farm*. London: G. Bell & Sons (1944).

Davies, Tony, *When the Moon Rises*. London: Futura (1975).

De Cunzo, Mario and Vega de Martini, *The Chartreuse of Padula*, trans. Françoise Chiarini Rodolfo Citro. Florence: Centro Di Della Edifimi (1990).

Deane-Drummond, Anthony, *Return Ticket*. London: Collins (1953).
—, *Arrows of Fortune*. London: Leo Cooper (1992).

Demetz, Peter, *Prague in Danger: The Years of Occupation, 1939–45*. New York: Farrar, Straus & Giroux (2008).

Denny, Harold, *Behind Both Lines*. New York: Viking (1942).

Di Raimondo, Armando, *Il Forte Del Castel Di Gavi (1528–1797)*. Genoa: Erga (2008).

Dumas, Alexandre, *The Count of Monte Cristo*. New York: Modern Library (2002).

Dutton, G. J. F., 'In Memoriam, Alastair Lorimer Cram MC, 1930'. *Scottish Mountaineering Club Journal* 35 (186): 745–8 (1995).

Edgerton, Robert B., *Mau Mau: An African Crucible*. New York: The Free Press (1989).

Edy, Don, *Goon in the Block*. Ontario: Aylmer (2010).

Elkins, Caroline, *Imperial Reckoning: The Untold Story of Britain's Gulag in Kenya*. New York: Henry Holt (2005).

English, Ian, *Assisted Passage: Walking to Freedom, Italy 1943*. Uckfield: The Naval & Military Press (2004).

English, Ian, ed., *Home By Christmas?* London: The Monte San Martino Trust (1997).

English, Ian and Harry Moses, *For You Tommy the War is Over*. Sunderland: Business Education Publishers (2006).

*Evening News*, 'Germans Shoot Southsea Major Trying To Escape From Camp'. *Evening News*, 2 September (1944).

Farran, Roy, *Winged Dagger, Adventures on Special Service*. London: Collins (1948).

Fimrite, Ron, 'Baron of the Court'. *Sports Illustrated*, 5 July: 56–69 (1993).

Fisher, Marshall Jon, *A Terrible Splendor: Three Extraordinary Men, A World Poised for War, and the Greatest Tennis Match Ever Played*. New York: Crown (2009).

Foot, M. R. D. and J. M. Langley, *MI9: Escape and Evasion, 1939–1945*. London: Book Club (1979).

Franz, Herbert, ed., *Moosburg, The City and the Camp, Stalag 7A*. Moosburg: City of Moosburg (1982).

Gammon, Victor F., *Not All Glory! True Accounts of RAF Airmen Taken Prisoner in Europe, 1939–1945*. London: Arms & Armour Press (1996).

Gilbert, Adrian, *POW: Allied Prisoners in Europe 1939–1945*. London: John Murray (2006).

Gill, Anton, *The Great Escape*. London: Review Press (2002).

Gillies, Midge, *The Barbed-Wire University*. London: Aurum Press (2011).

Graham, Dominick, *The Escapes and Evasions of 'An Obstinate Bastard'* Bishop Wilton, York: Wilton 65 (2000).

Green, J. M., *From Colditz in Code*. London: Robert Hale (1971).

Green, Peter, *The March East, 1945: The Final Days of Oflag IX A/H and A/Z*. Stroud: History Press (2012).

Harding, Thomas, *Hanns and Rudolf: The True Story of the German Jew Who Tracked Down and Caught the Kommandant of Auschwitz*. New York: Simon & Schuster (2013).

Hargest, James, *Farewell Campo 12*. London: Michael Joseph (1954).

Herbert, Ronald, 'Ronald Herbert's War'. Unpublished manuscript (1962).

Hill, Leslie, 'A Bit of an Outsider, Really. An Autobiography, Part 1: 1918–46'. Unpublished manuscript (n.d.).

Hoe, Alan, 'The Phantom Desert Major: Obituary of David Stirling'. *Guardian*, 7 November (1990).

—, *David Stirling: The Authorized Biography of the Creator of the SAS*. London: Little, Brown (1992).

Horner, Gordon, , *For You the War Is Over*. London: Falcon Press (1948).

Howell, Edward, *Escape to Live*. London: Longmans (1947).

Hurst-Brown, Alan, *War Memoirs*. Privately published (n.d.).

'J. M. G.', 'Long, Weary Journey: Young Airman's Escape in War'. *The Age*, 5 May: 5 (1951).

Jones, Priscilla Dale, 'British Policy Towards Nazi "Minor" War Criminals, 1939–1958'. Unpublished PhD dissertation, Cambridge University (1990a).

—, 'Trials of War Criminals'. In Israel Gutman, ed. *Encyclopedia of the Holocaust*. New York: Macmillan: 1488–99 (1990b).

—, 'British Policy Towards German Crimes Against German Jews, 1939–1945'. *Warburg Annual Yearbook* 36: 339–66 (1991).

—, 'Nazi Atrocities against Allied Airman: Stalag Luft III and the End of British War Crimes Trials'. *Historical Journal* 41 (2): 543–65 (1998).

Lamb, Richard, *War in Italy, 1943–1945: A Brutal Story*. New York: St. Martin's Press (1993).

Lauterpacht, H., 'The Law of Nations and the Punishment of War Crimes'. In *British Year Book of International Law, 1944*. London: Oxford University Press: 58–95 (1944).

Leeming, John F., *The Natives Are Friendly*. New York: Dutton (1951).

Lifton, Robert Jay, *The Nazi Doctors: Medical Killing and the Psychology of Genocide*. New York: Basic Books (1986).

Lloyd-Jones, Robin, *The Sunlit Summit, The Life of W. H. Murray*. Dingwall: Sandstone Press (2013).

MacDonald, Callum and Jan, Kaplan, *Prague in the Shadow of the Swastika: A History of the German Occupation, 1939–1945*. London: Quartet Books (1995).

Mackenzie, S. P., *The Colditz Myth, British and Commonwealth Prisoners of War in Nazi Germany*. Oxford: Oxford University Press (2004).

MacLean, Fitzroy, 'Obituary: David Stirling'. *Independent*, 6 November: 16 (1990).

Macpherson, Sir Tommy with Richard Bath, *Behind Enemy Lines: The*

*Autobiography of Britain's Most Decorated Living War Hero*. Edinburgh: Mainstream Publishing (2010).

Marshall, John, 'Obituary: Hon. Daniel Johnston Riddiford, MC, MA, Attorney-General 1971/72'. *New Zealand Law Journal* 1 April: 141–2 (1975).

Mason, W. Wynne, *Prisoners of War: Official History of New Zealand in the Second World War 1939–45*. Wellington: War History Branch, Department of Internal Affairs (1954).

Mastny, Vojtech, *The Czechs Under Nazi Rule: The Failure of National Resistance, 1939–1942*. New York: Columbia University Press (1971).

McLeod, Rosemary, 'Black Sheep of an Esteemed Family'. *North and South* (Auckland) November: 116–23 (1989).

McSweyn, A. F., 'Escape!' In *They Got Back: The Best Escape Stories from the 'RAF Flying Review'*. London: Herbert Jenkins: 32–60 (1961).

Medd, Peter, *The Long Walk Home: An Escape Through Italy*. Completed by his companion Frank Simms. London: John Lehmann (1951).

Metcalfe, Margaret, *All My Father's Children (A Personal Journey)*. Leigh-on-Sea: Skills Station (2002).

Millar, George, *Horned Pigeon*. New York: Doubleday (1946).

Morgan, Guy, *Only Ghosts Can Live*. London: Crosby Lockwood & Son (1945).

Mortimer, Gavin, *Stirling's Men: The Inside History of the SAS in World War II*. London: Weidenfeld & Nicolson (2004).

Muir, John, Untitled, unpublished manuscript (n.d.).

Müller, J. P., *My System: 15 Minutes' Work a Day for Health's Sake*. Copenhagen: Tillge's Bochandel (1905).

Murphy, W. E., *The Relief of Tobruk*. Wellington: Historical Publications Branch (1961).

Murray, W. H., *Mountaineering in Scotland*. London: J. M. Dent & Sons (1947).

—, *The Evidence of Things Not Seen: A Mountaineer's Tale*. London: Bâton Wicks (2002).

Newby, Eric, *Love and War in the Apennines*. Newton Abbot: Readers Union (1972).

Oliver, A. E. V., *Kriegie*. Maidstone: George Mann Books (1998).

Palmer, A. B., *Pedlar Palmer of Tobruk: An Autobiography*. Canberra: Roebuck Society (1981).

Pape, Richard, *Boldness Be My Friend*. London: Elek (1953).

Parrott, Robert F., Untitled, unpublished manuscript (n.d).

Pernice, Francesco, *Il Forte di Gavi*. Torino: Celid (1997).

Plunkett, Desmond L. and The Reverend R. Pletts, *The Man Who Would Not Die*. Durham: The Pentland Press (2000).

Pope, Michael, 'A Wartime Log'. Unpublished diary, 1940–45.

—, *For the Grandchildren*. Privately published memoir (1992).

Pringle, Jack, *Colditz Last Stop: Six Escapes Remembered*. London: William Kimber (1988).

Ratcliffe, James M., 'Escape from Germany', James A. Ratcliffe. ed. Unpublished manuscript (n.d.).

Read, Simon, *Human Game: The True Story of the 'Great Escape' Murders and the Hunt for the Gestapo Gunmen*. New York: Berkley Caliber (2013).

Reid, Ian, *Prisoner at Large: The Story of Five Escapes*. London: Victor Gollancz (1947).

Reid, P. R., *The Colditz Story*. London: Hodder & Stoughton (1952).

—, 'Escape! What I learnt on my break from Colditz'. *Observer*, 3 November (1974).

—, *The Full Story*. New York: St. Martin's Press (1987).

Renoir, Jean, *Grand Illusion, A Film by Jean Renoir* (1937), trans. Marianne Alexandre and Andrew Sinclair. New York: Simon & Schuster (1968).

Riccomini, James Arthur, Unpublished diary (1943).

Riddiford, Daniel, *Committed to Escape: A New Zealand Soldier's Story*. Wairarapa: Ruamahanga Press (2004).

Rollings, Charles, *Prisoner of War, Voices from Behind the Wire in the Second World War*. London: Ebury Press (2007).

Ross, Michael, *From Liguria with Love: Capture, Imprisonment and Escape in Wartime Italy*. London: Minerva Press (1997).

Lord Russell of Liverpool, *The Scourge of the Swastika: A Short History of Nazi War Crimes*. London: Greenhill Books. Reprint of 1954 edition with new introduction (2002).

Sedlák, Jan, ed., *The Path from Renaissance to Baroque: Great Buildings of Moravská Třebová*. Prague: Foibos Books (2012).

Steininger, Rolf, *South Tyrol: A Minority Conflict of the Twentieth Century*. New Brunswick, NJ: Transaction Publishers (2003).

Stewart, Angus, 'A Remarkable Advocate'. *Newsletter of the Faculty of Advocates*, September (2009).

Stewart, Leslie, 'Squeeze to Freedom'. *The Wide World*, July: 170–75 (1957).

Straker, Thomas, 'I Thomas William: An Account of the Life of Thomas William Straker', Parts I & II. Unpublished memoir (n.d.).

*The Times*, 'Tunnellers of Gavi, An Escape Scheme in Italy'. *The Times*, 14 December (1945).

Tobia, Simona, 'Questioning the Nazis: Language and Effectiveness in British War Crime Investigations and Trials in Germany, 1945–48'. *Journal of War and Culture Studies* 3 (1): 123–136 (2010).

Walker, David, *Lean, Wind, Lean: A Few Times Remembered*. London: Collins (1984).

Walters, Guy, *Hunting Evil: The Nazi War Criminals Who Escaped and the Quest to Bring Them to Justice*. New York: Broadway Books (2009).
—, *The Real Great Escape*. London: Bantam Books (2013).

Weaver, William, 'A Hidden Italian Masterpiece: The Certosa of Padula'. *New York Times*, 17 November: 8–9 (1991).

Whipplesnaith, [1937], *The Night Climbers of Cambridge*. Cambridge: Oleander Press (2007).

Williams, Eric, *The Wooden Horse*. New York: Harper & Bros (1949).

Wilson, Patrick, *The War Behind the Wire: Experiences in Captivity During the Second World War*. Barnsley: Leo Cooper (2000).

Wood, J. E. R., ed., *Detour*. London: Falcon Press (1946).

Wynne, Barry, *No Drums . . . No Trumpets: The Story of Mary Lindell*. London: Arthur Barker (1961).

Yarnall, John, *Barbed Wire Disease, British & German Prisoners of War, 1914–19*. Stroud: History Press (2011).

Yeoman, Allan, *The Long Road to Freedom*. Auckland: Random Century (1991).

## The British National Archive (TNA) files

Capt. P. H. Griffiths, WO309/1987

Holmes Report, Commission of Inquiry into African Courts, CO822/787

Ill-Treatment of Col. Kenyon at Luckenwalde, WO311/1021

Ill-Treatment of PsW at PG5 (Gavi), WO311/1200

Killing by Means Unknown, Deaths of Major Wadeson, MC, RE and Capt. Hugh McKenzie, WO309/244

Oflag VIIIF, Killing of Major Wadeson and Capt. Hugh McKenzie, WO309/1270

Operation Fleacomb and Filecomb, WO309/476

Pforzheim, WO309/125

POWs at Oflag VIIB Eichstatt Shooting, WO309/19

Proceedings and Findings Court Martial for Lieutenant Commander David A. Fraser, RN, Submarine H. M. 'Oswald'. Royal Naval Barracks, Portsmouth, April 17–18, 1946, ADM 156/272

Ravensbrück Case JAG, No. 225

Results of War Crimes Trials, WO309/479

Salinger, van Zouco, WO309/731

Shooting of 50 RAF Officers Stalag Luft III, WO309/523

The Trial of Six Kikuyu Guards on Charges Arising out of the Murder of a Kikuyu Prisoner, CO822/785

Verdicts of War Crimes Courts, WO309/1838

War Crimes CROWCASS, WO309/466

War Crimes Group, WO309/1673

War Crimes Group, (NWE) Rundown, WO309/9

Dr. Bruno Weber, WO309/472

## MI9 Reports

Colin Armstrong, MI9/S/PG (Poland) 1521
Hugh John Baker, PW/Ex/Switz/85

Norman Boddington, PW/Ex/Switz/426
Richard Phillip Carr, MI9/S/PG/LIB 166
Alastair Lorimer Cram, MI9/S/PG (G) 2988
Bedrich Dvorak, MI9/S/PG/LIB/22
L. G. Gaze, MI9/S/PG (G) 3086
James Hargest, MI9/S/PG (Italy) 1587
Leslie Alexander Hill, MI9/INT/SP 2962
John de Filek Jago, MI9/INT/SP1464
Peter Henry Joscelyne, MI9/S/PG/LIB 23
Gerald Barnard Keily, MI9/INT/SP 4904 and MI9/S/PG/LIB 1021
Christopher Gerald Lea, MI9/INT/SP 4421
Garth Armitage Ledgard, PW/Ex/Switz/1285
Jesse Maxwell Lee, PW/Ex/Switz/1293
Frank Christian Lorentz, PW/Ex/Switz/99
Ian Lauchlan Mackay M'Geoch MI9/S/PG (-) 1920
Ronald Thomas Stewart Macpherson, MI9/S/PG (Poland) 1520
Hugh Mainwaring, MI9/S/PG (-) 1474
Allan Frank McSweyn, MI9/S/PG (G) 1629
George Reid Millar, MI9/S/PG (G) 1716
Mark Ogilvie-Grant, MI9/INT/SP 2963
Maurice John O'Sullivan, MI9/INT/SP 2675
Ralph Buckley Palm, MI9/S/PG (G) 1628
R. F. Parrott, MI9/S/PG/LIB 245
George Robert Paterson, PW/Ex/Switz/1258
Albert Edward Penny, MI9/S/PG (Italy) 1038
Harold Andrew Peterson, PW/Ex/Switz/89
Desmond Lancelot Plunkett, MI9/S/PG/LIB/48
Michael Donald Pope, MI9/INT/SP1454
Trevor Allan Gordon Pritchard, MI9/INT/SP4757
H. E. Stewart, MI9/S/PG (Italy) 636
Denis Percy Swinney, MI9/S/PG/LIB344
Ivor Tonder, MI9/S/PG/LIB/101
Jack Ernest Stanley Tooes, PW/Ex/Switz/1883
George Tsoucas, MI9/S/PG (G) 1886
Frank Theodore Vlok, PW/Ex/Switz/618

Harry Mann Wakelin, PW/Ex/Switz/1065
Aubrey Charles Forster Whitby, MI9/S/PG (Italy) 1568

## Red Cross Reports

Colditz, Camp History of Oflag IVC, WO228/3288
Gavi, Camp 5 Italian POW Camp, WO224/10b
Luckenwalde, Stalag IIIA, WO224/6
Moosburg, Camp History of Stalag VIIA, WO208/3276
Oflag VIIIF, later Oflag 79 [Mährisch Trübau and Brunswick], WO224/77
Padula, Camp 35 Italian POW Camp, WO224/11
Rotenburg, Secret Camp Histories, Oflag IX A/Z, WO208/3294
Secret Camp Histories, Oflag 79 (VIIIF) Querum, WO208/3292

# Index